D0904106

The House of Make-Believe

The House of Make-Believe

Children's Play and the Developing Imagination

WITHDRAWI

DOROTHY G. SINGER
AND JEROME L. SINGER

Harvard University Press
Cambridge, Massachusetts
London, England
1990

This book is printed on acid-free paper, and its binding materials have been chosen for strength and durability.

Library of Congress Cataloging-in-Publication Data

Singer, Dorothy G.
   The house of make-believe : children's play and the developing imagination / Dorothy G. Singer and Jerome L. Singer.
      p.   cm.
   Includes bibliographical references and index.
   ISBN 0-674-40874-8
   1. Play—Psychological aspects. 2. Imagination in children.
3. Developmental psychology. I. Singer, Jerome L. II. Title.
BF171.S53 1990
155.4′18—dc20   90-355-3
                                                          CIP

To our children and their children

Preface

First there's the children's
house of make-believe.

Robert Frost, "Directive"

This is a book about the origins, the determinants, and the manifestations of the human imagination in childhood and early adolescence. We approach this intriguing subject primarily as psychologists, that is, as behavioral scientists attentive to available research and systematic theory. But we are also ordinary adults aware of our own memories of childhood play and those of our children, of their friends, and of the many other children we have observed over the years in nursery schools and daycare centers. As clinicians we have been exposed to the therapeutic play of disturbed children and the retrospective reports of adult patients in treatment. As avid readers with a special interest in the imagination, we have been on the lookout for memories of childhood play in published biographies and personal memoirs, and for childhood scenes in fiction. Our hope is that we can share this wide-ranging view of early imaginative play with a broad group of readers.

We address this book to behavioral scientists, mental health workers, teachers, parents, and those who are simply curious about the special mystery of how we develop our human capacity for mental travel through time and space. Yet despite its comprehensive coverage of the available research, this book is not a textbook. Rather, we have tried to combine a scientific and a humanistic approach in a series of essays that draw on both clinical and literary data while still according the greatest importance to systematic observation and experimental research.

The inherently private nature of imagination and fantasy presents an almost insurmountable obstacle to its definitive study through the relatively "objective" methods of laboratory observation and experimentation. Researchers of childhood have succeeded, nevertheless, in developing such observational and experimental procedures sufficiently to permit us to test the hypotheses, suggestions, and even the theories we generate through introspection and clinical experience. Yet without memories of play, conversations with children, and literary accounts, in which fine writers, drawing on reminiscence and observation, hold up mirrors to our own lives, our presentation of available knowledge might be spare and unengaging. We have therefore chosen to intersperse our review of theoretical issues and formal research findings with personal recollections as well as clinical observations in order to flesh out and vivify our subject matter. We hope we can help readers to recognize the value of the scientific approach to data collections, while also encouraging their personal involvement in our subject.

We thus begin with a series of childhood memories. In assembling them we have spent some wonderful hours poring through the remarkable biographical collection of Edith Cobb, philanthropist, social worker, and friend of researchers Margaret Mead and Erik Erikson. More than 250 volumes are housed in the special collection she willed to the library of Teachers College, Columbia University, which was being organized by Margaret Mead shortly before her own death. From these and other sources we have selected examples from the childhoods of the famous, or nearly famous, and those less well-known people who simply wished to record their life experiences. We believe they suggest many possible ways in which childhood imagination begins and develops. We could have carried out a quantitative analysis, memoir by memoir, of specific instances, but given the cultural diversity of these writers and their differing objectives, our effort might have proved only pseudoscientific. Instead, as we have suggested, we serve them up as a charming first course. But they are more than that. We recognize that childhood fantasies, like the childhood games we played, are not purely idiosyncratic but are indeed a reflection of our common humanity.

A book such as this could not be completed without valuable assistance from many people and, of course, the participation in our research of hundreds of children and parents, who must necessarily remain anonymous. The opportunity to make use of the great collection of autobiographies and childhood reminiscences housed in the Edith Cobb collection at the Russell Library, Teachers College, Columbia University, was of special importance for us. We spent happy hours reviewing the fascinating material available there, and we wish especially to thank David M. Ment, Head of Special Collections, for his hospitality and guidance. Marianna Kastner and Julie Sincoff aided us considerably in locating relevant research references. Virginia Hurd typed the many drafts of the manuscript on her word processor and was helpful in numerous ways. Comments on particular chapters by Marjorie Janis and Alan Kazdin were useful. Helen Glixon provided the valuable index. Finally, we acknowledge the sustained encouragement and concrete editing assistance of Angela von der Lippe and Linda Howe of Harvard University Press.

Contents

O hours of childhood
when behind the figures was more than merely the past,
and before us not the future.
Of course we were growing, and sometimes we were eager
to grow up soon, half in order to please those
who had nothing else besides being grown up,
and yet, in going our own way, we were happy
dealing with things that endure, and we stood there
in the region between the world and the play-thing,
in the place created in the beginning
for a pure act . . .

> —Rainer Maria Rilke, Fourth "Duino Elegy"
> (*translated by Ute and Thomas Saine*)

Memories of Childhood Play

Memory, as someone said, is the greatest of artists. It eliminates the unessential, and chooses with careless skill the sights and the sounds and the episodes that are best worth remembering and recording.

—Maurice Baring,
The Puppet Show of Memory

In her charming book, *The Ecology of Imagination in Childhood,* Edith Cobb observes that "memories of awakening to the existence of some potential, aroused by early experiences of self and world, are scattered through the literature of scientific and aesthetic inventions."[1] Cobb attempts to demonstrate that many geniuses have attributed their childhood sense of wonder to a cosmic sense, an awareness of the forces of nature that inspired their later creative endeavors.

We would like to go one step further and propose that this "sense of wonder" is found not only in the autobiographies and biographies of famous writers, artists, and scientists but also in the recollections of those ordinary people who are creative and imaginative—or who could be if they would get in touch with their earliest memories of play. We believe there are some common threads in early childhood that are linked to the appreciation of the cosmic Cobb felt to be such a necessary element in creativity and in the development of a capacity for fantasy and mind magic.

This cosmic sense, or appreciation of nature, is beautifully described by the black writer Richard Wright, who grew up in wretched circumstances, but whose ability to respond to the smells, sounds, and images around him allowed him some measure of refuge and beauty in the otherwise stark environment of a small Southern town. He appreciated the "drenching hospitality in the pervading smell of sweet magnolias," or the "suspense" he felt when he "heard the taut, sharp song of a yellow-black bee hovering nervously but patiently above a white rose," or the feeling of "limitless freedom distilled from the rolling sweep of tall green grass swaying and glinting in the wind and sun."[2] And later when, encouraged by his mother, he tried to read, words in books opened new possibilities for escaping from the poverty and bigotry that surrounded him.

The same sensitivity to nature appears in the work of other writers. In "There Was a Child Went Forth," Walt Whitman exclaimed that every day, the child became "the first object he look'd upon" and "that object became part of him for the day or a certain part of the day."[3] For Whitman, the lilacs, the grass, the "white and red morning glories, and white and red clover," everything the child sees and experiences is a part of that child. Remembering her childhood in Kenya in *The Flame Trees of Thika,* Elspeth Huxley recalls the golden light of a sunset and "its obliteration by the dusk, as if some great lamp had been turned down in the heavens." This disappearing sun filled her with a "terrible melancholy that sometimes wrings the hearts of children, and can never be communicated or explained."[4] Sarah Shears, describing her childhood in Kent in *A Village Girl,* wonders "what it would be like to live always in the woods and never go home."[5] Growing up in South Africa, Peter Abrahams communed with nature as he "climbed the short willows with their long drooping branches." In *Tell Freedom* he recalls the "touch of a willow leaf on the cheek" and his "feeling of cool wonder" and how lying on his back "on the green grass on the bank of the river," he would look up and watch "fleecy white clouds form and reform" into the shapes of people and things he knew. He "loved being alone by the river. It became my special world."[6]

If some children are sensitive to nature, others become acutely attached to a place. Edith Wharton's childhood houses inspired her love of architecture and figure prominently in her stories. Henry James, who spent much of his adult life traveling and living abroad, always recalled the "sweet taste of Albany." A clearer understanding of the etiology of play emerges from such childhood reminiscences. In the words of playwright John Van Druten, such memories are "like a dim glow of ruby-colored light through a dense patch of darkness."[7]

Some writers remember the simple furniture and household objects that abetted their play as children. In *Childhood, Boyhood and Youth,* Leo Tolstoy created a childhood gleaned from experience but shaped by imagination. He writes, "in the long winter evenings we decked out an armchair with shawls, turning it into a carriage . . . one of us took the coachman's seat, another the footman's, the girls sitting in the middle, and . . . with three chairs for horses, we set out on our travels."[8] Like Tolstoy, Swedish writer Selma Lagerlof used "beds, bureaus, tables, and chairs in the nursery" and covered them with blankets and quilts.[9] In this way, she created a "wall" as backdrop for a play she wanted to produce for her family, enlisting the help of siblings and servants. Inspired by a visit to the theater, where she had seen a performance of *My Rose of the Forest,* Selma wanted "everyone" to "understand that the table, the chair, and the stool represent the cottage where *My Rose of the Forest* lives with her grandfather."

In 1876 when Maurice Baring (an early twentieth-century journalist) was two, he received a large toy "bird" with yellow and red plummage for Christmas. He kept this "hen" on top of his nursery wardrobe and imagined all kinds of stories about it. When Elspeth Huxley was given a pony by her mother's friend, Lettice, she was "much too overcome for speech and gazed at the pony which gradually changed before my eyes. From a stumpy, rough-coated Somali it became a milk-white charger, fleet of foot and proud of eye." This treasured gift inspired Elspeth to make up stories about her horse; she envisioned him as an "object of romance and enchantment," pretending that at one time "he had carried princes on the tented battlefield and galloped through the night to bring new victory to maidens with hibiscus flowers in their dark hair, imprisoned in a moated fortress."[10]

If Elspeth played with a real horse, Chiang Yee, growing up in China at the turn of the century, recalls playing with a "bamboo stick about three centimetres in diameter and two or three metres long." He would place this "horse" between his legs and hold the upper end with his right hand while raising his left hand "as if wielding a whip." He and his friends on their bamboo horses made as much noise "as a cavalcade of real horsemen in full gallop." At other times, Chiang became a "horse" himself when a cousin tied a string on his back hair plait. Two of Chiang's other hair plaits became "horse's ears." Years later, Chiang could "still feel the pain of my hair being pulled and find my hand going involuntarily to the back of my head."[11] Just as Tolstoy and Lagerlof used furniture in their games, Chiang describes how he and his cousins put chairs and stools together to make a "Chinese shop." They then made believe that pieces of thick paper were either "cakes or sweets" or "money."

Our examination of primary and secondary sources suggests that the capacity for imagination is not the exclusive property of the "only" child, the isolated, the ill, or the handicapped but is found among the robust, in families with many children, among children raised in the city and in the country, among the rich and the poor. What we have discovered, however, is that there are certain essential ingredients that are conducive to fostering this willingness to explore the possible.[12] There must be a key *person* in a child's life who inspires and sanctions play and accepts the child's inventions with respect and delight. There must be a *place* for play, a "sacred space" (no matter how small), and *time*, open-ended and unstructured. And there must be simple objects or *props* to help inspire the adventure (sometimes a pet becomes the beloved playmate that turns into a "wild beast," a "baby," or a loyal keeper of secrets). With these essentials, and the "cosmic sense" we described earlier, children can create a world of wonder they will remember and carry with them throughout their lives.

A Person Who Plays and Encourages Play

Memories of pretend play are often associated with a special person who encouraged play, told fantastic stories, or modeled play by initiating games, who perhaps had a flamboyant personality that inspired imitation or gave wonderful gifts of puppets and picture books or shared exotic travel adventures—who above all showed a trusting, loving acceptance of children and their capacity for playfulness. In many journals and biographies a mother, father, older sibling, governess, friend, cousin, aunt, uncle, or teacher is mentioned repeatedly. Vladimir Nabokov's mother, for example, "did everything to encourage the general sensitiveness I had to visual stimulation."[13] Sometimes, he writes in his autobiography, *Speak Memory,* his mother, Elena Ivanova, would "produce a mass of jewelry for my bedtime amusement." When she brought out the various tiaras, rings, and necklaces from a small compartment in her room, for him they were like the "mystery and enchantment" of St. Petersburg during imperial celebrations, when colored electric bulbs "glowed with a kind of charmed constraint above snow-lined cornices on housefronts along residential streets." Nabokov's mother also read fairy tales to him, as did a "bewildering sequence of English nurses and governesses."[14] His cousin Yuri introduced him to "the dramatic possibilities of Mayne Reid books," Wild West fiction translated into Russian,[15] which he used in his adventure games in the park of Batovo. Nabokov's numerous childhood illnesses brought his mother closer to him, and she indulged him with lavish, sometimes unusual presents, such as the giant four-foot pencil that had hung as a showpiece in a local shop. His mother had an "intense or pure religiousness" that took the form of "an equal faith in the existence of another world and in the impossibility of comprehending it in terms of earthly life."[16] From her, Nabokov believes he inherited a sense of the "beauty of intangible property, unreal estate," that shaped his creative gift.[17]

James Barrie's mother, Margaret Ogilvy, also played an important role in her son's life. Delmont and Shirley Morrison suggest that the "romantic ideation" Barrie expressed in *Peter Pan,* with its theme of the "Lost Boys" who desire to remain young forever, stems from the intimacy he experienced during his mother's deep depression following the death of Barrie's older brother David.[18] Barrie was six at the time and spent many days sitting on his mother's bed as she told stories about David, her favorite child. One day, Barrie "conceived a glorious idea, or was it put into my head by my mother . . . the notion was nothing short of this, why should I not write tales myself?"[19] He did so, often in the garret of the house. His mother was his ideal, "sent by God" to "open the minds of all who looked to beautiful thoughts."

In *Life and I*, Edith Wharton describes one source of her impulse to write fiction drawn from her memory of a friend of her father's who came to dine every Sunday. He would "take me on his knee after dinner" and "tell me mythology." This was particularly important to Wharton, because while her parents and teachers *read* stories to her, this friend *told* her a story. "Our Sunday evening guest was the only person who ever showed signs of knowing anything about the secret story-world in which I lived."[20]

Goethe's "genial, indulgent mother" filled long hours with storytelling to "his and her own delight." His mother described how she sat with young Wolfgang as he listened, and how he would become angry if one of his favorite stories was not told "according to his fancy." Goethe's grandmother also told him stories, made a pet of him, and best of all, gave him a puppet theater on Christmas Eve in 1753, which he says "created a new world in the house."[21] This "new world" of pretend was encouraged by Goethe's mother, who transmitted to him her "love of story-telling, her animal spirits, her love of everything which bore the stamp of distinctive individuality." She would say, "I and my Wolfgang have always held fast to each other, because we were both young together."[22]

Anton Chekhov remembered his father as a stern disciplinarian who began to give him lessons before he was even five years old. The father was a talented man, an artist who painted icons and a violinist, but he could not tolerate children's play, which seemed to him a waste of time. In contrast, Chekhov's mother kept her children entranced by recounting fairy tales and "personal reminiscences of her adventures before marriage, when she had traveled all over Russia."[23] Yet Chekhov maintained a strong affection for his father and claimed, as had Goethe, that he derived his "talent" from his father and his "soul" from his mother.[24] Despite her numerous household chores and the burden of rearing six children, she truly appreciated her offspring and fostered Chekhov's love of make-believe, acting, and the theater—a passion he pursued during his years at the Gymnasium. Theater-going violated school rules, but Chekhov nevertheless managed to attend as often as possible, and as a young teenager he became part of a troupe that performed before small audiences in private homes.[25]

George Bernard Shaw's mother, Lucinda Gurly, whom he describes in his autobiography, was raised by a strict grandaunt to be a "lady" with "complete dignity." Shaw was convinced that she was "of a species apart from servants and common persons,"[26] yet she was a poor housekeeper, could not budget her small income, and viewed religion and discipline as "tyranny and slavery," nor did she concern herself about the everyday needs of her children, permitting servants who could neither read nor write to train them. She was, however, musical, with a lovely voice of "extraordinary purity of tone."[27] Shaw's father, a wholesaler in the corn trade, about which he knew next to nothing, was a drunkard. The household, a ménage à trois, was shared by George John Vandaleur Lee, a musical tutor and a colleague of Shaw's mother. Lee had a deep influence on Shaw, who described him as a man that ate brown bread, slept with the windows open, distrusted physicians, was skeptical of academic authority, and was a "teacher of singing so heterodox and original" that he was detested by his professional rivals.

Although Shaw's mother was uninterested in the everyday care of her children, she filled his head with nursery rhymes, while Lee and Shaw's maternal uncle, Walter—his "two supplementaries" as he called them—widened his "outlook considerably." Shaw studied these men along with his father and delighted in the humorous stories his father and uncle told. From his mother and Lee he learned to know and enjoy music, and later, when Shaw became a music critic, he claimed he owed it to Lee's early influence. As he commented, "had there not been imagination, idealization, the charm of music, the charm of lovely seas and sunsets, and our natural kindliness, and gentleness, it is impossible to say what cynical barbarism we might not have grown into." From his father he inherited a sense of humor and the ability to write comedy. Of his father he said, "the more sacred an idea or a situation was by convention, the more irresistible was it to him as the jumping-off place for a plunge into laughter."[28]

If Shaw's father was an impossible, easy-going drunkard, Elizabeth Barrett Browning's father, Edward Moulton Barrett, a proper, straitlaced man, was regarded by most people as a "tyrant." Browning did recognize a less obvious aspect of her father's personality, however—"his elastic spirit and merry laugh"[29]—but she was closer to her mother, who died when Browning was twenty-two. They spent long evenings reading together, and the list of books she read during that time is "formidable." Browning loved fairy tales, and at four-and-a-half "her great delight was poring over fairy phenomenons and actions of necromancers." She made up verses in "infancy," and as she grew older wrote "epics" and "tragedies" or planned charades and plays in which she and her brother Edward and her sisters acted.[30] Spiritually more at home in books and dreams, she lived on a beautiful estate called Hope End, which resembled a "Turkish house" with its minarets, domes, spires, and crescents. The family was large, loving, and well-off until a series of financial losses involving property in Jamaica finally forced her father to sell the house and estate to satisfy his numerous creditors. But her early years were important in shaping her creative mind, and she owed much of this to her mother's love of music and books.

Browning's brother, "Bro," was also an important person in her life, and in "Verses to My Brother," she remarks on the games and classical books they shared together as children. She was a "frail" child, and it may well be that her unusual interest in books was a form of compensation for her inability to participate in outdoor games and sports with her brother and sisters at Hope End. Her taste for books on history, religion and philosophy, and for all modern authors who had any claim to "superior merit and poetic excellence" was shaped before she was twelve and continued throughout her life.

Orphaned by the death of his mother when he was not quite two, and of his father when he was nine, Leo Tolstoy was raised by relatives and consequently drew closer to his brothers. He worshipped his brother Sergey, who "was always singing, drew extraordinary roosters with colored pencils, and raised chickens in secret." As Tolstoy wrote, "I copied him, I loved him, I wanted to be him."[31] His brother Nicholas also inspired him through his ability to tell "fantastic" stories and plan imaginary expeditions. In addition to the love and affection of his brothers, Tolstoy fondly remembered his grandmother, Pelagya Nikolayevna, "corpulent and white, in her night dress and white cap," making soap bubbles between her wrinkled fingers to amuse him.[32] Each night the children took turns keeping their grandmother company in her room. When it was his turn, his grandmother would climb into her bed, and Tolstoy into his, and a maid would put out the candles. Then a blind old man, a professional storyteller who had been brought to the estate many years before to amuse Tolstoy's grandfather, would sit in the bay window and tell stories in a drawling voice, mixing Russian folklore with tales from Scheherazade and lulling Tolstoy and his grandmother to sleep.

In his *Autobiography*, A. A. Milne remembered his father, a schoolmaster, and his mother, a former teacher, as simple, religious people with little money. But they respected nature and valued learning, and encouraged their three sons, Barry, Ken, and Alan, to do the same. The family lived in rooms adjacent to Henley House, a school Milne's father bought in the town of Kilburn, England. Here he had "lots of freedom." He woke early in the morning and with his adored older brother, Ken, roamed the fields collecting minerals, played with his fiery iron hoop, which was far better than any wooden one, enacted the adventures of Robin Hood, or daydreamed of life at sea. Inspired by reading *The Three Midshipmen,* the three boys played at being sailors, pretending they would "capture Arab dhows, knife sharks and swim through the heaving waters with a rope in our teeth."[33] The atmosphere at Henley House, with its slow pace and musty rooms, inky desks and inky boys, was conducive to daydreaming. In such an atmosphere, encouraged by his shy, scholarly father, Milne was able to read before the age of three. He was exposed to *Pilgrim's Progress, The Quiver, Line upon Line,* and other similar works deemed appropriate for the sons of a devout Presbyterian schoolmaster.

The various artifacts collected by Milne's father seemed exotic to young Alan and evoked many pleasurable fantasies. In the hall on the family side of the school, for example, hung the horns of a buffalo, a looped lasso, and a pair of Mexican spurs, so that "every time one slid down the banisters, one slid through Kilburn into a romantic world of which one's imagination was the only master." In this world, Milne and his two brothers "roamed prairies such as were never seen . . . wearing spurs as big as saucers, lassoing buffaloes as big as elephants, stamping rattle-snakes into the ground with our big, high boots, sliding under the belly of our horse when Indians went by, then regretfully leaving all this and sliding down the banisters again."[34]

Milne and Ken wanted to become writers, but Milne actually believed that his brother was the more talented, the true "writer of the family."[35] Although Ken was Milne's best companion, Milne idolized his father, years later telling his own son, Christopher Robin, that "everything we are is that way because that was how our parents made us. Every talent we have has been inherited."[36] For his children Milne's father was instrumental in opening doors to sensitivity and beauty. "He was the best man I have ever known; by which I mean the most truly good, the most completely to be trusted, the most incapable of wrong. He differed from our conception of God only because he was shy, which one imagined God not to be, and was funny, which we knew God was not."[37]

Later, when Milne became a famous writer, he was celebrated more for *Winnie-the-Pooh* and for his children's poetry, which were inspired by three-year-old Christopher Robin, than for his adult plays and essays. Milne came to believe that within him there were "unforgettable memories of my own childhood" and an understanding of children "based on the imagination which every writer must bring to memory and observation."[38] These memories—and parents who sanctioned his play—were crucial elements in his creation of an imaginary forest and its imaginary animal inhabitants.

Like his father, Milne endowed his own son with the gift of play. Although the joyful interaction of father and son led to a sense of pride and a love of books (Christopher Robin later became a bookseller), the son never measured up to the creative genius of his father. In *The Enchanted Places*, Christopher Robin sets forth a bittersweet account of what it was like to be the son of a renowned author.

Similarly, in a poignant autobiography, Vyvyan Holland remembers his father, Oscar Wilde, with great warmth, although he knew him only during the early years of his life. After 1895, Holland never saw his father again, but he described Wilde as a "real companion" to him who would go down on all fours and become "a lion, a wolf, a horse, caring nothing for his usually immaculate appearance."[39] He mended the children's toys and "played with us a great deal in the dining room," allowing the children to "clamber" all over him. Wilde was also a great storyteller, weaving adventure tales or recounting fairy stories to the children. Holland recalls how he and his brother Cyril spent long hours playing with forts and armies of lead soldiers, shooting toy cannons and taking prisoners. A special toy was a lantern with a beam that could be made clear or green or red, which allowed them to "play real trains, in the dark, complete with signals." This was "heaven and romance" to these small boys. But best of all were Holland's memories of Wilde singing Irish songs to his sons and inventing poems that held them spellbound. He was able to be so much of the child in his playful moments in the children's nursery.

At times, siblings rather than parents foster a playful spirit in each other. Charlotte Brontë was born on April 21, 1816, in Thornton, England. The three Brontë sisters, Charlotte, Emily, and Anne, were all to become writers, but it is Charlotte that we favor, and of course her childhood experiences were shared with her sisters and brother Branwell. In the parsonage at Haworth, where their father had accepted a perpetual curacy, a "little extra up-stairs room" was appropriated to the children for their use and called the "children's study."[40]

The children's mother had died in 1821 when Charlotte was five, and Mr. Brontë, possessor of a "strong, passionate, Irish nature," a man of "philosophic calm and dignity of demeanor," was usually "busy in his study," or, when he was with the children, spent the time teaching them their lessons until they were ready to go to school. The children were generally left much on their own, with two "rough, affectionate, warm-hearted" servants to care for them. They "did not want society" but were "bound" to each other, inventing and acting in their own plays, reading to each other, and playing games—they were their own support system.[41] Neither Elizabeth Branwell, an aunt who came to manage the household after their mother's death, nor Tabby, an elderly woman who joined the family when Charlotte was about nine, was able to enter the charmed circle of these precocious siblings. They had no childhood friends and did not mingle with the village children.

When Charlotte was eight, she attended a boarding school maintained for daughters of clergymen at Cowan's Bridge. Her older sisters, Maria and Elizabeth, died as a result of a fever contracted there, and Charlotte became the leader of her siblings back at Haworth. A gift to Branwell of wooden soldiers was the impetus for an "ever-lengthening series of games." The toy soldiers became "young men" whom the children cast as "make-believe publishers, authors, [and] antiquarians." These characters were credited with "exploits surpassing the achievement of ancient and modern masters." Later, the children invented a new game called "Our Fellows," in which each child created an imaginary island inhabited by such creatures as "Boaster," "Hayman," "Clown," and "Hunter." Charlotte eventually elaborated this game and created a "fictitious Island of Dreams where she erected a school which was to contain one thousand children." It was more "like the work of enchantment and beautiful fiction than sober reality."[42]

Thus, the significant people in the Brontë children's childhood were each other—Charlotte, Branwell, Emily, and Anne. They fired one another's imaginations and accepted one another's plots. Inspired by the books they read (especially *The Arabian Nights*), they eventually turned their childhood games into literary prose.

Places, Space, and Time for Play

Just as children need a special person to sanction and inspire their innate curiosity and their eagerness to explore, they also need a place to play and enough time to carry out their adventures. But the availability of large, open fields or houses with many rooms does not guarantee that a child will make use of that space for play without encouragement. One corner of a room or part of a table can be a magnificent play space for a child—if a parent or another adult permits it. Children often want to keep some of their play constructions intact overnight, and for this reason also, space is a necessity.

Time, too, is important. Children may play one game again and again. Each time, mastery of the materials, the language, and the plot is enhanced through repeated practice. When the novelty finally wears off, a variation of the game can develop or an entirely new one take its place. Children who are deeply involved in an enchanting game of pretend or a challenging game of skill find little reason to be bored.

In *A Village Girl*, Sarah Shears recalls the "Children's Hour from five to six o'clock every evening" when her mother played "quiet games" with the children or helped them with their spelling and sums. She remembers how "we sat together in the lamplight, with

Henry on Mother's lap, and it was so peaceful and pleasant." This quiet time, when the mother devoted herself to the children, is the kind of quality time psychologists recommend today for the busy working parent. The children in the Shears' household could count on its regularity "as our dose of Syrup-of-Figs." For Sarah, it was "solace and salvation" making life in her dreaded school almost tolerable.[43]

Nabokov's mother set aside time for reading to him each evening in the large drawing room of their country house. She would read stories in English—tales of "knights, whose terrific but wonderfully aseptic wounds were bathed by damsels in grottoes." And there were "large, flat, glossy picture books" and pop-up books. This was a special time for Nabokov and conjured up dramatic scenes that inspired his own powers of imagination.[44]

Helen Flexner, a Quaker, treasured the morning time she spent with her father. Every day, it was his custom to instruct one of the children—each in turn as he or she grew—"while he stood before his high shaving table with its small, round mirror and leather strop hanging at one side." He made a ceremony of sharpening his razor while "his little pupil of the year danced up and down at his side studying the picture at the top of the page, getting ready to read the big, black letters" and waiting impatiently for the next adventure in *The Black Cat Book*.[45] Helen could also count on other special times with her father as he drove around in his carriage doing the family marketing or paying his professional calls. During these hours, he would tell her stories and comment on the people and places they visited, and Helen would replenish her imagination just as her father replenished the food basket with each stop at the country food-stalls.

Samuel Chotzinoff, a pianist and music critic who later became music director for NBC radio and television, recalls that every evening after supper he was allowed to play for a while on the sidewalks or in the gutter in front of the house, where he would be seen from the windows and, when it grew dark, summoned to bed. His daytime playgrounds were the streets of New York; the tenement roofs where he would play tag; the backyards where he could climb up clothespoles; the alley behind restaurants where milk cans "served for games of leap frog"; and the rubble of demolished buildings. With his friends he played "hide-and-go-seek" "in the dim vestibules of the tenement houses" and "leave-e-o, prisoners' base, and one-o'-cat" on the sidewalks of East Broadway continuing on to the Bowery.[46]

In contrast to the New York City streets where Chotzinoff, a poor Rabbi's son, played, Nabokov's playgrounds were the fields of Vyra, his wealthy family's large country estate in the former province of St. Petersburg. Here Nabokov bicycled or rode his horse, explored the marshlands, roamed grassy wonderlands, played cowboy games with his cousin, and in particular, searched for butterflies, imagining himself as a famous "young Russian collector" or the discoverer of "the only specimen so far known." In *Speak, Memory,* Nabokov also describes one of his favorite places for play indoors when he was four: a "big cretonne-covered divan, white with black trefoils, in one of the drawing rooms at Vyra rises up in my mind, like some massive product of a geological upheaval before the beginning of history." This divan became part of "a primordial cave" that was an important component in his early make-believe adventures. With the help of an adult or anyone nearby, he moved the divan away from the wall so that he could crawl behind it, make a roof with the bolsters, and then have "the fantastic pleasure of creeping through the pitch-black tunnel, where I lingered a little to listen to the singing in my ears—that lonesome vibration so familiar to small boys in dusty hiding places."[47]

Such "hiding places" or "nests" are an important part of our own memories. Like Nabokov, one of us (DGS) made tents out of the bedclothes at bedtime. Or we spread an old sheet over a card table in the hallway to make a cave, an igloo, or an Indian teepee. Outdoors with a best friend, we commandeered a large glacial rock in a nearby park as a castle, store, house, hospital, or whatever structure suited the particular afternoon's pretend game. An arbor on an abandoned estate along the Hudson River only a short walk away was our fairy home where we danced, sang, and prepared magical spells to scare away demons and goblins. And on rainy days, in a corner of the kitchen, near the watchful and gentle presence of Grandma, we played with dolls, sewed, and colored, and were allowed to hang our finished drawings on the kitchen wall. These memories intrude upon us as we read about those of the writers we have sampled and verify our thesis that places and spaces are important components of play.

Among Edith Wharton's fondest memories are the days she spent at Pencraig, the family home in Newport. She had a pony of her own, beautiful gardens to delight her, a sheltered cove where she and her friends could swim, and places for walking and riding. But if the outdoors enabled Wharton to grow in body, the happiest times in her childhood were spent in her father's library, "a secret retreat from the rest of her young-girlhood."[48] Here, lonely child that she was, she gained nourishment from the books she read, and as her biographer, Cynthia Wolff, notes, she was like a "scavenger, rummaging through the family's literary leftovers."[49] A quiet place and time to read afforded Edith the opportunity to develop her intellectual gifts, which eventually allowed her to take "refuge" in writing fiction. Despite a cold, distant, and self-centered mother, who wanted Edith to become a proper young lady and even decided which books her daughter could or could not read, Wharton managed to maintain her impulse to write, and poured her fantasies into her many novels. In *A Backward Glance,* her autobiography, she writes, "I cannot remember the time when I did not want to 'make up' stories." Her loneliness in childhood (except for the summers at Newport) forced her to look inward, and she found companionship in "words."

A striking comparison is the early history of the famous and notorious nineteenth-century French novelist, George Sand, who like Wharton was born into an aristocratic family and experienced a lonely childhood. Sand wrote in her reminiscences that at ages four and five "I used to compose out loud innumerably long tales which my mother used to call my novels . . . They were stupefyingly boring (according to my mother) because of their length and digressions . . . I could not yet . . . read fairy stories; printed words . . . did not make much sense to me . . . through the telling of them, I managed to understand."[50]

Erich Kastner, who is probably best known in America for *Emil and the Detectives,* had a special place for playing when he was a child in Dresden. As he reports in his memoirs, "the staircase was my playground. It was here that I used to set up my fort—the medieval fort with loopholes, pointed turrets and movable drawbridge. Fierce battles took place here."[51] Kastner enacted battle scenes with his tin soldiers, intermingling troops from every century and every nation, mixing up battles and generals, allowing his imagination to take liberties with the facts in his history books. The other people living in the same building as Kastner's family had to take "enormous steps" in order to avoid crushing a regiment engaged in "victory or defeat." Neither the postman nor Frau Wilke who lived on the fourth floor could interfere with Kastner's "battles," for he was "Commander-in-Chief and Chief of General Staff of both armies. The fate of all the centuries and all the nations taking part lay in my hands."[52]

Long, narrow hallways also served as playgrounds for Richard

Wright. But these were the hallways of his grandmother's house in Jackson, Mississippi, with its "white plastered walls, its front and back porches, its round columns and banisters."[53] There were no tenants, such as Kastner recalled, to disturb the games of hide-and-seek in these hallways or under the stairs. For Wright, visits to his Granny's home were a welcome retreat from the otherwise bleak life of a black child in America. There were enchanting places to explore both inside the house and in the wide, green fields where Wright and his brother roamed, played, and shouted.

A forest for Nabokov, city streets for Chotzinoff, a quiet library for Wharton, and for Lillian Hellman, a fig tree in New Orleans, a "first and most beloved home." These were the sacred spaces that provided a place for pretend. In *An Unfinished Woman*, Hellman writes: "The fig tree was heavy, solid, comfortable, and I had, through time, convinced myself that it wanted me, missed me when I was absent, and approved all the rigging I had done for happy days I spent on its arms. I had made a sling to hold the school books, a pulley rope for my lunch basket, a hole for the bottle of afternoon cream-soda pop . . . It was in that tree that I learned to read, filled with the passions that can only come to the bookish, grasping, very young, bewildered by almost all of what I read."[54]

Props and Pets

Of all the "props" of childhood, none are more compelling or conducive to make-believe and fantasy than the books children read or hear read to them by a warm, loving adult. Shaw, for example, believed that he was "born able to read" and could not understand why he needed "poor Miss Hill," a governess, to teach him to read or write. He could not "recollect anytime when I could not and did not read everything that came my way." His "mind thirsted for a new idea." In remembering his favorites, *The Pilgrim's Progress* and *The Arabian Nights*, he claimed they showed that "I was as good a critic in my infancy as I am now, though I could not then give such clever reasons for my opinions." His mother encouraged him to read *Robinson Crusoe* and later he acquired a taste for Shakespeare, but he loathed children's books "for their dishonesty, their hypocrisy, their sickly immorality, and their damnable dullness."[55]

Erich Kastner also loved to read as a child and remarked that when a child learns to read and likes to read, "he discovers and conquers new worlds . . . The child who cannot read is only aware of what is under his nose." The child who reads is carried to faraway places and discovers "Mount Kilimanjaro, or Charles the Great, or Huckleberry Finn . . . or Zeus transformed into a white bull with the fair Europa riding on his back." Kastner "read and read and read. Nothing printed was safe from my eyes."[56]

The French plays that the English journalist, Maurice Baring, read as a child "fired" his "imagination as nothing else did."[57] Baring and his sisters acted out the stories using costumes and props made from anything on hand in the nursery and performed their plays endlessly.

As we have seen, just as the books and plays the Brontë children read served as the basis for their own inventions in their "children's study," reading was the salvation of Edith Wharton's childhood. When once Wharton discovered Washington Irving's novel, *The Alhambra,* she was in "ecstasy." Even though she could not read at the time, "from those mysterious blank pages I could evoke whatever my fantasy chose." Sometimes as she made up her own stories from the pages she was "reading," she held the book upside down, but she turned the pages as if she were truly reading, and alone in the room (parents and nurses peeping in), she continued her fantasizing. When she learned to read, reading became a "frenzy" with her, and she made up stories at a furious pace.[58]

In her autobiography, *Blackberry Winter,* Margaret Mead recalls that she filled her days with "reading, reading as many hours a day as I could manage between playing outdoors and doing formal lessons. Of course, reading was a good thing, but too much reading was believed to be bad for a child. And so it became, in part, a secret pleasure I indulged in at night when I was supposed to be asleep or in the daytime hours I spent curled up in a hollow at the roots of a tree while I was supposed to be off on some more active quest."[59]

Other "props," such as the rabbit and furry Spitz puppy Wharton owned as a child or the ponies of Nabokov or Elspeth Huxley, are also important elements in childhood play. Not only were these pets sources of love and affection for these children, but, for Huxley particularly, a little girl growing up away from her mother and English friends, the pony was a welcome companion.

Toys can also spark interest and engagement, and initiate elaborations in play and in language. They need not be expensive or complicated—a stick, even a piece of paper, offers endless possibilities. Although many of the creative people we have mentioned were inspired by a parent's story or a visit to the theater, which then became the impetus for pretend, they still needed certain materials to carry out their plans. Chiang Yee's bamboo-stick horse or a "green hat" Peter Abrahams wove out of "young willow wands and leaves" are reminders of the simple elements children enjoy using in their games. In *The Longest Years,* novelist Sigrid Undset describes the inventiveness of children in rural Norway, who were permitted to run about in a "withered, untidy, and wet garden" where they played "bakery" using bricks, a board, and mud: "With quick and practiced gestures she plunged her hands into a lump of mud that lay on the counter, rolled it into balls, and patted them flat: 'Is it to be a Christmas cake today, or would you like a seed bun?' " The children used pebbles for money, grass and mud for mincemeat, red brick-dust for cinnamon, and the iron steps nearby for the "house" where Undset "was supposed to live; she had thoroughly entered into the game. She was quite dizzy with delight."[60]

Like Undset, who described the simple, natural elements these Norwegian children used, we once watched a family who had come to the beach in Puerto Rico. The only toys the children brought were a shovel and a small doll, yet they played endlessly using sand, shells, fallen feathers, bits of driftwood, smooth ocean glass, or whatever "treasure" they could find on the beach.

Sometimes toys can be more elaborate. Vyvyan Holland remembers a "toy milk cart drawn by a horse with real hair on it" that his father gave him. Wilde then filled the churns and the cart with milk and permitted the children to tear "around the nursery table, slopping milk all over the place" pretending they were horses.[61] For Goethe, his puppet theater was his greatest joy, and so were the toy forts that Kastner and Holland treasured. But even these more expensive toys were not the mechanically operated, remote-control kind that do the same thing over and over. Rather, they encouraged open-ended play. Unstructured or semistructured toys, such as blocks, a dollhouse, or a fort, can lead to transformations as varied and creative as a child's own capacity to effect them. The Brontë children's toy soldiers assumed new names, personalities, and occupations to suit the young players' moods and desires. Nabokov's "boxful of tremendously appetizing blocks" were "infinitely precious things" and made perfect tunnels for his toy trains.[62] Puppets were important to the film director, Francis Ford Coppola, who contracted polio at the age of eight and spent almost a year in bed. There he would read or "tinker with mechanical things or gadgets." Like his heroes Thomas Edison and Alexander Graham Bell, he came to see himself as an "inventor." He invented stories. Alone in his room, inspired by books his brother gave him, "he played with his puppets, listened to 'Let's Pretend' on the radio and began to fantasize stories that he might tell."[63]

Puppets were also the delight of Maurice Baring. A servant in his household gave him a puppet theater equipped with scenery of a Moorish garden and a forest, and "a quantity of small puppets suspended by stiff wires." This theater was "a source of ecstasy, and innumerable dramas used to be performed in it."[64] Baring also played with a dollhouse and dolls, "but not as girls do, mothering them and dressing them." Instead, he used the dolls as puppets, "made them open Parliament, act plays and stories" or take the part of kings. He kept his play a secret, "knowing it to be thought rather eccentric and liable to be misunderstood," but it did not matter to him considering the pleasure he gained from his games of pretend.[65]

From these childhood memories and many others like them we are able to add to our understanding of the factors that lead to the imaginative adult. We believe that children who are left alone with no encouragement to play, no place to play, and nothing to play with might indeed play, just because children are inquisitive creatures by nature. But when we add a caring person, a sacred space, and a few props or toys, imagination bursts forth. Thus, when we recognize among the adults we know those who are a trifle more creative, more flexible, more willing to entertain the impossible, it may well be that their childhood experiences included some of the elements we have described.

Can we get in touch with those childhood experiences? Of what use are they? Will they help us become more creative adults if we can recapture that spirit of fantasy? Will our memories be a source of inspiration and guidance for our own children? Erich Kastner believed so. He said that our recollections "live right inside us. They are generally dormant, they are alive and breathing, and sometimes they open their eyes. They live, breathe and sleep elsewhere—in the palms of our hands, in the soles of our feet, in our nostrils, in our hearts, and on the seats of our trousers."[66]

2

Imagination:
The Realm of the Possible

> I dwell in Possibility—
> A fairer House than Prose—
> More numerous of Windows—
> Superior—for Doors—
>
> —Emily Dickinson

As a young mother hung up the telephone one afternoon, she noticed with surprise that her four-and-a-half-year-old son Danny had dragged his toy box into the kitchen and was hastily lining up a troop of toy soldiers on the floor. In response to her inquiry he shouted, "We're gonna try 'n' rescue Daddy! You said he couldn't come home for dinner 'cause he's all tied up at work!"

This incident encapsulates a most complex set of processes that reflect not only the special limitations of the cognitive capacity of a normal preschool-aged child but also the early manifestations of the vast reach of the human imagination. Little Danny has not yet developed the differentiated vocabulary that would enable him to grasp "all tied up" as a metaphor for a complicated series of transactions at his father's workplace; from his perspective it is what happens to Muppets or cartoon victims on "Fraggle Rock" or the "Smurfs" who must then be rescued by troops of "good guys." Whether or not our young hero really believes he can fetch his father home for dinner with his toy soldiers, he is displaying in language ("we're gonna try") and, presumably, in thought, a sense of *possibility*. The concept of "what might be"—being able to move in perception and thought away from the concrete given, or "what is," to "what was, what could have been, what one can try for, what might happen" and, ultimately, to the purest realms of fantasy—is a touchstone of that miracle of human experience, the imagination.

Whether in adults it takes the form of reconstructing one's past (for memory, as most cognitive research demonstrates, is rarely simply a vivid reexperiencing of actual events), planning what to do on the job, or merely allowing oneself to daydream about future vacations, sexual opportunities, or space adventures, the imagination liberates us from the tyranny of this place, these chores, these people. Through our human capacity for what the great neurologist Kurt Goldstein termed "taking an attitude towards the possible" (a capacity he believed reflected the optimal functioning of a healthy, intact brain), we are capable of exploring a range of potential futures or of traveling through time and space to a different or better childhood.[1] Sigmund Freud wrote that thought was a form of "trial action." Indeed, he built his theoretical concept of the ego around the principle that a human being can delay the impulsive, potentially damaging actions urged by the underlying drives of sexuality or aggression by imagining various outcomes. He proposed that such fantasies partially reduced the strength of drive pressures and allowed the ego time to plan more adaptive and effective means of satisfying the basic drives.[2]

We need not accept the specifics of Freud's hydraulic energy model to recognize the great importance of trial action through thought, which his theory emphasizes. Most of the great theoreticians of psychology have put imaginative exploration at the center of their efforts to construct a broad outline of the human organism. Kurt Lewin, who worked in Germany and the United States, wrote of "levels of reality and irreality" in the individual's life space; Lev Vygotsky in the Soviet Union attributed great significance to the role of reflective thought in avoiding impulsive action; and Jean Piaget in Switzerland proposed that symbolic or imaginative play was a critical phase in the emergence of mature thought.[3]

Freud also made a distinction between primary and secondary process thinking. The former mode of thought reflected direct expression of basic wishes and body-derived impulses (usually sexual or aggressive) and was found in daydreams and nocturnal dreams. Secondary process thought emerged through the influence of what Freud later called the ego; it was orderly, rational, and characterized by logic and the ability to postpone or suppress immediate sexual or aggressive desires in the interests of long-term satisfaction through, in effect, socially adaptive planning.[4] This conception, certainly a most suggestive and provocative notion when Freud proposed it at the start of the twentieth century, incorporated a developmental view of the primary process as more childlike and immature, a form of thought to be supplanted by the secondary process. According to Freud, most people might regularly revert to primary process thinking—a conclusion reflecting his inherently tragic view that our civilization can never really be free of the cyclic pressures of the biological drives of sex and aggression—but on the whole, mature adult life is characterized by secondary process thought. Only in the special activities of artists or writers can one observe socially adaptive applications of primary process thought. In his studies of artistic creativity, psychoanalyst Ernst Kris described these creative explorations of "primitive" thinking as "regressions in the service of the ego."[5]

A more modern view of human thought seeks to avoid conceptions that are built on "regression" to childlike processes. Instead, it proposes that thought operates in at least two general forms, both adaptive for particular sets of social and physical demands. Jerome Bruner has termed these the "paradigmatic" and "narrative" modes of thought or understanding, "ordering experience" and "constructing reality." The logical, sequential, paradigmatic mode is usually formulated in verbal terms in our own thoughts as well as in our communication to others; indeed, in its most advanced form it is expressed mathematically. This mode seeks for truth and is, as are all scientific hypotheses, ultimately falsifiable.

In contrast, the narrative mode, while sequential to the extent that it is communicated to others in a series of statements, may be thought of first in bursts of images, usually visual and auditory, but sometimes even olfactory, gustatory, tactile, or kinesthetic. It is expressed as a story and can also emerge, we would suggest, as what cognitive psychologists call "episodic" or "event" memories, or as fantasies and daydreams. As Bruner has proposed, the object of narrative is not truth but verisimilitude or "lifelikeness." One can identify gaps in logic in a story sequence, but those very features (as in much poetry, in the novels of Franz Kafka and Thomas Pynchon, or in Philip Roth's recent Zuckerman series) are designed to communicate the sometimes comical or playful, but often creepy or sinister, irrationalities of the human condition.

Both of these modes, formulating propositions about events into logical hierarchies and organizing our thousands of experiences into believable or "acceptable" stories, must be mastered by children growing up in what we call the Western industrialized countries. It may be that some cultures place more emphasis upon narrative thought and communication than others, but it is hard to imagine societies that do not require the paradigmatic or logical sequential mode of discourse, even if only for economic purposes and business transactions. We concur with Bruner when he asserts that "efforts to reduce one mode to the other or to ignore one at the expense of the other inevitably fail to capture the rich diversity of thought."[6]

Our objective in this volume is to explore the narrative mode of thought as it first emerges in the mind of the growing child. We are proposing that such thought first manifests itself in make-believe and pretend play interactions—such as "peekaboo" or "feeding the dolly"—between parent and child during the second year of life and that it becomes a more vivid feature of children's floor play (alone or in small groups) in the third through fifth years. Through play we hope to explore the consciousness of the kindergartner by observing sequences of naturally occurring or experimentally varied pretend and symbolic games.

A caveat is necessary at the outset. We cannot claim that children's imaginative play has been proven to be a forerunner of adult narrative or imaginative thought. It may well be that theories of development are untestable unless our society commits itself to intensive and extensive longitudinal data collection on a scale much greater than has hitherto been possible. And since we are functioning here in the paradigmatic mode, subject to the demands of scientific hypothesis-testing, we must also make some of our presuppositions clear. We assume that early imaginative play *is* a precursor of later fanciful thought, and we propose that such play has particular adaptive features. When children engage in symbolic games they are practicing mental skills that will later stand them in good stead, just as practice in walking, balancing, or swimming aids the development of motor skills. In a review of animal and child play research, P. K. Smith concluded that the cross-species data do not point to many identifiable social benefits of play that are evolutionarily adaptive.[7] But we concur with Brian Vandenberg that such a conclusion is irrelevant to the intrinsic mythmaking, reality-constructing nature of human beings. If the narrative mode of experiencing and communicating has an adaptive function (even if only to sustain hope and provide enjoyment), then its origins in children's play are worth examining.[8]

Imaginative Play in the Context of Cognitive-Affective Psychology

For the first half of the twentieth century American psychological theory and research was dominated by a curious, inadvertent conspiracy between psychoanalysis and behaviorism. Both systems of thought tended to focus on conceptions derived from Darwinian evolutionary theory and on the continuity between animal species and humans. This common focus was especially evident in their agreement that human behavior was motivated and steered by biological drives. Although at first the behaviorists limited their attention to hunger, thirst, and sexuality, the sorts of things one could vary in maze-running rats, in the 1940s they also began to include anxiety or fear-avoidance among the motivators presumed to be biologically rooted. Psychoanalysts, while obviously more mentalistic than behaviorists, still followed the libido or drive-energy theories that Freud had developed during the last thirty years of his life, which sought to reduce human motivation to two basic, presumably biologically derived drives, sexuality (Eros) and aggression (Thanatos).

During the late 1950s psychology gradually underwent a paradigm shift, a broad-based change in the ways that behavioral scientists conceptualized both human and animal information processing and learning. This "cognitive revolution" was occasioned by neurophysiological research questioning the conception that peripheral drives like hunger and thirst were sufficient to cause complex, motivated behavior; by studies of the sleep cycle, which led to an awareness of how much thinking goes on while organisms are in reduced stimulus states; by the new field of artificial intelligence, which sought to simulate thought through computer programming; and by other extensive advances in studies of how adults and children process information.

While psychoanalytic theorizing changed less drastically (in part because clinicians tended to be less aware of new research findings), a comparable revision in emphasis has occurred. The shift from drive theories to the so-called "object relations" notions that by the 1980s had come to dominate the psychoanalytic field reflects to some extent a shift toward a more cognitive model. The view that a sense of the boundaries between self and others, an ability to differentiate parental figures, and even a sense of "good me-bad me," "good mother-bad mother" are critical in children's development has a much more cognitive cast than do the earlier "vicissitudes of the instincts" or hydraulic-energy-like drive models that emphasized the pressures of hunger, sex, or aggression rather than the child's experience. The way in which objects (meaning the people in a child's life space) are represented through self-talk and imagery is now the major feature of the more orthodox psychoanalytic school. Under the leadership of Jung, Adler, Sullivan, and others, neofreudians had always emphasized interpersonal relationships, but now such concerns became part of the psychoanalytic mainstream. The direct observation of children by Vygotsky and A. R. Luria in the Soviet Union, H. Wallon in France, Jean Piaget in Switzerland, and Lewin in Germany and America had not had much affect on psychoanalytic theorizing about childhood. When John Bowlby began studying "attachment" to parental figures, however, his views gradually began to exert an influence in psychoanalysis, especially as careful experimental and observational studies by developmental psychologists supported the heuristic value of his studies.

Clinical studies by Heinz Kohut and Otto Kernberger have also been influential in shifting psychoanalytic theorizing to a relational (and, hence, cognitive) rather than a drive model of personality. Psychoanalysts such as Kohut have sought to maintain their "classical" credentials by proposing that the relational perspective—that is, the infant's awareness of boundaries between self and others, and its differentiation from and fusion with a "good" or "bad" parental image—is characteristic of infancy and babyhood, while drive conflicts of the classical oral, anal, phallic, and Oedipal stages operate to create neurotic problems or personality variations in children ages two to five. As Stephen Mitchell has cleverly shown, the attempt to preserve a drive theory by "tilting" the relational model back to infancy does not work; it is clear that such a model operates throughout the life span.[9] From the kinds of papers that fill current psychoanalytic journals it is apparent that the emphasis today is upon the perceived relationships through which children develop the meanings about self and others they assign, and the ways in which these internal perspectives on self-other relationships are played out in the face of direct social interactions in later childhood and adult life.

It seems likely that the information-processing view of the person will continue to prevail for the balance of this century. In effect, we now regard human beings from their earliest emergence from the womb as information-seeking creatures, curious and exploratory, striving to organize and integrate novelty and complexity but also most likely to feel comfortable and to smile (as Hanus Papousek's experiments with infants have shown) once they can experience control over novelty and assimilate new events into prior concepts and scripts about the sequence of events.[10] The "smile of predictive pleasure" described by Papousek and other observers of early childhood behavior and the comparable signs of positive emotion (laughter and smiling) associated with familiarity in the adults studied by Robert Zajonc suggest that, while cognition and emotion may be structurally different systems in the body, they are closely linked in human response.[11]

The theoretical analyses of Silvan Tomkins have played an important role not only in producing psychology's paradigm shift toward a cognitive model in the early 1960s but also in once again making emotion the center of active research in personality and social psychology. Tomkins has shown that a cognitive perspective, an emphasis on the human assignment of meaning and the organization of experience data into schemas and scripts, as the research of Hans and Shulamith Kreitler and of Roger Schank and Robert Abelson indicates, does not preclude a powerful, motivational role for affect or emotion. With the support of the extensive empirical research initiated by Carroll Izard, Paul Ekman, Gary Schwartz, Ross Buck, and, by now, many others, we can view humans as showing differentiated emotional response patterns that are closely intertwined or evoked by the novelty, complexity, and other structural properties of the information they confront from moment to moment.[12]

This cognitive-affective perspective broadens our view of human motivation considerably. Rather than reducing all motivation to some symbolic manifestation of infantile sexuality or aggression (as Freudians once did, and, alas, as many psychoanalytically influenced literary critics and scholars still do), one can propose that the basic emotions described across the human species by Ekman and by Izard are motivating for dozens of different situations along the four dimensions identified by Tomkins.[13] We seek first of all (1) to reexperience or to reconstruct events, interactions or thoughts that have evoked the positive emotions of *interest-excitement* or *joy* (smiling and laughter) and (2) to avoid in action or thought those situations that have evoked the specific negative emotions of *anger, fear-terror, sadness-distress* (weeping), or the complex of *shame-humiliation-guilt*. We also appear to be "wired up" (3) to *express* our emotions as fully as possible and, finally, (4) to *control* emotional expression where our social experience suggests it is necessary. Those situations that permit the experiencing and expression of positive emotions or allow for the appropriate control of negative emotions will intrinsically be positively reinforcing. Those situations that have

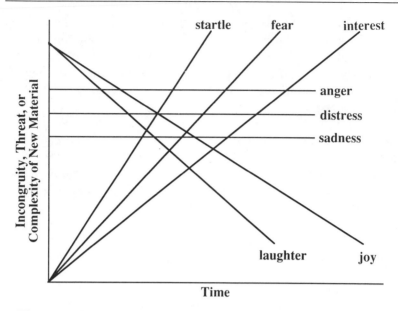

Figure 2-1. Reaction to a novel stimulus depends on the suddenness and incongruity of new information and the time it takes for that incongruity to be reduced through assimilation to established schemas. Note that laughter and the positive emotion of joy are aroused when an incongruity or threat is quickly reduced. If high levels of incongruity persist, the negative emotions of anger, distress, or sadness emerge. (Derived from proposals by Silvan Tomkins in *Affect, Imagery, Consciousness* and modified to emphasize information assimilation.)

evoked fear, anger, distress, or shame, or that have blocked the expression or socially adaptive control of emotions, will be inherently punishing or negatively reinforcing. If, as we shall describe below, the emergence of basic emotions is closely associated with the human tendency to organize, integrate, and assign meaning to novel information, we can see how a great variety of situations well beyond those that satisfy the biological appetites of hunger, thirst, or sex, or the dubious drive of aggression, can become motivating.[14]

One of Tomkins's most provocative hypotheses is that the specific emotions are triggered by the information-processing tasks one confronts at a specific time or across a restricted time period. A simple diagram may represent what we consider to be an extremely challenging conception and one that will help us later on in understanding the affective components in imaginative play (see Figure 2-1).

The diagram represents the relative rapidity with which we are exposed to different degrees of novel or relatively unanticipated information in our physical and social environment (or, we would add, in the stream of our own thoughts). Tomkins employs the term "density of neural firing" to suggest that anything from a sudden, unexpected loud noise to an unanticipated hostile outburst from a friend or spouse will evoke a great range of neural activity.[15] This concept of density is somewhat vague, although it may find some support in neoassociationist theories of memory, such as those of Gordon Bower or John Anderson, in which complex networks of semantic meanings may be activated in the rapid search to match stored meanings with the features represented in a sudden new stimulus.[16] We prefer to use the term "assimilability of new information," that is, the extent to which anticipatory schemas or expectations are already capable of being matched to the new material or the extent to which an array of such stored schemas are available to be matched with the new information once a rapid cognitive search process gets underway. Our position is also close to that of George Mandler, who has emphasized the role of the "interruption" of expected sequences of events, or "incongruities," and the "discrepancies" between ongoing plans or initiated actions and their outcome, both informational and physical, as the basis of emotional experience.[17]*

Figure 2-1 suggests that, while a highly unexpected, incongruous, or novel stimulus (social or physical) arouses the startle response and emotions of fear or terror, a more moderately paced, less extreme set of incongruities may chiefly evoke the positive emotions of interest or excitement. This is an important feature of Tomkins's position: incongruity stimulates exploration and curiosity, a "moving toward" response. Part of the reason earlier drive reduction theories floundered was that they could not account for the exploration and stimulation-seeking behavior Harry Harlow observed in monkeys and Jean Piaget in babies and toddlers. Indeed, the great psychoanalytic scholar David Rapaport has said (personal communication) that classical Freudian theory cannot explain natural curiosity.

Most theorists agree that those who are suddenly exposed to an unexpected event will react with fear even before they can formu-

---

* See Mandler, pp. 202–208 for a diagram and a discussion that somewhat overlap with ours.

late a clear meaning. If we are seated on the front porch on a quiet holiday afternoon, for example, and hear the sudden sound of screeching tires, we feel terror even before we can clearly add the cognitive appraisal, "An accident!" Since the combined suddenness and incongruity of the noise cannot be assimilated into our extant schema of the day's likely events, we are frightened. The noise may repeat but again, no explanation fits. Then we realize it is coming from the television set in a neighbor's house; it is Memorial Day and the Indianapolis 500 is being broadcast. When we can make this match with preestablished schemas, our sense of incongruity drops sharply; we experience relief and smile even if we feel a bit foolish about not having remembered the scheduled race or a bit peeved at the loudness of the neighbor's TV. This pattern, the reduction of the novel to the familiar to produce laughter or smiles, is a recurring one, and we will return to it in our attempt to understand children's joy during make-believe play.

Suppose, however, that the screeching of brakes and the squeal of tires does not stop and that the noise is not attributable to a television broadcast. Instead, a succession of "souped-up" cars or motorcycles speeds down the hitherto quiet street, something that has never before occurred in this peaceful country village. This persisting high level of incongruity first evokes our anger and then an inclination to take action, to remove the unexpected. We may express the anger by shouting at the drivers as they whiz by, by calling the police, or even by taking violent action if a weapon is at hand. A case in point is that of Washington journalist Carl Rowan, an adherent of strong gun control laws, who shot a strange teenager he found unexpectedly cavorting in his swimming pool in the middle of the night.

As time passes and we further assimilate new information into preestablished schemas, we may recognize, for example, that immediate action will not remove or resolve the unfamiliar situation. We may then react with despair, depression, or the weeping response of distress-sadness. A sudden bereavement exemplifies this effect. The unexpected death of a loved one produces shock, and then sometimes anger at doctors, at the victim for not getting medical help, at God, or at ourselves for some related failure. Gradually, as we assimilate the reality of the loss, we may no longer feel anger, but, rather, sadness as the sense of incongruity continues. Each time we undertake a task we once shared with the other or enter a room or a setting where the lost person would usually be found, our expectation of his or her presence is disconfirmed. It is this still moderately high level of persisting incongruity that produces the sadness of helpless mourning. In the tragic moments of an opera, play, or film our willing suspension of disbelief allows us to hope, with the temporarily revived Violettas or Mimis, that they *can* live, only to experience the crashing minor chords and despairing cries of their lovers as the reality of death hits home. As the curtain falls and we applaud and leave the theater, our suspended disbelief fades; we reduce the sense of incongruity with the smile of familiarity: "What a great performance!" or "That was a real tear-jerker!" We have assimilated the experience into the general schema of "an evening at the theater."

We have devoted a good deal of space to a discussion of the cognitive-affective position because it remains less well known to many intellectuals and even to many educators, applied psychologists, psychiatrists, and mental health workers than other approaches. We are also proposing that it is a central conception from which we can explore the nature of imaginative play and its role in childhood and speculate on the conditions that arouse, enhance, sustain, or interfere with the emergence of imaginative thought.

Human beings, as we have suggested, must make sense of the world they inhabit: the nursery, the family, the neighborhood, television (a new kind of environmental context), and the ever-widening social and physical milieus that growing individuals encounter. Beyond the cognitive demand for meaning assignment and organization (with the affective consequences we have just suggested) human beings confront a dialectic tension in their general motivation throughout the life span. This tension is between, on the one hand, the need to feel close to others, to be attached to or encompassed by, at first parents, siblings, and other caregivers, and later, friends or membership in a particular group (for example, religious, ethnic, or nationalistic); and on the other hand, the need to preserve a sense of autonomy, privacy, personal competence, and individualized skill development. This fundamental struggle—to achieve a balance between affiliation and a sense of community and at the same time to develop a sense of autonomous power—has been emphasized by a number of major personality theorists. Described with especial clarity by David Bakan as the tension between community and agency, the concept also appears in the earlier theorizing of the Hungarian psychiatrist Andras Angyal, who emphasized homonymy versus autonomy. Otto Rank, one of Freud's most brilliant early disciples, later moved away from Freud's sex versus aggression polarity to stress the tension between immersion in intimacy and relationship versus assertion of the individual will. Alfred Adler juxtaposed individualized power striving and the enormous importance for personal well being of what he termed the social interest, the need to relate to and serve others. Carl G. Jung's sweeping concepts of extraversion and introversion seem at least partly to represent this same polarity, cast in more purely psychological or intrapsychic terms.[18]

Jung also stressed a kind of male-female tension in all humans, which he called the *animus-anima* and which he linked characteristically to broad cultural symbols such as the Chinese *yang-yin* or sun-moon principle. Today we might propose that calling this tension one between male and female reflects a social stereotype, the fact that the traditional masculine role emphasizes power, autonomy, and achievement while the traditional female role favors affiliativeness and nurturance. Jung might agree that the polarity is not inherently gender-linked but characteristic of all humans and more developed in one gender or the other because of socialization or community expectations. Even Freud's Eros-Thanatos polarity might be reinterpreted as reflecting in Eros, or sexuality, a feminine-mother orientation and in Thanatos, or aggression, a masculine-father perspective. Louis Breger has provided a careful analysis of this dichotomy and the way in which Freud seemed eventually to move beyond the male-female stereotype in the subtext of his soul-searching book, *Civilization and Its Discontents*, to recognize that this tension is inherently human. Most recently, in the framework of an object relations psychoanalytic system, Sidney Blatt has sought to show how the early childhood struggle between attachment and individuation may, if one pole is overemphasized or becomes a focal area of conflict, eventuate in particular forms of psychopathology. George Bonanno and Jerome L. Singer have extended these views to identify a series of personality dimensions that recur in the literature along with particular affective tendencies, defensive patterns, variations in physical illness-proneness, and the emotional disorders as characterized by Blatt, all of which can be grouped schematically in a triangular diagram (see Figure 2-2).[19]

This conceptualization, still speculative but in keeping with some research evidence, suggests that optimal personality functioning and hardy physical health are found near the apex of the triangle

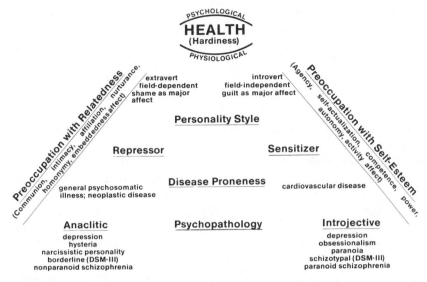

Figure 2-2. Diagrammatic representation by George Bonanno and Jerome L. Singer of the implications of the persistent human tension between relatedness or attachment and self-esteem or individuation for normal personality variations, psychological defenses, physical illness-proneness, and psychopathology. The further one moves to the sides of the triangle, in effect giving priority to attachment or to individuation, the more the likelihood of a one-sided personality style or, toward the base, of a particular type of pathological development. (Reproduced by permission.)

and toward the center, implying a reasonable balance between affiliation or relatedness and autonomy or individuation. Near the top of the triangle, an individual may be more focused on individuation or personal power but still sufficiently mindful of social needs to be labeled as introverted or field-independent in style without any likelihood of susceptibility to gross physical illness or neurosis. Only as the gap between the two sides of the triangle widens and an individual overemphasizes either autonomy or community do we see manifestations of some susceptibility to particular kinds of physical or mental illness.

To elaborate on all of the conceptual and research aspects of this view will carry us too far afield from our main focus on the child's imaginative growth. What we will stress as we move through our exploration of the child's make-believe world, however, is the extent to which, in both form and content, the pretend play of the toddler represents a continuous working out of the dialectical tension between the need for closeness and affiliation and the need for privacy, a sense of personal power, and individuality. This tension is perhaps fundamental to the nature of our cognitive system for, in a sense, we inhabit two worlds, each of which provides stimulation to which we must respond. Piaget signaled this when he distinguished between accommodation or imitation of the outside world and the attempted assimilation of new experiences into the limited store of available schemas.[20]

We would propose that by its nature, our memory storage system provides us with an ongoing source of stimulation in the form of intruding images and phrases, which call for some share of attention as do the stimuli in our external physical or social environment. We must learn to establish priorities in how we distribute our attention, whether toward the environment or toward material recurring from memory or forming itself into fantasies. Survival may well demand that we learn to give higher priority to processing external stimuli, what David Rapaport wrote of as the "permanent gradient towards external attention—cathexis."[21] Yet, as we shall see, effective development may also involve reflection, introspection, the capacity to enjoy and direct private experience, to plan, to create narratives, and to explore a range of future possibilities. For young children with limited motoric and linguistic capacities and a smaller, less differentiated range of schemas and scripts, the balancing of priorities may emerge in the relative amounts of physical, rule-oriented, social, and imaginative play in which they engage.

We have sought to position childhood imagination in the context of a cognitive-affective view of human beings and a community-agency dialectic. Before turning to specifics, we would like to examine the temporal role of imaginative play in the unfolding of the personality across the life span. As we shall see, imaginative play emerges toward the end of the child's second post-partem year, struggles fitfully toward a flowering well into the third year, and in the fourth, fifth, and sixth years is a significant factor in the child's behavioral repertoire. While Piaget seemed to suggest that imaginative play fades by the early school years as "operational" thought takes over, we shall suggest that it is merely submerged in the interest of the changing demands of school decorum and other social pressures.[22] As skill in internal speech and thought develop, make-believe play may become an ongoing fantasy activity, but the urge to play in this way may persist into adolescence, and, indeed, where social circumstances permit, even surface in adult life.

As Philippe Ariès has pointed out, pantomime, dressing-up, and play-acting were important features of the leisure of the aristocracy in the courts of Renaissance kings and princes.[23] In Edith Wharton's novel, *The House of Mirth,* we read of such entertainment among wealthy New York society members at the end of the nineteenth century, and it does not seem much different from the pastimes of the country gentry of England a century earlier depicted in Jane Austen's *Mansfield Park.* Adult play was ritualized in religious ceremonies and in quasi-secret societies like Freemasonry, the Order of Elks, the Foresters, and the Knights of Pythias. It was even more structured in the amateur theatricals of the English middle class in Charles Dickens's set or in the socialist circles where Karl Marx's daughter, Eleanor, and the young George Bernard Shaw tried performing Ibsen's *A Doll's House.*[24] Our attraction to make-believe games persists throughout the life span.

We stress the life span because modern psychology has moved beyond the psychoanalytic emphasis on personality formation in the first five years of life toward a fuller view of the human condition across time. Erik Erikson has of course been a key contributor in freeing behavioral scientists from the narrow conception, built around psychosexual stages in childhood, that prevailed among psychoanalysts and among many child care workers and researchers in the first half of this century. By showing how, in Western industrial societies at least, different age levels are linked to emerging general life crises, which require some resolution for further effective development, or at least satisfactory adaptation, Erikson broadened our conceptions. While perhaps not fully willing (because of psychoanalytic politics rather than theory or evidence) to give up completely on the oral, anal, phallic, or Oedipal stages, Erikson has shown convincingly that issues of trust, autonomy, industry, identity-formation, generativity, and so on are critical features of healthy human development. But by separating intimacy and identity as necessary phases of development at different chronological periods even Erikson seems to be adopting a more traditional, masculine point of view, as Franz and White have astutely observed. These investigators, in keeping with the polarity of communion and agency we have already described, have rewritten Erikson's well-known life-cycle diagram to propose that at each stage we must confront the same tension between attachment and individuation.[25]

Here, we present an even broader view of the life span, which incorporates the classic psychoanalytic model; Harry Stack Sullivan's juvenile "chumship" phase, for which data from the research studies by Thomas Berndt offer support;[26] Erikson's most recent modifications; and Franz and White's restructuring of Erikson's proposals.[27] But we also incorporate a fifth element, first suggested by Havighurst, Tryon, and Lillienthal and modified by us here,[28] which is the view that at particular ages, the very nature of human physical and mental skill development, as well as society, demands of us the performance of certain tasks. When we are infants our caregivers have expectations and provide environments that engage certain of our skills. At each subsequent phase we must respond to these familial or social expectations and find in ourselves, or in interaction with others, new skills and roles to deal with attachment-individuation crises and the other possibilities that our cognitive-affective structure or social milieu permit.

Table 2-1 presents an example of a life-span model that incorporates for each phase the Eriksonian view of specific conflict and its resolution, Franz and White's description of the individuation and attachment pathways that thread their way like a double helix through the life span, and our more specific identification of task demands and expectations. The Eriksons have recently added "wisdom" to the crises of old age, and Joan Erikson in a new book has proposed that the playfulness and openness to sensory experience that emerge between the ages of two and five must be sustained throughout life to permit humor and the emergence of wisdom in old age.[29]

Table 2-1 suggests that play and imagination are critical in the first three or four years of life, but each new life-task evokes new occasions for imaginative play, whether expressed in daydreaming, in amateur theatricals, in the enjoyment of reading, film, or theater, or simply in a humorous point of view that temporarily eases much of the inevitable bitterness and loss in human life as it moves inevitably toward death. In the chapters that follow we will explore the opportunities for play afforded by each level of social demand or each stage of cognitive growth, although we cannot provide evidence that either children's early imaginative play or the emergence of the "subjunctive mood" in thought and language establishes a foundation for all later imagination and play.

The Forms and Functions of Play

In a broad evolutionary and cultural context, play is a general biological phenomenon. Here we are indebted to observers like Charles

Table 2-1
Developmental tasks and their personality implications

Approximate age when task or social expectation first appears or is critical	Psychosexual stage	Developmental task life-crisis or societal expectation	Personality implication		
			Individuation pathway	Attachment pathway	
Infancy (to 18 mos.)	Sensory-oral (Freud)	Achieving secure attachment; giving and receiving affection; learning to walk and beginning to talk	Trust vs. mistrust	Trust vs. mistrust	
Early childhood (2–5)	Muscular-anal (Freud)	Developing self-control; beginnings of sense of right and wrong; communication skills	Autonomy vs. shame	Object and self constancy vs. loneliness and helplessness	
	Locomotor-genital (Freud)	Developing capacity for play and imagination	Developing private personality; initiative vs. guilt	Beginning to play with others and to "show-off"; playfulness vs. passivity or aggression	
Middle childhood (7–12)	Latency (Freud) School age (Franz and White) Juvenile chumship (Sullivan)	Relating to social peers, school groups, forming close friendships, learning new motor skills; developing cognitive skills, accepting or adjusting to one's changing body	Industry vs. inferiority	Empathy and collaboration vs. excessive power or caution	

Table 2-1 (*continued*)

Approximate age when task or social expectation first appears or is critical	Psychosexual stage	Developmental task life-crisis or societal expectation	Personality implication	
			Individuation pathway	Attachment pathway
Puberty and early adolescence (12–15)		Learning psychobiological and social sex roles; developing specific sexual "appetites" (hetero- or homosexual attractions); confronting issues of group membership, "popularity"; specific athletic, artistic, or academic skill development	Identity vs. identity diffusion	Mutuality interdependence vs. alienation
Late adolescence (16–19)		Learning to understand and control the physical world and the broader social milieu; developing an appropriate symbol system and conceptual abilities; learning creative expression	Identity vs. identity diffusion	Mutuality interdependence vs. alienation
Young adulthood (20–30)		Relating to the system of occupations; family formation, citizenship	Career and life-style vs. drifting	Intimacy vs. isolation

Table 2-1 (*continued*)

Approximate age when task or social expectation first appears or is critical	Psychosexual stage	Developmental task life-crisis or societal expectation	Personality implication		
			Individuation pathway	Personality implication	
				Attachment pathway	
Adulthood (30–50)		Relating to childrearing and to economic stress and opportunity; responsibility to older and younger generation family; community, citizenship, organizational relations, e.g., union, vocational groups, clubs	Life-style consolidation vs. emptiness	Generativity vs. self-absorption	
Maturity and seniority (55 and over)		Relating self to broader world and to universe; confronting retirement; grandparenting or aged parents; civic responsibilities; leadership roles; development of a life story; humor; planning for a sense of continuity by bequest or creative production	Integrity vs. despair; wisdom; existential identity; withstanding physical disintegration	Active participation vs. isolation and loneliness	

Darwin, who in the late nineteenth century identified those emotional and behavioral variations in human and other mammalian species that we call playful action.[30] At the beginning of the twentieth century, Karl Groos wrote *The Play of Animals* and *The Play of Man*, which have tremendously enriched our grasp of the role of play, not only in human development but across many animal species. Groos initiated in the Netherlands the tradition of keen interest in play and play theory that inspired Johan Huizinga's *Homo Ludens,* an intriguing work about the historical importance of play as a feature of human society. Huizinga's imaginative historicocultural analysis suggests that much adult human behavior can be understood as both a continuation of child's play and an outgrowth of the gamelike rituals and mythic forms developed in earlier societies (examples would include the links between Christmas and New Year festivities or between Mardi Gras and the Saturnalia of ancient Rome, with its pageantry and uninhibited sexuality). For Huizinga a certain quality of "gamemanship" is essential for effective life in our civilization; play is a critical forerunner of the later competitive strivings that characterize adult society. While current researchers on play are inclined to view Huizinga's position as relevant chiefly to games of skill and mastery, only one type of child's play, the influence of his position on modern entrepreneurial training is evident in the many popular books on game-playing and on training procedures for being "Number 1" or rising in the corporate world.[31]

More recently there have been important integrative efforts by Owen Aldis on play-fighting in animals, Robert Fagen on general play in a range of animal species, Peter Smith on the possible evolutionary adaptive functions of play across animal species, and Helen Schwartzman, who has brought together a vast array of anthropological observation, on children's play in human societies. Such research ranges broadly from marmosets to chimpanzees to human children in cultures as diverse as the Kpelle, a pretechnological modern tribe, and suburban nursery-school children in the United States. As Smith points out, some type of play behavior has been observed in primates, carnivores, pinnipeds, and ungulates, in sperm whales, wallabies, opossums, wombats, Tasmanian devils, and a few bird species. Usually reptiles are considered nonplaying species, but how can we tell, since snake behavior and metabolism are so far beyond our human frame of reference?[32]

We need, of course, some definition of play. While there may be some disagreement, especially about the animal species that are least familiar to us, most investigators draw a distinction between play and those animal behaviors that are directly related to survival and reproduction. Eric Klinger has provided a useful definition of play as "behavior *other than* (a) consummatory behavior, (b) instrumental behavior leading detectably to consummatory behavior or to a detectable goal extrinsic to the play behavior itself, (c) competition with a standard of excellence, (d) socially prescribed, institutionalized or ritual behavior when it occurs in a context in which the prescription is socially sanctioned and enforced and (e) behavior constrained by the requirements of social interaction" (italics ours).[33]

For young, nonhuman animals Smith has delineated three forms of play that generally follow Klinger's definition. These are (1) locomotor play, which involves jumping, sudden running, and dangling or crawling, and is generally carried out in solitude; (2) play with physical objects in a tool-like fashion but without a direct instrumental function; and (3) social play, which can include both of the above but also involves contact, usually with siblings or agemates, that calls for pouncing, grabbing, nonlethal biting, wrestling, mounting, grooming, or chasing. Such activities are sometimes signaled by a "play-face" in primates, by some other signal, or by their occurrence with species-appropriate "playmates" (almost never with adult males). Smith's review of the literature was designed to estimate whether such play behaviors have evolved through natural selection because they serve adaptive functions in the later development of the individual young animal. He concludes that there are enough indications to support the view that physical activity is useful, not in getting rid of "surplus energy" (as the poet Friedrich von Schiller's classic theory suggests) but rather as exercise—providing better muscle tone, physical skill, and agility— that permits more likely escape and hence, survival and reproduction. Play fighting, which is a widespread play practice in animals, cannot be shown, on the basis of current evidence, to have great adaptive significance for later development, although pouncing play in young cats has proved predictive of better prey-catching skills later in life, and wrestling behavior in male lion cubs seems potentially adaptive for later effectiveness in asserting one's power over a territory and a pride of females against other males. Smith proposes the as yet untested hypothesis that male lion cubs play more at wrestling, while female cubs (who later in life will do the hunting) engage in more stalking and pursuit play. Overall, Smith's review reveals little evidence of the benefits of play for growth in social and cognitive skills except in a few instances among the most humanoid primates. But he is very careful to point out that with human children, where language and apparent imagery or symbolic resources are involved, play, especially imaginative games, may have much more broadly useful roles. And he argues that as our society has become more complex and the skills needed to function within it more sequential and verbal, reliance on unstructured free play may be increasingly less useful than directed learning.[34]

Whether or not we can demonstrate that children's play has an evolutionary survival or reproductive developmental outcome is probably of little moment if we can show that it possesses other values within given societies. As Brian Vandenberg, Michael Lewis, Brian Sutton-Smith, Mihalyi Csikszentmihalyi, and other observers of childhood and adult play behavior have proposed, play is just plain fun.[35] In terms of cognitive-affective theory, most forms of play involve situations of moderate challenge, novelty, or incongruity. Playful interactions between self and others (or, in the case of pure fantasy play, self and symbolic others) or between self and objects usually result in a somewhat reduced level of novelty or incongruity that evokes joy. Such interactions may also produce the conscious or automatic realization that within the defined structures of play one can continue to experience moderate challenge along with a further reduction in incongruity. Such an approach seems to us more specific than Freud's postulation of a "repetition-compulsion" to explain why children play certain games again and again.[36]

For Piaget play emerges as a critical, if passing, feature in early childhood, where it takes the form of sensory-motor play, symbolic or pretend play, and games with rules. According to Piaget, all play serves a mastery function; he rarely discusses its affective function. Rather, he was primarily interested in epistemology, the sources of adult knowledge, reasoning powers, and morality. Sensory-motor play involves more than sheer "functional pleasure," to use the phrase of the Viennese pioneer of child development research, Karl Buhler; it provides the child with an increased sense of the differences between the textures, tastes, and smells in its environment and greater skill at reaching, grasping, and directed movement. Through symbolic play the child seeks to imitate and accommodate to complex adult actions and speech, gradually reshaping the externally generated material and assimilating novelty into its limited range of memory schemas, thus increasing the differentiation within schemas and gradually forming new ones. Games with rules range from the simple "Ring around the Rosy" (with hand-holding, circling, singing, and the dominant order to drop down on the signal, "All fall down!") or "Hide-and-Seek" to more complex street games such as "Red Light, Green Light," parlor games such as "Statues" or "Charades," and board games such as "Chutes and Ladders" or "Checkers." Such games are critical for mastery of orderly thought, moral judgment, and other phases of "operational" or mature thought.[37]

For Piaget, however, mature thought was chiefly limited to formal, sequential processes such as the shaping and reshaping of organized verbal meanings. Through his emphasis on ongoing internal representations of reality he played an important role in the shift from the stimulus-response psychology of the first half of this century to the cognitive approach that has emerged since the 1960s. But, as Brian Sutton-Smith and Inge Bretherton have shown, Piaget tended to devalue the importance of play as a source of mature adult imagery and as the foundation for playfulness in thought (and, we would add, for the daydreaming and fantasizing that add spice to adult experience and may lead to creativity and playfulness in social object interactions).[38] As Bretherton has noted, because Piaget viewed pretend play merely as an "assimilation of the world to the ego," a limited capacity of the growing child, he saw no role for it in those processes—seriation, classification, and conservation—that are the means by which we represent the "real" world in organized, ongoing thought. As Piaget wrote, "Symbolic games decline after the age of four, for reasons which it is very important to discover, since they also explain why these games are so numerous earlier. In a general way it can be said that the more the child adapts himself to the natural and social world the less he indulges in symbolic distortions and transpositions, because instead of assimilating the external world to the ego he progressively subordinates the ego to reality."[39]

Here we see the limitations in Piaget's emphasis on what Bruner has called "paradigmatic" thought and his corresponding neglect of "narrative" thought, and in Piaget's method, which included a very limited sample of children. It is clear from observing large numbers of children of diverse backgrounds that pretend play (as well as other kinds of play) goes on well into the early school years and continues either "underground" in the mind or in more socially sanctioned group forms well into adolescence. As we shall see, even "games with rules," such as the board game "Monopoly," often involve additional pretend elements or are the focus of private or shared fantasies well into adult life. The reshaping of "given reality" is as much a commonplace of human thought as the attempt to accommodate to the environment through coherent schemas, which Piaget's epistomology emphasized.

Play, then, is an inherent capacity of children, but it is often also a set of behaviors adults expect of children, especially when they are relatively free of the immediate need to find food or avoid life-threatening danger. But even when they engage in activities that are primarily instrumental, children naturally demonstrate an extra element of playfulness not unlike the tugging, pulling, sudden running, and mock wrestling described in the animal play literature. In *Oliver Twist*, Dickens describes crime-master Fagan's methods for training his troop of boys to be pickpockets in nineteenth-century London streets, and they include a great deal of make-believe and humor. Fiction, perhaps, but echoed in some remarkable documentary films made in the 1980s (and shown on TV's "Sixty Minutes") of the so-called "gypsy" children who harass tourists in Paris streets. These seven-to-twelve-year-olds, intent on pocket-picking, surround passersby. If, as sometimes happens, they are chased off by the kicks of their would-be victims, they still engage in noninstrumental "funny-faces," smirking, aimless leaps and runs, or verbal exchanges that create a play atmosphere, even though they are desperate to bring home wallets and purses to their hard gypsy bosses.

These documentaries also highlight a feature of human play that we sometimes minimize in our frequent references to the "constructive" or "socially adaptive" features of play behavior. For these street children, sold by Balkan parents to crime bosses in Paris, Rome, or Naples, or stolen outright, making fun of tourists or the police becomes the only way they can gain a sense of power, indeed, a subversive if small-scale sense of control over their true persecutors, their bosses or the parents who gave them up. At a less inherently tragic level, as Brian Sutton-Smith has pointed out, a great deal of children's play-fighting and pursuit, and even the grotesqueries of name-calling and teasing, reflects their attempt to create a miniature social structure in which they can try out, under "controlled conditions," being "bad" or disobedient.[40] For thirty years or more *Mad* magazine has prospered without commercial advertising by purveying cartoons that represent the outrageous, a ten-year-old's subversive look at the adult world. Alfred E. Newman, *Mad*'s exemplar, like the animated cartoon characters Bugs Bunny and Daffy Duck, reflects the modern Jungian trickster archetype, as appealing as Puck and Till Eulenspiegel once were to the generally repressed children (and adults) of medieval times.

We began this discussion with Klinger's definition of play as intrinsically motivated, noninstrumental, or life-preserving behavior. Within this general definition we can identify the three general classes of play proposed by Piaget: sensory-motor, symbolic, and games with rules. The first of these most clearly reflects our commonality with other animals—sheer physical exercise and, anthropomorphizing somewhat, a delight in sensual experience: the pleasant coolness of a breeze, the fresh scent of newly mowed grass beneath bare feet, the exhilaration of soaring high up in a playground swing. But, whatever the inner experience of animals may be, we cannot avoid recognizing that the human predilection for assigning meaning, the formation of scripts and of self- or other-schemas, and the beginning of the "as if" or subjunctive mood all introduce a symbolic play quality into both sensory-motor and rule play.

The tension we have described between self-esteem and social relatedness also informs our sensory experiences and, of course, our rules play, united through the creation of a make-believe dimension, a controlled, reduced-to-size realm that is the child's domain of personal power (agency). Within this private frame are enacted interpersonal comedies and tragedies: swinging may become a competitive besting of a peer or a sibling, the rule game a miniature war (as in chess or checkers) or the working out of a morality play in which one strives not only to play well but also to be on the winning team (community). One of the hypotheses we will consider in our exploration of children's play is that, whether or not pretending derives from evolutionary natural selection, it does have a host of important consequences beyond the sheer pleasure of the moment. We surmise that, while children may play at purely sensory or physical mastery games or engage in rule games (for the sake of communion or to demonstrate personal skill), those who fail to infuse play with pretend or symbolic meaning may not only be missing some additional fun but may also be handicapping their growth in certain cognitive and social directions. To assert that imaginative play has a variety of short- and long-term benefits may reflect a cultural bias, as Sutton-Smith has argued.[41] But, as we have already suggested, the subversiveness of cartoon humor demonstrated in *Mad* magazine or "Garbage Pail Kid" cards may serve an important balancing function for children in a world in which they are powerless and the tragedies of parental neglect or abuse, abandonment, illness, and death are increasingly apparent. Those children who do not experience encouragement or adult support through story-telling or pretending, who do not seem to be able to add a symbolic dimension to their repetitive physical play, rules play, or games of skill and chance may be condemned either to impetuous instrumental activity or to the apathy of isolation or extreme dependence on conventional ritual. We want to journey through the realm of make-believe in childhood to see if our hypotheses about the advantages of imaginative play throughout the life span are indeed supported by various research methods and observations.

3

The Beginnings of Pretending
and Baby Play

From the moment a mother holds her newborn baby in her arms, nuzzles its cheek, nibbles at its tiny toes, or allows the baby to curl its fingers around hers, she is engaging in various forms of sensory-motor play. This kind of bodily stimulation and interaction provides an initial opportunity for the mother—and other caregivers—to create and maintain optimal levels of arousal that will encourage the infant to explore and stimulate its curiosity about its environment.

A major question confronting those of us who study play is one of origin. Is the capacity for pretend play inherent—is an infant born with the ability to engage in ludic symbolism—or is pretend play taught? Perhaps, as Daniel Berlyne suggests, pretend play is a result of innate curiosity and, at the same time, of the natural exploratory drive described by Corinne Hutt. We look at play from the viewpoint of cognitive-affective theory, which we described in Chapter 2. As the baby glances at its mother's face and begins to explore her features, it is attempting to assimilate this strange but interesting object into its consciousness. Is this face "like a ghostly mask" looming so large overhead something to be feared or something to enjoy?[1] How can we assume that mother-child interaction eventually leads to pretend play and its whimsical characteristics? What is there in the baby that will cause it to respond favorably to its parents' smiles, vocalizations, or physical contact? How do the baby's initial facial expressions, which we label "puzzlement," "frowning," or "fearfulness," become the social smile that signifies delight, joy, and well-being? What really takes place, as Enid Bagnold says, in that "strange, concentrated life that no man knows, shared with the cat in the stable and the bitch in the straw of the kennel, but lit with questions of the marveling brain"?[2]

Early Smiling, Joy, and Play

Because the playful gestures of the mother toward the infant are stimulating, the baby responds with fleeting smiles from as early as four weeks; with cooing, babbling, and social smiles at three months; with genuine laughter at six or seven months; and with elation at twelve months—and thus a love affair with the human race begins. This mutual reinforcement is necessary for both parent and infant and creates a bond between them. Without the response of the baby, the mother becomes upset, frustrated, even depressed. Without the smiles and vocalizations of the mother, the baby begins to withdraw, remains passive, and in the most extreme cases may develop what René Spitz calls *anaclitic depression,* a refusal to eat, to smile, and to respond that can result in death. A mother may accompany her touch with kisses, smiles, and soft caressing sounds—all conveying to the infant that this is a pleasant experience. Such experiences cumulatively engender the beginning of a trusting relationship, the dyad that Freud, Sullivan, and Erikson viewed as essential for the development of children's future interpersonal relationships as well as their fundamental sense of their own trustworthiness.

A baby thrives on stimulation, but there appears to be an optimal limit. When stimulation exceeds normal boundaries (too much tickling or lifting up in the air) the infant manifests signs of distress and even anger. In their studies of mother's tempo in play sessions with three- and five-month-old-infants, Christina Arco and Kathleen Mc-Cluskey found that a natural temporal style of stimulation rather than a faster or slower pace led to the most positive interactions between parent and infant.[3] Mothers begin to learn how much to play, when to play, and when to allow the baby to entertain itself. The capacity for self-entertainment is important as the baby grows. Diana Shmukler's pioneering work with preschoolers in South Africa suggests that children engage in more imaginative play when mothers introduce a game or an idea and then step aside. An ever-present, hovering adult interferes with play.[4]

How does a baby know or recognize parents' playful intentions? Anthropologists have long studied play signals such as vocalizations and facial expressions, especially the open-mouthed play face, tail signals, and some ritualized body movements such as bounding, stiff-legged jumps, rhythmical head-shaking, and running with exaggerated stops among chimpanzees and other animals. The play face of raccoons, mandrill baboons, and certain species of bears, which open their mouths quite wide, differs from that of chimpanzees, whose mouth opening varies according to the intensity of their play. Animals may use open-mouthed play faces in wrestling, in chasing games, or during acrobatics.[5] Researchers are now finding a striking and remarkable convergence between the social systems of chimpanzees and dolphins. Like chimpanzees, the bottle-nosed dolphins of Shark Bay in Western Australia live in fluid and flexible communities within a common home range. Females are cooperative and form "playpens" around youngsters, allowing them to interact within a protective environment. At times, a female will "baby-sit" for another dolphin that may be occupied elsewhere. The behavior of bottle-nosed dolphins is so friendly and playful that they even permit tourists to stroke their flanks and feed them fish. These acts are reciprocated by the dolphins, which toss their visitors a fresh herring or a piece of seaweed.[6]

Among humans, smiles and laughter are universally considered to signal a play situation. The evolution of the human smile from the primitive grin seems rather clear, but the association of the smile with pleasure is more difficult to explain. As evidenced in baboons, the grin is evoked when animals meet each other and appears to be a defensive gesture that indicates friendly intentions. Perhaps the human smile has evolved in the same way, from a defensive reaction to one of pleasure and anticipation. Thus, what was originally a response to a startling situation, the approach of another animal, has become a sign of pleasure—in infants, a response to tickling or even to peekaboo games, in which the main idea is to surprise. The smile, involving movement of one of the facial muscles, the zygomaticus major, is found among all peoples, including those dwelling in the more remote areas of the world.

The Etruscans, a people of the Archaic Period (650 to 450 B.C.), carved "droll, enigmatic and outright goofy" smiles on the faces of the figures they produced in terra cotta, marble, and bronze.[7] In fact, the smile is the most pervasive facial expression in Etruscan art during this period, which, according to art historian Cornelius Vermeule, may represent a broader attempt to break away from Egyptian formality and focus on the ideal naturalism of the human figure. The smiling faces on statues of well-developed athletes, beautifully coiffed maidens and even votive beasts, whether real or mythological, are evidence of a playful view of the world. Some of them, especially those made of terra cotta and painted, display a smile "sweeter than a grin."[8] On a carving of a youth made about 540 B.C. as part of a funerary relief, we see a "smile of confidence even in death." One particularly engaging terra cotta sculpture of a monster's face with tight curls above its forehead wears a broad smile and sticks out its tongue in "piquant humor." "Smile wrinkles" are carved at the outer corner of each eye.[9]

The Maya, whose civilization flourished during the Classic Period

(A.D. 300 to 900), also introduced humor into their art. Although their main gods were carved with solemn restraint and have static faces, there are some subsidiary figures that suggest delight and joy. A long-nosed god carved out of bone wears an expression of "surprise" as he gazes at another god catching fish. A carved jaguar found in the ancient Mayan city of Copán, Honduras, has one paw balanced on its hip, sports "ridiculous pompons and flares at the end of its tail," and wears a loin cloth.[10] A creation myth in *Popol Vuh,* the sacred book of the Maya, describes the "Jaguar of Sweet Laughter" as one of the creatures to "come out human."[11] The Sovereign Plumed Spirit, an agent that exists above, before, or beyond nature recognized the human emotion of joy, expressed by laughter.

Although we do not have a clear understanding of what brain mechanisms control the smile, a neonatal smile is present in the infant soon after birth and before the social smile emerges. Even blind and deaf-and-blind children begin social smiling at roughly the same time as normal children. Perhaps this is not surprising: if we were to visit a strange land where we did not know the language or the customs of the people, we would probably rely on a smile to ease the situation and initiate friendly contact. The father who hides behind a pillow and then reappears with a big smile on his face and says, "Peekaboo," signals the baby that all is well, that he is "back again." The doctor who smiles at the infant and holds it in a relaxed position will have a more cooperative patient than one with a stern demeanor. The infant's smiling and vocalization, at least for the first eight to twelve weeks of life, are independent of the environment, that is, uninfluenced by learning, but after this period, the environment plays a much more important role.

How does the social smile come about? When a caregiver feeds an infant, whether by nursing or with a bottle, the removal of the discomfort of hunger, accompanied by the movement of the caregiver's features as she smiles and gently talks to the infant, becomes identified in the baby's mind with a pleasant, satisfying experience. As this experience is repeated, the "feeding-smile" association becomes established. The infant's memory of satisfaction leads to the sense of trust that Erikson describes as the first crucial stage in human development. Over time, this trusting relationship gradually generalizes from mother or father to whomever the baby sees on a regular basis. Eventually the infant will differentiate among the many faces it is exposed to during the early weeks of care.

By the age of two months, a baby will prefer to look at things that are complex, that are composed of different lines and angles or have specific shapes. If an infant is shown an incomplete face, one with eyes alone, it may smile. As the infant gets older, by about five months, it will easily smile at a face with all features present. A baby may initially be puzzled by a novel or strange facial configuration and may even register signs of distress as it gazes at a complex figure. But as it recognizes that the features resemble a familiar face, such as that of the mother or the father, the infant becomes interested, even delighted, and smiles. Silvan Tomkins stressed the importance of the face as a "major communicator" about affect. Just as the smiling adult face lets the baby know that a pleasant experience is taking place, an angry expression and harsh voice suggest fear, distress, or anger, to which a baby will often respond with crying.

A parent will soon learn to distinguish between an infant's cries of hunger, anger, and pain by their intensity in one-month-olds, and by their intensity, duration, amplitude, variability, and complexity in six-month-olds. This suggests that a baby is capable quite early on of conveying a sense of its needs to the caregiver. Ross Thompson has found nine types of cries among one-year-olds briefly separated from their mothers, which vary in intensity, rhythmicity, and continuity.[12]

Early Bonding and Social Interaction

By about six or seven months of age, the infant becomes attached to specific people: the mother, the father, the grandmother, an older sibling, or the caregiver if the parents work. We have noticed more expressions of joy when the infant is in the care of people whom it sees regularly and more indications of distress when a new babysitter or an unfamiliar visitor appears. Although the infant's crying may disturb grandparents who rarely see their grandchild, it is helpful for them to know that these distress signals signify "stranger" and are indications of the infant's intelligence in differentiating between familiar and unfamiliar faces. In a short time, a new babysitter or a grandparent can win the infant's trust by smiling and speaking gently, and by avoiding rushing in and trying to pick it up or approach too quickly. The infant needs times to inspect the stranger's face, absorb the features, and assimilate this novel person into its preexisting schema. Once this is accomplished, fear can turn to delight.

Jerome Kagan's research in different cultures suggests that children begin to show fear of strangers and to protest separation at about eight months. John Bowlby, Alan Sroufe, Mary Ainsworth, and Harriet Rheingold have also examined the effects of attachment and separation, and in general, in controlled experiments, have found that an infant will explore its surroundings if the mother remains fairly close by. If a stranger appears, the child will cling to its mother, peeking at the stranger from time to time but staying close to the mother as it plays. If the stranger is pleasant and smiling, the child will gradually begin to interact, but in a cautious way. If the mother leaves the room, the child will generally stop playing and cry or stand near the door immobilized until the mother returns.

What can parents do to foster more trust and acceptance of others in their child? We know that feeding is a major way in which the baby learns to trust the parent and attaches itself to the parent. The need for physical contact, however, is striking. If we recall Harry Harlow's experiments with infant monkeys, we became aware of how traumatic it can be for a baby to be denied the continued physical closeness and warmth of a parent. In the laboratory, a baby monkey spent more time clinging to a dummy mother covered with soft terry cloth than to a wire mesh dummy mother who provided milk. When frightening objects were introduced into the cage, the baby monkeys preferred to cling to the soft mother. What was most dramatic in the Harlow experiments was the behavior of the monkeys raised by a wire mesh dummy mother. The monkeys did not spend time clinging to the wire mesh mothers but after feeding time huddled in a corner, clutching their bodies and rocking to and fro. If a scary object was introduced into the cage, the monkeys would scream or curl up in a fetal position.

The contrast between the behavior of wire mesh and terry cloth reared monkeys is not too dissimilar to that of human infants. When a stranger approaches the infant, it is frightened and clings to its mother, but will gradually warm to the stranger if its mother remains close by for comfort, reassurance, and protection. With this security, the infant is more willing to explore a new situation, whether it is an interaction with a "stranger" or a new toy. The security the mother provides allows the child to add information to its existing repertory and permits its natural curiosity about new situations, objects, and people to emerge.

Here again, we see the importance of cognitive-affective theory in play. If a baby is not comforted or reassured, it will not explore the novel but will continue to cling and remain distressed. The baby that does feel secure enough to explore new ground may even laugh at the loud noise of a toy or the antics of a playful stranger. A trusting attachment between mother and child encourages the development of the child's natural exploratory, playful attitude. The child's later transference from mother to a special toy, blanket, or diaper indicates how important the proximity of a familiar object is to a child's sense of security. Many infants who sleep with a favorite blanket or stuffed animal, even as they get older (like Linus in the "Peanuts" cartoons of Charles Schulz), will feel totally abandoned and in despair if deprived of its comforting presence.

From Smiling to Laughter through Play

The peak time for face to face play with infants is between three and six months. During this time an infant may be exposed to numerous examples of facial expressions by caregivers. Mothers duplicate an infant's smile of pleasure, frown of discomfort, and wrinkled nose of disgust.[13] As the infant grows older, mothers may shy away from imitating negative expressions and reinforce a range of emotions they wish to encourage. Interestingly enough, we do see sex differences even in these early months. Girls tend to vocalize in response to stimuli (such as pictures of faces) more than boys do. And studies also suggest that parents respond differently to their babies: mothers show greater expressivity to girls than to boys[14] and in general, vocalize, smile, and touch their infants more than fathers do. This finding among American parents is similar to that of Michael Lamb with Swedish parents. In Sweden, however, fathers do not engage in as much rough-housing play with their male infants as fathers in America.[15] On the whole, American mothers and fathers tend to play more gently with their daughters.

If indeed a smile is a crucial socializing expression, laughter is even more infectious. According to Owen Aldis, laughter serves several functions. It can increase playfulness through a general arousal effect, which can condition a contagion effect. We have all had the experience of being in a group when someone starts to giggle. This "group glee," as Lawrence Sherman labels it, can be observed in nursery schools or daycare centers when children become convulsed with laughter.[16] When they try to stop, a mere glance can trigger the giggles again. This behavior seems to persist throughout life as anyone knows who watches teenagers "horsing" around or even a group of older men or women getting together for a night out.

Laughter is a signal from one person to another that actions are meant in fun, not fury. When a preschooler bumps his truck into his playmate's and laughs, his friend may join in the laughter and reciprocate in this "collision" game; without laughter a minor squabble might have ensued. Likewise, an adult who pushes a friend into the swimming pool amid squeals of laughter may be considered a fool, but the person he pushed will rarely be angry if he understands that the laughter is a play signal—and that the push was not meant to be harmful.

Laughter has a reinforcing effect as well as a signaling effect. If children perform a silly antic and we respond with laughter, no doubt they will do it again. The stand-up comedian needs our laughter; the most devastating blow is the deadly quiet of an unresponsive audience. For this reason television producers often use a laugh track in situation comedies to reinforce the laughter in the viewing audience; without it, many of the lines would fall flat.

Parents may use other play signals besides smiling or laughing. Facial expressions such as the "clown" or the "monster" with puffed out cheeks and distortions of the mouth or nose create silly or pseudo-scary images that children try to imitate. They quickly learn that these signals are introductions to play.

Imitation and the Onset of Spontaneous Play

As we have already pointed out, Piaget delineates three main stages of play: practice play, symbolic play, and games with rules. The earliest form of practice play is *imitation*, which involves "functional pleasure" games. From birth to about twenty-four months a baby displays a good deal of copying behavior without necessarily understanding what the movements mean. Much of the play of infants and toddlers is sensory-motor, experimenting with sounds, sights, and touch. Young children taste, chew, smell, lick, kiss, shake, and cuddle toys and eventually drop or toss them aside. When they discover the fact that objects fall, they amuse themselves by throwing everything to the ground and thus exercise their new power. Play is a constant learning experience, and although there might seem to be no overt purpose to repeated actions, there is joy in the experience of dropping—or what Piaget calls ludic play. Eventually, children will learn about gravity, but for now, they are satisfied merely to drop an object over and over again.

Facial imitation and finger and hand play are all part of the practice or mastery play Piaget describes as a preliminary to pretend or symbolic play. In the first several weeks of life, babies will stick out their tongues and open their mouths to mimic a parent's expression. Andrew Meltzoff and M. Keith Moore tested newborn infants ranging in age from 0.7 to 71 hours for their ability to imitate two facial gestures, mouth opening and tongue protrusion. They found that these newborns were able to imitate adult models under certain conditions. The babies, who were particularly alert, were tested seated in a semi-upright position in a well-padded infant seat. A white cloth in a spotlight was moved before the infant's eyes for at least twenty seconds to be sure the infant could fixate. The experimenter then put his face in the spotlight quite close to the infant's face and modeled either an open mouth or a protruding tongue. The data in this experiment contradict the view that infants have no capacity for facial imitations at birth. Meltzoff and Moore concluded that newborns accomplish imitation through an active matching process and "apprehend the equivalence between body transformations they see and body transformations of their own whether they see them or not." This is contrary to Piaget's theory that only eight- to twelve-month-olds can match a gesture they see with a gesture of their own they cannot see. To do this earlier than eight months, he believed, would be beyond their perceptual-cognitive competence.[17]

There have been attempts to replicate the Meltzoff and Moore study in Canada and Australia.[18] The Canadian experiment failed to find seventeen- to twenty-one-day-old babies capable of imitating either tongue protrusion or mouth-opening facial movements. The Australian researchers, however, although also failing to replicate Meltzoff and Moore's results, did not rule out the possibility that under certain appropriate conditions infants might imitate some behaviors. While more work needs to be done, researchers now believe that imitative behavior can occur much earlier than Piaget assumed.

Meltzoff has also been studying deferred imitation in babies and suggests that nine-month-old infants can imitate certain acts even twenty-four hours after the stimulus presentation;[19] infants were able, for example, to close a wooden flap, push a button, or shake a small plastic egg. The results argue for some form of memory in situations where infants only saw the adult model perform and were not given the opportunity to duplicate the act immediately. They also suggest that an infant may indeed watch an older sibling playing with a toy (one that is forbidden to the younger one while the older one is present) and, if the infant can secure that toy later, will attempt to remember how the toy works and play with it. Although earlier work by the same researcher found the capacity for deferred imitation in two-year-olds, the newer findings that young children (nine months) are capable of deferred imitation are important for understanding long-term memory in very young children. It may be that toddlers do indeed imitate behaviors they see that are not particularly directed at them. For example, in daycare settings where a number of infants and children are in contact, much vicarious learning may go on through the process of deferred imitation. Certainly these studies argue for the importance of caregiver-infant interaction in paving the way for future symbolic play and the development of a rich imagination.

The Beginnings of Emotional Development

Other important factors in parent-child interactions include the infant's capacity to recognize the facial expression of emotions. Would this ability to discriminate emotions be useful in the development of pretend play? Our own research supports the view that children who play seem to smile more and in general display more indications of positive emotions, such as joy and surprise. Play allows a child to develop empathy, the capacity for understanding another's point of view. The broad range of emotions a child experiences and learns to recognize in the early months of life may later on be utilized in games of pretend. The numerous activities that Piaget engaged in with his children, even during their first months, suggest that imitation of a parent's movements and gestures "can obviously be strengthened by a continual show of approval of the action, until assimilation becomes possible with the progress of intelligence."[20] Piaget encouraged imitation and joy in his children. He describes the smiling and laughter of his daughter Jacqueline when making bubbles or pressing her tongue against her lower lip to make a face or trying to imitate him as he put bread in his mouth and made it come and go between his lips. Jacqueline laughed when Piaget puckered his nose or when he put his face close to hers and opened and shut his eyes. There are numerous references in Piaget's *Play,*

Dreams and Imitation in Childhood to playful interactions between father, mother, and each child from birth on.

Parents attribute their children's facial expression to joy and interest more than to any other emotion; these are followed next by anger, with sadness lowest on the list. An identifiable facial expression of anger (lowered brows drawn together, eyes with a hard stare and bulging appearance, lips pressed firmly together with corners straight down, or mouth open and tensed in a squarish shape as if shouting) appears when a baby is frustrated.

To test frustration and anger, researchers asked, "What happens when a mother pulls an object out of an infant's mouth?" In an experiment with thirty seven-month-old infants, Craig Stenberg and colleagues (using a valid coding system) found that these babies exhibited facial expressions of anger when a teething biscuit was slowly but deliberately withdrawn, either by a female experimenter or by the mother.[21] The study supports the work of Paul Ekman and Silvan Tomkins, who claim that facial expressions specify discrete emotional states. The babies in the experiment exhibited more signs of flushing toward the experimenter (a stranger) than toward the mother, especially if the mother removed the biscuit first. Interestingly, if the mother's trial followed the experimenter's trial the anger directed toward the mother increased. The researchers interpret this to mean that the infant may have expected to be comforted when the mother's turn came, but when she did not offer comfort, the infant's anger became more intense.

Alan Sroufe's work on infant emotions suggests that the appearance of negative emotions, such as the rage of a newborn when its face is covered or when it is physically restrained, is the result of disappointment at three months, anger at seven months, defiance at eighteen months, and guilt at thirty-six months.[22] Not only do infants express these emotions, but it has been found that infants as young as ten weeks and five days can discriminate among facial and vocal expressions of happy, sad, and angry emotions. Charlotte Buhler has proposed that infants can recognize facial and verbal composites at five months, vocal expressions alone at six months, and dynamic facial expressions alone at seven months.[23] A beautiful example of this capacity appears in Irina Skariatina's recollections of her infancy in Russia:

> Expressions of faces became eloquent too, often even more eloquent than words, and so did movements and gestures. For instance she would

hear a new word and instantly look at the expression on the face of the speaker to find out what the new word meant. If she saw bright eyes and smiles she then knew that everything was all right . . . But if she saw dull and gloomy eyes and noticed that no smiles broke up the face into the lovely wrinkles that she admired so much—then she realized with a shock of fear that that new word meant something nasty and unpleasant and that in some way she was in danger.[24]

Current studies are finding that infants are capable of recognizing verbal expressions just as early as composite expressions. They can master sad-happy discriminations, whether vocal, facial, or composite, before angry-happy ones and generally discriminate expressions first through voice alone, regardless of which emotion an expression signifies. Work by Albert and Rose Caron and Darla MacLean supports the notion that neonates are most sensitive to vocalizations and that the voice may be a "primary channel of emotional communication" in early infancy.[25] Although mothers, as we have noted, are in general found to be more involved with their infants than fathers, it would be beneficial for fathers to use their time with infants in more vocalizing than has been reported.

It seems that parents' expectations about a child's capabilities at a particular age can influence their attitudes about what activities are appropriate for that child. If a parent believes a child does not understand language, for example, he may not see the need for vocalizing to the infant until the infant begins to speak. In a recent study in Israel, Anat Ninio and Nurith Rinott found that "fathers consistently believe that infants acquire cognitive skills and can participate in cognitively enriching or demanding activities at a later age than do mothers." This is unfortunate because of the numerous studies that demonstrate how essential it is for the adult to encourage infant vocalization. Such noise and sound play precedes what Catherine Garvey calls play with the linguistic system (phonological, grammatical, and semantic).[26]

Language and Early Play

Children in the two- to three-year-old age range use single word speech and simple verbal combinations, such as "go out," "me cookie," "baby come," "see bow-wow." In addition, they tend to use what Garvey calls action-identifying tags, such as "ding-a-ling" for telephone, "ruff-ruff" for a dog barking, or "bang-bang" for a toy drum. Their speech reveals a great deal of "playing" with sounds and noises and some rudimentary rhyming. Much of this language play goes on when children are alone, as Ruth Weir reported in her classic work, *Language in the Crib,* which studied the presleep monologues of her two-and-a-half-year-old son, Anthony.[27] When children play together, their speech tends to be more social. In preschoolers and kindergartners it may take the form of rhyming, or of fantasy and nonsense, such as making up funny names for friends or imaginary persons, or distorting or exaggerating words. Finally, language in play can be social conversation.

Before language begins, children often engage in games, and "a game in its way, is a little protoconversation."[28] A child who plays a game even before she has acquired language is, in effect, turntaking. The format a child uses in such early games—hiding or watching for the hidden person in peekaboo, feeding a doll or letting the doll feed her, moving a car or letting Mommy move the car—is known as the iconic mode. This mode of thought is a precursor to the symbolic mode, the ability to name an object or event. Through continued practice, a child begins to associate a particular game, or parts of a game, with words, whether "boo!," "yum-yum," or the actual word "car" in the games just described.

Many children begin acquiring language by pointing at an object or a person and saying a word, such as "da," as a signifier. Mothers or other caretakers reinforce this gesture by naming the object, by calling the child's attention to the object ("Look" or "What's that?"), or by agreeing, ("Yes" or "I see") and then labeling the object for the child. Thus, language seems to be acquired when, to use Jerome Bruner's term for this child-parent interaction process, two people "negotiate."

Recent work by Linda Acredolo and Susan Goodwyn provides evidence that symbolic gestures develop along with early language and that girls use gestures more than boys.[29] It is also clear from their studies that structured parent-child interactions are important in the development of these gestures. Children's gestures tend to depict the function of the object rather than the form. One small child combined her panting sign for "dog" and a knob-turning sign for "go out" to signal her mother that the dog needed to go out. Such gestures seem to be related to early vocabulary development and children's desire to communicate. Children clearly have a sense of the concept underlying the label of an object before they learn the word. Elise Masur found that mothers responded more frequently when children produced words with gestures than when children produced only gestures.[30] This suggests that some parents may not be aware that gesturing is a critical phase in their child's development and that they need to help by supplying labels. We have probably all seen babies wave "bye-bye" to someone just entering a room; eventually, through experience and repeated play with dolls and adults, they learn how to match words and gestures appropriately.

Piaget suggested that in the preoperational stage the preschooler uses egocentric speech, which he divided into three categories: repetition, monologue, and dual or collective monologues. The young child will repeat words and syllables for the mere pleasure of talking and may do this alone or in the presence of another child or a parent. "Spring Song," a short story by Joyce Cary, portrays an excellent example of a child's playful use of language.[31] Margaret (Mag for short) pushes her doll carriage along as she chants, "The akkerpeetie man—he was made of fish bones . . . and the tooboody came skinking along the collidor." When Mag's older sister Gladys tries to correct her, "Corridor, you mean," Mag insists that the word is "collidor" and that the "akkerpeetie" man had a "toople," an animal she calls a "singum" because "it came from Baffrica where all the dogs are scats." Exasperated, Mag's sister gives up, and Mag continues to enjoy her secret vocabulary in peace.

A monologue is composed of a group of phrases or sentences that are slightly more extensive than Mag's song in Joyce Cary's story. Children engaged in make-believe play often carry on elaborate conversations with themselves. At other times, when one child plays with another, they may engage in a collective monologue, but in this situation, each child may be carrying on his or her own conversation without necessarily interacting or responding to the other.

As the child gets older and enters the concrete operational stage, the pattern of speech changes from an egocentric mode to a socialized mode. Children can now adapt to another person through an exchange of thoughts and ideas. They can adopt the point of view of a listener and may argue or collaborate with others, criticize others, or use commands, requests, and threats. Children who use socialized speech ask questions that call for answers and answer questions in a meaningful way. Because socialized speech serves primarily for communication, it loses some of the playfulness of egocentric speech, which repeats the sounds children hear even when they do not understand their meaning (echolalia).

Sources of New Words

During the preschool years, from the ages of one-and-a-half to six, children learn over 14,000 new words, or about nine a day. Generally, language acquisition results from the dyadic interchange between caregiver and child, although some researchers have even included television as a possible source of novel words. In one study by Mabel Rice and Linda Woodsmall, three-year-olds were able to learn an average of 1.56 new words from even a brief exposure to television (fifteen minutes of two animated programs). The experimenters found that preschoolers could learn new words if the script was appropriate, if there was repetition, and if the words were coupled with a "clear, although not exaggerated, depiction of putative meanings."[32]

We believe, however, that parents can do a better job than television in teaching new words; and certainly they can provide a more loving interaction. The parent who speaks to a baby from the first day sets the stage for language learning. The baby sends out signals by cooing and babbling, and later by gesturing and pointing. Parents facilitate language acquisition by labeling, questioning, allowing the baby to explore their faces and limbs, and playing such games as "This little piggy went to market" and "I'm a little teapot" to help differentiate the parts of the body. By offering their babies a running commentary of continuous naming and interpreting, parents use "alter ego talk," which will be useful later in helping the child learn words and the appropriate emotional tone for various contexts. The early play of an eighteen-month-old, which may be functionally appropriate to an object (using a spoon to feed a doll), may later change to symbolic play (a stick can represent the spoon when the child feeds the doll). But whether the child uses a spoon or a stick, the accompanying vocalizations ("good baby," "yum-yum") suggest the affect the child associates with this experience. Sometimes we may even hear negative utterances ("bad dolly") and watch a child spank a doll, playing out an actual experience.

Parental communication styles also play a role in children's language acquisition. In some of our own studies we found that the amount of time parents spend in discussion and explanation, and in disciplinary or judgmental comments varied. Children whose parents used a discussion style acquired more information and more discriminating knowledge about their surroundings.

Early Metaphor

As children's vocabulary increases they begin to use metaphors in their speech. Some psychologists suggest that there is a difference between "child metaphors" and "real metaphors." In an excellent review of the research on metaphors, Stella Vosniadou presents her definition and criteria for labeling a word or phrase a metaphor. Metaphors must be "meaningful statements that communicate something about a concept by comparing it or juxtaposing it to a similar concept from a different conventional category." The two concepts that are compared must be based on "some perceptible similarity" and must "belong to different conventional categories."[33] Some researchers would argue that two-year-olds are incapable of producing a "real metaphor," since they cannot form conceptual categories, and that any apparent metaphor is merely generated by accident or based on the similarities between objects. According to Piaget, preschool children are unaware of the category to which each object belongs and may actually include completely different objects that may come from different classes within the same class.

Vosniadou suggests that when children use a block for a "cup" in pretend play it does not mean that they see any metaphorical similarities between blocks and cups; they may simply need the block for pretend drinking. Second, the use of the block as a "cup" is not meant to communicate anything about the object. Finally, the cup and block clearly are not similar in appearance. In general, in pretend play objects used to signify other objects need not be similar to them. A child we recently observed used a piece of irregularly shaped coral as a "telephone" in his play. Outside of this context his renaming is meaningless, and according to Vosniadou's criteria, cannot be called a metaphor. But such pretend renamings, which characterize much of symbolic play, are precursors of metaphors according to Vosniadou, and are based on "children's tendencies to impose a familiar schema on the object world."

Linguistic creativity seems to decline with age. According to Howard Gardner, elementary school children resist attempts to use figurative language. He has proposed that the development of metaphorical usage follows a U-shaped curve: metaphors are used by preschoolers, decline among elementary school children, and then increase as children reach preadolescence. Vosniadou, however, claims that Gardner's experiments with preschoolers did not "provide a direct test of metaphor comprehension."[34] Children younger than ten or twelve were unable to explain a metaphorical sentence or understand figurative language. John Waggoner and colleagues have also criticized Gardner for not using story context as support for interpreting metaphors in tests with children. When short sentences alone are used, they provide too narrow a base for children to make inferences about the meaning of a metaphor. Children might do better if the metaphor is surrounded by more meaningful material, which will lead to higher levels of comprehension.[35]

Piaget's notion of *literalism* or *realism* in language offers a further argument that children cannot interpret language nonliterally and are unable to compose real metaphors. A child who believes the "North Pole" is a wooden pole stuck in the ground and that "blackmail" means black stationery does not understand that these words do not refer to concrete objects. Danny in Chapter 2 clearly did not understand his mother's use of "tied up" when referring to his father's delay in coming home.

Vosniadou argues that metaphorical thinking in young children allows them to use their existing knowledge to explain and understand "new phenomena, phenomena that are not quite similar to anything they have experienced before." The two-year-old who uses a stone for a "cat" may imitate a cat's sounds and movements as he pushes it along the floor, hides it under a chair, or helps it "drink" pretend milk from a toy saucer. It doesn't matter if the stone is "cat" or "stone." What is important is that the child practices what a cat can do and imitates and controls its actions using an inanimate object in a safe situation.

As babies grow older, their receptive and expressive language capacities also grow, so that they can begin to use language to indicate their needs, wishes, and feelings. Language helps children to differentiate themselves from the environment, to see themselves as separate from their parents, and to gain a sense of themselves as a girl or a boy. Children's symbolic play, enriched by their capacity to express a character's personality, enables them to try out different roles and test their knowledge of what is possible. Piaget believed that language not only serves to communicate with others but may also give an individual "sufficient pleasure and excitement to divert him from the desire to communicate his thoughts to other people."[36] It is difficult for children, however, to keep thoughts entirely to themselves before the age of seven. Children tend to say everything out loud; before speech is used to socialize thoughts, it "serves to accompany and reinforce individual activity."[37] But adults, even in their private speech, "think socially" and continually have in mind "their collaborators or opponents, actual or eventual," to whom they will subsequently announce the results of their thoughts. Thus, when we observe children at play, a key focus is the language they use. Without children's verbalizations it is difficult to determine how imaginative or creative they are in their play.

In summary, we want to emphasize the blending of three facets of the infant's development—constitutional factors, the influence of the caregiver's personality traits and style, and the combined effect of these components on the baby's emerging cognitive skills (stability, for example, as reflected in the baby's capacity for habituation).[38] Whatever babies may bring with them at birth will be molded and tempered by the behavior of those entrusted with their welfare. Born with a powerful need to survive, babies kick, squirm, cry, and greedily root for the nipple. Their eyes follow light and movement; their fingers curl, grasp and stroke; their ears respond to noises and voices. Eventually they offer a smile to the world, and the enormous task of synthesizing their innate curiosity, their exploratory drive, and their caregiver's actions and responses begins. Parental style— easy-going or tense, joyful or depressed, talkative or noncommunicative, physically responsive or distant, involved or distracted, patient or irritable, as well as extremes or gradations of these behaviors—will affect a baby's temperament and development. Its natural curiosity, its ability to smile and laugh, and its physical growth, which is accompanied by greater finger dexterity, control over motor skills, and the coordination of these movements, all enable it to engage in rudimentary sensory-motor play, which will evolve into later pretend play.

Our discussion has centered on the influence of caregivers and their important role in encouraging play. In Chapter 1 we cited examples of the powerful influence a parent can have on a child's imagination and enjoyment of make-believe. But while we accept the notion of the parents' positive influence on a baby's innate attraction to the new or the unknown, Aldous Huxley's *Brave New World* (written when J. B. Watson's behaviorism was at its height) paints a dramatic picture of how eight-month-olds in a world of the future might be conditioned to shrink with horror at the mere sight of gaily-colored sheep.[39] Through electric shock conditioning, the infants, after "two hundred repetitions of the same or similar lesson," developed an "instinctive hatred of books and flowers."[40] Thus, babies with normal curiosity and a healthy desire to explore "clusters of sleek colours" learned to suppress their natural tendency to experience joy when exposed to brightness.

By fostering a playful attitude as the infant's language emerges through object labeling, by modeling the appropriateness of emotions, by adjusting flexibly to the baby's temperament, and by recognizing when to play and when not to, the parent becomes a partner in enabling the child to move from sensory-motor play to symbolic play, the period of heightened make-believe and sociodramatic games. When children can play openly and freely, they become good learners, developing their cognitive skills through the stepping-stones of play.

4

The High Season
of Imaginative Play

Unser mund sei voll lachens
(Our mouths are full of laughter)

—Johann Sebastian Bach,
Cantata no. 110

There are children "who spend hours in conversation with their dolls; who invest the smallest cast-off objects with secret significance; who on being interrupted at play react with blurred shock, flashing at the intruder the wary, glazed look of a suddenly awakened cat."[1] These are the children whose "mouths are full of laughter," the three-, four-, five-, and early six-year-olds who spend their time in make-believe play, completely enraptured by their own inventiveness.

Over many years of observing children in free play, we have found that those who engage in make-believe, what Piaget calls symbolic play, are more joyful and smile and laugh more often than those who seem to be at odds with themselves—the children who wander aimlessly around the nursery school or daycare center looking for something to do, who play in a perseverative way with a few blocks, or who annoy their peers by teasing them or interrupting their games.[2]

One of the major benefits of play is a feeling of well-being. It probably originates with what the mother (or other caregiver) conveys to the child in the first years of life and then continues during what Erikson calls the "play age" or Stage of Initiative versus Guilt (see Table 2-1). During this period (from approximately the end of the third year until age six) the child "enters into the infantile politics of nursery school, street corner and backyard. His learning now is eminently intrusive and vigorous; it leads away from his own limitations and into future possibilities."[3] This valuable period affords a child the opportunity to develop the sense of playfulness and creativity that Erikson believes sets the stage for the empathy, the resilience, and the sense of humor so much needed in old age.[4]

The Cognitive Skills Preschoolers Bring to Play

During the first three years of life, much of the play of children is devoted to making sense of the world around them through visual exploration and the manipulation of objects, and through what is called "mastery" play, the attempt to identify, compare, and categorize objects and events. Children are accumulating "a vast amount of 'first-time' knowledge about the world."[5] They organize, label, imitate, and through their first attempts at pretense—feeding a doll, bathing a toy duck, putting a teddy bear to bed, using a toy telephone, or making a clay cookie—simulate many of their daily routines. Pretend play develops through children's ability to include others in their make-believe games, to transform objects into elements needed to carry out a game (the clay becomes a cookie, the stick becomes a spoon), and to engage in related acts or themes that follow a sequence or order.

We find consistent theoretical analyses of symbolic play among the leading "play" researchers, from Jean Piaget's seminal conceptualization to the more current contributors to scientific journals. Piaget believed that symbolic play emerged in year two, increased over the next three or four years until age six, and then declined. He also believed that play became more realistic as a child's thoughts became more logical,[6] an assumption that does not stand up to the empirical data.

In agreement with Greta Fein, we accept the following as criteria for symbolic or pretend play:

1. Familiar activities may be performed in the absence of necessary material or a social context.
2. Activities may not be carried out to their logical outcome.
3. A child may treat an inanimate object as animate (offer food to a teddy bear).
4. One object or gesture may be substituted for another (a block becomes a pot).
5. A child may carry out an activity usually performed by someone else (pretending to be a doctor).[7]

As children get older, symbolic play changes. Simple, discrete actions become integrated into a game; children focus less on self and can include others in complex games, assigning roles and reversing roles; and children depend less on realistic objects, using nonprototypical imagery or invented objects in play. Four- and five-year-olds tend to organize their games around a specific goal. If they are playing a pirate game, the goal may be finding the sunken treasure. The preparation, in terms of finding costumes, making a boat, sailing the sea, and finally going under water to search for the treasure, involves integrated actions, multiple roles, imaginary objects, and the attainment of the goal: the treasure chest.

The earliest pretend acts, such as feeding a doll, occur at approximately twelve or thirteen months. Here the child is active and the doll is passive. Gradually, the doll "acts" on her own (the doll feeds herself), talks, walks, or, through the manipulations of the child, feeds another doll or its "mommy." Just as substitution behavior increases (in the use of objects at hand to substitute for actual ones) interactive or social play also increases, so that between the ages of three and six we see many more shifts from solitary pretend play to social pretend play with a concomitant increase in roles and themes. Edith Cobb has characterized this heightened period of social play as the time when a child can "draw in the wings of his surroundings at will and convert the self into a 'theater of perception' in which he is at once producer, dramatist and star."[8]

This delightful period in a child's life, the preoperational stage from birth to age seven, the early years before school, is characterized in Piaget's terms by distortions of time and space, by number confusion, by egocentric behavior, and by such concepts as animism, transduction, juxtaposition reasoning, artificialism, literalism, and a failure to conserve. *Animism* means that everything that has movement seems alive and conscious to the child: the blowing wind, a burning candle, and a bicycle that moves are alive; on the other hand, a burned-out candle and a bicycle lying still in the driveway are dead.[9] *Transduction* occurs when a child believes that simultaneous events have a cause and effect relationship: the whistle of the train makes the train go. *Juxtaposition reasoning* refers to the idiosyncratic or arbitrary way in which a child relates parts to a whole. When Piaget asked a five-year-old to group together objects that were alike, the child placed a woman next to a fir tree, a bench against a house, and a church together with a small tree and a motorcycle but with no understanding of why he had put these particular objects together. *Artificialism* refers to the notion that human or humanlike divine architects are responsible for natural formations such as valleys, mountains, and lakes. A child we knew believed that a godlike person up in the sky regulated rain, snow, and hail by turning on a specific faucet for each. *Realism* or *literal-*

ism, which applies specifically to language, accounts
charm of preschoolers.[10] The notion that a "frog in my
a small animal is lodged there or that the mailman v
hats" (his regular job and his part-time job in a loc
store) puts one hat atop another, makes us chuckl
literal interpretations.

Finally, the preschooler is unable to understand the notion of
conservation, the fact that objects or quantities remain the same
despite a change in their physical appearance: A certain quantity of
juice, whether poured into a tall, thin glass or into a short, fat one,
remains the same. Clay rolled out long and thin equals the same
amount rolled into a fat ball. Ten pennies, whether bunched together or spread out in a row next to another, shorter row of ten
pennies, always remain ten pennies, despite the preschooler's claim
that the spread out row (which looks longer) contains "more pennies" than the compressed row. Before the age of six-and-a-half or
seven, the child depends more on appearances than on logical reasoning, and as a result, responds in terms of what looks like
"more."[11]

Play is at its peak during the preoperational stage, especially
from ages three to six. As Piaget wrote, "unlike objective thought
which seeks to adapt itself to the requirement of external reality,
imaginative play is a symbolic transposition which subjects things
to the child's activity, without rules or limitations."[12] According to
Piaget, play is pure assimilation. We believe, however, that, despite its momentary suspension of reality and its quality of assimilation, play also enables children to make sense of their world and
accommodate to it by the very act of bringing it down to size. Play
allows children to experiment with different roles, acquire language skills, and gain control by organizing a game's plan or
themes and applying what they learn in a play sequence to the
everyday cognitive and social demands of life. We observed an il-
lustration of learning through play in a little girl who was attempting to wash a doll in a plastic tub filled with water. When
the piece of cloth she was using as a towel fell in the tub and became soaking wet, she hung it up to dry over the back of a small
chair in the nursery school and repeated to herself, "Tell mommy
not to drop *my* towel in *my* bathtub. Be careful." By the same to-
ken, what a child experiences at home or in school each day may
become part of the pretend play, but modified as required to suit
the player's moods and needs.

Emotions and Play

Compensatory play—play that enables children to express feelings —may actually help them to make personal sense out of a particular reality. Piaget gives us a good example of compensatory symbolic play in an everyday occurrence. When his daughter, aged three years and eleven months, was told not to go into the kitchen because of the pails of hot water being prepared for a bath, she said, "Then I'll go into a pretend kitchen. I once saw a little boy who went into a kitchen, and when Odette went past with the hot water, he got out of the way."[13]

Contrary to the opinions of some educators, who have considered it "in traditional education, as a kind of mental waste-matter, or at least as a pseudo-activity without functional significance, and even harmful to children," play has been given a somewhat more respectable status in American society.[14] The feeling of well-being rather than harm that play promotes in both mothers and children has also been noted in cultures other than our own. Judith Van Hoorn analyzed data based on observation of and responses from a diverse mixture of Chinese, Philippino, Mexican, and North American mothers of European descent during play interactions with their infants. She suggests that, despite some variations in the cultural patterns of the games the mothers and children played, the mothers' primary purpose was "mutual enjoyment." Games were "characterized by behaviors promoting mutuality, cooperation, and attainment."[15] Indications of the positive emotions of joy, surprise, and interest, which we referred to in Chapter 3, emerge when the parent engages in face to face play behavior with the child.

In one of our longitudinal studies that used eight nursery schools (which, over the course of time as the children moved on to kindergarten, encompassed forty-nine schools), we included the scoring of positive emotions such as liveliness, excitement, elation, and joy among a list of mood variables to be analyzed. We were interested in the social interaction patterns a child would manifest during free-play periods over a year's time. This study was one of the first to look at the patterning of emotions during a child's spontaneous play and to determine whether positive emotions related in any systematic way to imaginative play.[16] Our sample of 141 three- and four-year-olds was observed by teams of two assistants, who recorded verbatim the conversations of the children and their actions during a ten-minute period on eight separate occasions. Raters independently rated the children on each variable using a five-point scale. Children were observed both indoors and out on each occasion, and the appearance, mannerisms, physical build, sex, and age of each child were recorded, along with the time observed.

We found that positive emotions such as joy and liveliness were positively correlated with imaginative play. The children who enacted various make-believe transformations during play emerged across a year's time as those who were engaged in a good deal of smiling and laughter and were motorically active. Imaginativeness was negatively correlated with evidence of fearfulness, sadness, or fatigue. One could argue that the correlation of imaginative play and positive emotion is simply a function of the fact that children who speak a great deal more will elicit more positive ratings from observers. It was true that it was necessary for the children to speak in order for our research assistants to evaluate whether or not they used make-believe elements in the games. It could also be claimed that the relationship of imagination to positive emotions or to any of the other variables we used was in part a function of the general verbal expressiveness of the child. When we controlled for language by statistically eliminating the impact of verbal productivity, however, the relationship between imaginative play and positive affect was still significant.

Greta Fein has stated that "pretense provides an unusual opportunity for children to control their own emotional arousal and to maintain a level that is both comfortable and stimulating."[17] Only rarely did we observe pretend play among children who were very angry, anxious, conflicted, or hyperactive. We did see children employing their toys in fantasy games that involved aggressive acts, but these children were in control and used metacommunicative statements such as, "This is my bad guy. Make-believe he's chasing your guy." When children bring rage into their pretend play, the play tends to be fragmented, repetitive, and disruptive, and it is usually stopped by either a parent or teacher, or it may just disintegrate through its own lack of structure and thematic integration.

Other research, including work carried out by Jennifer Connolly and her colleagues, has yielded results similar to ours. After studying the social interaction of thirty-seven four- and five-year-olds during pretend and nonpretend play, she reported finding more positive and less negative affect during social pretend play than during nonpretend social activities such as putting puzzles together or playing a bowling game. Social pretend play was characterized by its longer duration, larger play groups, and an increased reciprocity of social exchange. In social pretend play children also attempted to influence the ongoing social interaction, and they complied more with other children's directives than children in the nonpretend play group.[18] Similarly, Roni Tower followed forty-three children between the ages of forty-three and seventy months and found that imaginative children were more lively, concentrated better, were more attractive to others, tolerated frustration better, tended to show less fear, and were generally more alert and joyful. Teachers, who did not know how the children had been rated by observers, described these same children as adventurous, curious, creative, and imaginative, among other positive attributions. Imaginativeness was measured during block play, nonblock prop play (with toy people, sand toys, miniature animals), dramatic play, and art.[19]

The joy and positive affect one child experiences during play arouses complementary pleasure in play partners. Children learn quite early to "read" the emotions of others. The data suggest that children discriminate the happiest expressions earliest and most easily (see Chapter 3).

Will a child's positive emotional expressiveness actually foster that child's popularity? Tiffany Field and Tedra Walden found that those children who could produce various facial expressions more easily and recognize facial expressions more accurately than other children were rated higher in sociometric ratings by their peers. In addition, children who were rated as less expressive by teachers made more frequent production errors; that is, they were less able to imitate facial expressions.[20] This study is important because it suggests that children are attracted to other children who tend to be more expressive and that teachers are also influenced by a child's capacity to express a wide range of emotions. In general the children made more errors in their judgments of fearful and angry expressions than of happy expressions. Joyful affects were the easiest for them to reproduce and identify.

Other research by Gary Ladd, Joseph Price, and Craig Hart suggests that children's behavior contributes to their social status among their peers. Those "children who played cooperatively with peers at the outset of the school year also tended to do so at later points in time, and this disposition was associated with long-term gains in peer acceptance."[21] Children who were arguers in the beginning of the year were rejected by their peers and remained so, even after they changed their behavior and became less disruptive. This study seems to support the idea that labeling a child as "bad" or as a "troublemaker"—which we have observed in our own work with children—continues to have a negative effect long after the child leaves that particular setting. The negative attention-getting devices some children use stigmatize them early on and may have deleterious effects later as they attempt to amend their peer relationships. Imaginative play, on the other hand, which, as our studies showed, is correlated with cooperation with peers, can lead to greater popularity and acceptance by other children.

The Structure of Imaginative Play

What forms does children's imaginative play assume? Since children may play alone or with others, the forms or patterns of play may differ within each context. We can recognize solitary or social play at every stage of a child's development. Infants and toddlers in the sensory-motor stage spend much of the day playing alone or with a caretaker. The infant who takes a swipe at a mobile suspended over its crib or crawls along the floor examining every piece of lint and selecting a tempting morsel to taste, who tries to stack cubes or put plastic rings over a small upright stick is quite content to be alone as it explores the immediate environment and "plays" with every colorful and intriguing object that catches its eye. Of course, such a child is delighted to interrupt these explorations if a willing sibling or adult is ready to play patty-cake or peekaboo, or assist in the cube-stacking or ring-tossing games. The play then becomes more fun, and the partner is there to be imitated, to assist with a complicated toy, or to serve as a parallel player. A toddler amuses herself as she plays in the presence of others and will occasionally try to reach for another child's toy, or her mother's book or sewing kit, but for the most part, the child under the age of two is engrossed in her own play world. This solitary play may take the form of simple pretend (which can appear at about twelve to thirteen months) when a child feeds a doll, moves a toy truck along the floor with accompanying noises, imitates a dog or kitten by crawling along the floor, dons a cowboy hat, or puts a stuffed toy to sleep. At times, two toddlers may play simple pretend games side by side, occasionally exchanging simple words or attempting to enact a role—carpenter, mommy or daddy, cowboy, or firefighter—but with little awareness or understanding of their playmate's part in the game.

As the child gets older, by about age three, cooperative social pretend begins and reaches its peak in the fourth and fifth years. Social play, according to Carolee Howes, is different from social pretend play in several ways. It emerges earlier[22] and involves some turn-taking and the consideration of a play partner's actions as well as one's own but includes no pretense elements. It also depends on the setting and the kinds of toys available. We see more social play in daycare facilities than in a child's home, where a parent or caretaker may not always be available to carry out the kinds of social interaction expected by teachers or aides in a communal situation. Some skill in the use of language also enables a child to engage in social play and join in a game earlier than one who is less verbal and communicative. Language helps to create, clarify, maintain, and negotiate the social pretend experience.[23] Social play in the early toddler period (thirteen to twenty-four months) is characterized by complementary and social interaction. Children can take turns and exchange roles through such actions as running and chasing, hiding and seeking, or giving and receiving a toy. As important as language is a child's understanding of the sequence of events and logical order. In the late toddler period (twenty-five to thirty-six months), social play can become social pretend play, and it is in this kind of play that we see imagination blossoming, especially if the elements we described in Chapter 1 are present: a time for play, a place to play, simple props, and most important, the sanction and encouragement of "make-believe" by an older sibling or an adult.

Children in the late toddler period become more socially competent.[24] They can assume complementary pretend roles ("You be the daddy, I'll be the mommy"; "You be the cowboy, I'll be the Indian") and share in nonliteral themes ("Let's be pirates") as they crawl behind the sofa, which becomes a "cave," or lie upon cushions, which become a boat. They can also reverse their roles: "Now, I'm the daddy and you're the mommy"; "I'm the pilot and you're the rider." In cooperative social pretend play, both players, in effect, follow a script, understand that their partner is playing a role, and use symbolic content in their play. According to Howes, social pretend play builds on the earlier form of social play the "reversal structure already established in complementary and reciprocal peer play."[25] In social play, children do not communicate the meaning of their actions, although they may reverse roles. Social pretend play therefore adds an important element, the understanding that the partner is acting out a role that is part of a simple story.

But even as children advance from solitary play to social pretend play, they may at times resort to the earlier form. Some highly imaginative players may choose to play alone for several reasons. First, a game that a child invents may have an elaborate plan, but his friends may not be able to follow the script. Here, the child has choices: either he can adapt and change his plan in order to include other players or he can withdraw and continue to play the game himself, thereby controlling the story line, perhaps with miniature toys that he can manipulate as he pleases. Second, children play alone when there are no friends around. In a daycare or nursery school setting, however, it is unusual to see a child who spends most of the time in solitary play. Finally, a child in nursery school or at home may withdraw from a social pretend game with friends because she needs her own space to work out a play theme that may be related to her own inner needs. (We will discuss this healing aspect of play in Chapter 9.)

We examined why children choose to play alone in one study we carried out with one hundred children. We were interested in changes in play and in the structure of play over a year's time. Research assistants observed three- and four-year-old children on eight separate occasions—twice a week in four probe periods three months apart. We accumulated one thousand samples of play behaviors. From these protocols, we selected forty children who scored well above or well below the group means over the year on imaginativeness of play and frequency of television viewing. Four groups were delineated: high-imaginative/high TV viewers; high-imaginative/low TV viewers; low-imaginative/high-TV viewers; and low-imaginative/low-TV viewers. Each group was composed of six boys and four girls, reflecting the trend in our data for boys to show somewhat higher scores on both TV-viewing and imaginative play. We examined the data for specific games played, roles assumed by children during make-believe, and indications of recurrent psychodynamic themes, such as cleanliness, orality, sexuality, dependency, and so on. We were also interested in different types of play, including games with rules and mastery play as well as make-believe. Seven categories were devised: (1) location and environmental features of play spaces and play things; (2) social structure of play; (3) major themes, for example, adventure, family, school, doctor; (4) roles assumed, for example, mother, father, baby, superhero, victim; (5) type of play: sensory-motor, mastery, rules-guided, symbolic; (6) dynamic themes: orality, anality or cleanliness, separation, rejection, sibling rivalry, and so on; and (7) television references in play. We then developed a *Play Protocol Analysis Chart* listing all the kinds of play and a scoring procedure.[26]

Some of the questions raised by our protocol reviewers were where did the child play, was play solitary or social, what space was used, what type of play was involved, what themes made up the content of play, was there evidence of pretend play and transformations (for example, a stick becoming an airplane), what specific roles did a child assume, and (to get at so-called psychodynamics) was there an emphasis on orality, cleanliness, sibling rivalry, sexuality, parental attachment, or aggression?

Our data, based on scores derived from 320 protocols (eight per child across the year) yielded seven statistical factors or clusters: (1) adventurous fantasy play; (2) domestic fantasy play; (3) gross physical activity (running, jumping) versus art play; (4) a more general emphasis on make-believe; (5) involvement with ritual games or dancing and singing; (6) play with pet animals; and (7) games with rules. Major results suggested that those children who were highly and consistently imaginative also engaged in more social play, participated in ritual games and singing, and were less likely to play alone. The imaginative children tended to be those who initiated games, who were rarely solitary, withdrawn, or defensive. They could occasionally play alone, but they did not carve out delimited territory in the course of their activities, nor did they play in more bounded space.

In keeping with the results reported by Howes, we found that over a year the larger motor activity of the children in our study tended to decrease, while their art play, ritual play, and singing and dancing increased, and they became more social. Themes of danger, disaster, and physical mutilation showed a steady increase. It may be that these preschoolers were now more aware of real-life dangers and could express these fears more verbally, but it is also possible that children choose plot lines that reflect danger, because these themes seem to be interesting to them and allow for more adventure and conflict in their play.

Consistency of Play and Imagination

The likelihood of finding behavioral consistency in young children is not very great, since they are in the midst of a period of rapid

physical and cognitive growth and are subject to all kinds of extra-
neous influence. Nevertheless, because we had eight different data
points gathered across a year's time, we were able to examine the
degree of consistency of specific behaviors among our sample of 141
children. Of particular interest here are the variables: imagination,
positive affect or emotionality (smiling and laughter), and aggression. For imaginativeness of play (a rating based on the degree to
which a child introduces elements of pretend and make-believe and
transcends the immediacy of time and place during free-play periods), 100 percent of the correlations between the various time periods were significantly better than chance: an imaginative child at
the beginning of the year tended to remain an imaginative child at
the end of the year. Similar results were found for positive affect or
emotionality: 50 percent of the intercorrelations across time periods
were significant. We found, too, that children who interacted with
other children at age three continued in this social behavior at age
four. Aggression also remained a consistent trait: those children
identified at the outset as aggressive (hitting others or damaging
property) were rated as aggressive one year later. It is striking to
note how behavior patterns in such young children became established early on and remained relatively consistent as they grew.

Dennis Wolf, Jayne Rygh, and Jennifer Altshuler have also found
"stable preferences for including or ignoring psychological information" in three-year-olds' representation of human actions.[27] These
researchers found that children ascribed internal experiences to
play figures along five specific developmental levels: Level 1—
talking to a doll, feeding it, placing it in a chair; Level 2—ascribing
speech and action to a doll; Level 3—ascribing sensations, perception, and physiological states; Level 4—ascribing emotions, moral
judgments, social relations; and finally, Level 5—ascribing cognitive processes such as thinking, planning, and wondering.[28] Their
sample was small, nine middle-class children, but their study is
significant in its attempt to assess children over time. When the
children were between the ages of one and three years, visits were
made to the children's homes for several hours a week; later, when
they were between the ages of three and seven years, visits were
made biweekly. Sessions were videotaped at intervals of approximately six months and later transcribed.

In addition to noting developmental changes in the way children
play with dolls, Dennis Wolf and Sharon Grollman have been interested in differences in children's imaginative styles as they play.[29]
Data selected from a longitudinal study of early symbolic develop-

ment conducted at Harvard University (Project Zero) focused on four girls drawn from a cohort of five subjects. Although this was a small sample, the study's conclusions offer ideas worthy of further exploration. Influenced by Howard Gardner's definition of style ("the characteristic features of compositions which mark the works of individuals or schools independent of the content of those works"),[30] Wolf and Grollman suggested two criteria for determining style. First, "stylistic differences must be conceptualized and shown to result from differences in the quality and not the developmental level of an individual's behavior" (thus, the differences must be independent of cognitive maturity). Second, individual differences must be stable across time. In examining the content of their subject's play, Wolf and Grollman identified two major styles in which children approached the materials. These they defined as object-dependent fantasy and object-independent transformational play.

Imaginative elements were either vocal or gestural attempts to alter a situation. These imaginative elements were further divided into those that were object-dependent and those that were object-independent. For example, object-dependent instances referred to events, objects or persons actually present (a child might use Play-doh for a cookie and put small pieces of paper on it for decoration). Object-independent instances of imagination were those that referred to nonpresent events, objects, or persons (a child might pretend he was making a cookie using gestures or pantomiming to represent adding salt or sugar and rolling out imaginary dough).[31]

Object-dependent children seemed to be more distracted from following the story lines in their play, used objects in their make-believe games (a block on a plate as a piece of cake, a stick as a knife), and tended to experiment with the physical properties of props at hand. The object-independent children easily assimilated new objects into their play, and "the play rules these children establish[ed], pursue[d] and enforce[d] have to do with the maintenance of fantasy—in particular the carrying-out of assumed roles and sustaining make-believe."[32]

Object-dependent players were labeled *patterners* and preferred items like blocks, clay, and markers. Object-independent players were named *dramatists* and preferred open-ended props, such as costumes and less structured toys, while ignoring puzzles, counting, or classification. They often made outlandish substitutions to fit their narratives. According to Wolf and Grollman, the patterners were sensitive to quantity, shape, size, and color, and excelled in visual-spatial tasks and in creating designs. The dramatists enjoyed sociodramatic play, arguments, and negotiations. Are these "styles" found in other samples of children, including those from different social classes? Do these styles persist over time? Is a child capable of shifting between the two? Finally, are there gender differences? Since Wolf and Grollman's work involved only girls, we have only a single-sex base upon which to frame answers to these questions.

In a study carried out with a much larger sample (twenty-two boys and twenty-one girls, with a mean age of fifty-nine months), Roni Tower identified two types of imaginativeness: one is constructive, with "some sort of environmentally-linked goals in mind," and takes "into account the constraints of reality intrinsic to the materials in use."[33] The other is expressive, motivated by internal associations and inner needs, focusing on the process of expression. Constructive Imaginative children operate with rules, but these are suspended within accepted environmental constraints, while Expressive Imaginative children set aside all external rules. The former resemble Wolf and Grollman's "patterners" except in one respect: they also carry on more elaborate fantasy play; the latter resemble the "dramatists." Constructive Imaginative children, however, were more tenacious in pursuing their goals and were somewhat less noisy and less fearful but more expressive of anger than the Expressive Imaginative children.

Sex Differences in Imaginative Play

A television commercial that particularly caught our attention a few years ago was a baby powder advertisement in which a proud father visits his wife and newborn son in their hospital room. The father has brought a large baseball mitt for the infant and beams at the baby, admiring his tiny hand. He is already imagining his son as a player in the major leagues. The baby powder container appears in the commercial to suggest that the product is helpful to the newborn, but the ad's human interest angle or "hook" is masculine pride and the father's dreams for his progeny. Studies show that even nonparents make conscious male-female choices in purchasing toys as gifts (a doll for a girl, a football for a boy)[34] and that adults act differentially toward infants depending upon the child's gender label (smiling more at females and encouraging gross motor activity with males).[35] Nancy Bell and William Carver found, for example, that women who expressed a belief in sex differences were more likely to choose a toy hammer when asked to interact with an infant labeled as a boy, while women who expressed little belief in sex differences were not affected in their choice of a toy by knowledge of the infant's sex. The babies' passive behavior was associated with a lower incidence of smiling by the mothers, more use of feminine toys, and lower ratings of activity and robustness. Babies who vocalized more were more likely to be offered masculine toys. What was particularly interesting in this study was the fact that "masculine and feminine toy presentations and ratings on stereotypically masculine and feminine traits were more strongly associated with the behavior exhibited by the infant than with gender label."[36] It would seem that infant behavior was a more important factor in eliciting responses in the adults than were adult preconceptions based on sex stereotypes.

We often like to observe children at play in daycare settings or in nursery schools. Recently, we watched a boy named Georgie play "work." He donned an old fedora, put a pocketbook over his shoulder, and climbed into a toy car. "I'm Mommy-Daddy, going to work," he said as he drove around the play yard. Georgie has two working parents and generally, as he plays, switches back and forth between male and female roles or, as in this instance, combines the two. Once we watched him "iron" a doll's dress. "Are you a mommy?" another child asked. "No, I'm Daddy." Clearly, Georgie was attempting to assimilate both parents' roles into his pretend play. But Georgie is unusual. Most of the time we see clear-cut differences in the way children play. Generally, boys are more vigorous in their activities, choosing games of adventure, daring, and conflict, while girls tend to choose games that foster nurturance and affiliation.

In their study Wolf, Rygh, and Altshuler observed some interesting sex differences.[37] Girls were more comfortable discussing internal states: their stories included more incidents referring to emotions and to psychological aspects of events than did those of boys. These authors were aware that both sexes from age three on are capable of describing the characters in their stories as both agents (taking action in an event) and experiencers (articulating internal states), but that girls tend to describe internal states and "knowing" more frequently and more explicitly using expressions that involve planning and wondering. The authors report on one instance in which a conflict arose during a "jungle" play scene. A girl resolved the fight by "setting to rights the internal or psychological worlds of the figures."[38] She allowed the story to take a more peaceful turn as the play figures joined in singing, humming, and dancing and were put to "rest" because they "love resting in ponds." In contrast, a boy resolved the conflict by having the play figures collide and knock down trees with loud cries; when all trees were down, he stated, "Then they don't fight over them."[39] Girls tended to adopt a more intimate, conversational strategy toward their play figures, while boys tended to talk about them from the point of view of an observer, emphasizing description—what they saw and how they handled obstacles.

Jack Block's summary of the research on the dynamics of personality development, which includes numerous studies on sex differences, suggests similar results.[40] He reviewed these differences using a model based on Piaget's notions of assimilation and accommodation. Block describes girls as socialized in ways that encourage "the use of assimilative strategies for processing new information, while boys, more than girls, are socialized in ways that encourage the use of accommodative strategies when confronted with informational inputs discrepant with prior understandings."[41] Girls are socialized to see the adaptive rewards of efforts to adjust, to, in effect, make peace, which thereby reduces any anxiety-inducing efforts to make changes through innovative accommodation. In the jungle incident described above, the girl adjusted to the existence of a pond and rested there, while the boy made the toy figures knock down trees in order to clear the way.

Block conceptualizes assimilation as a conservation of existing structures and accommodation as a fostering of social innovation and change. Such approaches, he believes, are based in the differential rearing patterns of females and males in our society. Girls are more restricted in their exploration and grow up with more strictures and directives. They have more household chores and are kept closer to home, and their play, according to Block, involves "model availability, instruction, and rule governance." Boys, on the other hand, prefer games that "require extemporaneity and the ability to be opportunistic in a momentarily advantageous situation."

In our own study of play themes cited earlier, we also found sex differences in the ways in which boys and girls played over the year's time.[42] While adventure themes, fantasy characters, superheroes, spacemen, or television-related roles (Bionic Man, Spiderman, the Fonz, Gilligan) seemed to comprise the favored pretend games of boys, girls' games showed a clear preference for family pretend roles (mother, father, baby), "house," and dress-up clothes.

The girls maintained the family games significantly more than boys during all eight probe periods over the year, while the boys played significantly more adventure and superhero games than girls in only one of the eight probes. What was fascinating was the finding that girls were moving closer to boys in their identification with heroic figures, adventurous achievement, and pretend aggression than previous data claimed. This appears to reflect changes in television action programs, where more female heroines now appear, as well as the increased willingness of parents to tolerate adventure themes in girls' play. Parents even make more purchases of the newly available female action toys (Masters of the Universe figures now include good and evil females).

We do not see a comparable trend among boys—that is, a movement toward playing female games and using traditionally female toys. Boys who spend time in preschool doll corners are viewed with suspicion by caregivers, who become anxious lest these boys appear to be "sissies" or develop homosexual characteristics. Despite the women's movement and the fact that more women are in the work force than ever before, most men and many women are reluctant to train their sons to be responsible for the day-to-day domestic chores required in a dual-career family or to encourage sons to move into such "female" roles as nurse, elementary school teacher, or secretary. These are, of course, lower paying jobs in our society and are consequently lower in status, but they also remain associated in many people's minds with females. Parents, especially fathers, emphasize task-oriented mastery and achievement behaviors in boys more than they do in girls, which may convey subtle messages to females in terms of future plans for vocational choices.[43] We may see some girls playing with trucks, cars, and space toys, or as they get older even joining Little League teams or racing in soapbox derbies, but it is rare to see boys willing to play "house," "school," or "dress-up" on a regular basis. Unfortunately, many nursery schools, daycare centers, and even kindergarten rooms are still designed with specific sexes in mind; they still include a dress-up corner (that includes more female clothing), a car and truck corner, a house and kitchen area, and a carpentry space. As one observes the children, it is quite common to see the sexes separating as they gravitate toward the designated areas. A sensitive teacher will use combinations of "sex-typed" toys in setting up play spaces in order to encourage greater cross-sex play.

Would children be motivated to try new pretend games if they were given access to a greater variety of toys in their usual play spaces? Corrine Hutt and Reena Bhavnani found clear sex differences in the ways in which children explored novel toys.[44] The investigators were curious about whether the individual differences they observed in patterns of play were enduring, stable traits or were a function of experimental situations, whether failure to explore a new toy related to a child's capacity for creativity or divergent thinking, and finally, whether there are sex differences in the ways in which children approach a novel toy. From a sample of one hundred children, forty-eight between the ages of seven and ten were tested for creativity and given a personality questionnaire. Teacher and parent ratings were also obtained. These children had been studied earlier when they were aged three to five. At that time they had been assigned to one of three categories depending on the way in which they had investigated a new toy. These categories were (1) *nonexplorers,* who looked at a new toy but did not inspect it, although they approached it; (2) *explorers,* who actively investigated the toy but did little else with it afterward; and (3) *inventive-explorers,* who after investigating the toy, used it imaginatively. Girls were found to be mainly *nonexplorers,* while boys were mainly *inventive-explorers.* A few years later, when the battery of creativity tests was administered, it was found that inventive play was positively associated with creative thinking in boys. On the personality questionnaire, nonexploring girls were self-rated as apprehensive, tense, and conforming, while nonexploring boys saw themselves as unadventurous and inactive.

The findings suggest that a failure to explore in early childhood is related in boys to a lack of curiosity and adventure, while in girls, it is related more to personality and social adjustment. The more inventive and curious a boy was in childhood, the more divergent a thinker he would be as he moved into early elementary school. Another study supported such a relationship between styles of play and divergent thinking.[45] Creative kindergarten boys were found to be more communicative, curious, humorous, and playful.

Hutt and Bhavnani suggest, as we do, that girls at the age of four are "linguistically and socially more competent than boys,"[46] and as a result, they believe (again as we do) that girls' creativity and pretend play may be more symbolic and covert. In our studies, we have found that girls closely identify with their mothers at around age five, and that the spontaneity of their language and play diminishes somewhat as they begin to enter into a new stage of socialization; they become more subdued, more organized, and more affiliative.[47] Boys, on the other hand, appear to be more explicitly active and exploratory. More inventive boys in the Hutt and Bhavnani study, however, were less socially well-adjusted than inventive girls. It appears that the daring, adventurous behavior of the active boys gets them into trouble more readily than does the behavior of the inventive girls. One must keep in mind the possibility that such a finding may also be specific to the particular culture under study.

A study of forty four- and five-year-old children from two Sri Lankan villages found that boys in both villages engaged in more negative behavior and scored higher on fantasy object play than girls.[48] The villages were similar with one exception: in one (upper district), fathers were regularly employed; in the other (lower district), fathers spent time seeking employment. In the upper district, mothers had less need to work away from home and spent more time attending to their children. There also was a greater tendency in the upper district for adults to interact with children, offering suggestions, participating, and helping to secure play materials. They also verbalized to the children ("Go and play") and monitored their activities. Despite the economic differences between the two villages, 70 percent of the children engaged in some sort of symbolic representational play.

Toy Preferences, Gender Role, and Imagination

Some of the earliest children's playthings known to us are the clay rattles, dating back to 2600 B.C., that were excavated in the ruins of the ancient city of Kish in Mesopotamia. This site also yielded a whistle and models of chariots. The rattles, which are hollow and have one or more pebbles inside to make a noise, are particularly intriguing because they are made in a variety of animal forms, including hedgehogs and goats, as well as the shapes that are more familiar to us today. In ancient times rattles were generally used by adults as musical instruments, but in India and Mesopotamia, they were clearly intended for children.[49]

In countries throughout the world children have amused themselves with simple objects: in New Guinea, for example, with toy bows and arrows, banana stalks for sliding down hills, string and finger games such as cat's cradle, and a variation on the Jew's harp or *tambagl;* in Australia, with spinning tops made of various objects, such as shells or old tobacco tins; in Yugoslavia and Sweden, with an arch game using the arms (like "London Bridge is falling down"); and in Switzerland, France, and England, with games of marbles. Among American Indian children one finds bone toys, such as those used among the Teton Dakota for the "deer game," or spinning tops made of ash, cedar, buffalo horn, or stone. Dakota children engage in seasonal games; boys and girls rarely play together. Among the Maori of New Zealand we find finger and hand games, knucklebones, stilts, whip toys, and string games.[50] What appears again and again as we browse through books describing children's toys, are the commonalities among playthings of various ethnic and national groups. Many of the most popular playthings are the unstructured toys made from natural or household materials—shells, bones, leaves, sticks, or string—which are used by both sexes but in different ways. Boys play games of skill and chase, while girls imitate domestic scenes with primitive dolls and shell dishes, or play intricate finger games with string.

American children originally did not differ from children in other countries in their preferences for simple games or in their use of homemade toys or natural objects. As the country began to prosper in the nineteenth century, however, children were given more freedom and more opportunities to play. During this same period, theories about child-rearing also began to change, so that children were recognized as developing individuals and seen less as miniature adults. Advancing technology and prosperity brought more elaborate toys, and board games, puzzles, and blocks began to appear in the stores. The toy industry expanded in the 1880s and the cast iron banks, miniature trains, and fire engines that are now collector's items were eagerly desired by children. Gradually, the toys we have today—the roller skates, bicycles, dolls, dollhouses, costumes, masks, and toy soldiers—became available. The vast majority of American children, however, had few manufactured toys and relied on their parents to make dolls, toy wagons, small boats, and even sleds.[51] Today most children, except for the very poor, own many of the toys advertised on television, or are at least aware of them. The well-known Erector Set and Tinkertoys have been replaced by Legos, and the electronic boom has led to a proliferation of personal computers and video games, and of talking animals and dolls. Many toys are operated by remote control and require batteries to power them. The microchip has become the voice-box of teddy bears that can talk to children or record and repeat their words.

We wonder how such mechanical toys equipped with voices affect a child's imagination. Are they enhancing or inhibiting? It seems to us that the limited repertory of statements by the programmed bears and dolls is not conducive to vocabulary building. Those that repeat a child's words are somewhat better, since it is the child who initiates the conversation and then hears her words repeated by the toy. But talking to a teddy bear that responds in a distorted recorded voice seems less appealing to us than listening to a child talk to a bear and then supply the bear's response in his own "bear" voice. The ultimate travesty we envision would involve two bears (triggered by a child) talking to each other in a playroom, each one repeating one another's words until we enter, turn them off, and try to regain our sanity.

Obviously, toys are desirable for a child, but as we mentioned in Chapter 1, a very simple toy or object can stimulate a lengthy imaginative game. Mary Ann Pulaski found, for example, that significantly more varied themes and richer fantasy were elicited by the minimally structured materials presented to children from kindergarten through second grade than were elicited by highly structured toys.[52] Minimally structured toys in her study included drawing paper, paints, Play-doh, wooden blocks, cardboard cartons, pipe cleaners, rag dolls, and costumes. Highly structured toys included plastic molds or cutters for use with Play-doh, a service station, a metal dollhouse, Barbie dolls, a G.I. Joe doll, and specific outfits for these dolls—a nurse's uniform, a bride's dress, an army uniform, and an astronaut's suit.

In another study, four- and five-year-old children, who were observed in small groups as they played, used dress-up materials, a phone, puppets, and stuffed animals more often in social pretend play than such items as puzzles, Legos, small blocks, and coloring materials.[53] These low-structure items were used more often in a social nonpretend context. Large blocks and a miniature airport and farm were used equally in both contexts. An interesting finding is that nontoy objects such as a wastebasket were used more often in pretend than nonpretend activities, which seems to suggest that children do enjoy using an object in symbolic ways and that by the ages of five to seven will carry out transformations more often than younger children.

Pulaski comments that, by the age of five, children have a "well-developed fantasy predisposition which affects their functioning regardless of sex and circumstance."[54] Certainly, our longitudinal study suggested that children at age three are already evidencing signs of a predisposition for fantasy and that such a trait is consistent over time.[55]

Other studies show that very young children need more structured toys representing commonplace objects in their environment (home furnishings, dolls, vehicles) in order to engage in pretend play. As children's representational skills become more developed, they are able to use less realistic objects in their play (blocks, clay, pipe cleaners, boxes, cardboard tubes) and consequently, can make more transformations. As their use of language increases and they are able to communicate more about their pretend acts, children's dependence on more realistic objects decreases. Many of the studies focused on middle-class children, who have had greater exposure to all kinds of toys than have poorer children. When they are presented with a wide array of toys in an experimental setting, it is not surprising that children in lower socioeconomic groups initially play more imaginatively with highly structured toys because of their immediate meaningfulness and novelty.

In her study of low-income, predominantly African-American three-and-a-half- and five-year-olds, Vonnie McLoyd found that highly structured toys increased the frequency of noninteractive pretend play among three-and-a-half-year-olds.[56] Her results are consistent with our belief that younger children will play more with replicas of everyday objects. The older children in her study engaged in many more substitutions with low-structure objects in their play than the younger ones, which again is consistent with the idea that pretend play increases with age. The older children, especially the girls, also played more cooperatively than the younger ones, but highly realistic toys did not influence this cooperative play. The type of roles the children enacted was not related to the structure of the toys. Girls, for example, most frequently played familial games, while boys preferred fantastic games, a finding similar to our results.

In a review of the role of toys in pretend play, McLoyd points out some of the methodological flaws in this kind of study. First, definitions of high- and low-structure objects vary from study to study (as an example, she refers to dress-up clothes, classified low-structure in Pulaski's study and as high-structure in her own). Second, studies have not examined the differential effects of toy structure on middle-class compared to lower-class children. Third, studies vary considerably in terms of the ages of the children studied, ranging from as young as eighteen months to as old as seven years. We would add another problem that frustrates comparability, the use of single children in some studies and of pairs, triads, or groups in other studies. Finally, it is rare to find studies that measure the long-term effects of toy structure on a child's pretend play. McLoyd admits her own failure to find support "for the claim that low-structure objects enhance pretend play," but she goes on to say that "systematic exposure to these objects over longer periods of time may result in effects different from those found" in her study.[57]

We have seen children play with elaborately constructed toys, motorized toys, wind-up objects, even Transformer cars, for a short while because the familiarity of the toy matches their preestablished schemas and evokes the affect of joy (see Chapter 2). But these toys often end up at the bottom of the toy chest, their batteries dead. Children choose large blocks, Legos, miniature people, and makeshift objects for longer periods of sustained play. We have also observed that children will initially respond to an opposite-sex-typed toy, but then go back to same-sex toys for longer play periods. Studies seem to verify common sense.[58] Yvonne Caldera, Aletha Huston, and Marion O'Brien found that children as young as eighteen months displayed sex-stereotyped toy choices.[59] Nancy Eisenberg, Kelly Tryon, and Ellen Cameron reported that four-year-old children played more with same-sex toys than opposite-sex toys but played most with neutral toys, such as clay, books, board games and puzzles.[60] In addition, the researchers found that play with opposite-sex peers was significantly and negatively related to a preference for same-sex stereotypic toys. When once a child chose a toy that matched his or her sex type, playmates of the same sex approached the child. As the authors state, "children played with same-sex peers more than opposite-sex peers during sex-typed and neutral (for boys only) play, but not during opposite-sex play."[61]

Working under the auspices of the Yale Family Television Research Center, Rena Repetti observed slightly older children (aged five-and-a-half to seven-and-a-half) in order to explore how their sex stereotyping might be linked not only to their parents' sex-role attitudes but also to their television-viewing patterns. She found that there was a strong maternal correlation with children's toy stereotypes. The children who chose the more traditionally sex-linked toys were more likely to be those whose parents responded to gender role questionnaires in very traditional ways.[62] Repetti showed pictures of ten different toys to preschoolers and asked them to indicate whether it was "for boys," "for girls," or "for both boys and girls" to play with. The children were also asked about sixteen adult occupations and whether the job was for men, women, or both. Children seemed to be aware of traditional sex stereotypes, assigning planes and jeeps to boys and toy mixers and dolls to girls. The tendency to sex type toys was significantly related to the child's tendency to stereotype occupations.

The kind of toys children play with may also determine their uniqueness of response. Brian Sutton-Smith presented kindergartners with male- and female-sex-typed toys and asked them for alternative uses for these toys. Although the children were familiar with both kinds of toys, their play experiences with them had been different. As a result, if the toy was same-sex, the child ascribed more unique responses to the toy, which suggests that play experiences with a toy contributed to a child's ability to create such responses.[63] Yet another study also sought to examine sex-typed toys and children's ability to suggest new or innovative ways of using them. Such toys were presented to children in grades 1 to 3 by Erica Rosenfeld.[64] The children were asked to think of strange, exciting, and interesting ways in which they could change the toys so that boys and girls might have more fun playing with them. Both girls and boys presented more varied ideas for improving the masculine toys. It appears that these toys had more potential for unique or creative use. Girls' toys may indeed lead to more passive or less varied play. James Johnson and Joan Ershler, observing functional, constructive, and dramatic play, found that preschool girls engaged in more onlooker behavior, more constructive parallel play, more reliance on props, less dramatic play, and more sedentary activities than boys.[65] The more passive stance among girls noted by these authors was also found in a study of siblings and friends as they played. Girls were more likely to accept "managee" roles than boys, and as would be expected, younger children were more compliant, while older peers did not differ in roles they assumed.[66]

We have seen that make-believe play takes many forms, depending on the setting, the sex and age of the child, and the kinds of toys available for play. We have noted that during this preschool period, the good pretend players seem to be happy, cooperative, and creative and to engage in more fantasy play than children who play chiefly in solitary fashion or who make few transformations as they play. In general, most of the research suggests that there are stages within this preschool play period, characterized first by simple pretending and then moving toward social pretend games involving more complex substitutions, more language, and less dependency on realistic objects.

As children reach ages six and seven they begin, at least overtly, to relinquish their symbolic, make-believe play and move on to what Piaget calls the stage of "games with rules." But, contrary to Piaget's view, we believe that this shift reflects the constraints of school and adult expectations rather than a fundamental cognitive change. Because of children's increased capacity for logical thought, more complicated motor skills, longer attention span, and increased ability to concentrate, their general play changes style and function. Many more group activities evolve; children join organizations such as Cub Scouts, Brownies, Little League, and 4-H Clubs. Children roller-skate, ride bicycles, use skateboards, work on puzzles, try out various arts and crafts, and begin to read.

For the middle-class child, a typical week may include music lessons, team practice, religious studies, and after-school clubs. Those moments alone or with one or two friends who have previously shared the child's world or make-believe become increasingly rare as school work and recreational activities crowd the days. Solitary activities may take the form of reading, playing alone in one's room with some favorite childhood toys, or mastering computer games. The plush toys get tucked away in closets, but girls may keep them on their beds or dressers waiting to go off to school to keep vigil in dormitories. Despite the rage of Cabbage Patch dolls one year, Atari or Nintendo the next, those cuddly soft "friends" of childhood remain the best-sellers every year, reminders of the many happy pretend moments of the high season of play.

5

Imaginary Playmates and Imaginary Worlds

From A. A. Milne's Christopher Robin dragging his stuffed bear Edward (also known as Winnie-the-Pooh) bumpety-bump down the stairs to Charles Schulz's cartoon child, Linus (locked for a quarter of a century into a preschool identity), tugging his blanket along as he pursues Charlie Brown, children's literature and popular culture include numerous examples of the phenomenon of early experience we call the "make-believe companion." A preschool child we observed in our research had as an imaginary friend an invisible (to adults) fox cub named "Sadie," whose attributes, which his parents described from the boy's spontaneous talk, included "warmth, cuddliness, bravery, strength, intelligence, and magical abilities."

For six months, three-and-a-half-year-old Josie sustained an invisible friend named Louisa, for whom an extra chair and place setting were required at dinner. Indeed, an extra pillow even had to be put on the child's bed at night. One day Josie was caught in a heavy rain shower. Later, when she sat down for lunch, her sympathetic grandmother asked if Louisa was hungry too. Josie said, "Don't you know? Louisa was drownded in the big puddle!" Her grandmother then assumed that no additional chair and place setting were necessary, but Josie burst out, "Oh no! You have to put a place for my new friend, Frogman! He's not afraid of puddles!"

Research studies and anecdotal accounts make it clear that a significant number of children show evidence of imaginary playmates between the ages of two and six. It is difficult to be certain just how common the phenomenon is either at various age levels or across subcultures or national groups, and how much such an experience can be carried into adolescence or adult life with or without the sanction of a given culture. We may well smile at literary representations of invisible companions—a stuffed tiger in the comic strip "Calvin and Hobbes" or a human-sized rabbit in the stage play and movie *Harvey*—yet how far removed are normal adults from such beliefs?

Sigmund Freud's provocative book, *The Future of an Illusion,* proposed that all religion is built around the continued adult yearning for an invisible father and mother and for the companionship of powerful siblings who are represented by Greek or Roman gods, sacred humanlike animal spirits, ancestral ghosts, bodhisattvas, genies, or saints.[1] The anthropologist Philips Stevens, Jr., proposes to avoid a head-on conflict with established religions by distinguishing between majority beliefs that are sanctioned by mainstream institutions in a culture or a society and the "occult" beliefs that operate on the social fringe without establishment sanction. As Stevens points out, "superstitions" and a belief in a magical world of ordinarily invisible spirits have continued almost unabated from earliest recorded history and operate in human thought somewhat separately from the structure of formal religion. The very individuals whose scientific and philosophical work led to the so-called "Age of Reason"—Francis Bacon, Johannes Kepler, Isaac Newton, and John Locke—all wrote about malign spirits, witches, and occult magical powers. The great seventeenth-century chemist, Robert Boyle, suggested that the coal and iron miners of England be interviewed and asked to describe the shape, manner, activities, and the intentions of "subterraneous demons." As Stevens notes, "a Gallup poll in June, 1984 showed that 55% of teenagers aged 13 to 18 believe that astrology works . . . In April, 1985 (*New York Times,* April 18 and April 25, 1985) a beleaguered Proctor & Gamble . . . remove(d) its 100-year-old man-in-the-moon logo from its packaging in reaction to thousands of phone calls and letters denouncing it as a satanic emblem."[2]

If a significant proportion of the adult world continues to hold an active belief in invisible spirits, let us not be so surprised at our children's creation of make-believe friends or societies. In the past, when we have written or talked to groups about some of our own research on children's invisible friends, we have occasionally received letters from apparently socially adjusted people, including teachers, who claim that children, because of their innocence and freedom from adult guilt or complexes, are directly in touch with the invisible spirit world. Their "imaginary" friends, these people write, are not make-believe at all!

In this chapter we propose to look more closely at this intriguing feature of childhood imaginative play: the emergence and development of imaginary companions and their presumed assimilation into the thoughts of the older child. In the adult, such companions persist in the internalized representations that form a key feature of adult daydreaming and interior monologue, and, perhaps, in religious or superstitious belief. For a smaller number of children and adults these companions come to inhabit elaborate imaginary worlds or societies. These pretend worlds, dubbed "paracosms" in the research of Robert Silvey and Stephen MacKeith, offer a fascinating link between the imaginative games of childhood and adolescence and the often powerful and influential literary and philosophical creations of such writers and thinkers as Plato (*Republic*), Thomas More (*Utopia*), Thomas Hobbes (*Leviathan*), B. F. Skinner (*Walden II*), and J. R. R. Tolkien (*Lord of the Rings*), eventuating also in dozens of Sword and Sorcery or science fiction novels. More recently, George Lucas's *Star Wars* film triology, viewed by millions, has spun off, through lucrative licensing, popular toys that may be inspiring a whole new trend in childhood paracosm creation.

Transitional Objects: Blankets and Teddy Bears

The British child psychiatrist Donald Winnicott struck a responsive chord in professionals and the general public alike when he pointed out the psychological significance of children's attachment to soft clothes or furry toys as babies and young toddlers.[3] The clutching, cuddling, and dragging around of these objects, even the child's occasional ripping or tearing of them to vent anger, represent, he proposed, the first steps in establishing a sense of self, an experience of "this is *mine* but *not* a part of me." Their soft, cuddly qualities, Winnicott proposed, reflected the warmth and closeness of the mother now transferred to an object conveying the mother's sensuous texture but completely under the child's control. Winnicott's label, the "transitional object," suggests that these soft blankets or furry toy animals represent a major developmental step away from a sense of self as fused with the mother, and from the pure narcissism of the first six months or year of life, toward a sense of self differentiated from caregivers and physical objects. The blanket or teddy bear is, however, not a complete step toward independence; the stroking of the cloth (often also associated with thumbsucking) may seem to mirror the child's position while being bottle-fed or nursed at the mother's breast. In the United States and England the diaper or blanket thrown over the adult's shoulder during feeding, or afterward when the child is burped, often becomes the child's transitional object. One boy lugged such a diaper and a soft furry "dog" around with him until his fourth birthday, when he declared his attainment of a new stage of independence and maturity by standing at the top of the staircase outside his bedroom and tossing his "Burpee" and "Bow-wow" down for good.

Winnicott identified a series of qualities associated with the transitional object. These included a sense of "entitlement" to possession, to which adult caregivers acquiesce (perhaps an echo of our primordial sense of a personal right to social security pensions and medical care in old age); and a sense of continuity, a result of the unchanging nature of the blanket or toy (often surreptitiously washed by concerned mothers). Even natural damage doesn't do away with this continuity: some little girls may carry just a fragment of a blanket in their play purses; girls moving into their cabins at summer camp and, yes, even college girls moving into their dormitories, bring a surprising number of well-worn rag dolls or now-eyeless stuffed animals with them.

For Winnicott, the key to the transitional role of the transitional object is that the object is palpable. In this sense, it differs from the imaginary playmate. Presumably it is gradually "decathected," that is, the child's attachment wears off and the transitional object does not become "internalized" as part of the child's thinking process. Nor is it missed or yearned for once given up, as the case of the boy flinging away his "Burpee" and "Bow-wow" demonstrates. Marian Tolpin has likened this process to that of the cicada, which sheds its skin once a new layer has formed.[4] She differs from Winnicott in suggesting that this can occur because the child, following repeated experiences of mislaying or losing the object, has learned to use thought as a soothing activity and no longer really needs a physical security blanket.

Perhaps the imaginary playmate is one manifestation of this internalizing process. A key step in this sequence may be the cognitive theory proposed by the renowned student of infancy, René Spitz, working with David Metcalf. They suggest that the transitional object emerges in that phase of early childhood when the capacity for recall memory in the absence of a real object is not yet well developed. Recognition memory, the identification of a previously observed stimulus from an array of others, is one of the simplest capacities of human memory; evoking a stimulus when it is not shown is always more difficult and less precise. The soft blanket or stuffed toy evokes the cuddliness of the primary caregivers in their absence without requiring the emergent recall memory to produce a mental image.[5]

There is a considerable speculative literature on the meaning of the transitional object to the infant, baby, or toddler, especially since psychoanalysis in this era of "object relations" is preoccupied with the first year of life. There seems little likelihood that we will penetrate the consciousness of the preverbal child, certainly not through retrospective accounts of adults in psychoanalysis, by which time layers of complex new meanings have encrusted our memories. It seems more useful to concentrate on accurate observations of the patterns that characterize the emergence of such behavior in babies, their generality across cultures, and their relation to other facets of child behavior, such as secure attachments, stress reactions, or playfulness.

Carol Litt's careful review of the observational literature shows that the use of a soft piece of cloth as a transitional object generally occurs before the age of twelve months, while a stuffed animal or soft doll is more likely to play that role after eighteen months. Litt's more focused inquiry methods revealed that 77 percent of a sample of middle-class American children showed some kind of transitional object attachment between the ages of two and five. Such behavior seems to some extent culturally bound, since higher incidences emerge from American and British studies and much lower rates are reported in Italian, Israeli, Japanese, and Korean samples. There is no good evidence linking the phenomenon specifically to breast feeding or to sleeping arrangements, birth order, or gender, or to the number of persons regularly involved in caregiving. In Israel, where variations on sleeping arrangements and caregiving in two types of kibbutz as well as in a nonkibbutz setting could be compared, the incidence of attachment to soft clothes or toys among Israeli children was relatively low compared to American children and was unrelated to the three types of early experience in feeding and sleeping arrangements observed.[6]

We are handicapped in making cross-cultural comparisons about the transitional object because of variations in the way inquiries have been conducted and because of the great differences, at least superficially, in child-care traditions, or in what is expected of children at various age levels, in diverse cultures. Helen Schwartzman's remarkable review of anthropological studies of play indicates how little attention field observers have paid to variations in children's play at different age levels within given cultures.[7] The transitional object phenomenon is scarcely mentioned at all in anthropological studies of dozens of cultures, not because it may not occur in some form in those cultures but because the theory and tradition of field research did not focus on it sufficiently so that it was looked for or asked about. Yet a simple inquiry about their early play to adults reared in different cultures can immediately evoke descriptions of such practices.

We have heard an interesting example from a Parsi woman. The Parsis are a very small minority group in India who migrated from Persia in Asia Minor about one thousand years ago. They are worshippers of Zoroaster who preserved elements of their ancient culture by remaining separate from the great Hindu and Moslem populations around them, prospering in business, shipbuilding, and science. The conductor, Zubin Mehta, is perhaps the representative of this group best known to Westerners. Our Parsi friend, reared in India and now a distinguished research scientist in an American university, reported to us that from her earliest childhood she carried around a piece of an old sari that her mother had torn off and given to her. She did so for at least her first five years and then preserved it, even after it was no longer "essential," among other keepsakes. The same practice was common, she insists, throughout the culture. As a matter of fact, her father, a successful businessman, still sleeps with a small remnant of his childhood sari rag under his pillow and occasionally uses it for various functional purposes, such as covering his eyes to shut out the light when resting or as a bookmark.

Litt's study of American children showed that 21 percent of her parent respondents indicated that they encouraged their child's attachment, much as Parsi mothers do. We wonder, however, if the parental role is not more extensive than Litt's data suggest; possibly many parents or early caregivers scarcely notice the ways in which they use cloths, diapers, or furry animals to soothe children. Certainly once the use of a transitional object starts it continues with parental tolerance. Litt's review makes it clear that prolonged attachment to a transitional object is a relatively common and essentially normal occurrence. She calls attention to research data (usually based on parents' reports rather than on direct observations of children) which indicate that there may be practical benefits in an attachment to security blankets or soft toys. In comparative studies, children with transitional objects, which they clung to at bedtime or when distressed, actually had fewer sleep disturbances and were reported in three out of four studies to be more tractable, self-confident, independent, and affectionate to caregivers. Retrospective studies with adults suggest that college freshmen who responded to a questionnaire indicating early transitional object attachment also scored as more impulsive, sensitive, and extraverted on personality tests. On the other hand, Litt's own research with children between ages eight and eleven, who stated that they had been attached to blankets and soft toys, indicated that such children fell within the normal range on various personality measures. A comparison group of children who reported no such early attachment showed significantly higher scores (but within a normal range) on a behavior problem scale, with indications of a greater tendency toward hyperactive, aggressive, and antisocial behavior. These differences were especially strong among the boys, suggesting that those who had been attached to transitional objects were *less* likely to be physically impulsive or aggressive. Retrospective reports from individuals suffering from severe personality and developmental disorders also indicate a low incidence of transitional object attachments.[8]

Such data cannot in themselves argue that the Linuses of America will grow up to be psychologically healthier. After all, the correlations we are seeing may be explained by other factors—parents who accept such behavior may also be benign in many other ways; retrospective reports may reflect cultural expectancies or a desire to please the interviewers; or the sheer availability of soft toys may reflect less stressful or economically deprived family circumstances. For our purposes it seems sufficient to recognize the essential normality of the attachment to transitional objects and the possibility that such attachments may become forerunners of imaginative play. This seems especially likely when we observe the child beginning to cuddle a cloth animal or doll, make room for it in the bed, and occasionally spank it or try to feed it. One might surmise, although the data are lacking, that the diaper or blanket is more like a security fetish, while the soft teddy bear or doll may lend itself more easily to the beginnings of imaginative interaction and may either serve as a transition to an imaginary playmate or actually become one as it is assigned human properties by the increasingly verbal child.

Most American adults reared in modest circumstances in the 1920s, 1930s, or earlier, can recall a favorite rag doll or stuffed animal. But social circumstances change, and today we are witnessing an explosion of interest in soft toys fostered almost certainly by the power of television commercials and increasingly attention-grabbing store displays. Will such a plethora of stuffed toys in a growing child's environment have any special effect on imaginative play and the phenomenon of transitional objects?

We Americans are inveterate toy givers. Remembering perhaps our own experiences in childhood or influenced by television commercials, we bombard babies with stuffed creatures. Indeed, a major factor in the success of the billion-dollar toy industry is what the manufacturers call the "plush product," everything from soft dolls like the Cabbage Patch Kids to huge stuffed bears, tigers, and pandas. Clearly, whatever the reason for a baby's interest in such objects in other societies or in the more innocent pretelevision days of A. A. Milne's *Winnie-the-Pooh,* our present culture fosters such a tendency. Learning to be a proper baby or toddler in American society means relating to stuffed animals, talking to them, and (as is possible with the new embedded tape recorder feature) listening to two teddies repeating each other's phrases! One wonders whether such heightened "reality" and the increased availability of stuffed toys will interfere with self-engendered play and fantasy or if it will enhance it. We can surmise that the extreme mechanical complexity of such toys may attract a child initially but will soon lose its "play value" as the novelty wears off. And what of the large numbers of such toys now provided to all but the very poorest children? Will children still select a favorite one to cling to and use, not only as a transitional object but in their first experience of imaginative play? We will have to wait and see.

Imaginary Playmates in Their Earliest Forms

One can find autobiographical references to what appear to be imaginary playmates in the work of nineteenth-century writers as diverse as Johann Wolfgang von Goethe, Leo Tolstoy, Robert Louis Stevenson, and Mark Twain, and literary examples in a number of Twain's novels and stories. It may well be that this great American humorist briefly developed a demonic make-believe friend, because he describes his mother's constant references to Satan when he was very small. Indeed, she may have been one of the few good Christians who prayed for Satan, since, as the world's greatest sinner, who needed prayers more?[9] We know that Twain translated dozens of early friends, acquaintances, and childhood experiences into the stuff of his vast literary output. The appearance of Satan as the invisible friend of the boys in *The Mysterious Stranger* may reflect the author's own childhood fantasies as he sought to deal with his mother's vivid references to this fallen angel.[10] In current psychoanalytic terminology, to which we briefly referred in discussing transitional objects, the invention of a clearly evil figure to represent all of the negativity, greediness, and "sinfulness" of the child is termed "splitting." As we shall see, splitting off one's traits into dichotomous characters may include not only the good and the evil but also the childlike and the adult, the timid and the audacious, the powerless and the superheroic. As Josie, the child in the vignette that began this chapter, pointed out, Louisa (perhaps representing her frightened or weaker alter ego) "drownded" in the puddle where Josie got so wet, but then Frogman, a more heroic new friend, appeared, clearly impervious to the dangers and discomforts of water.

In the earliest attempt at a scientific report on imaginary friends, C. Vostrovsky, writing in 1895, pointed to the stabilizing, possibly adaptive role such characters may play for the child.[11] Researchers in the early 1930s were less certain of these advantages and instead expressed concern, without the actual follow-up data, that children reporting pretend friends might be at risk for later psychopathology. Piaget was one of the earliest investigators during that period to suggest a more adaptive role for the child's invention of imaginary friends and to view the phenomenon as intrinsic to cognitive development.[12] In the 1970s more extensive collections of data began to appear, and it became apparent that the phenomenon was more common than had been supposed. Studies of preschoolers in Texas, conducted by Martin Manosevitz and Norman Prentice, indicated that almost a third of the children exhibited such phenomena. Those with make-believe friends were reported by parents to be happier in day-to-day activities and were also more verbal in communication. They showed no special inclination toward shyness and easily gave up play with make-believe friends when "real" peer-play opportunities presented themselves.[13] These results are similar to what we have found in our own studies.

The accounts of imaginary friends that have emerged from clinical studies have tended to emphasize their conflict-related, defensive, or compensatory quality. Certainly one way a child can deal with loneliness, helplessness, or fear of the dark or unknown might be to invent such a playmate or magic helper. In a study by Jerome L. Singer and Bella Streiner comparing the fantasies and dreams of matched sighted and blind children, it was the blind children who almost always reported having a sighted imaginary friend.[14] This result was not the case for deaf children, who showed no difference from hearing children in reports of pretend companions according to data obtained by Dorothy G. Singer and Marie Lenahan.[15]

As studies have accumulated in the 1970s and 1980s, the evidence for the prevalence, "normality" and, indeed, constructive, adaptive role of imaginary friends has increased. An extensive survey by V. K. Masih in the 1970s, and more recent reviews by Jana Somers and Thomas Yawkey, among others, point even more strongly to the creative and useful role of such playmates.[16] The latter investigators conclude, "research evidence suggests that the belief in imaginary play companions is linked with creative and intellectual growth. The development of sensitivity, elaboration and originality are creative aspects linked with imaginary play companions. From a cognitive perspective, the key elements connected to intellectual growth include symbolic functioning, decontextualization, object relations and symbolizations."[17] Somers and Yawkey go on to propose constructive "guidance strategies" that adults might employ with children in both school and home settings. We shall examine some of these approaches in Chapters 9 and 10.

Obtaining Evidence of Imaginative Playmates in Preschoolers

We should like to exemplify a research approach and some key findings about imaginary playmates by presenting the results of a study we carried out with assistance from John Caldeira.[18] There were two ways in which we obtained information about the belief in imaginary playmates among the children in our study. As part of the imaginative play interview each child was asked whether or not he or she had a "make-believe friend." This item was one of a group of items that provided the score for this measure. In earlier research there had been indications that such an interview would be useful in estimating the extent to which the child would show imaginativeness in spontaneous play or in other situations, or be able to tolerate delays as part of a game.

We also considered it appropriate to obtain more detailed information from parents in order to identify any patterns in their children's invention of imaginary companions. Accordingly, we prepared a questionnaire to mail out to parents. We asked them:

1. Has your child ever had an imaginary companion? Yes - No - More than one.
2. Did this imaginary friend appear only once, more than once, or is it a steady companion? Only once - more than once - steady companion.
3. Does your child talk to the imaginary companion? Yes - No.

Other questions sought information about the sex and age of the imaginary companion, any names assigned and their possible origin, the age at which the child first developed an imaginary companion, whether or not the child shared the imaginary companion with other playmates, siblings, or family members, and so on. A list of sample television characters was also provided to parents so they could check off whether any of these had emerged as imaginary playmates in the course of the children's home play. We believed that, since children watch, on average, more than four hours of television a day, its content ought to be reflected in their choice of make-believe friends.

To establish quantitative scores for each child estimating the frequency of play with an imaginary companion we created an imaginary companion index. This was based on cumulative scores from the questionnaire to parents indicating the presence or absence of a companion, the frequency of play, and active interaction with the imaginary companion.

A total of 111 parents returned imaginary playmate questionnaires for their children. To check on the possibility that we were getting some type of selective response pattern, we compared the parents' responses on this questionnaire with the self-report obtained from the children in the imaginary play interview. No differences were found between the frequency of imaginary playmates in children of parents who did respond and the frequency reported by the children of the small number of parents who failed to respond. Children in general reported a higher frequency of imaginary playmates than did their parents. In fact, 65 percent of the children answered "yes" when asked whether they had some form of make-believe friend compared to 55 percent of their parents. This is not unreasonable because the children would know better than their parents whether or not they had an imaginary friend; and some parents might have failed to notice or perhaps suppressed this information.

When we identified those children described by their parents as showing a good deal of play with imaginary playmates and compared them with those whose parents reported little or no such play, we found no differences between the two groups in age or IQ. There were no statistically significant gender differences in frequency of imaginary playmates, although there was a tendency for girls to be more often described by their parents as having more make-believe friends. Boys were more likely than girls to have animals as make-believe playmates, while girls were significantly more likely than boys to have a pretend companion of the opposite sex. Of those girls who had imaginary playmates, 42 percent mentioned at least one imaginary male friend, whereas only 13 percent of the boys reported any imaginary female playmates.

About one-third of the children named their imaginary playmates after real people, often actual friends. More than 90 percent of the children were described by their parents as actually talking aloud to the make-believe friends at one time or another. Children without siblings were clearly much more likely to have imaginary playmates. This result seemed especially strong in the case of girls but held true for both sexes. These data suggest that imaginary playmates may have some adaptive and compensatory quality for the growing child. They may very well reflect an effort to "people" one's world when left to one's own devices, but at the same time they also engender opportunities for practicing imagery and conversation in the absence of external social stimulation.

It is worth noting that, in general, in our studies we have found a higher frequency of occurrence of imaginary playmates than have other researchers, whose percentages are closer to one-third of the children. This discrepancy may in part reflect somewhat different ways of asking the question, some difference in the ages of the children, and also some difference in the definition of an imaginary playmate. Jersild, Markey, and Jersild at Teachers College, Columbia University, have reported that 79 percent of the children in a study they conducted had at least some dolls or objects that they clearly anthromorphized.[19] Our data do include parents' reports of their children's transformations of stuffed animals, which assume living, humanlike properties. We did not, however, count teddy bears or dolls where these were simply carried around or treated in the concrete fashion of the transitional object. Rather, to be included they had to be endowed by the child with definite human qualities and be treated as a friend or playmate. In this sense, Winnie-the-Pooh, Christopher Robin's little stuffed bear "come-to-life," would fall into the category of an imaginary playmate, as would Calvin's tiger, Hobbes.

The sex differences we observed seem particularly interesting, since they indicate several important changes that are taking place in role relationships between boys and girls. The girls were more likely to transform their imaginary playmates into humans rather than animals, and according to Louise Bates Ames, this would place the girls higher on an "imagination gradient."[20] Certainly, this seems in keeping with the generally greater verbal development of girls, and it is also in accord with the results described in other studies by Masih. Thomas Jersild has argued, however, that these gender differences may simply reflect a cultural artifact, because boys may be less willing to reveal private fantasies than girls.[21] We know from our earlier studies of free play in nursery schools that four- or five-year-old boys express imagination through more overt methods than girls do, but in reports of home play we find more indications of imaginative behavior on the part of girls.

The findings that girls more frequently choose opposite-sex playmates and that boys emphasize same-sex companions are comparable to results reported by Manosevitz, Prentice, and Wilson at the University of Texas in Austin.[22] Changing patterns of children's play in the twentieth century across several generations suggest that girls are moving in the boys' direction as far as games and playthings are concerned. Boys, conversely, have made very little movement toward adopting girls' games or toys.[23]

We have also observed an interesting trend in television programming: there are now female superheroes with whom girls can identify. Indeed, some of the girls who participated in our study included Bionic Woman or Wonder Woman among their fantasy friends, although they also included characters such as Superman or Batman. Boys, conversely, showed no similar tendency to choose imaginary female companions and in general limited themselves chiefly to male superheroes when they chose characters from TV. It is likely that this reflects a persistent dilemma in American society. Girls are encouraged to broaden the scope of their own role relationships and identification patterns, but a pervasive if subtle concern about homosexuality or emasculation, presumably picked up from parents, prevents boys from moving as freely toward adopting female fantasy playmates. It is unfortunate that the heroic television characters available to little girls are primarily action-oriented, aggressive females. It would be valuable if boys could be encouraged to move toward greater tenderness and nurturance, the admirable traits that women have always shown.[24]

In general, then, our data indicate that the children we studied from low to middle middle-class families have a considerable number of imaginary playmates. It would be hard to argue that the occurrence of such make-believe friends sugggests an inherent emotional disturbance or is a sign of serious conflict. Rather, make-believe friends seem to be common, at least among the children who made up our sample. It is also clear that at least some make-believe friends are drawn from television personalities, although the majority either reflect actual friends children have, or are combinations of figures from stories or television or simply creative original products of children's developing imaginative capacity.

What does the invention of a make-believe friend indicate about a preschool child's general imaginative tendencies? We had hypothesized that if imagination is evident in home play, at least in this form, it should manifest itself in the child's spontaneous play in nursery school and should be linked to more positive emotionality, more persistent and elaborated sequences of play, less overt aggression, and more extensive language usage. We were also interested in determining whether there might be an inverse relationship between the occurrence of imaginary playmates and the frequency of television viewing.

One way of looking at the data is to divide children into those with and those without imaginary playmates and then to examine each group's scores on behavioral variables across an entire year. We measured children's free play at daycare centers at least four times, and our assistants rated the children for styles of play and recorded their language, emotions, and aggression or cooperation. In general, those children reported by their parents to have imaginary playmates at home also showed more imaginativeness in their spontaneous play in nursery school, more positive emotionality during such play, more cooperative behavior with adults, and somewhat more extended language usage. Parents' viewing logs, maintained periodically over the year, also indicated that the children who had imaginary friends were watching less television.

Our data are even more clear-cut when we rely on the quantitative scores from the imaginary companion index and the frequency of play with imaginary companion scores and include these in statistical multiple regression analyses predicting play variables, language variables, and TV viewing. The advantage of multiple regression is that it takes into account the overall patterning of a group of variables as they predict a single criterion and, in a sense, comes closer to the way things work in real life. When we included the imaginary companion index along with the child's age, IQ, socioeconomic status, ethnicity, imagination interview, and an inkblot estimate of imagination as predictor variables in looking at the children's scores on overt behavior and language, indications were that the imaginary playmate scores were consistently and independently good predictors of the child's later behavior as seen in the daycare center.

When we sought to predict imaginativeness of play among boys, one of the best predictors was the imaginary companion variable. Attempting to predict the occurrence of positive effect, that is, indications in the observations of the child across the year of frequent smiling, laughing, curiosity, and excitement during play, the imaginary playmate variable was evidently the strongest single variable in the equation. This outcome is quite comparable to the findings reported by the Texas researchers, who also found that, according to parental reports, children who had imaginary companions seemed to be happier and showed more positive attitudes. But they relied on parents' reports about their children, while our data are based on direct observation of the emotions shown by the children during play. We also found that our imaginary playmate measure predicted greater persistence in play as observed over the year for those children who showed more make-believe friend activity.

Of special importance were the findings from our effort to predict overt aggressive behavior in boys. Our results suggest that boys who have imaginary playmates at home and who watch relatively few action-adventure TV shows are much less likely to turn out to be aggressive in their overt behavior as observed over the year by assistants who did not know the children's scores on imaginary play or TV viewing.

Of particular interest also is the attempt to predict the degree of cooperation with peers—the sharing and helping the child shows in overt behavior with other children. Here the imaginary companion variable for boys again turned out to be the major contributor to a highly successful prediction, along with other variables that included heavy viewing of the usual fare on commercial (in contrast with public) television. Similar results were obtained for a number of emotional variables, and the imaginary companion variable was more likely to occur as a predictor of specific positive emotions and was negatively linked to somewhat more negative affective states, such as fatigue and sluggishness. Particularly striking were indications that children having an imaginary companion were less likely to be fearful or anxious during a later play situation.

Results for girls showed some differences. Our predictions again moved in the same direction but were not as effective when imaginative play, aggression, and positive emotionality were our criteria. Television viewing seemed more important than imaginary friends in determining these reactions in girls. But the index of imaginary friends was a strong predictor for girls of persistence in play and of cooperative behavior at school. In terms of emotions, girls with imaginary playmates were less prone to anger and fearfulness during play behavior, and this finding was very strong for sadness. Combining both genders yields results generally like those found for boys alone.

In our attempt to predict the children's language use during the play, the best results were of course obtained for age and IQ. For boys, the number of words spoken by the child and the average length of the utterances produced during play periods were at least partially explained by the imaginary playmate variable. For girls, however, the imaginary playmate variable did not contribute strongly to the prediction of language usage. We also found that boys who had no imaginary playmates were watching more TV. When the same analysis was performed for girls, however, no clear results emerged.

The ability of the imaginary playmate variable to predict imaginative play, persistence, cooperation with peers, and general happiness during spontaneous play seems to indicate that the extent to which a child has such fantasy companions at home may indeed provide a more general indication of the child's imaginative capacity. The data are somewhat stronger for boys than for girls, perhaps because girls tend to be more likely to have imaginary companions than do boys and thus show somewhat less variability.

Our results clearly do not support the popular belief that shy or maladjusted children are especially likely to have imaginary companions. If anything, the evidence that a child has an imaginary playmate seems to be an especially powerful predictor of the likelihood that a child will play happily in nursery school, will be cooperative with friends and adults, and may use somewhat more extensive language, while also being somewhat less likely to watch a good deal of television. Again, the evidence of cooperative behavior with adults is comparable to the report of Martin Manosevitz and his collaborators in Texas, who found that children with imaginary playmates turned out to be more adept at talking with adults, according to their parents' reports.[25] Our findings also indicated that those children who had imaginary companions were more likely to be watching educational or public television programs, such as "Mister Rogers' Neighborhood" and "Sesame Street."

The Ways Children Manifest and Use Imaginary Playmates

So far we have emphasized studies of the imaginary playmate phenomenon that used fairly large numbers of children in order to establish what might be termed the normative basis of the phenomenon. Intriguing questions remain. How do individual children develop their invisible companions? What are the sources of the names and identities they assign? Do imaginary playmates serve a common function for all the children who develop them or many different functions? What is the fate of imaginary playmates as children reach early school age and move from the relative openness of the daycare center, nursery school, or kindergarten to the more formal constraints of the classroom.

At this stage of our knowledge there are no formal research studies even to shape approaches to answers. Instead, we must rely on anecdotes accumulated from interviews with parents, volunteered reminiscences, or the reports of clinicians who have directly observed children in therapy or recount the memories of their adult patients. Such data are suggestive and hypothesis-engendering, perhaps, but they cannot provide adequate tests of theoretical propositions.

Psychoanalytically-oriented observers of the imaginary companion phenomenon have placed considerable emphasis on its function in the development of the defensive cognitive process of "splitting," separating out one's (or another's) desirable and undesirable characteristics and behaviors, or those that are socially sanctioned and socially punished, into polarized extremes rather than recognizing them as capable of integration into one coherent schema. This phenomenon is important in current object-relations theory because psychoanalysts such as Otto Kernberg have identified this form of sharply dichotomized thinking as a special feature of "borderline" adult patients, who hover between serious maladjustment and frank psychosis.[26] Multiple personalities, extremely few in number but much celebrated in books and movies, generally show alternating "good" and "bad" or "uptight" and "licentious" sides within the same individual. And, of course, romantic fiction and legend have long celebrated such splits, whether within one body, as in Robert Louis Stevenson's *Dr. Jekyll and Mr. Hyde,* or within one's choice of life-styles or love objects, as in Richard Wagner's opera *Tannhäuser,* in which the hero is torn between the Greek goddess Venus and her orgiastic troupe and the pure, saintly maiden, Elizabeth. The concept of sacred and profane love that has threaded its way through European literature for almost a thousand years exemplifies this phenomenon.

Selma Fraiberg, one of the most influential psychoanalytic observers of child behavior, described the way a boy named Stevie used his imaginary playmate Gerald as his regular scapegoat for acts that Stevie himself carried out, although he knew they were unacceptable, such as breaking his father's pipe. In a sense this arbitrary splitting, in which Gerald is always the author of Stevie's misdeeds, allows Stevie to identify clearly what the expectations of his parents and other adults are and gradually to internalize them by meting out punishment and criticism to the offending invisible friend.[27]

In a girl named Karen described by Bruce Klein, the author of a thoughtful clinical study of imaginary playmates, we also see the splitting phenomenon, but here linked to some extent to dramatic changes in her life between the ages of three and nine. Karen's father died before she was two, and her imaginary playmates Jeff and Julia appeared soon after her mother began regularly dating the man she soon married. Jeff was mischievous while Julia was good, and Karen generally played the role of the parent who reprimands or punishes. Perhaps Karen was maintaining an association with a positive female, her mother, through Julia while shifting her anger at her lost natural father or her intruding new father onto the shoulders of Jeff. Even less transparently split are two other companions she created, Happy and Maddy.[28]

The persistence of splitting as a significant form of thought into adolescence and adult life may well have ominous implications as a feature of the borderline personality as defined in the current psychiatric description of the disorder. But we have no evidence that the splitting observed in preschoolers with imaginary playmates portends any such fate for a given child. On the contrary, evidence from maladjusted adult individuals who resemble borderline patients suggests that they are less likely to recall playing with imaginary companions. One might speculate that, while a childhood dilemma might initiate the emergence of imaginary figures, suggesting a splitting pattern, an opportunity for the child to use her capacity for fantasy, usually with parental tolerance, may actually help to resolve the dilemma and avert a more serious persistence of "good me" and "bad me" beliefs. In the case of individuals exhibiting multiple personalities, there is some evidence of a high incidence of early child abuse; for these children, it is likely that the split components emerged defensively but could never be controlled or internalized as pure thought because the children lacked the benign parental sanction that would help them recognize these alternative selves as part of a playful environment.[29]

Make-believe friends also emerge for other purposes that often seem to meet compensatory needs in confronting loneliness, childhood fears, or a sense of weakness in relation to adults or older children. When the Yawkeys at Pennsylvania State University studied children reared in single-parent households, they found significant correlations between this family structure and imaginary playmates. The children reported having more imaginary companions, revealed more signs of frequent conversation with their invisible friends, and more generally showed a good deal of imagination when playing alone. Only children or children separated in age from other siblings by about five years are somewhat more prone to generate make-believe friends, as our studies and several others have suggested.[30]

At the age of two-and-a-half, one only child began communicating with a companion he called "Poh." He also soon invented another less frequent friend called "Chanukah." When taking baths the boy would report that "Poh," who was in the tub with him, was afraid he would wash down the drain, and the boy urged his parents to be especially careful. The parents knew their child had developed a fear of this "danger," since he was somewhat consoled on hearing Mister Rogers sing on television that "You can't go down the drain!" They speculated that the name "Poh" came from the Hebrew word meaning "here," which was shouted out by older children during roll call in a religious school the little boy had visited and where he also heard about Chanukah.

A woman we know remembers that she created imaginary playmates during a period when, as a preschooler, she often heard references to her father's recurrent illness. These friends included

Phena and Barbara Tall as well as Ultra, Violet, and Ray. She often worked them into a pretend radio series she made up based on a popular program of that time, "The Quiz Kids."

Sometimes children seem to create imaginary friends with special strengths or abilities they themselves lack. One boy we observed had an invisible companion named "Giles," who shared his bed in the new house to which the family had recently moved. Giles was in fact the name of a rather independent, aggressive child the boy encountered in his nursery school. Another boy in one of our studies had an unnamed imaginary elfin companion who could frighten off monsters and transform small objects into large ones by sprinkling magic dust. The boy often called on this elf when he was frightened. One four-year-old girl we encountered, who came from a family in which various relatives had recently married and where there was a great deal of contact with much older cousins, generated five imaginary husbands. Four were conventional, with common names, but the fifth, named "Flier," a mischievous young man who attended college and often engaged in high jinks on a school bus, was her favorite.

Bruce Klein has described a similar instance of a compensatory imaginary figure. A boy named Allen, already almost six but painfully shy and slower than two much older and very successful brothers, had a friend named Gerry, who could do many things Allen could not. He even owned a plane, which he let Allen fly. As Allen moved on in school his companion became less prominent, but when the boy faced a situation that required chatting with newly met adults he offered to let Gerry do the talking. With this magical touch Allen could then move more smoothly into natural conversation.[31]

As we have mentioned, in our own studies we have found that children frequently create imaginary playmates named after television superheroes such as Superman or Wonder Woman. Initially, such compensatory figures may be merely for consolation, but over time they may also provide the child with modeling opportunities for trying out new physical or social arts or creating new and more interesting games. In a curious way we see the same techniques employed in modern cognitive-behavioral therapies, in which adults seeking to develop greater self-assertiveness are encouraged by their therapists to engage in covert modeling practice or to conjure up inner guides or magical healers. How far removed are children's efforts at self-treatment and self-motivation through make-believe friends from the reliance of religious adults on patron saints and guardian angels? And did not Charles VII owe his coronation as King of France to the courage of an Alsatian farm girl, Joan of Arc, a courage gained from the invisible saints who spurred her on to serve her nation?

We know relatively little as yet about imaginary playmates that are shared by two or more children. One example that has come to our attention is that of two young English girls aged three and five, who between them generated an ethereal imaginary creature named "Fetiss." She was treated as a real child, sharing their bed at night and accompanying them everywhere. When we questioned their mother in some detail about the circumstances surrounding the origin of this figure, she remembered that she was pregnant when the children first developed the mutual fantasy. Had the word *fetus* been used within earshot of the girls? Did they give their mysterious invisible sister a premature birth as their companion in an effort to deal with their puzzlement about what was happening to their mother and to the family? We cannot know, but it seems a reasonable hypothesis.

On the subject of shared imaginary companions we have found relatively little evidence of ambiguity in children's behavior in terms of their belief in the reality of their invisible friend. Shared fantasies, such as the Ant People developed by Tolstoy and his siblings, seem to emerge at somewhat later ages and take on a quality more like that of a pretending game or a paracosm.[32] It seems more likely that the "pure" imaginary playmate is a special feature in the development of an individual child's imagination, a transitional stage of possession and unique control out of which a belief in selfness can emerge. As in the case of the transitional object, a step toward greater maturity and self-possession is often manifested by a refusal to share the fantasy and by its voluntary abandonment. Benson and Pryor have described an instance of a girl named Lynn whose parents acquiesced in her companion fantasy, even packing extra clothes for the invisible friend when a trip was impending. Her grandfather entered actively into the fantasy by asserting, after he had closed the garage door using a remote control device, that her companion had done it through magic. Lynn dropped the companion for good after this incident. Bensen and Pryor suggest that the sense of personal control was crucial to Lynn's need for the fantasy, and once it was not so controlled by her she gave it up.[33] Bruce Klein also reports a similar incident in which a girl named Sharon dropped two imaginary companions after a visit to her grandparents, during which her grandfather had become actively involved in playing with the unseen figures. Klein quotes the mother as saying, "It was like she lost control of her friends."[34]

Children probably hover between a sense of the reality of these playmates and an awareness that they are part of their pretend play. When adults "butt in" uninvited, children not only lose a sense of privacy and possession but may also fear that adults are ridiculing them or have somehow stepped out of adult roles. Studies of more general imaginative play, including our own and those of Marc Gershowitz and Diana Shmukler, have shown that children may welcome the initiation of fantasy play by adults (from whom they get plot ideas) but quickly give up the game if the big people persist too long or become too childish.[35]

What is the later fate of imaginary playmates? Do they all disappear somewhere between the sixth and eighth years? Perhaps in their most primitive forms—as "Poh" or "Fetiss"—there is no place for them in the increasingly socially influenced consciousness of the child. But very likely the *process* of peopling one's private thoughts with companiable souls, whether as introjected parental figures, friends, or religious figures, goes on indefinitely. Social traditions make possible internal monologues with dead ancestors (as in pre-Communist China) or saints. Tevye the dairyman's chats with God as depicted in *Fiddler on the Roof* reflect some of this process. One of us (JLS) used to while away long subway rides to high school at age thirteen by imagining that an ancient Roman gentleman (not unlike Cicero, whom he was studying in Latin class) had appeared in twentieth-century New York City. He had to satisfy this person's curiosity about tunnels, bridges, trains, automobiles, and airplanes through careful mental explanation. That such a fantasy may not have been unique is suggested by the appearance of a recent novel, *The Far Arena*, by Richard Ben Sapir. A champion Roman gladiator whose living body was sealed in ice in the North Sea in A.D. 80 is resuscitated by cryogenic scientists. His rescuers must then explain the modern world to him.[36]

The persistence of imaginary companions in some modified form in adults often appears to be associated with aspects of the creative process. The Greeks personified this notion in the Muses, and many writers, painters, and composers have mentioned the experience of sensing an almost real presence near them that seems to dictate words or music or direct their artistic efforts: Dickens often spoke of the tremendous sense of reality his characters assumed in his mind when he was immersed in writing his novels; Robert Louis Stevenson wrote of the quasi-reality of the Brownies who visited him; Woody Allen humorously represents similar visitations from the dead Humphrey Bogart in his film, *Play It Again Sam*. Along with the other functions of the imaginary playmate we have already described, it may well be that it is also a precursor, or at least a sign, of a longstanding creative interest, if not actual talent. In a study of adolescents Charles Schaefer found that those rated by teachers as most creative significantly more often reported that they remembered having imaginary playmates.[37] When Germany's two great writers, Goethe and Thomas Mann, chose to depict the creative impulse and the struggle to attain mastery, although writing one hundred and fifty years apart, they both employed the metaphor of a pact with the Devil.[38] Were they reflecting some private personification of the struggle between ease, conventionality, conformity, and traditional values and their decision to forgo such paths through a selfish, almost sinful commitment to art—a split reflecting the imagined companionship of that evil spirit?

Imaginary Societies or Paracosms

An early form of shared fantasy that may result in a more complex, individually or mutually elaborated form of companionship is described by the English journalist, Maurice Baring. In writing of his early childhood days in the 1870s he describes how he and Hugo, a younger brother, developed a "maddening, to grown up people" imaginary language. "Yes" was "Sheepartee" and "No" was "Quilinquinino." "We used to talk this language, which was called 'Sheepartee' and which consisted of unmitigated gibberish, for hours in the nursery." Eventually his older sisters complained, and in response to threats of whipping these conversations were terminated. There is actually some research on the grammatical properties of languages invented by children, but our concern here is rather with the fantasy elements of the process. Maurice and Hugo then progressed to a new game, which persisted well into their school years. They created and acted out a game called "Spankaboo," which involved an imaginary continent with countries, towns, wars, and a noble class. Lady Spankaboo and her husband, a country gentleman, were leading figures, but eventually hundreds of characters were involved, each with special intrigues and a unique personality. The boys shared roles and played the game in the garden or after they went to bed. "Everything that happened to us and everything we read was brought into the game—history, geography, the Ancient Romans, the Greeks, the French, but it was a realistic game, and there were no fairies in it and nothing in the least frightening. As it was a night game, this was just as well."[39]

The development by one child or several children of a "paracosm," an elaborated private society or even alternative world, is one of the least studied phenomena in the child development literature. The late Robert Silvey and Stephen Mackeith have been almost alone in attempting to explore the range, origin, and implications of this form of childhood imagination and play.[40] Silvey was an audience researcher and executive with the British Broadcasting Corporation; Mackeith is a psychiatrist in England. They were attracted to the subject by Silvey's own recall of his childhood paracosm and by the belief that, since paracosms are among the few childhood fantasies that are retained into adult life and are very often written down, they represent a kind of fossilized reflection of actual childhood imagination. To be considered in this research, a paracosm had to meet three criteria. It had to (1) be clearly distinguished by the child as imaginary; (2) sustain the child's interest over a period of years; and (3) inspire a sense of importance about its conception, a feeling of pride in its devising, and a desire to maintain consistency.

Silvey and Mackeith used radio talks and newspaper advertising to solicit respondents to the very detailed questionnaire they developed. They obtained data from fifty-seven individuals, three children and fifty-four adults, who described a total of sixty-four paracosms. Their analysis indicates that 19 percent of the paracosms were actually developed by children between the ages of three and six but that they peaked between the ages of eight and nine, a period we might note when more overt make-believe play has disappeared or generally moved "underground" into private thoughts. The earliest ones (invented by children in the three- to six-year age group) are built around animals, stuffed toys, or special locations. As might be expected, these societies are characterized by wish-fulfillment, shifting structures, and some inconsistency. They seem more clearly like the make-believe friendship patterns we have already discussed and probably reflect a transitional phrase. Silvey and Mackeith describe a girl named Holly who created a country called "Branmail," which one reached by climbing "Bumpety Banks." All the inhabitants except Holly were cats, and one, named Kitty, seemed to represent a mischievous scapegoat whom Holly could blame for her own misdeeds. The inhabitants engaged in numerous adventures, and Holly acted out her stories with parental approval.

In a reminiscence not cited by Silvey and Mackeith, Tolstoy describes a paracosm that, like Holly's "Branmail," demonstrates the limited cognitive capacity of the very young child. It was Nicholas, Tolstoy's older brother, who initiated the stories about a pretend society when Leo was almost certainly of preschool age. The younger boy became caught up in the adventures of the Ant people and tried to follow Nicholas's account of a society in which sickness would disappear and love would prevail. The term "ant" people, as Tolstoy realized later, was formed by his assimilation of an unknown term into a limited set of cognitive schemas. His older brother had somewhere picked up the name of a Bohemian religious sect, the Moravian Brothers, which he used to designate his idyllic paracosm. For the much younger Leo this sounded like the word *muravey,* which meant "ant," hence his concept of an "ant brotherhood."[41]

Silvey and Mackeith organized their collection of reported paracosms along a five-part continuum: (1) toys, animals, and family groups; (2) particular places and local communities; (3) islands, countries, and people; (4) systems, documents, and languages; and (5) unstructured, shifting, and idyllic worlds. They suggest a rough correlation between the age level of the child and the form of the paracosm, with higher numbered dimensions more characteristically emerging at older ages. According to their data, most paracosms had changed from active preoccupations into only occasional activities by the age of twenty-one. The long persistence of paracosms may be explained by the fact that they provide a welcome distraction from otherwise routine, boring duties or chores for somewhat introverted, shy persons. Silvey and Mackeith cite the example of a now-retired scientist named Darius who generated an island society named "Pacifia," which was made up of a very intelligent, high-technology-oriented citizenry. At the time, Darius was twenty-one and serving a boring tour of duty in the military.[42] During early high school years one of us (JLS) developed a mythical ancient Greek society, passing tedious class time by drawing elaborate classical busts of various rulers in this benign, kingly dynasty, depicting the adventures of its heroes in cartoon form, and reflecting in a somewhat naive fashion on the early development of science and philosophy by its intellectual and cultural leaders, who were faintly reminiscent of Plato and Aristotle.

In addition to mitigating boredom and providing an escape, the paracosm also serves affective purposes by generating a sense of joy, personal control, and power. These reactions emerge in the reports of Silvey and Mackeith's participants, but they are also evident in the published descriptions they reviewed and in the autobiographies we surveyed. Perhaps the most famous childhood paracosms were those of the four Brontë siblings, Charlotte, Branwell, Emily, and Anne, all of whom went on to further literary pursuits.[43] Raised in relative isolation, the children shared a series of imaginary societies (see Chapter 1) over a period of more than ten years. Inspired by the set of toy soldiers given to Branwell in 1826 when he was nine, they created imaginary kingdoms, with elaborate battles and intrigues, and eventually began to write down their stories, Charlotte and Branwell calling their kingdom Angria, and Emily and Anne calling theirs Gondal. Their characters are a pastiche of the English leaders in the recently concluded Napoleonic wars, and their plots are drawn from *The Arabian Nights* and *Blackwood's Magazine*. What emerges from these early writings is the sense of control the children gained from manipulating their characters, their shared excitement, and their practical division of labor according to their interests (Charlotte was stronger on characterization and plotting, for example, while Branwell was better on geography and social structure). Living in reduced circumstances, trained in solitude by a remote and bookish father, they became their own small community as creators of fantasy while also developing their literary skills in these first attempts at writing.

We should like to propose that paracosms represent an even more advanced and imaginative way in which children and adolescents come to terms with the inevitable tension between agency and community, which we discussed at the outset of this book. Often enough, the children who invent imaginary worlds have already used their imaginative skills in play. Now they apply these themes to developing a sense of community without having to confront the often cruel or unpredictable behaviors of actual extrafamilial peers. In the community of the created society, children, and even adults, can maintain some individualized pride in their constructive skill and a feeling of nearly godlike power.

Silvey and Mackeith's participants most often described themselves as "imaginative," "bright," and "dreamy," as well as "bad at games" (presumably peer sports), "timid," "apprehensive," "solitary," and "unmechanically minded." The accounts of paracosms in the published autobiographies and biographies of such well-known persons as Anthony Trollope, Kenneth Grahame, W. H. Auden, C. S. Lewis, sculptor Claes Oldenburg, and actor-playwright Peter Ustinov attest to the use of this mechanism in coming to grips with isolation and, at the same time, expressing a sense of control and individuality. But paracosms are not always associated with defensiveness and compensatory reactions; they are often natural extensions of individual imaginativeness, curiosity, and exploratory tendencies. In summarizing their research findings, Silvey and Mackeith assert that, in addition to a desire for control, power, and independence, "the creation of an imaginary private world, like other imaginary activities, seems to be encouraged by such factors as cultural and familial tolerance of fantasy generally, the existence of leisure, the hearing of stories, the reading of books and the availability of suitable material on radio and television."[44]

Are paracosms harbingers of possible madness? On the basis of our own research and that of Silvey and Mackeith we see little evidence that children who have developed such imaginary societies are likely to forgo genuine personal interactions in order to dwell in private worlds. Studies of psychotic individuals, usually schizoid or schizophrenic, rarely indicate such developed fantasy lives. On the contrary, most of the patients tested show little evidence of rich, organized fantasies, and even paranoid delusions tend to be externally focused and lack the sense of control, enjoyment, and discrimination between reality and fantasy that characterize paracosmists. Two especially dramatic case histories, however, report paracosms in individuals under treatment for mental illness. In one instance, Hannah Green, the fictionalized adolescent patient of the real Dr. Frieda Fromm-Reichman (in the ever-popular *I Never Promised You a Rose Garden*) certainly seemed to have lost control of her demonic fantasy world.[45] Yet the paracosm might well have augured great imaginative potential, for with sensitive therapy, the patient was not only able to move into a normal life but emerged as the well-respected, successful novelist, Joanne Greenberg.

Another even more elaborate adult paracosm was described by psychologist Robert Lindner in his case study, "The Jet-Propelled Couch."[46] Here, the proponent was a successful nuclear physicist who had developed—and was increasingly living within—a science-fictional planetary domain. Lindner was able to reach the young man by sharing his fantasy for a time and through this means exploring the highly personal psychodynamic conflicts that underlay the patient's distress. So compelling was the fantasy world that Lindner reports nearly being sucked in himself and mildly regretting its dissolution when the patient finally abandoned it (not unlike the four-year-old who threw his Burpee cloth and stuffed Bow-wow downstairs) and moved on to a new stage of realistic living.

Imaginary playmates and paracosms may chiefly represent the vast creative potential of inherently talented people, but in less elaborated forms, they may also represent what childhood imagination can offer to the growing person. Humanity has already benefited from the paracosmic visions of Plato, Thomas More, Aldous Huxley, Thomas Hobbes, Arthur Tappan Wright (*Islandia*), and J. R. R. Tolkien. The imaginary playmates created even as late as the age of twelve by the young Steven Spielberg later appeared in the film *E.T.,* which brought pleasure, and perhaps a shock of recognition, to millions of adults and children. The film's depiction of adults, generally viewed at waist height through a child's eyes and clearly impervious to the child's world, captures one sense in which imaginary playmates function to overcome childhood powerlessness. A case in point is the scene in which the mother of the protagonist children barges into the kitchen, preoccupied with her shopping bags and the responsibilities of household management as a single parent, opens the refrigerator, and, without seeing the presumably visible E.T., knocks the appealing alien flat with its door.

It remains to be seen whether films about fantasy playmates such as *E.T.* or *Meatballs II* will gradually encourage children to use such playmates more constructively and more openly or whether those like George Lukas's *Star Wars* trilogy will foster the invention of other imaginary worlds. What we believe emerges from our extensive survey is that we need to appreciate the human imagination and its potential when we see children asserting their power, self-control, and sense of possession, and, in a curious way, resolving the tension between individuality and social concern through make-believe friends and pretend societies.

6

Cognitive and Emotional
Growth through Play

We have the good fortune of being grandparents, which has afforded us a second chance to observe children's behavior in a home setting rather than as intruders in a nursery school. So, as the auto bumper sticker says, "Let us tell you about our grandchildren."

Grace, who is eighteen months old, has been given a small toy airport with some rather simple airplanes and trucks. Once the toy set is unfolded she sits at it and manipulates the objects, choosing a plane or a truck and moving it around in the air or on the field while producing a "brrrr" sound. As her game goes on she stands up enthusiastically and swings the vehicle she is holding in wider arcs, continuing her very limited range of sound effects. She can sustain this game for as long as fifteen minutes if she is not distracted by the activity or conversation of her older sister, Cory, aged six-and-a-half, or of the adults in the room. Since she lives in a mountainous rural area, she has had much less exposure to airplanes or airports than many children, so it is doubtful that she has a very differentiated cognitive structure about airplanes and how they are different from automobiles or trucks. More likely, what she is doing is repetitively mastering her ability to hold and move objects, to imitate the sounds of the cars and trucks she does see often, and to gain some sense of power and competence, as Brian Sutton-Smith has suggested, by moving and controlling miniaturized versions of the huge and often frightening vehicles that rumble along the road. Grace clearly takes delight in the game—she smiles as her father unfolds it on the floor, shows intense interest as she sorts out the objects and manipulates them, and laughs aloud between periods of onomatopoeic vocalizations.

A little later, she and Cory engage in a game that goes on for almost twenty minutes and indeed, might have lasted longer if the impatient adults had not terminated it by calling the children away. Cory crawls into an empty kitchen cabinet, crunches herself up to fit into its narrow confines, and closes the door. One of the adults calls out, "Where's Cory?" and Grace starts to inspect the cabinet, finally grasping the door by a knob, pulling it open, and peering inside. Cory shouts, "Here I am!" Grace is first startled and then laughs in delight. Soon the game continues in an increasingly smoother form, with Cory shutting the door, Grace looking momentarily puzzled and then pulling it open and laughing as she finds Cory inside. Occasionally Grace tries another cabinet door, but soon she focuses regularly on the correct one. We observe a smoothing of movement (a sign of perceptual-motor learning) and less startle effect, but continuing laughter and smiling as Grace discerns the figure of her sister in the cabinet's shadowy interior.

Readers knowledgeable in psychoanalysis will recognize in this vignette a parallel to Freud's much-cited description of his own eighteen-month-old grandchild's repetitive game of throwing a pole-attached spool onto a bed so that it disappears and then reeling it back into view with the joyful cry of "Da!" (German for "There!"). Freud used this example to elaborate his conception of what he called the "Repetition Compulsion," and, characteristically, he interpreted such a game as being "related to the child's greatest cultural achievement—the instinctual renunciation (that is, the renunciation of instinctual satisfaction) which he had made in allowing his mother to go away without protesting. He compensated himself for this . . . by himself staging the disappearance and return of the objects within his reach." Freud goes on to hypothesize other motives—an effort at mastery by turning a passive experience of abandonment into an active one—and also gives particular emphasis to the motive of revenge on the mother for leaving him: "All right, then, go away! I don't need you. I'm sending you away myself."[1]

Today, in contrast to Freud's reduction of the game to the specific issue of conflict resolution and mother-child attachment, we take a broader perspective. For one thing, Piaget's concept of "object permanence" has taught us that a great deal of early childhood activity involves efforts to establish the constancy of all kinds of objects as they fade from view in the distance or disappear, as our arms and legs do, under blankets. The corpus of experimental and observational research on toddlers' separation or stranger anxiety over the past thirty years makes it clear that important properties of the cognitive capacity at different stages necessitate a range of "coming and going" experiences. Many of these are achieved in spontaneous play or in peer- or adult-initiated games of peekaboo or hide-and-seek, which gradually integrate the child's limited memory schemas with new information and new skills, such as the ability to manipulate imagery.[2]

The psychoanalyst Ernst Schachtel, in his great book *Metamorphosis,* also writes of the repetitive "hide and return" game in terms of the discovery of the consistent structure of objects and people. One's power to regain the missing feature, whether by crying for the parent, reeling in the spool, or, as in Grace's case, manipulating the cabinet door to reveal the hidden Cory, polish one's skills at searching, and develop what we would today call a schema or script for establishing confidence that objects temporarily out of sight or reach will later be available intact. Of special importance for pretend play is the capacity to sustain the object in *thought,* that is, to develop an image, cognitive map, or plan of it in its physical absence.[3] This latter gain from repetitive play cannot be overemphasized. Kurt Lewin's 1929 film depicting a toddler's difficulty in sitting on a stone graphically demonstrates this phenomenon. The child *faces* the stone as he crawls onto it. But to sit, he must actually *turn away* from the stone, a case of "out of sight, out of mind," and thus for the child a puzzle.[4] One of the most tragic experiences we share in this regard is observing an old man stricken with Alzheimer's disease who can no longer sustain a mental image of a chair and who thus resists lowering himself into it with his back to the seat lest he fall to the ground.

Schachtel makes a telling point about the repetitive nature of play:

> Much of what impressed Freud as repetition compulsion in the child's need to repeat a story or a play activity over and over again turns out to be neither the result of a desire to return to an earlier state nor the effect of the principle of inertia, but an essential requirement of the gradual exploration of the environment, the world of reality, and the child's relations to it. Exploration by many acts of focal attention is possible only if the object of exploration is repeatedly available and is unchanged; and orientation in the environment would become quite impossible if one could not depend on its relative constancy. This does not mean that no other motives are present in the child's need for repetition of experiences. The enjoyment of doing that which one already masters, as compared with the hazards of any new venture, are ever-present competitors in man's life . . . [The] tendency to prefer safe mastery of the familiar to the challenge of the unknown often plays a role, especially if his natural curiosity and desire to venture have been inhibited or stifled by an overanxious or forbidding parent. In the child's

insistence that not a single word be changed in a story, there may also be the desire, born of anxiety, to control the situation and the reading adult. *But the possible presence of such other motivations must not blind one to the fact that exploration and discovery of unknown aspects are constantly going on in what may impress one as mere repetition* [italics ours].[5]

We have italicized Schachtel's last sentence to stress the issue that to us seems a critical feature of how repetitive play and adult story-telling are linked to children's cognitive development and to differentiated schema formations. Once an adult has heard the story of "The Three Bears," its repetition presents nothing new, but for a child, who is still struggling with what a bear is, how a child named Goldilocks could stumble into a bear's house, what chairs or beds are, and how bears use them, these elements all present novel features that arouse the affects of interest and surprise again and again. Thus, exploration and repetition often go hand in hand during play and eventually produce new kinds of schemas and scripts. As a parallel experience, adults may recall their own reaction on first hearing a great symphony. While certain melodies or moments of orchestral power might have struck them at once, they probably required repeated hearings to feel that they "knew" the work. Indeed, one can listen twenty times to Beethoven's Third, Fifth, Seventh, or Ninth Symphonies, or to Brahms's First or Fourth, and still make new and exciting discoveries. The "simple" world of a hide-and-seek game or a pretend play activity may hold similar novelties for the child.

One final example of Grace's play can conclude this part of our discussion of play and cognitive growth. In this example, Cory has been drawing a picture of an elf and proudly signs it "Cory 1988," evidence of her recent acquisition of reading and writing. Afterward, one of us reads her a fairy tale, during which time Grace watches and listens for a few minutes but, clearly uncomprehending, moves away to other activities. The story over, Grace returns, takes a crayon from the box on the table, dabs at a paper, then opens a book and starts to "read." She reads in a firm, clear voice but in a continuous babbling language, punctuated only occasionally by an English word from her extremely limited vocabulary: "Cory," "bye-bye," and "moo" (pointing to a picture of a cow). She turns the pages as she babbles, varying her intonation and occasionally laughing out loud, so that a foreigner or a space alien might actually believe she is reading. Here again in this very early form of pretend play we see a combination of Piagetian accommodation and assimilation, a practice of mastering speech intonation in advance of an adequate vocabulary, and, in addition, some perceptual motor learning about holding a book and how to identify recognizable objects in it, such as the cow that evoked a "moo" or the car that evoked a "bye-bye."

Early Play and Cognitive Learning

In our discussion of the life span in Chapter 2, we called attention to the kinds of demands imposed on physically growing children by their newfound capacity to move in different ways and by the increasing expectations of adults or older siblings. How do children acquire specific new skills, practice them, find out for themselves what new capacities, motor or intellectual, they have attained through normal growth, and, finally, employ these skills to attain a sense of attachment or other forms of reinforcement from those around them? The baby and toddler must maneuver between what we described as the three basic human motives—to organize and integrate schemas and meanings about the world; to develop motor skills, images, and a sense of autonomy (for example, walking alone, manipulating blocks); and to obtain signs of approval, love, and nurturance from caregivers. These motives drive children to explore and play. One of the key questions we will address in this chapter is the special role imaginative play may have in helping children move smoothly through the physical, cognitive, and social demands of toddlerhood and early childhood.

According to David Caruso, although we can demonstrate that babies remember objects they have seen and sounds they have heard, and that they can become conditioned by both classical and operant forms, at such young ages they cannot be said to have "understood" the features of their environment; by "understand" we mean assimilating these features into the organized mental structures psychologists call schemas. True schema formation implies some more active process of manipulation or intervention.[6] Experiences conducive to meaning assignment, schema formation, and primitive labeling are produced by exploration and play (as we saw with eighteen-month-old Grace). While exploratory behavior was once conceptually separated from play, we now see them both as part of a continuing process. Physical manipulation through sucking, biting, and grasping may reduce some of the extreme novelty of objects (and the fear they arouse). As we discussed in Chapter 2 in connection with cognitive-affective theory, this kind of experience may render an object or situation only *moderately* novel, thus evoking the positive emotion of interest. Further exploration of the object may take the form of play, in which a repetitive shaking, a hide-and-seek movement, or even a crude storylike theme now helps the object become assimilated as a "toy" into the child's limited range of schemas. Pretending not only provides practice in manipulation of objects *and* symbols, it also involves a continuing exploration of the new physical and mental structures created by the game itself.

Research by Jay Belsky and Robert Most involved observing the exploration and play of babies ranging in age from seven-and-a-half to twenty-one months and then scoring the observer's recorded descriptions along various dimensions.[7] Their data indicate a rather consistent, almost orderly, progression across the age span. The earliest form of play is simple handling or tasting and mouthing, followed by what they call *functionally correct play,* such as pushing a toy car or making a small plastic horse gallop along the floor. The naming of objects (*enactive naming*) is a precursor of pretend play, which is followed by *pretending with self* (as when Grace produced sound effects and moved a toy airplane or pretended to read) and *pretending with others,* the kind of make-believe that eventually flourishes between ages three and five. These later stages include *substitution pretend* (a block becomes a car), *sequence pretend* ("I'm going to work now. Now I'm home!"), combinations of these, and, finally, *double substitutions* (pretending a plastic horse is a child and then pretending to bottle-feed it with an elongated block). The data from this and other similar studies suggest that each new phase builds on the prior one and that the sequence is relatively orderly through each successive stage. As Caruso points out, "At each level of play in the sequence infants are able to build a more sophisticated understanding of their world based on the new skills available in play. For example, children using functional or relational play are able to use information about the specific properties of objects that was not available to them when they used only mouthing or simple manipulation."[8]

In the past decade investigators have looked much more closely at infant, baby, and toddler behavior during the first two years of life. It has become clear that play and exploration are indeed closely linked and that in combination they generate cognitive growth from simpler to more complex structures. It also seems that the variety of play behaviors or appropriate uses of toys may be more predictive of later intellectual competence than the sheer amount of time spent at one form of play. The level of spontaneous rather than experimenter-elicited play predicts later intelligence test scores. The work of investigators like Jay Belsky, David Caruso, and their collaborators also points to the role of environmental resources and parental interactions with children as stimulators of exploratory competence and more advanced spontaneous play. More and more children are being raised from their earliest years in settings outside their own homes (in family daycare homes, nursery schools, or daycare programs in church basements or storefronts, and perhaps some day soon, in public elementary school annexes) and by professional caregivers outside the nuclear family. Establishing the particular environmental resources and parental or other caregiver skills that encourage cognitive-growth-enhancing play becomes increasingly important. In this chapter we will consider what specific benefits for the children's cognitive and emotional growth may accrue from the special features of make-believe and pretend play and what particular settings or adult activities can promote such play.

What a Child Must Learn and What Pretending Play Can Teach

In a remarkable work of imagination, scholarship, and poetic writing, *The Origins of Consciousness in the Breakdown of the Bicameral Mind,* the psychologist Julian Jaynes develops a far-reaching hypothesis about human consciousness.[9] He proposes that consciousness is reflected in our ability to recognize our thoughts as thoughts and not sense data, or percepts, to create narratives from perceived events or memories, to think of "I" or "me," and to lie and deceive or to guess at the thoughts of others. Consciousness emerges as a consequence of the evolution of separate functions for the two hemispheres of the brain. Drawing on some remarkable analyses of excerpts from ancient texts—Egyptian and Sumerian writings, the Homeric Greek *Iliad,* and the Hebrew Old Testament—he proposes that almost no evidence of consciousness is apparent in human communication until after the period between 1500 to 1000 B.C. He hypothesizes that during that time a series of natural disasters disrupted organized traditional societies. Only those whose brains had evolved to the point that differential functions of the hemispheres were operative and who could separate private thought from public utterance or pretend and deceive were able to survive when thrust among strangers. (We need not go into great detail here about the theory he proposes or the evidence he offers, although we do not believe his thesis should be ignored or dismissed out of hand. We once invited Jaynes to a dinner party along with Yale scholars of ancient Sumerian, Hebrew, Egyptian, and Greek, and they were quite impressed with his technical knowledge of the texts they study.)

What is especially important for our purposes is the conception of consciousness that emerges from Jaynes's analysis of metaphors and analogies, and his idea that effective human thought requires a model of one's own mind and those of others as well as theories that relate such models to how people behave or how causality operates. If we fail to develop a system for representing mental processes, Jaynes implies, we are doomed to believe that our thoughts and memories are the voices of our gods, our parents, or tribal authorities. We then lack a basis for discovering whether others are thinking what we think or whether we (or they) are capable of error or deception.

Quite recently the British psychologist Alan Leslie has proposed a very detailed and analytic theory of the special role of pretend play in developing in the child a model of mind and of mental states, which seems to us to be very similar in conception to that of Jaynes.[10] Leslie considers what for him is one of the major puzzles of development: "If a representational system is developing, how can its semantic relations tolerate distortion in these more or less arbitrary ways? . . . [How] is it possible that young children can disregard or distort reality (as in using a banana as a telephone) . . . Why does pretending not undermine their representational system and bring it crashing down?"

His argument contends that a major step in development involves the "decoupling" of direct representations of objects, persons, or situations from a new set of metarepresentations, that is, symbolic or mental representations of the same original set of objects but now treated as part of a system that one can manipulate, modify, analogize, transform to metaphor, and so on. If we walk into a room and unexpectedly see a long, thin object on the floor, we may jump because we think it is a snake unless we recognize it with relief as a telephone extension cord. This is "error" because we had no reason initially to treat the objects in the room as other than percepts. If on another occasion we say to a child playing "explorer" with us in the same room, "Look! There's a dangerous snake!," we are treating the telephone cord in its metarepresentational mode, and its only casual resemblance to a snake suffices to permit a distortion of what would ordinarily be a fixed representational and semantic structure.

Leslie's conception, with our modifications, is presented in Figure 6-1. A theory of mind implies that humans have available a domain of metarepresentations they can manipulate to make inferences about causes and predictions about future events, to recognize the consequences of ignorance, to distinguish reality from fantasy, to acquire a language of words and phrases depicting mental experiences or states, and to infer motivations. Such development begins perhaps in the middle of the second year but doesn't really flourish until the third and fourth years, although some children may use words like *know, remember, pretend,* and *dream* by the end of the second year. As Leslie puts it, "Pretend play is thus one of the earliest manifestations of the ability to characterize and manipulate one's own and others' cognitive relations to information. This ability, which is central to a common sense theory of mind, will eventually include characterizing relations such as believing, expecting and hoping, and manipulating these relations in others, for example, getting someone to expect something will happen by promising."[10]

Although pretend play begins to emerge by the end of the second year, as Greta Fein's work in particular has suggested, when parents interact more with children, it takes two more years before children seem able to move from comprehending the manipulation of object representations (as in using an empty cup to pretend to drink) to being able to understand the possibility that others may have erroneous beliefs. Consider the "false belief" experiment: A child (the target participant in the study) watches as another person hides a piece of candy in a box (A) and then leaves the room. Someone else then moves the candy to another box (B). Asked where the candy is now, the child correctly points to box B. When the person who first hid the candy returns, the child is asked where this person will look for the candy. The evidence indicates that only when they are around four do children regularly predict that the deceived original hider will look in box A rather than in box B.[11] This experiment has been employed by Leslie and other researchers not only to show the egocentricity (in Piaget's sense) of the child, but also to demonstrate that even severely retarded older children can master the "false belief" concept, although autistic children with higher IQs than the retarded children have great difficulty in doing so. Autistic

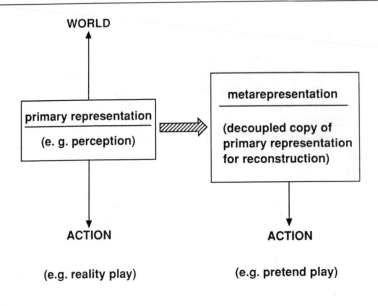

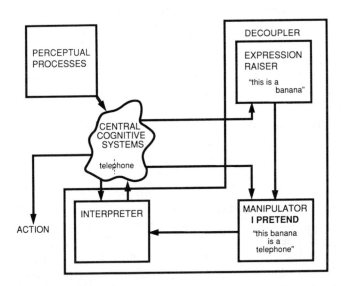

Figure 6–1. Alan Leslie's proposed models for how children develop metarepresentations in which perceived real objects and their mental images are transferred into a system that allows the child to treat them as possibilities. The upper half depicts the general system, the lower half the specific process by which a perceived object (banana) can be transformed by the child (telephone) for play purposes. (Reproduced from Figures 1 and 2 in Leslie's "Pretense and Representation" with permission.)

children seem to have a special deficit in such perspective-taking and perhaps more generally in their ability to develop a metarepresentational world decoupled from primary representations. And we know from our own studies and those of others that they show very little capacity for make-believe play. Recent observations of babies and toddlers born of "crack" cocaine-addicted mothers also seem to indicate findings comparable to those for autistic children. These children, despite apparently average general intelligence, seem deficient in play skills.[12]

If we return to Grace manipulating her cars and planes or "reading," we may well argue that she is probably not yet showing true pretend play, although she may be on the threshold. Her vocabulary is too sparse to include words like *pretend* or *make-believe,* so we cannot know what she thinks. But it seems unlikely that what we see is more than purely functional play, a correct use of objects. Her reading too may be little more than pure imitation but, of course, it may ultimately help her to discriminate pictures from text and learn to turn pages, and in effect, prepare her for being comfortable when her cognitive structures for actual reading are in place some four or five years from now.

Grace is at least on the right track to beginning make-believe play and developing the capacity for an "attitude toward the possible," in Kurt Goldstein's phrase: evolving a consciousness of self and establishing for herself a metarepresentational domain that will make symbolic manipulations and the emergence of a model of mind possible. Such advances will be reflected in her being able to ask her sister Cory to "make-believe you're a doggie" or her parents to "promise" they will take her to a friend's party. Pretend play will also help her confront the human need for narrative, to organize the seemingly random events or social interactions that occur in her milieu or that recur in her memories and dreams into story sequences.

We posed a question at the outset of this section about what a child must learn. What we have suggested in our brief discussion of Jaynes and Leslie is that the major and most complex cognitive demands in the third through fifth years are the development of consciousness and a metarepresentational model of mind, and then the ability to formulate and express narrative. Is imaginative play just a concomitant expression of such development or is it a necessary, or at least a very useful, process for accelerating or deepening the development of mental models? We cannot answer that question definitively, but we can examine some evidence from particular studies that link make-believe play to cognitive functions.

In formulating the major dimensions of the cognitive capacities needed for the child's development, Piaget did indeed emphasize that symbolic play was a useful way of indicating how much progress a child was making in separating the symbol from what it originally stood for. But, as Inge Bretherton and Brian Sutton-Smith have pointed out, Piaget tended to minimize or simply ignore the inherent cognitive significance for maturity of such symbolic processes because his focus was on logical, sequential, orderly thought.[13] The kinds of tasks and problems he generally employed to estimate what he termed operational thought involved taxonomic structures (what sorts of objects or classes of objects logically belong together) and hierarchic classifications (what classes of objects subsume other classes). Bretherton notes that current analyses derived from studies of consciousness or from attempts to program computers to simulate human thought have led to a recognition that thinking involves not only logical operations but also figurative representations. In such schemas or scripts, events are depicted in the spatial, temporal, and presumed causal linkages between the actors and the objects upon which they act. But schemas do more than reflect events; they also allow us to anticipate and interpret new experiences. Thus, they have an independent mental existence comparable to, or "isomorphic" with, real objects and events, as Leslie also suggests, but perhaps they are even more basic to thought than the groupings and hierarchies that Piaget stressed. Bretherton suggests that the literature on children, as well as schema research more generally, implies that those "taxonomic hierarchies, roles and problem-solving strategies" that Piaget used as his outcome measures to indicate the growth of the mind might in themselves be derived from the organized mental representations we call schemas or scripts.[14] Studies of children's play by Katherine Nelson and by Maria Kreye, using language or conceptual structure as the measures, further suggest that meaning structures like scripts or schemas seem more basic than the logical organization or dictionarylike definitions of terms that so many cognitive studies following Piaget have emphasized.[15]

If we return now to our question—what cognitive skills must a child learn and what can make-believe play contribute?—we would offer the following: First, children must expand their vocabulary and learn not only how to name objects but also how to form sentences or phrases by linking objects with actions and how to use descriptors such as adjectives and adverbs. Children must learn about object constancies and about persistence in dealing with objects. They must form event schemas and scripts about what one does or expects of others in a variety of situations, from eating out in restaurants to attending birthday parties or keeping doctor appointments. Children also need to learn strategies for solving problems, from the simple uses of sticks as levers to problems of orderly sequence, number-object relations, and cause and effect. Generally speaking, psychologists following Piaget have emphasized problems and thought processes that yield only one answer, what we call *convergent* cognition. But as we increasingly realize, effective human thought also requires creative processes, that is, the ability to produce varied and flexible associations, what is called *divergent* cognition.[16] As the recent research and theorizing of both Howard Gardner and Robert Sternberg indicate, effective thought or intelligence calls for abstraction, combinatorial skill, and a rich vocabulary, for fluent and flexible divergence, and for skill in practical "street knowledge."[17] Finally, following on the position of Jerome Bruner we stressed in Chapter 2, the child needs to learn a flexible use of narrative thought, the ability to shift between, on the one hand, the need to remember or anticipate events, and on the other, the need to engage in formal logical thought and clear communication.

The research on make-believe play has only begun to address some of these issues of cognitive growth. Much of the available work has involved specific correlations between imaginative play and various forms of language usage, the ability to solve Piagetian tasks, such as conservation or problem-solving strategies and convergent or divergent task performances. With older children we begin to see some studies linking pretend games to the beginnings of reading, writing, or story comprehension.[18] Such correlational studies are suggestive, but they often cannot resolve the issue of whether, for example, a richer vocabulary enhances imaginative play or whether play serves to provide vocabulary and more general language usage practice. To estimate the possible causal role of imaginative play in improving cognitive skills, investigators have resorted to training procedures designed to determine if children trained in pretend games (as compared with those not trained or subject to other types of adult intervention) show gains in language or other cognitive performances. This formal training approach also has obvious implications beyond theoretical tests: if training in play abets language or comprehension skills it should be of value in early childcare program curricula and may be useful as a guide to effective parenting. While we don't wish to provide a detailed critical review of the literature, we will point out some typical findings and how such research is generally carried out.

Some Approaches to Studying Language and Play

One of the first studies to look systematically at language usage by kindergarten children who differed in their spontaneous use of sociodramatic or fantasy play was reported by P. H. Lewis in her doctoral dissertation at Ohio State University. She showed pictures to a sizable group of children and asked them to interpret what they saw. The comprehensiveness, clarity, and organization of their responses were scored along with the number of kinds of words they used. Those children who had already been identified as playing more imaginatively also excelled in the picture interpretation task and in the extent and use of their vocabulary. When asked to produce "free association" the children who had played more fantasy games also demonstrated more associations and used more words, but they also used more references to objects or events remote from themselves or their home environment. They were also more likely to categorize and link up the words they produced rather than using them in the random associations that were more characteristic of the less fantasy-play-oriented children. To make sure that these results were not simply a function of general intelligence differences, Lewis looked at the results for the high IQ groups in her sample, comparing those who showed a great deal of imaginative play with those who showed relatively little. Her high IQ-high pretend play group yielded very clear advantages in their language organizational ability compared to the high IQ-low pretend play group. While a study of this type cannot clearly distinguish between the possibility that a predisposition to use language well fosters make-believe play and the reverse notion that such play enhances language, it is certainly suggestive of a mutually enhancing interaction between pretend play and language complexity and richness. Such findings have emerged in a number of studies over the past quarter century.[19]

We can gain some insight into how pretend play may contribute to better organized, more extended language usage from several very careful studies carried out by Katherine Nelson and Susan Seidman at the City University of New York and by Lorraine McCune-Nicholich and Carol Bruskin at Rutgers University.[20] The latter team carried out precise monthly home observations of levels of play and language use for five girls aged fourteen to eighteen months. By recording actual word usage they were able to show that the girls produced more combined words either during sessions of play rated as higher in symbolic level or during sessions just following earlier evidence of more pretend play. For such young children language combinations emerge almost necessarily from efforts at make-believe. Thus, Mira's longest utterances are, "It's a mop," "It's two baby," "Mommy where a baby?" and "Mommy where soup?"; and Meri's "I did it all gone'" or "a baby phone." McCune-Nicholich and Bruskin attribute the combined enhancement of early language and of beginning symbolic play to new underlying skills, "(1) the ability to combine symbols in relation to context . . . and (2) deferred imitation."[21]

It is hard to disentangle the mutual influences of language and play, but as these investigators note, even if

> both symbolic play and language are dependent on the development of underlying representational capacities, symbolic play may prove a useful tool for assessment and intervention with language-delayed children. For example, if two children whose language is below age level differ such that one exhibits age appropriate symbolic play and the other does not, this suggests both different etiologies for the language delay, and perhaps different strategies for intervention. In the first case language training can proceed directly based on the assumption that the symbolic system is appropriately developed. For the child exhibiting neither age-appropriate play nor language, perhaps, cognitive intervention should supplement the language program. Training in symbolic play may prove an appropriate intervention vehicle. The strongest evidence for the basis of language and symbolic play on shared underlying structures would be the transfer to language of skills trained through play.[22]

In the studies by Nelson and Seidman we see further indications of how the organized action schemas that are part of pretend play may function to extend language usage. They observed white children from lower socioeconomic backgrounds during their free play in nursery schools. They found that when children were engaged in play organized around some theme ("scripted play") the conversations recorded were longer and more coherent. Simple requests for objects or expressions of emotion ("I'm not your friend then") led to brief bursts of talk, while themes of "baking" or "working in McDonald's" elicited extended sentences and conversations. In effect once the children jointly entered into the framework of a little pretend story, the inherent properties of the script evoked more verbal give and take, longer sentences with more complexity, and, one may surmise, more practice in both make-believe play and in the "art" of conversation.[23]

In our own studies* we obtained data from much larger samples of children. We recorded the language of seventy-nine boys and sixty-two girls, ages three and four, observed in eight separate ten-minute free-play sessions over a year's time. Our observer teams recorded all words used in several basic categories, such as spoken number of utterances, and mean length of utterances; and for various linguistic categories, such as the percentages of verbs (of total words used), descriptive adjectives and future verbs, and so on.

From our extensive tables of the language employed during these eight ten-minute periods, we found, for example, that if we look at the number of words used during ten minutes of spontaneous play, four-year-old boys score significantly higher than three-year-old boys, who use only about 60 words during a ten-minute period compared to the more than 100 used by the four-year-olds. Four-year-old girls are obviously far above the boys, using close to 130 words during the period, whereas three-year-old girls are speaking on the average of approximately 18 more words during a ten-minute period than the boys. What follows during the year is a dramatic acceleration in language for the three-year-olds of both sexes with an even more striking increase for boys than for girls. By the fourth probe, the initially three-year-old boys use actually somewhat more words than the initially three-year-old girls. Indeed, the acceleration is marked, and the contrast between the initially four-year-old boys and four-year-old girls is so great because of the significant drop-off in speech in this fourth probe, so that we see the four-year-old boys speaking approximately 190 words in a ten-minute period while playing, whereas the four-year-old girls are speaking only 112 words.

We can conclude from our data that the actual spontaneous output

---

* These were never cited by researchers on early language development, perhaps because they were reported in a book called *Television, Imagination and Aggression: A Study of Preschoolers* and thus did not get into the "right" abstract compendia.

of words during free play increases as much as 50 percent for our total sample, with boys nearly doubling their verbal output over the year. Were it not for the drop in language for the four-year-old girls shown in our fourth probe, a sizable growth might be in evidence across the sexes. The number of separate utterances shows a 30 percent increase, and the average number of words within an utterance, although remaining close to four words, shows an increase especially for the boys.

A closer examination of the language changes suggests that the major pattern of change is reflected in (1) a decrease in questions; (2) a decrease in personal pronouns or in possessive pronouns (I, my, mine); (3) sizable increases in the usage of descriptive adjectives; (4) increases in past tense verbs along with a decrease in present tense verbs; (5) increases in onomatopoeia (usually sound effects); and (6) some increase in qualification sentences, analogies, and metaphors ("This is like that" or "Pretend this is a train"). Although our analysis of parts of speech is of limited value, it seems likely that we are primarily observing an increase in sheer verbal output and expressiveness. Most language use still involves declarative and imperative sentences or questions, but there is an apparent reduction in the egocentric frame of reference and a broadening of temporal perspective as the past tense becomes somewhat more evident. Although future verbs do not show much growth overall, we did find that an even broader time perspective emerged among those children who were oriented more toward imaginative play. Future verb use is generally one of the only language classes besides output that shows links to behavioral variables.

Another way of looking at the data, following the suggestions of Bruner (see Chapter 2), is to consider the uses of subjunctive, conditional, and past and future verbs. Here, too, the general trend was one of increase across the year's time for three-year-old girls and three-year-old boys and more of a stabilization at the four-year-old level. These changes were also coordinated with ratings of imaginative play for the children during the year.

Language use is also related to the imagination variables, our imagination interview, the Barron Inkblot score for human movement, and whether or not the child has an imaginary companion. Those children who scored high in imagination tended to use more words and a greater number of utterances. Could this result simply reflect the fact that brighter children are more verbal and by saying more increase the chances that they will be scored as more imaginative? It is difficult to separate play from language, but when IQ is taken into account statistically, the relationship between language and imagination persists. When the effect of the number of words is statistically eliminated, correlations between imagination variables and other behavior variables such as persistence or cooperation with peers remain stable. One of our main theoretical problems is to determine whether or not symbolic or imaginative play can indeed be occurring when the child manifests no overt language. It seems that language and play are interacting continuously, and we cannot yet determine which takes precedence.

A substudy carried out on a sample of our language protocols by Shlomo Ariel, a linguistics specialist now at the University of Tel Aviv, indicated that one could identify play patterns suggesting imaginativeness without the use of language. He then examined the frequency of language usage and the utterance lengths of the children's communications when they were not actively involved in make-believe games, asking the teacher for a drink, for example, or drawing, or cutting and pasting. He found that the number of words and the length of utterance during imaginative play were correlated with language in other situations but that nonverbal imaginative play did not correlate with more general language usage.

The number of words, number of utterances, mean length of utterance, and use of declarative sentences seem to reflect mature forms of speech because they correlate positively with age and IQ. Pronouns, verbs, and imperative, interrogative, and exclamatory sentences correlate negatively with IQ and age and seem to be more closely related to the egocentric nature of the younger child, who is clearly seeking help or information or is exclaiming about each event, and is more concrete and action-oriented than the older child.

In general, our language data suggest a much greater spurt for the boys during the year's time. The indication is that girls, who initially started well ahead of the boys in language expressiveness, may be entering into a new phase of socialization by five years of age. Perhaps older girls are now ready for a more organized kind of experience. It may also be that certain socialization pressures on girls are also beginning to emerge. In general, this pattern seems to go along with a change in television-viewing by the older girls.

As we noted in Chapter 5, the boys in our sample who had separately reported that they had one or more imaginary playmates were also more likely to use more words and longer utterances in their spontaneous language usage during free-play periods. We carried out factor analyses averaged across the year's observations to identify the behavioral and language variables that clustered together. We found a "playfulness" factor in which both imaginative play and extended language usage, including the use of future verbs, were heavily involved. When imaginativeness was measured by more "internalized" procedures—questions about private fantasy or inkblot associations rather than by make-believe play scores at school—the "home" imagination of the children was strongly linked to the average size of their spontaneous verbalizations at school (mean length of utterance).

Training in Imaginative Play: Some Influences on Language and Cognitive Performance

One approach increasingly employed in assessing the advantages of imaginative play is that of providing children with structured experiences and adult leadership in pretend and sociodramatic games. Pioneering work in these areas has been carried out by Sara Smilansky and also by Dina Feitelson, who worked in Israel at a time when that nation was seeking to assimilate large numbers of Sephardic Jewish immigrants (chiefly from Arabic countries) into its then predominantly Western Europeanized cultural tradition.[24] The studies indicated that training in various forms of imaginative play not only enhanced the spontaneous tendency to engage in such play but also yielded evidence of better adjustment to school, better reading readiness skills in language usage, and (in the case of the Feitelson group) more signs of divergent or creative thought.

In the United States, Joan T. Freyberg used a similar approach with a group of inner-city educationally disadvantaged kindergarten children. With just a little more than two hours of actual training time (eight twenty-minute sessions of exposure to various play themes, such as "boat and sailors in a storm," "family around the dinner table," and "a magic genie performing tricks"), the scores for spontaneous schoolyard make-believe in the experimental group doubled, while there was almost no change in the untrained control group. Along with these demonstrated increases in imaginative play there was also evidence of greater positive emotionality, and signs of better persistence in play and in more general behavioral sequences. The children exposed to training showed more verbal communication when observed later in the schoolyard, used longer and more complex sentences and more verbal labelling, and were more discriminating in their use of language.

Similar training approaches are now widely found in the literature.[25] Some controversy remains over whether this kind of training has special advantages over other kinds of more direct and focused training in enhancing cognitive skills. While admitting that studies have shown fantasy play training to have resulted in significant improvements in verbal intelligence, mathematical readiness, perspective-taking, concentration, complexity of play, conservation or object-constancy performances on Piagetian tasks, originality, and group problem-solving, Peter Smith raises the issue of whether such play training is better than instruction that focuses only on the specific ability in question. At the same time, he believes that such training is valuable in dealing with emotional problems and in reducing conflicts, and that it may also foster more motivation and peer interaction, a finding we observed in our own studies.[26]

Eli Saltz of Wayne State University in Detroit, who has conducted some of the most extensive studies on thematic play as a stimulant for cognitive and emotional development in poor, inner-city children, has also reexamined various findings, including his own, using play training. With Jane Brodie he has shown that attempts to attribute the positive effects of fantasy play training on verbal skills primarily to better "rapport" or "verbal encouragement" cannot explain the results. His own studies involved four to six months of training with groups ranging from 30 to 150 participants. These represent some of the most extensive and careful training studies thus far available. Saltz's thematic play training yielded evidence comparable to Freyberg's in vocabulary usage. He and Brodie acknowledge that short-term training, which enhances performance on measures of originality, leaves open the question of how extensive such results may be. Will they generalize to creativity in other situations? Our data from specific studies are as yet too sparse to be certain, although we do have evidence that adults who are more creative report (as our biographical accounts in Chapter 1 also suggest) that they were more likely to play imaginatively, daydream, or have imaginary playmates as children.[27]

While some remain skeptical about the advantages of thematic or fantasy play training, especially in relation to specific cognitive objectives, most careful observers of children's play in the past decade have recognized that, as Charles Brainerd expresses it, if "the goal is to promote social competence, emotional development, or the general well-being of the child, other techniques (besides training in conceptual skills) will probably be necessary, and dramatic play may be an appropriate choice."[28] Despite Brainerd's belief that no evidence yet exists to support play training for emotional growth, the findings of Saltz and his group showed that thematic play training led to greater self-control and longer waiting ability in children, and Freyberg found more positive emotions and persistence. Some of our own studies also indicated more evidence of positive emotionality and persistence after just a few weeks of make-believe training.[29] Although we will discuss some of the approaches to play enhancement for daycare programs and parents that have emerged from research and clinical efforts in Chapter 9, we wish here to point out that, despite a very few inconclusive studies and very little "hard" evidence for its long-term advantages, many training studies and concurrent observational studies point to the general value of imaginative play for the naturally developing cognitive skills of the growing child.

The Potential Contributions of Imaginative Play to Imagery and Behavioral Control

Apart from training studies, we must chiefly infer the advantages of imaginative play from other observations, for example, that children who engage in more make-believe play during their toddlerhood and preschool years seem to function more effectively in a variety of situations than children who exhibit less of such behavior. Of course we must be able to eliminate any underlying variables, such as general intelligence or language skill, that may account for this inclination or capacity for pretending and for other behavioral advantages (such as self-control). As we have already seen in the case of language skills, this is a difficult distinction to demonstrate. But an analysis of what a child has to learn in the continuing effort to sustain a pretend game, alone or with other children, suggests that there is much to be gained from further practice of this activity. It is reasonable to believe that the child who engages in extended play in which objects are transformed (a rag doll into a baby, a stick into a rocket ship) is likely to be enhancing skills in the use of imagery, in reshaping mental representations more generally, as Leslie suggests, and in forming more and more coherent scripts. What are the potential advantages that may accrue to those children who, whether because of some underlying cognitive readiness, training, or parental encouragement (see Chapter 7) engage in more frequent imaginative play?

Imagery Enhancement

Imagery is the capacity to reproduce in its absence an object that has been presented to one of the sensory organs. Imaging was extensively studied by psychologists in the nineteenth century, in particular because it seemed to be a uniquely psychological phenomenon. It was at once a form of external stimulation processing and a private response invisible to others, determinable chiefly by verbal report. The importance of imagery in human cognitive functioning was minimized during the behaviorist domination of psychology in the first half of the twentieth century.[30] Although the use of imagery has been viewed as a characteristic of children that gradually fades in later life, there is other evidence to suggest that the elaborative skills needed for effective vocabulary development in childhood hinge considerably on the development of imagery.[31] Complicated transformations seem to some extent to require the child's interpolation of a private visual or auditory image. As we saw in Chapter 4, the indications are that as children get somewhat older and their play becomes a more complex form of make-believe, they prefer less well-defined objects and choose more unstructured playthings because these lend themselves to more varied private transformation and do not conflict with their private images.[32]

Alan Paivio has examined the value of various imagery methods within the context of our overall capacity for storing information and recalling or eventually communicating it effectively, and his work has evoked a host of recent research.[33] What we are proposing is that helping children to develop greater skill in make-believe is likely to lead to a fuller capacity for imagery and, ultimately, a richer life experience. Children who play at make-believe may be attempting to construct sights, sounds, smells, textures, and tastes as part of their games and in this way may actually be practicing and sharpening their capacity for imagery. Much has been written about the fact that, apart from its use in describing events, imagery heightens esthetic experience and human sensitivity.[34] Imagery skills may be an aspect of our capacity to appreciate the beauties of nature and in retrospect to reexperience beautiful music or a lovely sunset. A sensuous approach to a fine painting may help us to appreciate what Bernard Berenson called the tactile values in the best art of the Renaissance masters: the delight we take in first viewing the sunlit hills of Tuscany may actually be enhanced because we see them in memory in the paintings of Pollaiuollo or Verrocchio.

This proposed linkage of fantasy play to imagery remains partly speculative, although the work of Rohwer documents to some extent the importance of imagery elaboration in children's learning during the preschool period and in the development of reading readiness. Rohwer's position suggests the likelihood that imagery skills may develop once some system of language has emerged. In a comparison of lower- and middle-class children, aged five through eight, he found that those of higher socioeconomic status were significantly better at tasks involving learning and imagery methods, except on the task in which pictures and names of objects were presented simultaneously. He proposed that this discrepancy depended on the degree to which the child requires individually elaborated conceptual activity. Thus, when children only hear the name of an object, they must supply a verbal label. In the case of a sentence, an action image coincides with the verbal label. If children are shown a picture, they must also apply a verbal label. If the children are given a picture and the name of the object illustrated together, however, they need not supply anything on their own. Rohwer suggests that middle-class children have learned to elaborate on what they have been shown and have thus developed a readiness for private elaboration. He stresses the importance of aiding vocabulary learning by setting it within the context of a meaningful procedure that asks the child to provide some form of spatial relationship or anticipated action along with the single word.

Although Bruner proposed that iconic or pictorial imagery probably takes precedence over verbal skills, Rohwer's data suggest the likelihood that imagery skills, even if manifested early, require additional support from verbalization and training in contextual settings for full development.[35] Piaget and Inhelder reported that anticipatory imagery can be contrasted with simple reproductive imagery and that the former emerges only during the sixth to eighth year.[36] The data do not indicate, however, whether the children's ability to experience anticipatory imagery was influenced by earlier practice in engaging in imaginative play. It is intriguing to speculate on the possibility that some of the changes in the direction of anticipatory or "fantasy" types of imagery may also be occurring as children begin to limit overt verbal expression of their make-believe games in favor of an apparent internalization of speech and overt play behavior.[37] This is also a time when there is more motor inhibition and increasing evidence of imaginative responsiveness as measured by the Rorschach test.

Some additional small bits of evidence tie imaginative play to specific imagery behaviors. Litt compared the self-reports of imaginative play by ten-year-olds, which were based on our interview techniques.[38] He found some indication that children who still showed evidence of make-believe play and imaginary companions at this age (which included perhaps 40 percent of his sample) were also likely to score higher on measures of imagery, particularly in its vividness. Litt also found support for the association between an involvement in imaginative play and the divergent production or creative fluency measures derived from the work of Guilford.[39]

Earlier we mentioned research using the Rorschach inkblot test. Children's movement responses to the inkblots, particularly the percentages of humans in action, may be seen as a reflection of private imagery. Even in children under six (who exhibit only a small tendency to report such movement responses) the relation between Rorschach movement and spontaneous imaginative play does emerge, albeit modestly. Studies indicate such findings for children as young as three or four and as old as the early high school years.[40] In a study by Diane Franklin, a significant correlation emerged between evidence of fantasy play in children and the production of a greater number of movement responses to the Barron Movement Threshold Inkblots, a variant of the Rorschach inkblots.[41]

Much research still remains to be done into the relationship between imaginative play and the development of imagery skills. Clearly, this is an area that demands more careful analysis, particularly in view of our increasing awareness of the importance of imagery in normal day-to-day thinking. There has been an unfortunate tendency to view imaginal process thinking largely as a form of regression or primitive thought. Systematic study of imaginative play should help us to understand the miniaturization of memories and the transformation of the make-believe games of childhood into the sophisticated ability to plan ahead and symbolic thought of the adult.

Verbal Fluency or Divergent Thinking

We have already indicated the extent to which imagery and verbal skills may interact in children's early make-believe activities. An obvious feature of pretend games is that children in their uninhibited way think out loud in what Piaget has called "egocentric" speech.

⌐One of the characteristics of this talking out loud is that children, to some extent, hear their own vocalization. In other words, in the absence of adults who talk directly to the child, the child's own words during make-believe play provide an ongoing source of verbal stimulation. The sound effects or scraps of dialogue the child emits in a pretend game create a stimulus field to which she may make further response, or from which she may acquire further information, in the same way our ongoing thoughts provide an alternative stimulus field. Garvey and Berndt have carried out a fairly molecular analysis of pretend play. They point out the extent to which, once initiated, a format or plot line brings together a host of object and identity transformations to which the child can then make further response. As they also point out, the actual social pattern of pretending depends heavily on varied and extended efforts to communicate. There is considerable redundancy in vocalization, motor gestures, and verbalization in the elaboration of a pretend situation. The authors put it well when they state that "the communication of pretend provides a rich source of information for students of play as well as for the pretenders themselves."[42]

The various outlandish possibilities provided by children's attempts at accommodation and assimilation in a still-limited differentiated schema system probably provoke from them in the controlled atmosphere of a play situation the positive affects of surprise and interest. These positive emotions may explain why make-believe play in general includes longer sequences and complex combinations. The child seeks out situations at moderate levels of increasing novel stimulation and when reducing that novelty by matching them with already familiar memories (schemas) also experiences joy, in accordance with Tomkins's theoretical propositions. We would thus expect that the child would not only make progress in the convergent processes of actually refining word definitions through the feedback from ongoing make-believe play, he would also become aware of the odd and divergent possibilities in vocabulary usage from his initial makeshift efforts at including adult gestures or snatches of conversation. Longitudinal data, so vital in the study of imaginative play and its relation to cognitive and socialization functions, are still lacking in the areas of verbal skill development and divergent verbal processes.

Two studies directed by Dina Feitelson examine the effect of training on the level of complexity of play and of children's creativity as measured, for example, by instruments developed by Torrance.[43] The overall findings of these studies suggest that both novel ways of looking at material and more sophisticated combinatorial behaviors result from increased opportunities to model or otherwise observe make-believe play.

Research assessing the effects of play on fluency, designed specifically for use with minimal intervention but with careful controls for the type of interaction, was carried out by J. L. Dansky and I. W. Silverman.[44] Preschoolers from middle-class socioeconomic backgrounds were instructed to play with a set of unstructured playthings. They were presented with the opportunity to play, to imitate adult behavior, or to learn coding systems. Other controls were involved. The children were then tested on their ability to identify sets of objects similar to and different from those presented in the exercises and on their ability to produce new associations and identifications. Whether play was social or solitary, interaction with the objects promoted a greater number of associations and also generalized more readily to situations quite different from the play situation. Play increased the children's ability to demonstrate associative fluency, even when they were asked to respond to stimuli that were rather different from those to which they had been exposed. Dansky and Silverman concluded that the ability of the children to produce both common and unusual associations after playing with objects is not attributable simply to the fact that they manipulated more of them in their play; rather, their play behavior seems to establish an attitude that prompts them to produce novel sets of responses, even to unrelated materials. The researchers go on to describe the advantages of a playful attitude and propose that playful behavior may be even more useful than formal instruction in the cognitive development of children.

The work of Eli Saltz and James Johnson has shown that the systematic make-believe play training of children in an urban ghetto area was effective in enhancing their ability to produce more thoroughly rounded thematic stories and, in general, in stimulating their story-telling capacities.[45] Litt's study, cited earlier, shows that children who report more imaginative play in their day-to-day activities at ten years and older are also more likely to score higher on the measures of divergent thinking derived from Guilford's work. These measures, of course, depend heavily on effective vocabulary expression.

Pulaski found that five- and six-year-olds who were predisposed to make-believe play (an evaluation based on Rorschach scores and interviews about their own home play activities) were much more inclined to play imaginatively with unstructured blocks. In addition, they could shift their point of view when asked to play with an object in a different way than they had before; that is, if they had played with a figure as a cowboy, they were asked to play with it as a flyer or a pilot. The more imaginative children (based on other measures) responded easily to this transformation.[46]

The studies cited thus far have been carried out independently and without systematic overlapping of some of their procedures, but they seem to suggest that opportunities for make-believe play, whether spontaneous or fostered by more formal modeling or training procedures, seem to lead to an effective use of more complicated narrative lines during the play itself or to thematic responses to material presented by adults. It would certainly appear that we are on the threshold of some rather important discoveries with implications for educational policies and methods. Teaching children readiness for school or even the use of language and arithmetic may be more effective when cast in the form of playing and story-telling that evokes their active participation.

Fantasy and Reality

Earlier, on the basis of clinical observation and theoretical speculation we proposed that the experience of engaging in make-believe play might actually help children discriminate between fantasy and reality. Our reasoning was based in part on the notion that children's ability to produce transformations helps them to recognize not only the sequences they produce by themselves but also those that are demanded by others or are characteristic of the physical environment. Another consequence of the active repetition of make-believe sequences may be an increase in differentiated memory schemas.[47]

Using reasoning of this kind, Jane Tucker carried out a rather broad investigation of the role of fantasy in cognitive-affective functioning. On the basis of the notion that differentiated schemas are associated with playing out fantasy sequences over a period of time, she hypothesized that children possibly recall an adventure story presented as fictional more completely and accurately, and with more embellishments, than a story presented as true. In addition, she proposed that subjects who showed a high fantasy predisposition (as measured by their human movement responses on the Rorschach inkblots) would recall an adventure story more completely and accurately and with more embellishments than subjects who showed little predisposition to fantasy, whether or not the material was presented as fictional or true. She further proposed that a high fantasy predisposition would lead to more effective recall of fictional stories than stories described as true and suggested some hypotheses about the differential functional set and the duration of time after full recall.

Her subjects (134 children between the ages of nine and twelve) were asked to listen carefully to a story and to be prepared to write down its details from memory as accurately and completely as possible. In the first test situation they were told to write immediately after the conclusion of the story, which was repeated twice; in the second, they were tested for recall three hours later. The story, an adventure involving children the same ages as the subjects, was identified as fictional or true, and the meaning of these words was appropriately defined. Pilot work attested to the story's believability.

The results indicated that there was little support for Tucker's first hypothesis. The differences in recall for the groups did not vary significantly whether the story was identified as fictional or true. Her second hypothesis, however, was consistently supported. The high-fantasy group yielded superior performances on completeness of story response, accuracy of story response, and story embellishments. There was no interaction between a fantasy predisposition and the fantasy or remoteness recall situation or presumed truth or falsity. A more detailed analysis of the specific kinds of errors made by subjects in their recall indicated that the high-fantasy subjects showed significantly fewer disruptive errors, that is, breaks in continuity, serious distortions, or the introduction of new information. This contrasted with the relatively small differences between the groups in the number of simple mistakes, such as the total number of people engaging in the "search for the lost children" and other details of story content.

The children's fantasy predisposition was also measured at the end of the experiment in a questionnaire, which inquired about spontaneous imaginative play characteristics. The correlations between fantasy play behavior based on self-reports and performance on the recall test indicated that the children who were prone to engage in make-believe games or to report an imaginary companion were also more likely to show a higher level of accuracy of recall of story units and to have made fewer mistakes, particularly fewer disruptive errors. It should be noted, incidentally, that neither of the measures of fantasy—the inkblot measure or the interview on spontaneous play behavior—correlated significantly with intelligence. In general, then, this study remains perhaps the first that approaches the question so often raised about the possible risks of imaginative play. A group of eleven-year-olds who are predisposed to make-believe turns out to be more accurate in recalling story material and less prone to introduce gross distortion than one that lacks a comparable imaginative predisposition. This approach, which examines recall in the context of emotionally laden material, would appear to open a new avenue of exploration and seems to come closer to addressing clinical questions about the value or danger of fantasy behavior in childhood. We cannot, of course, be sure that the make-believe play of the preschoolers or kindergarten children we have been emphasizing is continuous with the imagination measures in middle childhood.

Waiting Behavior or Self-Control

A significant advantage of children's capacity to engage in imaginative games or that of adults to engage in waking fantasy is the likelihood that such behavior creates a novel stimulus field. In some circumstances this might be viewed as an escape from an unpleasant environment, but it might also be considered more broadly as a characteristic response to an environment in which there is considerable redundancy—a routine bus trip or, for a child, the endless wait in the doctor's office before a medical examination. In such waiting situations, without some form of self-entertainment the time seems to drag endlessly. Extensive research indicates that "filled time" appears to pass much more rapidly than unfilled time. The adult riding a bus can read a magazine or a newspaper, or contemplate the advertisements above the windows. But if the individual can generate an elaborate fantasy (about the occupations or lives of some of the other passengers, for example) or anticipate a forthcoming vacation, the bus ride will seem to end very quickly indeed.

For the young child in a waiting-room, the situation is more difficult: reading is less likely and appropriate reading materials may not be available. The child becomes restless, and even if wandering around the room is a manifestation of constructive activity, it may quickly evoke the displeasure of a parent or other adults if the child knocks into furniture or bumps against a plant. For children with few private resources who cannot occupy the time with a game of make-believe, even with relatively unstructured playthings, the likelihood of coming into conflict with adults in the many kinds of waiting situations they will inevitably encounter is great. Indeed, clinical indications are that active children who have difficulty concentrating in this area are often subject to a negative reaction from adults and after a while are labeled "bad," "wild," or "pesty." Under such circumstances waiting can degenerate into a display of screaming and whining and may even lead to blows. There is evidence that those individuals who, based on Rorschach scores of human movement, have already shown indications of imaginativeness are likely to be able to tolerate waiting-room situations with a minimum of restlessness and in the case of mental patients are less likely to be impulsive or aggressive in their ward routines.

Evidence on children is also available, but it is not so extensive. Anneliese Riess found that children of kindergarten age who had numerous human movement responses to the Barron inkblots were more likely to remain quietly occupied during an extended waiting period. In their study of adolescents, George Spivack and Murray Levine reported that those subjects who showed more evidence of imaginative behavior, as measured by inkblots and other indices, were more likely to avoid serious disciplinary problems, while children low in imaginative tendencies exhibited difficulty in self-regulation and were more often involved in acts of delinquency and other antisocial behaviors.[48]

An early study specifically addressing the question of children's waiting behavior and its association with ongoing play behavior involved children between the ages of six and nine who were given the opportunity to simulate spacemen by sitting quietly in an imaginary capsule for as long as they possibly could. The results showed that those children who reported more make-believe play as part of their ongoing activities and more imaginary companions were more likely to tolerate the long wait and to hold out during the simulated capsule situation. Observations of the children's pattern of dealing with the enforced delay indicated that those who had reported more make-believe play to start with sustained themselves during the waiting period by introducing play elements into the situation, mouthing sound effects, and occasionally gesturing as if they were actually participating in a space flight.

Again, results from this study and another subsequently carried out with three- and four-year-olds have generally supported the notion that imaginative play behavior may be associated with a somewhat greater ability to concentrate and with a friendly and emotionally positive demeanor. In a study we will describe further shortly, Diana Franklin found that preschoolers' expectations of positive reinforcement were correlated with their predisposition for imaginative play (as measured by interview and inkblot scores) and with the duration of their spontaneous imaginative play.[49]

The work of Walter Mischel and his collaborators has indicated that when children engage in some form of consistent self-communication or in producing playful imagery, they are able to maintain a longer period of gratification delay or to defer overt responsiveness more effectively.[50] Research by Donald Meichenbaum has also pointed out the possibility that children who engage in self-communication and practice a variety of imagery-related cognitive procedures can learn to control impulsivity.[51] Although these students do not deal specifically with imaginative play, the continuity between the extensive self-communication that is a part of make-believe play and these more focused approaches seems apparent.

Working closely with us, Diana Franklin carried out an intriguing study of block play in four-year-olds, whom she observed in a daycare center.[52] This was an elaborate experiment comparing "objective" block play modeling and "fantasy" block play modeling by adults to determine what each approach yielded in terms of subsequent imitation and spontaneous use of blocks by the children. In general, the study anticipated by about a dozen years the distinction, which we have pointed to in Alan Leslie's work, between objects as concrete givens and objects as manipulable mental representations. Of particular relevance here is the finding that in later sessions children were more likely to show traces of the fantasy use of blocks in spontaneous play than concrete demonstrations of their properties. The fantasy play exposure led to longer play periods and more persistence and positive affect in the daycare observation periods. Children who had been identified from interview and Rorschach inkblot scores as imaginative did indeed show more fantasy play during both the initial modeling and later spontaneous floor play sessions. The more imaginative players also showed a greater tendency to be reflective and to attribute positive events to their own actions while assuming that negative events were externally caused, a result generally found for normal rather than depressed persons in studies of attribution.[53] This "illusion of control" of happy events may well emerge from the way in which fantasy play provides the child with opportunities to practice manipulation and power over a miniaturized world.

We have already mentioned the extensive studies carried out by Eli Saltz and his group in Detroit. These investigators used some of the same "waiting" or simulated astronaut situations we have described. They found that children trained in thematic fantasy play were far more able to sustain impulse control and "think of something pleasant" during waiting situations than children who received other kinds of training not involving pretend play.[54]

Although it cannot be argued that all the links in the chain have been forged, imaginative play as an ongoing procedure, or the predisposition for imaginative play as a personality trait, may play an important part in children's capacity to tolerate delay or wait quietly in situations in which external stimulation is minimal. As Freud surmised long ago, "waiting one's turn" is one of the distinguishing features of civilizations.[55] Imaginative play may be an important asset in the socilization process, which eventually helps children to develop the capacity for deferring immediate satisfaction that is part of growing up.

Emotional Differentiation and Self-Awareness

We next ask whether imaginative play can contribute to a child's ability to recognize, express, or control emotions or whether such play is implicated in the emergence of a differentiated sense of self. Here, alas, we must rely less on reasonably controlled, systematic research and more on the anecdotal reports of child observers and clinicians. We will consider clinical accounts of play in Chapters 9 and 10, when we refer to the mental health implications of imagination. Here we will point to some of the ways in which, at least in theory, children's pretend play may assist them in differentiating their own sense of self from that of others and in forming schemas and scripts about how emotions are expressed. That fantasy play is intrinsically enjoyable and associated with positive affect we have already stressed in previous chapters. Let us now consider some ways in which make-believe games function to evoke the discovery and schematization of the emotions of others and to create a greater sensitivity to self-other relationships. The following examples will also call attention to some of the psychodynamic or conflictual areas of personality, as well as the beginnings of romance and the "war between the sexes" as they emerge in interactive fantasy play.

We have drawn some examples from the late Rosalind Gould's fine collection of transcriptions of spontaneous nursery school play.[56] First we present Mike, a three-year-old boy who seems to be struggling to find a sense of uniqueness, which emerges only after a mildly traumatic, self-inflicted injury:

> Mike is playing with Stuart in the indoor gym. He cries, "I'm ready for another trick," barely able to wait his turn. Stuart says, "Go ahead. I'm an acrobat." Mike: "I can throw myself like a ball. I'm a basketball." (To another child who has jumped.) "How about to swim, stupid!" (He dives and rolls about freely.) "Watch a big one!" (Jumps vigorously onto the mat and performs a somersault.) The teacher asks, "Are you a circus clown?" and Mike replies "No, I can jump." (He jumps and dives.) "I slipped like a knife. Now I will be a jet plane." But, alas, this time he has bumped his head, has risen quickly without crying and headed for another room saying, "I better go in the room. I have a headache." There he takes out his favorite toy, a mailbox, and puts cards into it. "I have a headache" he says to the teacher who then asks him why his head hurts. Mike: "Mommy hit me this morning" ("Why") "Because I hit Markie" (his younger brother). "Mommy hit me because I hit Markie . . . he was fighting with me. I don't like him. He took things away from me." Mike's play with his letter box has gone on and he then says, "I will give you a letter. I will give Mrs. Crowe a letter, a star. I will hold it for her" (his favorite teacher). "Markie, 'may not take things away from me' " (as if quoting the teacher).[57]

In this example, Mike's effort at make-believe also seems tied to physical prowess, to attempts to establish a sense of a more powerful identity, and, later, in playing with the mailbox, to an effort to find a "better" mother in his teacher and to internalize her admonitions. Apart from the psychodynamic significance of this episode (emphasized by Gould in relation to aggression and sibling rivalry), one also discerns a series of "trying on for size" a variety of selves and relationships, the beginnings of differentiated self-schemas.

"Digging for a Princess," an especially charming instance from Gould's protocols, highlights how ongoing make-believe play can also provide a theater in which four-year-olds can rehearse what they have picked up about the sexes from adult talk, stories read to them, and television and how by reshaping these themes they begin to clarify further their experience of self. We note that the boys, caught up in their manipulation of pretend symbols—Alan Leslie's metarepresentations—are relatively impervious to the efforts of the "real" girl, Olivia, to insinuate herself into their game.

Yard time, May 1964

Chris: I hate women!

Teacher: Why do you say that, Chris?

Chris: Because when ya' marry them ya' hafta get your blood tested.

Teacher: What else do you think about women, Chris?

Chris: I think they're kookie! I think I'm gonna marry a princess . . . because they're better—they're prettier.

Jim: Yeah, because they have jewels and gold—and they have crowns.

Olivia (comes over to the boys): What are you doing?

Jim and Chris: We're digging and looking for princesses.

Olivia: Well, I have a bride dress at home.

Chris: Aw, who cares about that.

Jim: Yeah. Ya' need a princess suit. (To teacher): Don't tell her we're gonna marry a princess.

Chris: Princesses have to wear their princess suits all the time or else they'll be stripped of their beauty.

Olivia (to teacher): What means "stripped of their beauty?"

Chris: Aw, go away! We hafta keep diggin'.

Teacher: Digging for what?

Chris: Digging for a princess, of course.

Jim: Yeah, ya' don't find them in New York. We're digging our way to find one.

Chris: Well, ya' just don't marry one like the regular way. Ya' hafta save one first. Princesses fall in love with princes. Did ya' ever eat a princess?

Jim: NO! (They dig for awhile silently.) I dream about army things.

Chris: Well, I dream about that I'm a lieutenant with a lovely princess.

Olivia: Boys! Boys! I just found a real live earring from a princess. (She hands them a piece of crumpled paper.)

Jim and Chris: Get out of here! (They chase her away.)

Chris (running around the hole he has dug): Romance! (Running full circle again.) Princesses! (Running full circle a third time.) Jewels! Let's get digging for those princesses!

Jim: No, we don't really want them. We hafta wait till we're grown up for that.

Chris: Yeah, till we're twenty-one!

Jim: Yeah.

Chris: And then we can buy a real drill and shovel and a pick.

Jim: And a whole car and one of those things that go rrr-rrr-rrr.

Teacher: You mean a pneumatic drill?

Jim: Yeah.
Chris: But I wanna dig for princesses.
Jim: No!
Chris: Oh shucks. Josh, do you wanna marry a princess?
Josh: Sure I do.
Olivia: Do you know where you could get a real princess?
Josh: Sure I do.
Olivia: Do you know where you could get a real princess? In Ireland or England or something.
Chris: Yeah, then we could find one and . . . we could see the Beatles while we're there!
Jim: I love the Beatles. Yeah! Yeah! Yeah!
Chris (running back from the group of girls in another part of the yard): I just went up to the princess' house and guess what—they scared me away.

This vignette of "digging for a princess" speaks for itself as a vivid example of how imaginative play permits the integration of scripts, the identification of possible selves, the formulation of gender identity, and even a self-as-child versus self-as-grown-up identity. What we cannot be certain about is whether children who do not regularly engage in make-believe play are significantly disadvantaged by the lack of opportunities to try out different roles, possible selves, and scripts about real or potential human experiences as Chris and Jim do. We believe that those children who have less opportunity, encouragement, and (possibly in the case of autistic children) less constitutional predisposition toward regular make-believe play miss an important phase of becoming fully human, developing complex self-schemas and learning how to express and to experience emotions. More generally, they miss the chance to incorporate into their repertory of skills the capacity to miniaturize the complex world into a format they can control.

We have traversed a long path from the fantasy play of Grace at the beginning of this chapter. Whatever the limits of the research literature and the clear need for much more investigation, we cannot avoid the belief that imaginative play serves important purposes in the emergence of the psychologically complex and adaptable person. Individual differences in the frequency and variety of such play seem to be associated not only with richer and more complex language but also with a greater potential for cognitive differentiation, divergent thought, impulse control, self-entertainment, emotional expressiveness, and, perhaps, self-awareness. The training studies on the whole suggest that there are wonderful opportunities for child caregivers in nursery schools, daycare centers, and private home daycare settings to foster thematic play and thus to assist children in fuller cognitive growth and emotional adaptability. Imaginative play is fun, but in the midst of the joys of making believe, children may also be preparing for the reality of more effective lives.

7

Creating an Environment for Imaginative Play

The room has been transformed: a large old blanket is draped over the card table, cushions cover the floor, blocks are scattered about, and a cardboard box sits near the couch. We grown-ups are drinking coffee while two four-year-olds play "camping." The covered table is the "tent," cushions are "row boats," blocks are "fish," and the box is a "monster's den." We have been in the dining room for about an hour, and only occasionally has one of us found it necessary to settle a squabble, to help with a suggestion (providing clothespins and string for a fishing pole), or to offer a new word when asked to name a specific "fish." The children periodically come to us to tell us what they have caught and eagerly await our approval and our signs of wonder and surprise as they describe "sea-monsters" or "sharks." They tell us about strange noises they hear when they sleep in their "tent," and feign fright with much giggling and scrambling for cover behind the couch, which becomes an "enormous mountain," or run to one of us who now must play the "sheriff" and come to the rescue.

These friends are happily engaged in the kind of dramatic, social pretend play we have described in Chapter 4, and we, the parents, are there to provide what Carl Rogers called the external conditions of psychological safety and psychological freedom.[1]

Rogers believed that a creative environment for child-rearing also included three internal psychological conditions on the part of the parent: an openness to experience, an internal locus of evaluation, and the ability to toy with elements and concepts. Children experience psychological safety when they are accepted unconditionally and treated with empathy. They experience psychological freedom when caregivers allow them to express themselves symbolically and with few constraints. Children must not be teased or laughed at if their play appears silly or unrealistic. Dina Feitelson, for example, reported that in her work with Kurdish mothers in Israel, many of the mothers could not accept the Play-doh figures the children were taught to make. To these mothers, clay was clay—not "oranges" as the teacher had suggested to the children.[2] In her study the attitudes of the mothers hindered the playfulness of the youngsters and squelched their creativity, at least insofar as such an orientation was important in helping the children adapt to a more westernized culture.

In Chapter 1 we stressed the importance of the play environment by looking at the childhood experiences of creative people who remembered with affection their toys, their secret places, and their daily periods allotted to play. In practically every instance, they also mentioned the support and encouragement of some adult who fostered their play by providing the internal and external conditions delineated by Rogers.

Where Children Play: The Social Context

It is difficult for an unprepared observer to identify when a child has shifted from simply exploring a room into what Leslie has called the metarepresentational mode of pretend play. If, for example, a stranger entered the room where the four-year-olds had set up "camp," a rather different interpretation of the situation might suggest itself. Is the card table a tent, cave, or house, or merely a table covered with an unusual tablecloth (the old blanket) awaiting the dishes? Are the blocks the scattered results of a collapsed "building"? Are the cushions on the floor just more comfortable for sitting on there than on the couch? Are the clothespins and string part of a clothesline? And what is that box? Did someone forget to take out the garbage?

Nancy King suggests that "children are experts on the meaning of their play—the researchers are the novices."[3] In order to truly understand what the game is about, we need to observe children at play and then listen to them as they interpret their actions. We also need to study children's play where it *naturally* occurs and be aware of its particular physical and social setting. In addition, we must understand the history of children's relationships with each other and how these relationships change as settings change. Reviewing the many studies of children's play in the laboratory—singly or in dyads or triads (even if the children seem comfortable with each other)—seems an artificial way to study play, unless as Helen Schwartzman says, "we wish only to generalize on how children play in unfamiliar places."[4]

Lev Vygotsky emphasized the importance of the social context of play.[5] Children play differently in different places. They may play more imaginatively in their own home if a parent is open and accepting, or in a friend's home if the friend's parent also encourages symbolic play. Children also play differently in open and in closed spaces. There is more running, climbing, and jumping in large, uncluttered rooms or outdoors than in smaller confined spaces. The high-spirited, boisterous play of the playground may become more subdued when the same children move inside. Play differs too according to the personalities of the children and their playmates. Leaders and followers complement each other, and as long as their styles match, they can sustain many pretend games. Bossy, aggressive children are rarely missed when they are absent, and the tone and climate of play in their playgroups change radically on those days.

Modeling and Its Effects on Make-Believe

The majority of the studies we have reviewed in preparing this book used laboratory settings to investigate both the purposes and the effects of play on a child's emotional, social, or cognitive development. Very few researchers actually observed children in their natural settings, either at home or on the playground. But whether the setting was a laboratory or at home, nearly all the studies concerned with intervention effects stressed the importance of the caregivers' guidance as well as the need to be sensitive to children's own cognitive level as they play. Barbara O'Connell and Inge Bretherton express this succinctly:

> Mothers are active and willing teachers of their children but their strategy appears to be the provision of wide-ranging guidance rather than tuning in to the level of their child's ability. Children in the course of mastering any of a variety of activities rely simultaneously on their own cognitive skills and constructive processes as well as on any assistance that may come their way from the architects in the social world.[6]

A study carried out by these researchers found that a greater diversity of play occurred when twenty- or twenty-eight-month-old children played in collaboration with their mothers than when they played alone. Older toddlers were also more likely to follow the mother's suggestions for symbolic play than younger ones. The mothers in this particular study, however, did not seem to be as sensitive to their children's needs and did not adjust their behaviors to the children's ages or cognitive capacities as much as mothers in other studies did. Younger children did not appear to understand fully many of the mothers' suggestions. One example given by the authors related to putting "peg people" into a car. Although the twenty-month-olds inserted the figures, they did not always place them facing in the correct direction nor did they then "drive" the car. The twenty-eight-month-olds were more careful in placing the people in the holes facing in the appropriate direction and then were able to drive the car along the floor with appropriate accompanying noises. The older children were cognitively better equipped to follow the mothers' modeling of the activity; the younger children accepted only those directions that were compatible with their levels of functioning and did not heed other suggestions.

In brief, O'Connell and Bretherton believe that children "tend to take advantage of mothers' suggestions more frequently when the content of these suggestions coincides with tasks the child is currently trying to master than when these suggestions represent domains that the child has already mastered or those beyond the child's capabilities."[7]

As Vygotsky has written, "in play a child always behaves beyond his average age, above his daily behavior; in play it is as though he were a head taller than himself. As in the focus of a magnifying glass, play contains all developmental tendencies in a condensed form and is itself a major source of development."[8] He believed that instruction was important for the development of the child, but like O'Connell and Bretherton, he argued that a child must achieve some specified level of functioning before he can incorporate or integrate any aspects from his environment. Vygotsky also described what he called a "zone of proximal development," the distance between what a child can do by himself and what a child can do with assistance. Instruction is useful and important, but it is contingent on the development of a child's skills in the zone of proximal development.

Robert Hodapp and colleagues attempted to demonstrate that the zone of proximal development is present in infancy.[9] These researchers were interested in Bruner's notion that a caregiver provides a social scaffold for the acquisition of skills. In other words, the caregiver is an enabler who can help the baby participate and respond to cues in a variety of games. Two games, "roll the ball" and "peekaboo," were used to test maternal scaffolding. Three behaviors (repetition, mutual involvement, and alternate turn-taking) were observed between seventeen pairs of mothers and their infants, who were aged eight to sixteen months. What is interesting here is that more mothers and infants played more rounds of a game when the child was mastering a game-relevant skill than they did either before or after that time. It seems that both mother and child became excited by the new skills and increased the rounds until the novelty wore thin. Joint attention was also important for the mothers' assistance or scaffolding to be effective. Mothers directed and channeled their infants' behaviors until the infants acquired a skill through the mothers' cues (for example, holding hands out in roll the ball, vocalizing while hiding in peekaboo). Maternal aid appeared to help these infants achieve higher levels of skill, and certainly the social context of the games enhanced skill acquisition. Hodapp and colleagues present a good example to explain this. They describe how infants show the ability to grasp and drop objects well before they can manage to return objects to adults. A child can return the dropped object *only* when there is someone nearby to encourage that return and offer the infant the reinforcement of a smile or words of pleasure. Similarly, a child can build a simple block tunnel, but when the parent moves a small car through the tunnel, the toddler may make the connection and then, if she's ready, imitate the act with appropriate car noises.

Other work by Jay Belsky, Mary Kay Goode, and Robert Most attests to the need for caregivers to be sensitive to their infants' developmental status when stimulating them.[10] The researchers operationalized the concept of stimulation and described three physical and three verbal strategies for stimulating a child. Physical strategies included pointing, demonstrating, and moving a child's hands. Verbal strategies included instruction/questions, highlighting (describing an object), and naming objects. The study used eight infants at four stages: nine, twelve, fifteen, and eighteen months. In addition to their conceptualization of stimulation, they coded three levels of play (juxtapositional, functional, and pretend) and three categories of behavior (extended exploration, attending to mother, and imitating/complying). During the last quarter of the children's first year, mothers used both physical prompts and language as part of their mediation, but as the children began to develop more linguistic skills in the second year, mothers relied more on verbal devices to stimulate the toddlers. In a second study using sixteen one-year-olds in an experimental and a control group, Belsky and colleagues found that children whose mothers were made conscious of their own spontaneous stimulating behavior through the experimenter's reinforcement of such behaviors, engaged in more competent play than control infants.

Arietta Slade was also interested in maternal involvement and its effect on symbolic play.[11] The participants in her study were sixteen mother-toddler pairs who were assessed at bimonthly intervals when the children were between the ages of eighteen and thirty months. Her data, however, cover the free-play sessions at twenty, twenty-two, twenty-six, and twenty-eight months only. Slade used a carpeted playroom equipped with a couch, chairs, a chest of drawers, and a standard set of toys—a toy iron, telephone, baby doll, and doctor's kit. She measured the length of each symbolic play episode and the level of the episode using five distinctions, ranging from presymbolic (action naming) to planning and enacting a pretend sequence (feed doll, search for doll and bottle). Mothers were scored for their degree of involvement. Results indicated that both the duration and level of play increased with age, as one would have expected. The level of pretend play increased when the mother was available to play, and, just as O'Connell and Bretherton had reported, the symbolic play episodes were enhanced by the mother's availability at twenty-six months. The level of play was highest when the mother both initiated play and actively participated with the child. Verbal commentary was especially effective in increasing both the level and duration of play.

Vygotsky's assertion, echoed by Bretherton, that a parent needs to adjust to a child's knowledge base, was further verified by Joan Lucariello, who found that when a child was familiar with a theme, the child and mother participated in advanced levels of symbolic play activity, but when play involved unfamiliar themes, the children in her study (aged twenty-four to twenty-nine months) had difficulty in integrating the actions of a novel game, such as playing with a castle.[12]

Some mothers may actually be more aware of the language they direct at younger children than at older children. Robert Kavanaugh and his colleagues report that mothers used more fantasy utterances with two-year-olds than with eighteen-month-olds. They were able to talk about nonexistent imaginary objects and ask the child to extend a play episode by providing new fantasy elements.[13]

Age is not the only factor to be considered in any intervention strategy. If a child is comfortable, in a state of equilibrium in which all basic needs—thirst, hunger, sleep—have been met, the child is motivated to explore the environment and is more receptive to maternal guidance or intervention. Trying to "teach" children a new game when they are sleepy or hungry just increases their irritability and frustrates the caregiver. Robert White's excellent treatise on motivation suggests that a child can only be effective and competent, or master an act, when physical and psychological conditions are harmonious.[14]

Learning theorists have long considered a state of readiness an essential ingredient in learning new behaviors, and this seems particularly relevant to the maternal intervention studies that deal with symbolic play. In summary, it appears that four conditions are necessary if maternal or caregiver interventions with children are to be effective: (1) a state of readiness, both psychological and physiological; (2) a set for learning in terms of intellectual level; (3) a social context in which a caregiver is present to interact with the children by modeling, directing, or channeling behavior; and (4) a caregiver who is sensitive to the child's needs and who is able to provide both the internal and external affective conditions described by Carl Rogers.

David Harrington, Jeanne Block, and Jack Block actually tested Rogers's theory of "creativity-fostering environments."[15] Their investigation was longitudinal, involving 106 children and their parents when the children were three and four, and later when the children were approximately eleven-and-a-half. The authors carried out their study by translating Rogers's theory into indices of child-rearing practices and parent-child interactions that were then applied to their subjects. For example, "I respect my child's opinions and encourage him to express them" is typical of the statements consensually judged most typical of a creativity-fostering environment. Examples of items used in a teaching strategy incorporating Rogers's ideas were "parent encouraged the child," or "parent was warm and supportive." These indices were then applied to the data available in a longitudinal follow-up of children during preschool and early adolescent years. In addition, a composite index of creative potential in early adolescence was used and compared with the earlier measures of parents' child-rearing practices.

The data support Rogers's notion that children raised by parents who provide conditions of psychological safety and freedom will develop their creative potential more fully then will children whose parents do not adhere to his position. When controlled for the effects of sex, preschool intelligence, and preschool creative potential, the results were significant and "compatible with a number of personality theories."[16] Erik Erikson, for example, called attention to the importance of establishing a sense of basic trust during the child's early years, and emphasized the need for a child to express his independence and autonomy in the preschool period, Stage 2 of the Eight Stage theory of development.[17] The authors caution that their data are correlational, so that we have no cause and effect results, and that they do not know whether creative early adolescents will become creatively active and achieving adults. What is clear in this study, however, is how important parents can be in fostering the creative potential of their children by permitting the psychological freedom Rogers proclaimed as a necessity in child-rearing patterns.

Diana Shmukler and Idva Naveh's work is particularly relevant here.[18] Working with 116 economically disadvantaged preschoolers in South Africa, they found that children made significant increases in imaginative play behavior and in other aspects of play, such as positive emotionality, social interaction, cooperation, and concentration, as a result of play training when compared to children who were in control groups either receiving mastery training or no intervention. The children who received play training also improved in verbal fluency, flexibility, originality, and imaginativeness of stories, and in verbal IQ. What is pertinent to our discussion of Rogers's theory and the study by Harrington and colleagues is Shmukler and Naveh's statement that encouragement, endorsement of imagination, protection, modeling, and warmth were the factors that were "powerful" in the experimental play intervention groups regardless of whether the type of play intervention approaches were structured or unstructured.[19] They are careful to point out that a supportive atmosphere in itself did not account for the social gains in increased imaginative play, since a similarly supportive atmosphere was present in the control situations but without the play training component.

Shmukler's earlier work had demonstrated the importance of the parent as a motivator for play, but she proposed that there is an optimal point for such facilitation.[20] If the parent is too intrusive the child plays less imaginatively than when the parent starts a game, makes a suggestion, and then withdraws. Shmukler also found that children who showed more imaginativeness and positive affect had mothers whose own behavior was rated by observers as reflecting more imagination, warmth, and involvement. The best predictors of a child's imaginativeness were the scores based on observations and home reports, which included evidence that "mother tells stories" and "mother accepts child."

Our own research corroborates this finding. More imaginative older children significantly more often reported to us that their parents told them stories or played fantasy games with them.[21] In more recent research, we found that preschool children who were read to in the evening or who had a settling-down time before bedtime, and whose television viewing time was controlled, were less aggressive and more imaginative than children without such soothing or television control, and who did not experience encouraging mediation by parents.[22]

It seems reasonable to conclude that children need to learn through imitation, encouragement, and practice how to attend to their ongoing thoughts, how to transform the objects in their environment into playthings they can at least temporarily control, and how to recreate in an accessible, miniature form some of the many complex, confusing, and even frightening scenes they have experienced. The role of a benign adult seems essential in helping the child achieve this imaginative skill. The parent, grandparent, or concerned caregiver who lovingly sanctions a child's first attempts to invent stories and pretend games permits the child to continue strengthening her imagination, which then becomes an important ingredient in the adult personality, acting as a buffer in moments of anxiety. The adults who foster imagination offer children a sense of security and closeness they remember long into adulthood. Was it an accident that Dickens used the family name of his childhood story-telling nurse, Miss Weller, when he chose the surname for one of his warmest and most delightful characters, Mr. Pickwick's servant, Sam Weller?[23]

The Home Atmosphere and Symbolic Play

How can we find out if Rogers's theory of constructive creativity truly depends upon psychological safety and psychological freedom in the home? Over a four-year period we followed up sixty-three children (thirty-one males and thirty-two females) from preschool to early elementary school. They represented a fair range of socioeconomic status, ethnic background, and intelligence. We examined the parents' own personality characteristics, their child-rearing patterns and household management, and the home television environment. Home visits to families by specially trained interview teams unfamiliar with the study's hypotheses or with children's scores on specific variables were carried out. Interviewers administered a Family Style Questionnaire and observed how households were organized. Parents were also questioned at the research center about their personal values, methods of discipline, and specific child-rearing attitudes, as well as their television viewing habits.[24]

Using a self-report measure developed by a colleague, Roni Tower, we obtained information about a parent's style or value orientation according to three dimensions: *resourcefulness* (based on a selection of adjectives that included "imaginative," "resourceful," "curious," "creative"); *reliability-stability* ("competent," "organized," "practical"); and *relationship-sociability* ("outgoing," "hospitable," "helpful").[25] We also examined measures that dealt with family structure, such as single-parent versus intact family, number of children, family stress (bereavements, illness, accidents), and mother's work status. Household routine data were obtained about suppertime and bedtime hours, the kind of bedtime routine used, hours of sleep, regularity of daily routines, cultural activities (museum visits, library visits, music lessons), and the family's emphasis on outdoor recreation and sports. We also obtained data on the children's verbal intelligence and their television-viewing patterns during the four-year period.

Children were assessed for their degree of imagination using three separate estimates: human movement responses to a form of the Rorschach inkblots; responses to an imagination interview; and observations of their block play fantasy using a scoring system established by Eli Bower.[26] The human movement associations to the random patterns of inkblots (usually labeled as M responses) have been shown to be associated with other measures of imagination. We also had measures of the children's intelligence and their television-viewing habits.

We found that children who were imaginative (as measured by their association of more movement responses to inkblots) were more likely to have parents who were resourceful, that is, who described themselves as valuing imagination, curiosity, adventurousness, and creativity. These parents were also those who used inductive child-rearing approaches rather than physical punishment or who instituted clear rules as part of their discipline. In addition, parents of creative children were those who used more orderly routines, attended more cultural activities, and were less oriented to outdoor recreation. Parental emphasis on imaginativeness predicted the children's degree of imaginative play several years later.

Tower's earlier findings in her study of preschoolers suggested that mothers who scored high on resourcefulness had sons whom the parents perceived to be more artistic, higher in expressive imaginativeness, and in general also higher in resourcefulness. Fathers' scores in resourcefulness yielded a different relationship to their sons than mothers' scores; sons of such fathers were low in dramatic and global imaginativeness. We may speculate that fathers were so involved in their own creative activities, they did not share these experiences with their sons. When parents agreed on their self-ratings, however, Tower found that such agreement predicted a great degree of imaginativeness in block play and in art, and a general imaginative style in their children regardless of sex. The "optimal" rating reflected what teachers considered an adaptive, appropriate behavior pattern. It may mean that when parents seemed to agree in their value patterns their children showed a more well-adjusted play pattern.[27]

In view of the very extensive work on the human movement response in the Rorschach literature and in clinical use, our home visit study provides one of the few instances in which specific familial factors and their possible relationship to imagination were examined across time. Psychoanalytic object-relations research, which places great emphasis on the internalized representation of parental or other human figures, has led to many important inferences about particular childhood or family patterns derived mainly from reconstructions of adult clients' memories. Studies using natural settings and direct family observations can help us better understand how a child's milieu can stimulate the development of private images and internal story-telling capacities.

The parental values measured by Tower may influence children because of the specific patterns of action the adults engaged in. When the attitudes, values, and behavior of thirty-nine parents of gifted and nongifted three- to five-year-olds were compared, it was found that parents of the gifted children spent considerably more time with them on school-related activities, reported unconditional love for their children (similar to the inductive style we found), and were more willing to foster independence than parents of nongifted children.[28] It is interesting to see how important this inductive style is in the rearing of children, especially when compared to a power-assertiveness style. For example, in a study of parental influence techniques using participants aged five to adult, it was found that power assertion produced external attributions, that is, indications that children perceived an individual's fate as dependent on external events and discounted altruistic traits in story characters. On the other hand, when the parents showed more modeling and spontaneous helping behavior, the children showed more internal attributions, that is, an emphasis on self-directed causality and stronger inferences about the presence of altruistic traits in story characters.[29]

Research evidence supporting the importance of a parent's attitude and modeling behavior is further demonstrated in a study that compared boys who were rejected, neglected, or popular with their peers in a physical play situation. Twelve boys, ranging in age from three to five, were observed in interactions with their parents at home. Fathers of boys who were generally ignored by their peers engaged in less affectively arousing, physical play than fathers of popular or peer-rejected boys. The rejected boys were also overstimulated or understimulated compared with popular boys. The overstimulation we conjecture may lead to more wild, disorganized, and less socially acceptable patterns of play among peers.[30] The results of this study suggest the need to relate affect and sensitivity on the part of the parents to a child's ability to handle stimulation. The study also suggests that there are links between parent and peer social systems in terms of social competence.

Kevin MacDonald and Ross Parke found similar results.[31] Twenty-seven preschoolers (thirteen boys and fourteen girls) were videotaped while playing separately for twenty minutes in their homes. Their social competence with their peers was independently evaluated by using teacher rankings of their popularity with peers, Q-sort ratings of their competence by their teachers, and assessments of their social interactions with three other preschoolers on separate occasions. Findings suggest that fathers engaged in significantly more physical play with their children than mothers, while both parents talked more to girls than to boys. Boys showed a consistent profile: positive characteristics were associated with paternal engagement and physical play, and with maternal verbal behavior. Maternal verbal behavior and paternal physical play and engagement that were associated with teacher rankings of popularity were "related to an observed pattern of harmonious, relaxed and dominant interaction with peers. Similarly, paternal directiveness—a variable that was related to low popularity ranking—was correlated with an abrasive peer interaction for boys."[32]

Through play with parents, children learn social communication skills, the value of their own "affective displays," how to use these signals with their peers, and how to decode the social and affective signals of their peers.[33] As we have reported in earlier chapters, MacDonald and Parke also state that when the parent generates positive affect in the child during the course of play, this affect is carried over into peer relationships. Alan Sroufe and colleagues have also found this pattern, the consistent relationship between affective expressiveness and peer social competence, in their work on children's play.[34]

If an atmosphere of positive affect and verbal parental engagement with children is more conducive to fostering socially competent children, can peers also influence the quality of their play with each other? Neil Cohen and C. Tomlinson-Keasey investigated four social settings: (1) mother-toddler; (2) toddler alone; (3) mother, toddler, and peer; and (4) toddler and peer. The level of play (oral, tactile, active, explorative, and creative) and the amount of play (wandering, fleeting, and sustained) were measured.[35] The procedures (ten-minute observations) were carried out in the homes of twenty-six toddlers using a familiar friend in the peer setting. The results indicated that the mother-child setting facilitated exploration of the unique qualities of an object for both boys and girls. When girls played with their mothers or by themselves, they were the most creative. Boys, on the other hand, played most creatively with their peers. This may suggest that boys encourage each other to devise novel uses for their toys, are more willing to be adventurous than girls, and stimulate each other in ways that mothers do not. As we pointed out earlier in this chapter, the sex of a child and the social setting have a bearing on the quality of play.

Some parents do not value peer influence and may try to isolate their preschoolers by choosing not to send them to nursery school even when they can afford to do so. There have also been cases of parents who have attempted to educate their older children at home, avoiding any formal school training. One of the most unusual families we have read about is described in Michael Deakin's *Children on the Hill*.[36] The parents deliberately chose to rear their four children (at the time the book was written they were five, seven, nine, and twelve) in an environment far removed from any city influence. They came to Wales in 1964 to live in a dilapidated cottage. Both parents were well educated. Maria, the mother, an Italian by birth, although quite poor, not only had a partial university background in

Greek philology but had taken a course in Montessori teaching. Martin, the father, was Jewish, raised in England by parents who had left Poland at the turn of the century. He grew up during World War II, and his childhood was an unhappy one. Eventually, as a young man he took up residence in Milan, where he supported himself by giving English lessons. He soon went on to Rome to study and the couple met at the university.

The goal of the parents was to raise each child in a unique way to enable each to find a suitable method of self-expression. Maria felt it must always be "the child who led, not the teacher."[37] Since both parents had had unhappy experiences with peers, they saw no need for their children to have friends in their preschool years. The parents maintained certain rules of conduct, used a positive pattern of reinforcement, never restricted the children's curiosity or their need to explore space or distance, and even permitted freedom concerning excreta or other bodily functions. When the children played "potty bombs," Marie permitted it, just as she permitted a mess in the bathroom. She felt they would satisfy their curiosity by their expurgation of taboos, and the messes would not be repeated. The parents continually named objects in the cottage, used sandpaper letters to help the children learn through a kinesthetic approach, and made a set of rods of different colors for one child who was fascinated by numbers. Through the manipulation of these rods he learned about simple mathematical functions.

For years this unusual family remained insulated from other children and the pressures of the outside world. When each of the older children was ready for the first formal school experience at age six, it was a difficult adjustment for them to deal with rowdy children and a narrow-minded teacher. These were gifted children, reared according to a philosophy that allowed for total self-expression. The oldest boy was expert in mathematics; the next was a gifted pianist who at age seven won a music contest in London; the only daughter, Ruth, had artistic talent, painted, and played the flute; and the youngest was gifted in computer skills as well as mathematics.

When the youngest child turned five, the family left rural Wales and moved to an industrial city so that the older children could advance their studies. Maria and Martin believed their philosophy provided an environment that benefited their children during their preschool years in ways that would have been impossible if the children had experienced typical peer relationships or typical nursery or daycare-center training. Maria believed the major guiding principle to be "freedom from outside pressures, be they of guilt or violence or doubt, and a feeling of total 'togetherness' with the children." Her precepts, not very different from those of Carl Rogers, included

(a) *Environment:* in itself simply a cocoon allowing for this freedom from outside pressures which is of such paramount importance.

(b) *Freedom from objectives:* the release from any pressure to success or early achievement of educational goals. Quite literally, the course must be one of *laissez-faire*—the child should choose its own speed and the parent simply see that its footsteps don't falter on the way.

(c) *A reciprocal approach:* rather than an authoritative one. By recognising the early egocentricity of a child and helping it rather than opposing it, vital energy is spared, both by the child and the mother. This will then lead to a speedier embarkation on the seas of true education.

(d) *Self-sacrifice by the parents:* only by giving themselves totally to the "process" can parents hope to succeed. The release from inner pressures of this surrender, the freedom from guilt about "doing the best thing for the children" can make this sacrifice less difficult than the uninvolved would suppose.[38]

Many of the ideas Marie and Martin proposed have been used coincidentally in home-based intervention studies in the United States and in Bermuda in a more formal way in the Mother-Child Home Program (MCHP), and have been researched with support from private and government agencies.[39] These studies focused primarily on cognitive, social, and emotional training through the use of a Toy Demonstrator, who taught preschool children in their own homes using toys and books. Mothers were encouraged to model the demonstrator's techniques and to assume responsibility for each interaction with their children.

Despite good family participation during home visits in both studies, neither was able to report significant long-term effects from such expensive intervention programs. The investigators who were involved agree that continued experimental evaluation efforts are still needed, and that effects might be stronger in different samples than the ones used in these studies. Modifications of the MCHP program should also be made in the future to meet the needs of specific samples of children. In addition, if such programs are used, it is important to be sure that the samples involved are truly educationally at risk before such intervention programs are prescribed and before so much money is invested by school districts.[40]

We are not discouraged by the findings of these studies and believe that play training can still be taught in the home to individual parents, or to small groups through contacts with child-care centers, or in kindergartens. Since the studies mentioned above concentrated primarily on cognitive gains and emphasized such skills in their training, it would be interesting to see if a different approach, one focusing more on play, would have yielded better results.

The School as a Creative Environment

Bernard Spodek, an educator, believed that a teacher needs to guide children, not merely set the stage, and should judiciously intervene if play is to be educationally useful. According to him, such guidance requires "an awareness of and sensitivity to the children's play activities, a sense of what the teacher hopes the children will derive from the play, and an ability to move into the children's play on occasion, make suggestions, even become a player if that can be done without distorting the children's play."[41] Spodek echoes Diana Shmukler's philosophy of the parents' role and applies it to teachers, whom he calls "social engineers."[42] Setting out materials for a child is not enough; there must be active but sensitive guidance.

Friedrich Froebel, one of the great educators and the founder of the first kindergarten in 1837 in Blankenburg, Germany, proposed that a child belongs to both family and society. We have reviewed many studies dealing with the parents' role in developing a child's imagination, but like Froebel and others after him, we also accept the important role of the teacher as a stimulus to the child's imagination. Froebel attempted to relate his mystical religious philosophy to education. He believed in a unity of man and nature, man and God, and man and other men. Children should play, and if tasks given to a young child aroused delight, Froebel labeled the task or the employment "play." He recognized that play can help strengthen bodies, exercise the senses, and acquaint a child with nature. To achieve his goal of applying his philosophy to education, Froebel developed three approaches to be used with children aged three to six. According to the first, children were taught to use *gifts,* small sets of manipulable materials such as yarn, wooden spheres, cylinders, and cubes, which were to be combined into various forms in a prescribed sequence that symbolized different aspects of the universe. The second was *occupation*. Children learned to weave, cut, draw, paint, and model clay. The third was *mothers' play*. Children were taught songs and games dealing with the social and natural world derived from the play of peasant women with their children.

This early pioneer in children's education had an enormous impact on preschool education in Germany and in Western society in general for many years. Maria Montessori's Children's House, established in 1907, used many of Froebel's and Pestalozzi's principles concerning the potential of play to enrich a child's imagination. Montessori was particularly sensitive to the fact that children have much to offer adults, and that "our first teacher, therefore will be the child himself."[43] Sandra Scarr and Kathleen McCartney would agree that much of the work in developmental psychology "consists of family studies in which no consideration is given to child effects on adults, to the sources of naturally occurring covariations in parental and child behaviors, or to the role that children play in creating their own environments."[44] Montessori believed that order and discipline are necessary for education, but that such order came from children through "hidden, inner directives, which can manifest themselves only if the freedom permitting them to be heeded is given."[45] This can be achieved if the teacher designs a constructive environment that can lead to spontaneous activities.

One of the earliest studies of play as a means of producing positive effects in the behavior of disadvantaged preschool children adhered to the principles of the constructive atmosphere in emphasizing the child's "potential abilities and knowledge" and combining his "scattered experiences in a flexible way."[46] Sara Smilansky recognized that sociodramatic play was one of the best and most natural means to meet the needs of culturally disadvantaged children and that the school was a natural place to carry out her work, since most schools allow children free-play periods and have the necessary equipment. Smilansky's study took place in Israel and involved thirty-six kindergarten and nursery school classes in which the ages of the children ranged from three to six years. The classes were divided into two groups: eighteen with middle and high sociocultural backgrounds and eighteen with low socioeconomic backgrounds, primarily children of immigrants from other Middle Eastern countries. The experimental group consisted of 420 "Oriental" disadvantaged children. The control group included 362 Oriental children in one condition; another control group consisted of six classes of disadvantaged and six classes of advantaged children of European descent totaling 427 children.

In this elaborate study the experimental group played for ninety minutes each day, five days a week throughout each three-week period devoted to each of one of three themes. Treatment lasted for nine weeks, a total of sixty-seven hours. The experimental group was subdivided into three and each received different intervention techniques, such as outings, stories, discussions, and actual "teaching" of sociodramatic play. The children who received comments, suggestions, and demonstrations, and experienced teacher participation made significant progress on outcome measures of make-believe play, persistence, interaction, and verbal communication. The stimulation by the teachers allowed the children to draw on their own memories and abilities, which then became rich material for play themes. Smilansky reports that the teachers encouraged and helped the children to do what they wanted to do "instead of abandoning" them to life with the "immense task of solving all the problems" they "encountered in [their] efforts at self-expression, alone and unaided."[47] Visits to the homes of the disadvantaged children of Middle Eastern descent provided some indications that the parents in these homes, although they provided a warm emotional atmosphere, did not equip children with the verbal, cognitive, and social abilities required for sociodramatic play. Nor, according to Smilansky, did these parents provide any encouragement in the basic techniques needed for such play, which as Diana Shmukler states, is necessary for play to thrive.

A community-based center, the Bromley Heath Infant Day Care Center in a city-run housing project in Boston, Massachusetts, set up objectives similar to the Israeli project. The goal was to establish a setting where people could learn to become responsible and creative teachers of preschoolers, to provide daycare for parents in order to allow them to develop their own potential and thus increase their effectiveness as parents, and finally, to provide a stimulating environment that would be emotionally supportive for the children.[48]

The curriculum that was developed focused on infants and toddlers from one to two years old. Play was an important component, and the curriculum emphasized teaching a play skill that was within the child's developmental level. Just when a child is developing a pincer grip, for example, teachers or parents should be on the alert and provide small, soft, safe edible objects. Or to simplify an activity to be learned, they should offer only one part of a nested cube to an infant until the child learns to make several fit together. Teachers and parents were also shown that they could focus attention on important parts of an activity by pointing to a picture or to the right shape in a shape box and that they could guide the child by actually holding a hand or a leg or telling the child what to do next using words the child could understand.[49] The curriculum also suggested many kinds of toys that were both age appropriate and conducive to developing simple pretend play.

Other programs have developed various exercises for promoting imagery skills that can be demonstrated by teachers even if they themselves have had little training or experience in the use of imagery. These programs are spelled out in a step-by-step fashion and use few props[50] and sometimes only imagery methods, movement, and music.[51]

Material on "playing what if" is readily available if teachers are inclined to use these ideas. A major problem in the implementation of a play curriculum is the current attitude in many preschool centers, which emphasizes developing cognitive skills such as counting, learning letters, reciting the alphabet, and participating in reading readiness exercises. We can support such early learning of such skills as a precursor to formal schooling provided that the caregiver or teacher approaches these "lessons" through enjoyable play. Such preparation can be effective only when children are cognitively capable of forming connections between ideas learned in play and the "real world" of school. A child who has considerable experience in playing will benefit in many of the areas we discussed in Chapter 6.

The current introduction of computers to some middle-class kindergartens has been viewed by many as inhibiting to children's creative process, since children will be forced to work with clearly defined programs. But in one school, at least, the computer has become "an invitation to play." At the Developmental Research School at Florida State University, kindergarten children have been given the opportunity to experiment actively with print in novel ways. Children make repeated patterns of letters on the computer and accompany their configurations with "soundmaking," especially after they create unusual configurations using numbers, large and small letters, dollar signs, slash marks, and so on. The exploration of sounds, words, and patterns has led to the creation of stories in which children use their own rules and language. The teachers found that "repetitive soundmaking—including phoneme/grapheme relationships, sound order, length, duration and tonal quality accompany and facilitate writing to help children to organize print and to construct meaning."[52] The use of language, which is so important in play, can be encouraged through experimentation with letters, words, and patterns on the computer, yet another technique useful for imaginative training.

Libraries and Playgrounds

In the 1970s, "toy libraries" sprang up around the country—an initially successful one in Glassboro, New Jersey, funded by the Carnegie Foundation, was followed by many others.[53] Toy programs under this same Carnegie Foundation grant were then extended to twenty-six isolated villages in remote regions of Alaska where children had an opportunity to explore toys and games that would not ordinarily have been available. In establishing these toy collections, libraries found that if they offered a "course" to parents, toys were more likely to be borrowed and used; otherwise, many of the librarians who organized a program in their libraries found that parents did not borrow the toys to the expected degree.[54]

In addition to school and home play training, computers, and toy-lending libraries, playgrounds can be wonderful places for fostering make-believe and imaginative play. One New York City playground designed by Arthur Weyhe is located in a churchyard and features play sculpture that has been a great source of pleasure for neighboring daycare centers. One teacher described how children "pretend they're in a boat going over water filled with sharks—or that they are cowboys riding horses, or astronauts on a rocket."[55] The children have stretched their imaginations to describe a "sculpture" made of very long cedar poles that cross one another asymmetrically and are bolted together. It is used in pretend games, or for running along, or for swinging on, or just for nestling up to while they "build their castles in the sand."

If parents cannot create playgrounds in their own backyards, there are places where children can find unusual play areas. Robert Leathers, an architect who has designed more than 480 playgrounds in twenty-five states, has used children as his consultants. When children are encouraged to let themselves go, they have suggested such items as a "banana split slide," a "hunk of cheese" with holes to climb through, a "volcano" that spews sand, a "bouncing mushroom," an "octopus" with seats, and more.[56] Some playgrounds, called "adventure playgrounds," are composed of materials that look like buildings—huts, walls, forts, dens, tree houses. These playgrounds generally require special landscaping and structures that are simple but sturdy, and usually have "play leaders" who manage the play areas. Successful examples have been built in England, Sweden, Canada, and Norway.[57] Some "playgrounds" are actually mobile vans. Those in Stockholm, Sweden, are filled with easily portable toys and games of all kinds for children to borrow during recess and after school or to play with in the van itself. Architects Jay Beckwith and Richard Dattner have been leaders in playground design, and others have also planned indoor and outdoor environments that are whimsical and practical. Children are collectors and need storage space for their treasures. They also like cozy areas or "nests" for settling down to listen to music, browse through a picture book, play with a favorite toy, or daydream.

Two books on children's play spaces that we particularly like describe a variety of settings that are esthetically pleasing as well as functional.[58] In both books the designers are aware that children drop paint, spill water, run toys along a floor, jump on beds, and bounce balls against a wall. Floors are designed to handle spills and messes. Washable walls can be scrubbed when sticky or dirty fingers touch them, or when the artist in the child decides that wall space is better than paper. A creatively designed room can be planned inexpensively as long as it is "a place where space, color, and form work to stimulate, delight, and stretch the child's mind and body."[59] Unfortunately, such expansive room arrangements at home are limited to families with the space and economic resources for implementing the proposals. The principles in these books may serve, however, as guides for operators of home daycare settings or larger nursery and child-care facilities.

Getting in Touch with One's Own Playful Spirit

In this chapter we have described studies that relied on a variety of intervention techniques to promote make-believe play: verbal guidance or the use of comments and suggestions; pointing behaviors in which the adult actually puts a finger on an object; physical actions such as moving a child's hands or legs to demonstrate a desired movement; fantasy training in which a child is told a story that is discussed and then acted out; imaginative play training where transformations are encouraged and where puppets and simple props are used; and finally, imagery training in which a child might be told to picture in her head a person she knows and then imagine that person in different scenes. Richard de Mille, a psychologist, has written a useful book in this area, *Put Your Mother on the Ceiling*, which is filled with clever imagery exercises that parents or teachers can employ to help a child work through feelings about people or social situations.[60]

Whether to choose one technique or another depends on children's age and intellectual level. But in order to try out any of the techniques we have discussed, adults must first feel comfortable about their own fantasy and imagery skills in order to enter the child's world of make-believe. Very young children have difficulty separating fantasy and reality, and to them a monster may seem very real. Parents or teachers should accept such emotions as a part of the child's reality. If they allow the child to play the monster game again and again, such fearful feelings may eventually dissipate. As we suggested in Chapter 2, affect theory would indicate that as the child places frightening things into familiar cognitive schemas, the balance shifts to the positive emotions of joy and interest. As we will see in Chapter 9, fearful feelings can be expressed and worked through in play, music, art, pantomime—and just talking.

What are some of the things we can do to understand a child's world? Through observing children at play, we recognize what their worries, concerns, and fantasies are. We learn about their basic needs, their feelings of love and anger, their rivalries and fears of failure, their secret wishes and desires. Another way to understand children's make-believe worlds is by remembering our own childhoods and pleasant early experiences, whether a birthday party that was particularly meaningful, a visit to a place that turned into a great adventure, or a childhood playmate. Remembering toys of childhood, games we played, secret clubs, friends with whom we shared special times—all these early memories help adults open the doors to their playful selves. Keeping track of nighttime dreams permits us to get in touch with our own deep-seated fantasies and wishes, sources of inspiration for pretend, which can help us realize how hard it is for children to separate reality from fantasy. Relaxing in a chair and allowing ourselves time to daydream and play out fantasies in our minds moves us away from the mundane tasks of everyday life and brings us a little bit closer to the magical realm of childhood. What is sometimes called "hypnotic age regression" is simply an extreme form of concentration on our childhood settings. It allows us to "become" a three- or four-year-old again and experience images or fleeting memories of childhood. Finally, playing with a child, actually getting down on the floor, can be an exhilarating experience. For a brief moment we can participate in the game of "space people," or "deep-sea diver," or "going shopping" and share the fun of "pretend."

We set the scene for make-believe play when we stimulate children and participate with them, but as adults we must remember to retain a sense of dignity. The caregiver who becomes too "babyish" may upset a child, who expects the adult to be in control. We can be the big, friendly giant, the captain of the ship, or a large cuddly animal, we can change voices and make sound effects, but we must remember when to withdraw from the game and allow children their own space to play. Maria and Martin believed that the environment needed for creativity must contain a "reciprocal approach." The parent or teacher and the child must work together to achieve the conditions that encourage the child to learn how to transform the physical objects in the environment into a flexible, symbolic world.

· 8 ·

Television-Viewing and
the Imagination

*Like the sorcerers of old, the television set casts its magic spell,
freezing speech and actions and turning the living into silent
statues so long as the enchantment lasts.*

—Urie Bronfenbrenner
in *Social Science and Social Welfare,*
ed. John Romanyshyn

What is it about television that keeps children glued to the set
(depending on their ages) from one to six hours a day? When school-
age children are asked why they watch TV, they claim they watch
it for escape (it's fun and exciting), for fantasy material, for company, for learning about ways of behaving and dressing, and last,
for getting general information about the world.[1] Most children are
indiscriminate viewers, that is, they rarely use a guide to help them
decide in advance whether or not a program is worthwhile or appropriate for someone their age. Generally, they switch on the set
and watch whatever appears; or if they have a remote control device,
and especially if they also have cable, they may "zap" from channel
to channel.[2]

Educators, professional mental health workers, and parents are
concerned about the number of hours children spend in front of the
set and about the content of the programs they watch. One parent
we know has hidden his TV set in the basement. Another has tried
to control his children's viewing by constructing an ingenious device: He took a bicycle, made a stand for it in the TV room, and
hooked it to a car generator and a twelve-volt battery. Using "pedal
power," his children are able to operate a portable twelve-inch TV
set. On a busy night, parents and children take turns pedaling,
storing electricity for five-minute recesses; they take breaks during
commercials.[3] Not all parents are about to take such drastic steps,
but certainly, many parents do express their concern about television's possible impact on their children's development.

We became interested in studying the effects of television on children, and particularly on their imaginations, in 1972 while we were carrying out a research project dealing with play in preschoolers. What piqued our curiosity were the references many of the children made to a television production of "Peter Pan" they had watched one weekend. Some of the children dressed up like Peter, Wendy, and the pirates and imitated the characters as best they could, acting out parts of the plot and adding their own interpretations. The inspiration to study television using empirical methods evolved from the observations of these children during their free-play periods. We began to ask ourselves whether television might be a new element in the child's early experience that enhanced imagination or whether it might have features that hindered creative thinking.

After years of studying the associations between television and children's behavior and reviewing the research literature, we are convinced that television pervades the consciousness of children. It is manifest in the clothes they wear, the toys and games they play with, the characters with whom they identify, and the cereals and candy they eat. No other extraparental influence has penetrated the lives of children as television has. The "magic" of television takes us all over the world and has almost brought about the "global village" described by Marshall McLuhan.[4] In the remote Amazonian rain forest village of Gorotire, Brazil, for example, a satellite dish brings "He-Man" and "The Flintstones" to the naked Kaiapo Indian children. The villagers call television the "big ghost." The nature of their community is changing. They no longer gather at night to meet and to talk, to pass on information, or to tell stories. Beptopup, the oldest medicine man, says, "The night is the time the old people teach the young people. Television has stolen the night."[5]

Television has stolen the day as well as the night from many people in the United States. The average American family watches approximately twenty-eight hours of television a week, while preschoolers average about twenty-one hours.[6] It is difficult to believe that all these viewing hours are filled with programs that are both edifying and entertaining. One study has found that children between the ages of three and seven watch cartoons and comedies, with some leveling off between five and seven.[7] Boys watch more cartoons, action adventure, adult informational (including sports), and variety-miscellaneous programs than girls. Stability of viewing was found to be generally high in this age group, indicating that this is a "critical period for socialization of television-viewing patterns, and that such patterns have long-term implications for children's development."[8] Between five and seven is the period when boys shift their viewing to action adventure programs and children of both sexes shift to comedies.

What can this medium be doing to our thoughts and feelings? The literature dealing with the effects of television on social, emotional, and cognitive development is vast and has been summarized in major reports funded by the National Institute of Mental Health[9] and by the Office of Educational Research and Improvement.[10] In this chapter we focus on the relationship between television-viewing and imagination in young children because we believe that cognitive-affective theory is relevant to the way in which television affects our ability to process information, develop schemas, and enhance our imaginative growth.

Cognitive-Affective Theory and Television

According to cognitive theorists, humans organize experience through anticipation and planning based on a storehouse of memories. If information is presented to us too rapidly to be matched against already existing ideas or memory schemas, we may react by being startled, surprised, afraid, or even terrified. If novelty and incongruity remain at a very high level we may become angry, sad, or distressed. When novelty and incongruity are presented more gradually, however, we become interested and begin to explore the situation; we experience curiosity and a pleasant feeling of anticipation about learning more. Children react with some anxiety in a new situation if they are unprepared, but if they have information about it through pictures or prior discussion, they may respond joyfully with a laugh or a smile. We may wonder why a young child experiences distress while visiting an amusement park we thought would be fun. But if we are aware of the cacophony generated by the whirling of machines, the shouts of hawkers, the screams of people on various rides, the music of merry-go-rounds, and the "bangs" of guns aimed at targets we can realize that this overstimulation can cause fear rather than joy.

Despite considerable experience watching TV, many kindergarten-age children, and certainly many preschoolers, are still confused by special effects such as zooms, fades, ripple effects, and split-screens. Thus, what may seem like a typical television convention to us may be distressing to a child. As adults, we recognize that eerie-sounding music suggests an upcoming dramatic or even violent scene, but the young child may not be as well-prepared to recognize this convention, and when such an event does occur may be more frightened because of it.

We can summarize some of the implications of a cognitive-affective theory for the television environment as follows:

1. By framing and miniaturizing novel and complex situations in a box, the television set reduces the range and intensity of emotional reactivity, in contrast to the big screen in movie theaters or the traditional stage in dramatic productions.

2. The emphasis on rapid shifts in sequence and on changes in sound effects and background music maximizes our orienting reflexes and holds our attention, and especially that of children, to the set. These effects may appear to create a pattern of almost mindless or unresponsive watching.

3. Because of the close tie between emotion and the degree of development of children's store of memories and information-processing capacities, programming for children must be carefully designed to be specific. Artistic or dramatic effects and plots that may seem desirable to adults may be confusing or even misleading to children. A first-grader watching the "Bionic Man" running in slow-motion to catch an enemy asked, "Why is he running so slowly if he wants to get the bad guy?" The director was attempting to create an esthetic effect of tension, something adults can grasp but which made no sense to this child.

4. Because television viewing is pervasive, the medium could play an important role in education and in the constructive socialization of the child. When parents talk to children, read them stories, and explain human relationships or natural forces such as thunder or rain to them, they are, in effect, reducing the outside world to a manageable size. Then, children's own games of make-believe and their use of imagery can eventually help them assimilate these into memory schemas. If parents are too busy, too stressed, or unavailable to play this mediating role, however, television, *with age appropriate programming,* can be especially valuable in reducing the big outside world to manageable proportions and stimulating the imagination and positive emotions in children.

One TV program that is especially sensitive in helping the preschool child make sense out of a confusing world is "Mister Rogers' Neighborhood." The host, Fred Rogers, acts as a surrogate parent, explaining through verbal repetition, music, puppets, special guests, and trips to various locations some of the confusing elements in a child's environment. He deals with facts—how balloons float in air, how crayons are made, or how wood may be carved. He introduces imaginative elements through a make-believe world of puppets ruled by King Friday. He also helps children face feelings and emotions by discussing jealousy, love, and anger; he has even touched on birth and death. He can help a child deal with a first day at school, a visit to the doctor, or a stay in the hospital.

Unfortunately, such programming is rare, although research has demonstrated the effectiveness of "Mister Rogers' Neighborhood" in promoting social skills such as sharing and cooperation and in influencing the imagination.[11] Many adults claim to be bored by Fred Rogers's slow, deliberate speech pattern, but preschool children, as we have observed them watching the program, are obviously enthralled. We know that children like his repetition of words and ideas. How many times have we read the same story to a child (who, by the way, will not tolerate any attempt to skip a phrase), yet each time the child eagerly anticipates the climax. The familiarity of the plot fits in with the child's previously encountered schemas and is therefore satisfying. In addition, children rarely master information they only hear once. Each time they hear a story read, they gain more information they can add to their repertory. This desire for repetition explains why children replay their favorite records or videotapes, watch reruns of old TV programs, and, as we noted in Chapter 4, play the same games over and over.

We can see, then, that carefully thought out programs can actually enhance a child's imagination and inculcate socially desirable behaviors. Unfortunately, quality children's programming is unavailable on the three major commercial networks on a regular basis, and unless a family has access to cable television or tunes in public television, the commercial networks, with their cartoons and situation comedies, provide the bulk of the programs that children view. As the research indicates, after children graduate from information-giving programs like "Sesame Street" and "Mister Rogers' Neighborhood," they make some choices about which adult programs to watch; comedies seem to be the least demanding and are thus among their favorites. They usually watch other adult programs with their parents, who influence these program choices.[12] Children's viewing of adult programs tends to be passive simply because the level of comprehension and interest in these programs falls outside their range. Given the freedom of the set, children will generally choose cartoons, or, in the case of boys especially, the action adventure programs that contain numerous acts of aggression and violence.

Television and the Toddler

What is particularly disturbing to some observers is the age at which children begin to watch television. Infants as young as nine months of age have been exposed to an average of about one-and-a-half hours of television a day.[13] What is the effect of television viewing on such young children? There is some evidence that television can be a source of stimulation and even serve as a modeling device for babies. Dafna Lemish and Mabel Rice carried out a field study over a six-month period in which sixteen babies ranging in age from six months to three years were each observed in their homes four or five times while the television set was on.[14] These babies and toddlers (depending on their age and verbal ability) exhibited such behaviors as pointing to characters in the TV screen and naming them verbally, asking questions related to the medium, repeating single words or phrases, or commenting on a character's mood. One twenty-three-month-old, watching a commercial, reflected, "Coke is it. Coke is it. Coke is it."[15] Another, at only twenty months, who spoke abruptly, without conversational intent, while the television set was off, said, " 'Sesame Street' is a production of the Children's Televsion Workshop." We wonder if either of these toddlers really understood what it parroted.

Parents in this study were, like their children, engaged in pointing, labeling, and attention-calling, and corrected their children's errors. They also repeated words and phrases after a child did so or after TV characters spoke, thus acting as reinforcers of vocabulary. Lemish and Rice comment on the "richness of the interactions surrounding the television influence."[16] Children in the study "viewed and conversed while they ate, played, had their diapers changed and generally went about their ordinary routines." Work by Albert Hollenbeck and Ronald Slaby found, as Lemish did, that infants can imitate vocalizations from television.[17] Their results indicate that televised presentations of discrete, repeated vocalizations influenced the vocal pattern of infants in their study, whose average age was twenty-eight weeks. They see possible uses of television as a speech stimulus, and perhaps under certain conditions, where speech is delayed, this technique might be useful.

While we agree that television has the potential to teach children, as the above studies sugggest, we fear its use as a babysitter and as a substitute for the warm, loving parent-child interaction that results from human contact. If young children imitate the positive features on the television set, why would they not imitate some of the negative ones as well? For this reason, we believe that parents must be present when a toddler watches television. While our own feelings on the subject would suggest that children under the age of three not be exposed to television at all, since there is more to be gained from play, in this changing society of single-parent or two working parent households, we can understand why the television is on while a parent is busy with household chores after a busy work day. But what we are concerned about is its overuse or abuse based on the results of our work and that of other researchers, especially since data dealing with the relationship between aggression and television indicate that aggressive behavior in children and heavy television viewing of specific kinds of programs (action adventure) are positively correlated.[18]

Children like to imitate the superheroes they see on television. If they do so, elaborating on the themes they have seen, some imaginative play may result. But in many instances, we see children wearing their Superman or Batman capes (usually a towel fastened by a safety pin) simply running around the nursery school or day-care center knocking down other children's block constructions, bumping into still other children, and even hitting some. Teachers begin to scold, remove the capes, and stop the game. This kind of perseverative play and subsequent aggression is usually found among our heavier TV watchers.

It is understandable that children want to play Superman, Batman, Spiderman, Wonder Woman or He-Man. Most of the time they feel small, helpless, and dependent on the adults in their lives. A superhero game affords children power and makes them feel magical and strong. Teachers and parents can accept these feelings and permit the cape-wearing and the transformation into superheroes, but they can also channel the motivation and energy into socially acceptable and imaginative games. A child then gains attention for positive play rather than for acts of aggression.

In Chapter 1, we emphasized the importance of an adult figure in a child's life who encourages make-believe and who even helps a child start a game. The teacher or parent who recognizes that children express particular basic needs through play will accept the character a child chooses to imitate but will help the child move beyond the costume and trappings to develop a make-believe game. As we have reiterated in earlier chapters, children who engage in pretend play smile and laugh more, have longer attention spans and more satisfying peer relationships, and are less aggressive than children who do not know the joy of make-believe play.

The American Academy of Pediatrics and the American Psychological Association have both issued resolutions about the negative effects of television on children's aggressive behavior. We therefore caution parents to be aware of the kinds of programs their children view and the number of hours they spend in front of the television set. Most important of all, we feel that adult mediation, explanation of stories, and discussion of motives and characterizations will help children make sense out of what they watch and adopt a more critical stance toward television programming. Our own studies of family mediation indicate that when parents impose rules for television use and mediate television viewing, they promote "scaffolding": children begin to see the world through the perspective of "the other" and to consider alternate viewpoints and interpretations.[19] If, for example, a child is watching a situation comedy in which a character makes snide remarks or "puts down" another character (reinforced by the laugh track), a parent can explain to the child that in real life, if we behaved like that we would no longer have any friends because we would hurt their feelings, or that we might cause someone to become so angry they would want to hit. Parents can even help a child express concern and empathy for a character on TV who may be treated unfairly by another character in the story. A child begins to understand, then, that television stories and characters are fictional, that television writers exaggerate negative personality traits, and that plots are designed to make us laugh, sometimes at any cost. When adults mediate, children begin to view television more actively and critically. Research by Gavriel Salomon and others suggests that when children expend mental effort, which he calls AIME (amount of invested mental effort), they learn more from television than when they view in a passive way.[20]

Research indicates that the comments of mothers to elementary school children about the content of television programming, moral issues, and historical, geographic, or scientific details, and their statements about aspects of TV that are true-to-life are related to a general family communication style.[21] While this study was carried out with somewhat older children (the average age was eight years) we still believe that mediation can be carried out with preschoolers. Work with younger children suggests that an adult mediator could help children understand the concepts presented on "Mister Rogers' Neighborhood" and gain in imaginative play when compared to children who view the program alone and without such explanation.[22]

Some researchers have made statements we believe to be irresponsible, claiming that the evidence on aggression and cognition (reading, language acquisition, and imagination) is questionable. One researcher has even stated that doing homework in front of the television set may be all right.[23] Without experiments to substantiate this remark, it seems to us that it merely opens the door to further problems for those children who may already be experiencing difficulties in school.

We are not totally opposed to the use of television as a learning device for children, and as Andrew Meltzoff has found, babies as young as fourteen and twenty-four months can imitate a TV model manipulating a novel toy in a particular manner.[24] Influenced by Albert Bandura's social-learning theory. Meltzoff attempted to determine whether or not infants could observe an action on TV on one day and then on a later day direct their behaviors accordingly, a phenomenon, called "deferred imitation." His results indicated that the youngest children were able to imitate the TV actions of a model after a twenty-four hour delay. Babies do look at television, but whether their learning has any long-term effect at so young an age needs further exploration beyond the few studies dealing with the effects of television on infants. And again, we see this early imitation as a double-edged sword. Is it possible that a toddler watching something aggressive on the screen will imitate it in a social situation later on by hitting another toddler?

Television and Attention

Our interest in attention to TV stems from our involvement with imagination and children's ability to incorporate elements of a television story into their existing schema. Julie Duck and her colleagues in Australia researched "Playschool," a program designed for preschoolers, and found that children will consciously and visually attend to switchpoints (the points in time that mark the beginning of every segment and serve as signals for the approaching segment).[25] These switchpoints serve as markers of content chunks. Children may take their eyes off the screen, however, and rely on auditory clues to imitate TV actions such as twisting and twirling. Visual attention enables children to establish a "set," or an understanding, of what transpires in a program, but their auditory attention may be sufficient to enable the child to continue to focus on the content. The belief of these researchers, which is in keeping with the production philosophy of "Playschool," is that children should be able to reflect on a program's content and absorb it by withdrawing their attention from the screen and that they should be able to stop viewing if they so desire. These researchers state that "dragging children's attention back to the screen" by means of "formal features" (activity, camera cuts, auditory changes, intermittent music, special effects) may be counterproductive.[26]

We have long argued that if children's programs are designed to foster imagination, they must follow a philosophy similar to that of "Playschool." Children must be allowed to remove their gaze from the TV screen in order to process the content, repeat the phrases to themselves, and internalize the material. We have found, for example, that children who watched segments from "Mister Rogers' Neighborhood," in which the pacing is slow and moments of silence occur, were more imaginative after only a two-week exposure to the program than they had been prior to such exposure.[27] Many of these children moved away from the set and played with toys but continued to listen to the words as they carried out their play. Sometimes we observed them glancing back at the set, but they did not remain fixated on the screen. This has caused some controversy about their ability to attend to the screen, which refers to the notion of "attentional inertia," meaning the longer a viewer continuously maintains an episode of visual attention, the more likely it becomes that he or she will do so.[28] While some researchers believe that attentional inertia actually reduces distractibility, Morton Mendelsohn found that with infants as young as four or seven months, attentional inertia was not in evidence.[29] Mendelsohn believes that infants perform a series of "looks" to gain meaning rather than the single look that proponents of attentional inertia believe is a meaningful unit of attentional behavior. This finding is similar to what we have observed in our studies of preschoolers. Children look away from the screen, back again, and away again as they actively process and internalize the information presented. Exposure to cartoons, however, seems to depress active processing. The repeated visual and auditory sequences in cartoon programs maintain high levels of visual attention and seem to preclude social exchange and play.[30]

Reading, Radio and Television, and Imagination

We have been asked on numerous occasions when we speak to various groups whether reading, more than television, stimulates imagination. In general, reading is more conducive to the creation of personal images, but as we have pointed out, some carefully thought out television programs for children can inspire imaginative games and play. Reading, however, is a more active process than television viewing. When we read we encode the words from the discrete letters on the printed page. A string of words generates thoughts that turn into images. We can control our reading in many ways: by rereading a sentence, pausing to reflect, pondering a difficult word, stopping to consult a dictionary, flipping back the pages in the book to an earlier section or even peeking ahead if we want to, skipping over sentences we don't enjoy or understand or savoring sentences that have particular beauty or meaning for us. We control the pace when we read. We can go quickly or slowly. We can read with intent or we can skim. We can finish a book and then start all over again—immediately, if we so choose.

In watching television, unless we have a VCR and take the trouble to record the program, the words come too quickly, and we must process images and words simultaneously. As one writer describes it,

> Television, as its critics keep telling us, reduces its contents—dramas, sports events, elections, situation comedies, game shows, the world news—to a cereal of blandness, and the most powerful mechanism in that silent grinding is the medium's forgettery. The show goes on and ends, and then there is another show, and when we reach back and try to hold a picture or a scene or an issue that seemed to seize us, it has already slipped away. "Did you see that—wasn't that *something?*" we say to a friend, but even as we speak we can't quite recall what the something was.[31]

On television there is no instant replay if we miss some conversation. Instant replay is reserved for sports events where we can view a tackle or home run repeatedly and in slow motion. The action on TV is enhanced by lighting, music, cuts, and zoom shots. Special camera effects can distort images, create ripples or dreamlike sequences and slow or fast motion, or "split" the screen so that two or more events appear simultaneously. Editing can make things disappear or go backward, jump up or seem to float. The chroma-key process can give us the illusion that a reporter is in front of a famous landmark when indeed he is still in the studio and the landmark merely a projection on a screen behind him. Yet despite all this camera magic, television can turn us into what some Americans call "Couch Potatoes."

Studies examining the effects of reading, radio, and television on children's imagination seem to differ in their results depending on the methodology used. Two studies, for example, that both compared a "radio" (tape recorder) and a television version of a story differed in their findings. Mark Runco and Kathy Pezdek compared a television and a radio rendition of two folk tales.[32] Children in third and sixth grades (thirty-two in each) were instructed to attend to either the television or radio version and were then presented with a test of creativity requiring them to generate ideas in response to a hypothetical situation that followed each story. Their responses were tape-recorded and then evaluated by two trained coders for fluency (the number of ideas given by the child), flexibility (the number of distinct and different conceptual categories of ideas used by the child), and originality (the number of unique ideas generated by the child compared to the sample as a whole). No differences were found between the effects of the two forms of media in terms of fluency, flexibility, or originality.

In contrast, Patricia Greenfield and Jessica Beagles-Roos followed up some of their earlier work comparing radio and television[33] and found that radio, or audio, "was more powerful as a stimulus to imagination, while material presented in an audiovisual or television format was more memorable."[34] This study, more complex than that of Runco and Pezdek, used 192 middle- and working-class children, black and white, drawn from the first through the fourth grades. All children were exposed to two stories (the same used in the Runco and Pezdek experiment), but half of the children of a particular age, class, and ethnic group saw and heard an animated version of a story that had all white characters and heard an audio version of an African folktale using all black characters. The other half was exposed to an animated television version of the story with black characters and an audio version of the story with white characters. Within the two treatment situations, half of the subjects were exposed to television first and half to radio first, yielding four conditions. At the end of each presentation the experimenter asked each child to tell a story about what she thought would happen next. The two testing sessions were about a week apart. Radio versions led to significantly greater creation of new story material—

imaginative events, specific characters, and imaginative words. Television versions stimulated a significantly greater production of words found in the stimulus story, which the researchers considered to be the opposite of an imaginative response.

What is particularly interesting in the Greenfield and Beagles-Roos study is the impact that radio, as the medium encountered first, had on imagination. Hearing the story first stimulated a response to the television version of the other story in the second interview that was more imaginative than the response to the radio presentation of the second story by the children who saw the televised version of the first story. Details, however, were remembered better from TV than from radio, where the story was presented verbally. As the authors state, "The presence of dynamic visual images seemed to be a detriment to the imagination but a boon to memory." In the audio-visual format children remembered action better; while in the audio version they remembered dialogue better.

The results of this study support our contention that radio allows us to construct our own images, just as we believe reading does. We recall with pleasure our favorite radio programs, which we listened to regularly when we were children. We can still describe in vivid detail Buck Rogers' features, hair coloring, clothing, and physique as he pursued adventures in outer space, although we only heard his voice and never saw pictures of him during our growing-up period. What is fascinating is that each of us envisioned him quite differently when we compared notes years later. In the same manner Jack Armstrong, the Shadow, and the Green Hornet all came to life on radio through words and sound effects. In adulthood these images from childhood remain, despite comic book and movie versions of our radio heroes. We especially appreciated Woody Allen's film, *Radio Days,* because of our identification with various family members and their involvement with radio. We, too, remember saving our pennies and boxtops in order to send for secret rings, emblems, and other trinkets that denoted participation in the imaginary world of our radio friends' lives.

When results favor television, or find no differences between radio and television, it may be that in terms of information alone the television version of a story, which uses both an auditory and a visual presentation, reinforces facts so that they can be remembered but does very little to help generate ideas that transcend the material presented. A study by Jessica Beagles-Roos and Isabelle Gat, for example, indicates that a radio story elevated the use of knowledge unrelated to the story in children's inferences.[35] The radio presentation induced children to go beyond the explicit and implicit story content, facilitated the recognition of expressive language in forced choice questions, and stimulated the use of verbal content. In contrast, television stimulated the use of action and an awareness of the number of vaguely defined characters used to tell a story. Similarly, children and adults exposed to a radio and TV story with identical soundtracks demonstrated better recall of expressive and figurative language, dialogue, and sound effects after the radio version.[36]

Although television can be helpful to children in fostering visual skills, it is less helpful in developing imagination. Laurene Meringoff and colleagues found that children exposed to radio, television, and picture book presentations and asked to draw pictures later produced more imaginative drawings after the radio version; in terms of quality, however, the drawings after the television presentation included more details, and these were portrayed from unusual perspectives.[37] This reinforces Greenfield and Beagles-Roos's findings that children remembered details better from a visual presentation and suggests that each medium has its own advantages and disadvantages.[38]

Certainly, adapting a story to film or TV causes some problems. Much of the dialogue may be changed, and the characters' inner thoughts and feelings may not always be conveyed as the author intended. As Ray Bradbury remarked after the film version of *Fahrenheit 451* appeared, "I have heard those cries in the past of outraged authors whose books have just been gang-raped by a studio."[39] Unlike these authors Bradbury himself truly believed that the director, François Truffaut, had "captured the soul and essence" of his book and was "careful and subtle in his shadings and motions."

But much of television is neither careful nor subtle, and generally, language plays a role secondary to action. Despite the common belief that television "teaches" vocabulary because of all the words programs use, we have found that children who are heavy viewers of television have less well-developed language than light viewers. As we have pointed out, lighter television viewers used more adjectives, more adverbs, and more complex sentences than heavier viewers.[40] John Murray and Kathy Krendl found similar results in a study they carried out in a small Michigan community.[41] Younger children in grades one and three who were light TV viewers produced longer stories than heavier viewers of the same ages when they were asked to tell a story based on a television program they had recently seen. Older children who were heavy viewers produced longer stories as well. It may be that the younger children (who watched less television) were using non-television time to play more and gained vocabulary through social interaction, a finding we have reported,[42] while older children are simply better at retaining television plots. It appears that learning from television in the early years may not be as efficient as later on, when comprehension improves. Heavy viewing in early childhood is more detrimental to the learning process, and before the age of seven children have less ability to process either the conventions of television or its vocabulary and complex story lines. Children need to use a word in a sentence in order to understand its meaning. They need to repeat the new word and have it explained to them, or it is meaningless. With the fast pacing of American television programs, it is rare, if ever, that someone on television stops to explain an unfamiliar word. This occurs only on the public television channels in instructional programs designed for that purpose.

There are some who argue that television is a return to an oral culture and lower levels of thought[43] while others believe that television offers more stimuli than books because of its iconic and linguistic codes. Still others suggest that once we learn television's forms it is possible that we will recognize that it demands comprehension and discover that watching this medium is similar to listening to plays, lectures, or stories.[44] The data we have presented above seem to disagree with this last premise, however, and when we examine the effects of television on reading and creativity we see that some harmful results occur.

In a village located in a valley in Canada, a kind of geographic blind spot, the available television transmitter did not provide adequate reception for most residents.[45] This town, called "Notel" by the researchers, was the focus of a study before and after the installation of an improved transmitter and is therefore a particularly useful source of data on what the effects of the "big ghost" are. A few homes in Notel did have reception, but it was poor and according to the researchers, most people were unable to watch television in their homes on a regular basis. Although some residents did watch TV on occasion at home or when they visited friends in other communities where TV was available, 76 percent of the children in this town watched no TV at all during the first phase of this study.

Before the children in Notel had access to regular TV-viewing, their creativity and reading scores were obtained and these were then compared to their scores at regular intervals after the improved TV reception was available to all families. In addition, before the advent of television, the Notel children had higher creativity scores than those of children in the two towns with TV that were used for comparison in the study. After television was introduced to Notel, the children's creativity scores dropped and were similar to those of the children in the comparison towns who had grown up with TV.

The Notel children had been better readers initially than the same age children who had grown up with TV, but on tests after two years and then again after four years of television exposure, Notel children read no better than the same age children in the other two towns who had more TV-viewing years. The researchers suggest that reading development may be hindered by the availability and attraction of the television. Results of creativity and reading tests may reflect the fact that television watching requires little or no mental elaboration. It may instead supplant the time needed for reading practice, and in terms of creativity, it may also displace activities and experiences that are conducive to problem-solving. The fast pace of television programs and their entertainment function may interfere with the process of reflection needed for reading comprehension and creative thinking.

A study of the reading achievement of junior high school students in El Salvador found results similar to those in the Canadian project. When television was introduced in one town, acquiring a TV set was associated with slowed development in reading achievement as measured by group tests administered in the schools.[46] Japan, England, and Norway all reported a drop in the number of books children read when television was introduced into various communities.[47]

Many correlational studies have been done on the relationship between television and reading; some have found positive relationships and some negative. One study, for example, reports a positive relationship between TV and reading for viewing time of up to ten hours a week, when the relationship becomes negative.[48] This relationship is stronger for high IQ children and especially so for girls. In our work, we have found that there is a positive relationship between TV viewing and reading among children of lower classes, but only if parents are involved with their children and are self-described as curious and imaginative.[49] It may be that these parents actively mediated while their children watched TV. Children whose parents were less imaginative and curious did not show the same reading results if they were heavy TV viewers. Parental interaction with children during TV-viewing hours (and its effect on gains in children's cognitive functioning) is extremely important, as was shown in earlier studies of "Sesame Street."[50] When parents encouraged children to watch "Sesame Street" and commented on the content, children learned numbers and letters more easily than when children viewed alone or without such commentary.

Television-viewing may reduce a child's interest in reading, since it is easier to process a television story. It is possible that parents who do not themselves emphasize reading as a pastime, and who are themselves heavy TV viewers, set the scene for their children to follow this pattern. Thus, parents serve as role models for their children, who then adopt a more negative attitude toward reading. Studies have found that parents who have a high interest in reading have low TV-viewing levels, and they may communicate these values to their children.[51]

There is some evidence that television reduces children's perseverance in a task and increases restlessness. We have found, for example, that children who are heavy TV viewers are less able to sit still in a waiting-room situation and are described as more restless by their parents.[52] Another study suggests that during early reading acquisition, those children who do less well in task perseverance may have more difficulty in later reading achievement.[53]

As part of a large longitudinal study that we began in 1976 and carried over until 1982, we were interested in the cumulative effects of television-viewing on children's later reading acquisition skills.[54] We had complete data on a subsample of eighty-four children. By studying preschoolers before they began to read and following them until they began to read, we were able to look at both causal and correlational data. We had information on television-viewing, family life patterns, and cognitive and behavioral functions that had been gathered since their preschool years. We identified the children, matched for intelligence, socioeconomic status, and sex, who could be separated into two groups according to the amount of TV they viewed at age four. These children were then studied at ages seven and eight through a series of psychological tests and situations designed to ascertain their reading abilities, attention capacity, delaying ability, imaginativeness, and behavioral tendencies. We were thus able to determine the extent to which earlier patterns of TV viewing might relate to current differences between the groups and also to examine contemporary correlations of TV viewing and cognition, imagination, and behavior.

With light TV-viewing, the average reading score of a middle-class child significantly exceeded the average score of a lower-class child as measured by standardized reading tests. With heavy TV-viewing, the difference between the two groups disappeared. The scores of the middle-class children dropped and those of the lower-class children improved. Our data showed that the effect of TV exposure interacted with the child's socioeconomic indices. Thus, for middle-class children, the mean reading scores were significantly lower for heavy than for light viewers, while for the lower-class sample, the trend was in the opposite direction—the scores were slightly higher for heavy than for light viewers. This interaction was significant on tests of both reading recognition and reading comprehension. Under the influence of heavy TV exposure, any edge that middle-class children had over lower-class children was lost. This finding provides direct support for George Gerbner's "main-streaming hypothesis," which suggests that television has a leveling effect; it tends to remove differences due to the advantages of either nature or nurture.

The results of a study we carried out with about two hundred middle-class children in a New England town in grades three, four, and five indicated that they were watching about fifteen hours of television a week, atypical compared to the national norm of twenty to thirty hours for these ages.[55] The children's IQ and reading scores were recorded, and here, too, we found that their IQs and reading levels were somewhat higher than national norms. We did find differences, however, between light and heavy television viewers in terms of preferences for particular programs and interest in reading. Children with higher IQs in the study spent more time reading, watched fewer fantasy programs, and had limits imposed on their TV viewing time by their parents. When IQ and grade level were taken into account, the children who read more books tended to watch fewer game shows and variety programs. Children who were heavier viewers tended to have younger fathers who watched more television. The children's interest in television reflected their parents' viewing habits.

If the data from various studies do report depressed reading levels as a result of heavy television watching, we might ask what accounts for this effect. It is possible that the time needed for mastering the skills critical to reading is displaced by the TV set, and it is also possible that television simply reduces interest in reading. As Gavriel Salomon also suggests, children may perceive television as easier than reading: less AIME (amount of mental effort) is expended in front of the screen.[56] It may also be that the skills needed in processing television program content are different from those needed in encoding a text. Television requires both audio and visual input. Quite possibly, this combination of modalities may be an impediment to reading, where only the visual sense is needed and where an early reader must either vocally or silently decode the text. Children accustomed to heavy television viewing process both the auditory and the visual cues afforded by that medium simultaneously and may become lax in generating their own images when reading.[57] More research needs to be carried out in this area to determine the validity of this last hypothesis.

Television and Fantasy

Some researchers believe that people actually seek out television programs that are suspenseful or frightening in order to master their own fears or to gain vicarious satisfaction.[58] George Gerbner and Larry Gross take an opposite point of view. They have data to suggest that heavy viewers of television actually become more anxious and view the world as a more frightening place as a result of their viewing.[59] Curious about children's fantasy life and its relationship to television, Robert McIlwraith and John Schallow tested eighty-two first-grade children using a fantasy life measure, the Imaginal Processes Inventory for Children.[60] The children also answered a Television Identification Measure, which consisted of photographs of characters and scenes from network programs, and a Peabody Vocabulary Test to obtain a measure of intelligence. Children who were heavy television viewers reported more anxious, hostile, and generally unpleasant fantasies. Although in this study, pleasant, imaginative fantasy was not hindered by TV and appeared to be independent of TV-viewing, the authors were concerned that there was a correlation between aggressive and anxious fantasies and the use of TV. They suggest that research should focus on whatever promotes adaptive fantasy and less on TV as a threat to fantasy development.

The issue of a reality versus a fantasy understanding of television stories is a crucial one and has been covered in a chapter in the NIMH report.[61] Since that report, research has continued in this area but not to the extent the issue merits. Among the heavy viewers in their study of elementary-school-age children, Murray and Krendl found that the fifth graders who watched a good deal of television (an average amount of 25.5 hours a week) were more likely to believe that characters and actions in television programs were "real" than lighter viewers, who disavowed the reality of television.[62] Children who were lower in fantasy predisposition also preferred more action-adventure programs and turned to television when they were lonely, while children who watched fewer action-adventure shows were more likely to turn to books or friends when lonely. We reported similar results in the study of third-, fourth-, and fifth-grade children mentioned earlier; higher IQ children spent more time reading and watched fewer violent fantasy programs.[63] In a previous study, we found that children in third, fourth, and fifth grades had difficulty with the notion of "realistic" TV characters such as Fonz ("Happy Days") and Mary Richards ("The Mary Tyler Moore Show") and confused the actors' real names with those of the characters they portrayed.[64] Although by the age of seven, a child begins to think more logically and moves into the stage of concrete operations, it is surprising to find that children even older than seven have difficulty differentiating between reality and fantasy on television and in understanding the camera effects that enhance the illusion on the screen.

Television Curricula

Because research indicates that children are confused by camera effects and have difficulty comprehending many plots, even embellishing stories with characters that do not appear in the plot,[65] we designed a curriculum to teach elementary school children about television.[66] A segment of the curriculum deals with camera techniques, the process of animation, and the special effects used to create fantasy on television. Results indicate that elementary school children who were taught how to become critical viewers performed significantly better on specific measures than control groups. We feel that it is important to educate children about television and its formal conventions. Other curricula have been developed with similar goals, all based on the belief that in-school intervention is necessary to help children interpret and use television more wisely. Because there is so little parental mediation in television viewing, TV curricula may actually be effective against the persuasive and dominating force of the medium.[67] In-school intervention using television can teach children to read, provide serious discussion about program content, enhance critical thinking skills, present information about the production techniques of a program, induce skepticism about advertising and entertainment messages that use stereotypes or values that a family may deem unacceptable, and influence what children do with the information they get from television.[68]

Even adults may not understand how television, through clever editing, can present information that may not be totally accurate. A cameraperson focusing on one aspect of a situation, for example, an angry group of citizens shouting and pushing during a town meeting or a demonstration, may omit from the camera's eye, intentionally or by chance, the majority of the people, who are calm and orderly while seated in the room or standing in the street. A lively, more inflammatory scene simply makes better television and captures the attention of the home viewer.

The very nature of the quick cuts and changes of scene that characterize American television may lead to confusion and misunderstanding in adults as well as in children. We remember quite vividly the "kickoff" three-hour film designed to introduce a new television series, "Battlestar Gallactica." The show began with an apparently American president being captured in the White House by dark-colored alien robots. After some further adventures in which the defeated Americans prepared to escape into outer space, the program was interrupted and the symbol of the American presidency flashed on the screen. President Jimmy Carter, flanked by Prime Minister Menachem Begin of Israel and President Anwar Sadat of Egypt, proceeded to announce the Camp David accords. How could this not confuse the mind of a young child trying to make sense out of this sequence of events? Who was the real president? What happened to the robots? In actuality, a number of local ABC stations received calls from adult viewers complaining about the interruption of the program by this live newscast of a major international event.[69] Could it be that they were annoyed by the reality invading their fantasy? Or were they as confused as the children?

In addition to curricula prepared by various groups to teach children how television works[70] there have been programs designed to teach college students and teachers about the impact of television in our lives.[71] One graduate course, for example, focusing on television literacy, succeeded in giving teachers a keener awareness of their own viewing habits and reactions to TV. They learned how the industry works, both economically and technically, and then looked at some methods for developing critical viewing skills in their students and building an educational bridge between students' television experience and the school curriculum.[72]

Television and the Future

If by the time they are eighteen years old, American children will have spent more time in front of the television set than in any other activity except sleep, it behooves us to gain control of this electronic member of the family. We join with others who have suggested that parental mediation and control can make a difference.[73]

In a study of sixty-six kindergartners and first graders, whom we saw at home and at the Family Television Research and Consultation Center over a two-year period, we found that a combination of several family communication and discipline variables and parental mediation in the first year of the study were positively related to a child's reading recognition, ability to discriminate between fantasy and reality on TV, and comprehension of TV plots in the second year of the study.[74] As the children advanced into the early primary grades they developed more sophisticated linguistic and intellectual skills that enabled them to make better use of their parents' explanations. Children were better able to follow their parents' cause-and-effect answers to "why?" questions, and they showed increased attention spans and greater facility in asking questions. They were more empathic at this age than they had been earlier, and could appreciate another person's point of view. One other facet of the mediation process is worth noting. Parents who filter and explain television programs create an atmosphere conducive to curiosity, and children are rewarded in their efforts to make sense out of the confusing television world. It is important to begin this process early, even though children may not fully grasp an adult's explanations. The earlier the mediation, the more children will adopt an active stance as they watch the TV set.

We have also suggested that curricula developed by educators and introduced to the schools can help children become more active and more critical television viewers. We strongly believe that the commercial networks and cable companies must begin to offer programs geared to various age groups and guided by developmental theory. Organizations such as Action for Children's Television (ACT), the Children's Advertising Review Unit of the Council of Better Business Bureaus, the Media Action Research Center, and the National Coalition on Television Violence have all been strong advocates for children in regard to advertising and programming. And we must not overlook the alternatives to television—books, toys, games, cultural activities, and conversations—that we can offer our children. We can also encourage quiet moments for daydreaming.

A final word: We dread the proliferation of the new "interactive toys" that allow children to use hand-held weapons to "shoot" the villains on the television screen. We would prefer to see interactive toys that would be more conducive to encouraging a child's budding imagination. The technology is there to create such interactive games, but the marketplace is filled with TV games that promote weapons rather than more wholesome fare. Pamela Tuchscherer calls the new high technology a threat to children, and we agree with her eloquent statement that "violent entertainment is being pushed to its technological limits and is directly interacting with young viewers through their toys. How our children perceive the world and how they respond depends on us. Childhood is short and irreplaceable. Let us not relinquish this time to the unconcerned and insensitive but rather use it to nurture a joy for discovery and knowledge and empathy for others. For in childhood is the essence of humankind."[75]

9

Play as Healing

The close association of play and myth suggests that play therapy can also be conceived as a process of providing children with
new myths that more directly and successfully address the
sources of fear and dread in their lives and offer new hope . . . If
we view humans as fundamentally myth making creatures . . .
play becomes a more centrally important function in human life.
Not only is play a manifestation of myth, it is also, in children,
the overt expression of wish and hope, and play therapy is a
method for utilizing these attributes of play in a healing context.

—Brian Vandenberg, "Play, Myth and Hope"

So far, we have emphasized imaginative play as a natural feature of
the child's cognitive and emotional growth rather than the more
clinical view of it as a coping strategy, defense, or escape from anxiety and conflict. Yet the self-healing properties of pretend play need
not be minimized, even within our broader perspective of normal
growth. We will begin our exploration of some of the ways in which
pretending provides children with opportunities for expressing their
puzzlement, psychic bruising, and terror by examining two
examples—one drawn from the spontaneous play of a child after a
specific traumatic event and the other from the clinical play therapy
of a distressed child.

When Toby, our neighbors' pet retriever, developed a stomach
tumor and suffered severe pain, they decided to bring Toby to the
local veterinarian and have him put to sleep humanely. But the
young parents were faced with a dilemma: what to tell Michael,
their three-year-old. They finally told him that Toby was very sick
and that it was necessary to go to the vet, the "dog doctor," who
would try to do what he could to help, but that Toby might die.
Michael asked no further questions. Toby did not come back. One
afternoon shortly afterward, Michael began to play with his large
cardboard blocks, and his "house" evolved into a "dog house." He
then transformed his mother into "the doggy" and led her on all
fours into the dog house. At first he was rather gentle, feeding her

a bone, scratching her ear. Then he scolded his dog—"bad doggy," "bad doggy"—and "locked" her in. "You can't come out! Stay there!" Finally, he made up with the "doggy," gave her a bone, and let her out of the house. He then pretended he was driving to the vet, and told the doggy to follow him. When they arrived at the vet's house, the game was over. Michael forgot about his mother and moved on to other activities. Through play Michael was able to express his feelings about Toby's loss: first love, then anger that Toby was ill and had left him, then love again. Finally, there was a resolution, or trip to the vet. Michael has no real comprehension of death, but his parents' reassurance that they did everything to help Toby and to relieve her pain was comforting to him. Through his play, he demonstrated his concern, his anger at both his mother and Toby, and then his acceptance.

The next example is drawn from the play of a disturbed child. Mark's parents divorced after many months of quarreling, which had resulted in some ugly scenes in front of the child, a bright but socially isolated six-year-old. His world was falling apart. Weekly visitation rights were assigned to the father, with monthly sleepovers, but many of these weekly visits were canceled because the father's occupation required considerable traveling. Mark's reaction to the divorce and the frequent cancellation of time with his father necessarily led to disappointment, frustration, and anger. His behavior in school became intolerable: he hit other children, threw a chair at a teacher, and bit another child. He also had difficulty paying attention and concentrating.

In play therapy, Mark acted out many of his conflicts through games of "Superhero." At these times he was in control of everyone around him, bullying, commanding, and always winning whatever battle he staged. One particular incident early in his therapy demonstrated his acute reaction to the divorce. Hurricane Gilbert had recently struck the South and was often shown on television. Mark pretended that Hurricane Gilbert was approaching the large dollhouse in the playroom. He knocked down furniture and toy people and threw objects out the windows. He then took his "doctor kit," made believe it was a repair box, and put everything to rights. He played this game over and over in several sessions. Each time, rampant destruction of the house was followed by repair. One cannot avoid the belief that the cycle represented Mark's attempt to try to bring his parents together through his repetitive play. This effort seemed to reflect a self-healing process. As he began to accept the divorce, and as the therapy began to help him understand that he could still have both his parents' love, albeit in two separate houses, Mark gradually stopped playing at the destruction of the house. He began more and more to use the miniature dolls in a more tender manner with games involving caretaking, nurturance, and having fun together. This change in his play therapy was also reflected soon afterward in improvement in his school behavior and in some coming to terms with each of his parents and the new life-style of week-end visits to his father.

The Troubles of Early Childhood

If, with Brian Vandenberg, we are to propose that imaginative play can serve a useful function in the child's self-healing and adaptation or, as in the case of play therapy, in clinical intervention to ameliorate a child's distress or maladjustment, we need first to consider what can go wrong.[1] Sigmund Freud is usually credited with puncturing the mythic balloon of an innocent and joyful childhood sustained in nineteenth-century Victorian belief. He did so first by calling attention to the origins of neuroses in adults, which were occasioned by the sexual seductions they had experienced as children. When he came upon evidence that suggested that some of his patients' "memories" of such incidents might not be accurate, he was deeply troubled but eventually "saved" his theory of the sexual origin of neuroses by proposing that all children progress through a series of psychosexual stages. Memories of seduction may often be reflections of children's own wishful or fearful fantasies. Those first five or six years of a child's life, Freud suggested, are not all sweetness; children are sensually aroused and develop conflicts around their oral desires, their pleasure in anal and phallic excretion, and their attraction to opposite-sex parents along with their fear of punishment from their parental "rivals."

We need not concern ourselves here with the controversy about why Freud modified his earlier theory, whether he went too far in emphasizing childhood sexual fantasy and thus encouraged his followers to neglect the actuality of childhood seductions by adults, or even whether there is currently any merit to his ordering of human development according to oral, anal, phallic, and genital (Oedipal) psychosexual stages.[2] Whatever the ultimate fate of his classical psychoanalytic theory, Freud opened the way for child researchers to take a much closer look at the real problems and potential sources of conflict, confusion, and troublesome fantasies that bestrew the path of the emergent personality. It is much clearer to us today that growing up involves a complex and subtle interaction between the genetic temperamental variations children start out with, the expectations of their parents, the influence of parents' behaviors on the children, and, as Eleanor Maccoby has shown, the influence of the children's temperaments, cognitive skills, and socially determined reactions on the parents.[3]

Our greater awareness today that some children are born shy, others hyperactive, some more sociable or emotional, some more prone to activity and exploration need not preclude the important role of the family milieu in providing the child with coping strategies as well as dilemmas, fears, and experiences of helplessness or mistrust.[4] We are not prepared to give up some sense that children are indeed innocent seekers after structure and meaning in a complicated world. Often enough, it is our unrealistic adult expectations, our projections of our conflicts with family members onto them, our own fears of illness and death, our frustrations at work, and our yearnings for love that make children's tasks—reducing ambiguity, establishing autonomy, and feeling a sense of communion—so difficult. Older children may carry a terrified toddler into the bathroom and threaten to flush the child down the toilet several times before persistent screams finally arouse an adult reaction: "Cut it out!" or "Stop the teasing." Adult "playfulness," such as an uncle's pretending to pull off a child's nose and then displaying it as a thumb held between his fingers, may soon be forgotten by the adult but may persist for the child as a frightening puzzle for days. Indeed, a chance encounter with someone who has a flattened nose may reinvoke a chill of terror in the child weeks later.[5]

What we are suggesting is that the accommodation-assimilation cycle Piaget proposed as the way in which children progress in comprehending their milieu is often far more complex than just determining whether chairs stay the same when overturned, whether numbers of objects are conserved even in different positions, or whether clouds are alive. Children must find ways of assimilating into their limited range of schemas complex social interactions, including not only malevolent acts of sibling rivalry but even the insensitive, if "well-meaning," actions of adults like the uncle above or of parents or caregivers who tell ghost stories or let the children watch horror films on television. Playing with a few dolls or soft toys, creating a miniaturized setting, taking a bus trip or paying a visit to Grandma's house may allow the child to assimilate recently experienced ambiguity and incongruity into some new kind of organized structure over which the child feels some control. The "fun" of children's play (as we suggested in Chapter 2) may be a consequence of the gradual reduction of a high level of ambiguity or extreme novelty in a stimulus complex to a manageable cognitive structure the child can manipulate and over which, in contrast with the "real" adult world, he or she can experience some power.

For play to serve its function of helping the child to reduce incongruity requires at least two critical steps. The child must, first of all, be prepared to play imaginatively. While all children show initial tendencies in this direction, some forms of support from adults and older peers and a setting conducive to play are necessary. Although we as yet have no evidence of a genetic factor or of constitutional variations in the predisposition to make-believe play, the role of adults in initiating, supporting, or encouraging pretend play seems clear enough from the research.

What then of the child who has not received such assistance from caregivers? Eleanor Pavenstedt's careful case studies of children from multiproblem families call attention to the effect of parental or older peer interference when early school-age children do initiate pretend play. Pavenstedt and her collaborators describe a boy who, returning from school with a crude wooden plane he has constructed, holds it up and pretends to fly it. His father laughs in mockery, "Oh yeah, big deal. What a piece of junk!" In a few minutes the older siblings have torn the airplane apart while the boy stands by in silence. Is it any wonder that school observations characterize such children as apathetic, disorganized, and lacking in themes for play and the ability to sustain a game?[6]

A second factor in providing a basis for the role of play in assimilation or new schema formation has to do with the richness and complexity of prior schemas. To what schemas can a child subjected to the sudden death of a grandparent or to gross humiliation assimilate these unanticipated experiences? Some preparatory framework must be available, whether in the form of a religious structure (if the child is old enough) or some type of myth or legend to which the new experience can be linked. A preschool child observing the family grieving over the death of a sibling was informed that the angels had come to take her away. After that, the boy suffered from night terror, constantly on the lookout for angels who might be on the prowl for him. "Angels don't have headlights, do they?" he asked a counselor, reflecting his attempt to reconcile the difficult notion of angels with the more familiar schema that drivers turn on their headlights to see in the dark.[7]

One of the critical responsibilities of adult caregivers must therefore be to help children in the development of a sufficiently wide-ranging and differentiated set of schemas. Ordinarily, they do this by explaining, providing labels, and in general, organizing the complexity of the environment into manageable chunks. "See, that's a doggy. He's wagging his tail because he's happy when you pat him." Brief stories about real or make-believe events intrigue the child, foster imaginative play (as Diana Shmukler's work has shown),[8] and assist children in their own increasing formation of schemas, which, when matched with previously formed schemas, can reduce the fear or confusion engendered by the novelty and incongruity of the surrounding world. For the child it often makes little difference whether the schemas are mirrors of "reality" or whether they are legends, myths, or fairy tales. Indeed, one might as well point out that myths of an afterlife or of religious salvation provide us as adults with fairly effective schemas into which we can assimilate unanticipated bereavements, natural disasters, or sudden illnesses.

But what of those children whose parents or caregivers have not provided them with very many kinds of organized mental representations into which they can integrate new experiences? We have conducted studies of parental communication patterns using examples of how adults deal with children in different situations. These patterns vary along a continuum we label at one pole as Prescriptive Peremptory Talk and at the other as Discussion-Mediation. The communication of parents whose scores fall at the Prescriptive end of the scale is characterized chiefly by remarks like, "Stop that! Do this! You're being a pest again!" In contrast, parents whose behavior is more frequently scored at the Discussion end of the scale are likely to be labeling events for the child, telling stories about situations, describing events before they occur, or clarifying what happened after an experience is over. They are also likely to be explaining or talking about situations on television.[8] Children whose parents fall at the Prescriptive end of the scale may well be less likely to form a sufficient array of schemas, and what are called "event-scripts," to which they can relate unexpected new events—the sudden serious illness of a sibling, grandparent, or pet—and must suffer continuing confusion or fear over a longer period. Play can help only to the extent that some prior scripts are already available. As we shall see, the art of the play therapist involves providing miniaturized materials (toy dolls, toy parents) and suggesting possible scripts.

One of us was treating a four-year-old who had been sexually abused by an adolescent cousin over a period of time. Because the parents had discovered the situation and a family furor had erupted, the child knew that something very strange and obviously distressing to adults had happened that related to his and his cousin's lower bodies, but he did not understand what it was. Since he seemed to have little predisposition to imaginative play, he was gradually introduced to such activity through the provision of toys and a few relatively neutral plots. Once launched in play he was encouraged to nurture and wash a standard doll, and he engaged in this game with obvious pleasure for several sessions. An anatomically correct boy doll was then introduced, and the child undressed it for its bath. On seeing the penis, he jumped back, covered his genital region with his hands and shouted, "I don't have a pee pee!" When asked where it was, he answered "My daddy has it." After play had progressed over a few more weeks, and he continued to nurture and bathe the new boy doll, the child was able to assert quite spontaneously, "I *have* a pee pee. But no one can touch it except me or my Mommy and my Daddy."

Apart from the ravages of physical neglect, the pain of beating, or other gross corporeal insults to the child, much of the distress in early childhood results from inexplicable, unexpected events: the sudden withdrawal of a loved person or the sudden withdrawal of love, confusion over conflicts between parents, or terror aroused by witnessing one's parents or other close adults engaging in childlike behavior when drunk, psychotic, or severely physically ill. Some play-experienced children may find that they can gradually assimilate such events through pretend games, especially when they have already heard fairy tales about bewitched parents or princesses, biblical tales of how characters like Joseph have overcome adversity, or even family accounts of how parents or grandparents have dealt with dangers. For those children who have not been much exposed to make-believe play or who have not had the opportunity to develop organized mental representations about a range of possibilities through adult story-telling, the continuing high level of negative emotions, such as anger, sadness, or shame occasioned by incongruous experiences must be as painful as physical starvation.

Such children may desperately imitate the aggression they have witnessed at home and become even more mired in difficulty at school. They may seek to change their mood through impulsive flight, drug use, food indulgence, or other conduct that can only heighten their distress, the distrust of others, and the sense of helplessness that is the precursor to depression.[9]

An early but still quite clinically relevant series of case studies by the child psychiatrist Joan Fineman contrasted two groups of children, those whose spontaneous play involved a great deal of pretend and those whose play showed very little. Over a year's time the children in the latter group showed no appreciable change, even as they moved into other developmental stages. The more imaginative children, however, continued to engage in pretend play and were able to use it to get through conflicts and external traumatic events. As Fineman writes, "It should be added here that . . . these children are capable of relinquishing [pretend play] when they are called upon to do so, and begin to be able to define the boundaries between imaginary play and the often contradictory elements of external reality. In these children the intrusion of the real world into the imaginary one seems fraught with less conflict and there is less recourse to regressive attempts aimed at maintaining a fantasy world which would jeopardize the eventual acceptance of the reality principle."[10] In contrast, the children who showed little imaginative play continued to remain on a more infantile level, constantly seeking maternal attention and need gratification through demands for food or other direct physical satisfactions.

Naturally Occurring Play as Self-Healing

We began this chapter with the example of Michael, a normal preschooler who used pretend play in an effort to come to some kind of resolution about the disappearance of his dog, Toby. In this instance, the boy initiated play, and his mother, sensitive to the issue, went along with the game without trying to guide, direct, or interpret as a play therapist might have done in a clinical situation. Our own direct observations of children in nursery schools have provided us with many instances in which the theme of a make-believe game initiated by a child who has experienced some family trauma or who is in the throes of sibling rivalry engages the interest of others, so that a kind of psychodrama evolves. Even when the other participants do not share the same initial problem or conflict, the nature of pretend play seems to draw children to take on roles, to make suggestions, and, even when stepping briefly out of the play frame, to label objects or characters in ways that sustain the game. In effect, as the various close observational studies of Corsaro and Tomlinson, Giffin, King, and Gould have indicated, the shared make-believe frame creates new schemas that reflect not only the specific personal conflicts of the child-initiator but the more general issues of dependency, loss, and fear of the unknown that all the children share.[11] The year-long research of Helen Schwartzman in a Chicago nursery school demonstrates how children's play not only reflects the individual themes they bring to school but also some of the hierarchical structure and power issues that have evolved in the peer group and between children and teachers over time.[12]

An example provided by Rosalind Gould from her collection of nursery school transcriptions indicates how in the course of a make-believe game children create new schemas that can then encapsulate psychodynamic concerns about loss, aggression, and orality while also reflecting issues of in-group/out-group structure or power. The children are four-year-olds.

Laura and *Aries* (taking a board as a broom and starting to hop around): We're pretending we're witches and it's Halloween night.
Seth: Can I play?
Aries: You can be an assistant witch.
David: If I can't be the grandfather witch, I won't be your friend.
Aries: No you can't!
David (crying): I'm not your friend. I hate you!
Aries (softly): I was just asking Laura.
Laura: You can be a ghost, or a goblin or a witch.
David (very serious, up close to Laura): Well, what do witches do again? I'm not sure.
Laura and *Aries* (making faces of amused superiority): They take children and turn them into gingerbread.
David (nodding): Oh yeah. They put a "spell" on them.
Laura (serious): What's a spell.
David: They cut them up and put them in jail.
David (under shed): Well, I tell you, we have lots of supper tonight. I put people in the oven.
(David, Aries, Laura, and Seth sit down.)
David (handing out): One for you, one for you, one for you. (All pretend to eat. Suddenly David lets out): Oh! Oh! We have only three people!
Seth, Laura and *Aries* (all starting to count each other): One, two, three, four. Four. Four!
David: No, I mean only three people in the oven to eat.

Aries: I'm eating Celeste.
David, Seth, Laura: I'm eating Celeste's head, I'm eating Rondi's, George's
    arm. (Eating motions.)
(They jump up, jump on their "brooms" and go for George, Celeste and
    Ronnie.)[13]

In this instance, David, while not the initiator, seems especially
caught up in the game; he has found a framework for expressing
some of his special concerns about his grandfather, the mysteries of
disappearance, his fears (not uncommon to preschoolers) that children *can* be eaten up, and his eagerness to find a sense of communion with the other children. The game also reflects an in-group/
out-group issue in the school. Here the pretend play did not work
completely because the anger aroused about the out-group of George,
Celeste, and Ronnie provoked the "witches" to charge toward them.
The teacher, presumably unaware of the nature of the game, broke
up the sequence. She might under other circumstances have steered
the children into incorporating the out-group into a further variation of "Hansel and Gretel" with a more constructive and adaptive
outcome, thus providing the children with new schemas about play
and conflict resolution. As we shall see in some of the more verbal
make-believe interactions that characterize play therapy, especially
with older children, a key feature in helping children to use pretending as a means of ameliorating distress is the therapist's assistance in reformulating their story lines. By this means, new and
presumably more socially adaptive schemas can provide alternatives to children's unsuccessful efforts at assimilating the distresses
of family experience.

Another way of characterizing imaginative play in the normal
growth process has been suggested by the Swiss anthropologist and
educator Heinz Herzka:

Play also connects imaginative conciousness and fantasy with material reality. A child is given the opportunity to actualize impulses
from his imaginative consciousness and fantasy and, in the process, to
experience what the possibilities and limits of reality are and, vice-
versa, that is, real experiences become the stimulants for his imaginative consciousness. The dialogical union of both forms of consciousness
prevents imaginative consciousness from being severed from reality.
Such a severance can be seen in the condition of drug states or in
psychosis. The neglect of imaginative consciousness in our upbringing
and education is presumably also one reason why so many youths and

adults turn to drugs, that is, in order to once again have access to their own imaginative consciousness.[14]*

Herzka goes on to describe how play reflects the poles of autonomy and of solidarity (interpersonal affiliation), since much play involves not only private fantasy but also a sense of relatedness with the other players (see Chapter 2 for our own views on this). Play involves a series of polarities: "doing *and* experiencing, the physical *and* the psychic/spiritual, individuality *and* community, time *and* space . . . These contradictions and inner or social conflicts are not to be resolved. Rather, they are characteristics . . . of the vitality of human life itself. In play, a child has the chance to practice living with these contradictions and tensions, to endure them and to hold them within boundaries which are bearable for his own self and for his social surroundings."[16]

A special opportunity for somewhat older children to use play in the ways Herzka has described is exemplified by a program for inner-city early elementary school children at the Martin Luther King, Jr., School in New Haven. Marjorie Janis set up a special environment, the Discovery Room, consisting of attractive but inexpensive toys, props, and construction materials, where individual children could come at certain times during the school day. The opportunity for children to try out a variety of fantasy games and to learn how to play following judicious hints from a teacher proved to be a very useful addition to the general effectiveness of the experimental educational program conducted at the school.

Examples of how exposure to opportunities for imaginative play may be beneficial are especially poignant in instances where children are chronically ill, retarded, or institutionalized because of parental difficulties. Melissa Johnson, J. Kenneth Whitt, and Barclay Martin of the University of North Carolina carried out a careful experiment with twenty-six chronically ill and twenty-six healthy children between the ages of five and nine. The children from each category were randomly assigned to either an imaginative play/fantasy facilitation group or a control group that received a comparable degree of personal attention but without the encouragement of imaginativeness. The children's mothers were actually the persons

---

* Herzka's assertion about drugs may not be so far-fetched. Research we conducted at Yale University and at Murray State University in Kentucky, which included a thousand students, yielded indications that heavier drug use was also associated, among other factors, with less evidence of a fluid and varied imaginative experience.[15]

trained to provide either the fantasy encouragement or the loving attention built around straight communication and interest. While the chronically ill children were initially much higher in evidence of anxiety than the healthy children, both groups of children whose mothers had encouraged imaginativeness showed impressive reductions in their anxiety. In contrast, the control groups showed no changes in their anxiety levels.[17] Comparable findings of the benefit of imaginative play or fantasy for an older group of children are described in a clinical report by Lonnie Zeltzer and Samuel LeBaron of the University of Texas Health Sciences Center in San Antonio.[18]

Many years ago we conducted studies providing evidence that congenitally blind children or children born deaf showed certain limitations in their imaginative experience and expression compared to otherwise matched nonhandicapped children. Sarah Sloane has shown that a focused series of exercises designed to provide models of imaginative performance using poems and stories that employ alternatives to typical "visual" words can enhance spontaneous fantasy processes in the visually handicapped. Indeed, an increasing number of stories suggest that some form of imaginative play training or encouragement offers advantages to children who confront serious physical, environmental, or intrapsychic difficulties.[19]

One reflection of the recognition by lay and professional groups of the potential of imaginativeness training for children has been the emergence of clown training programs for children. These approaches afford children, often inner-city, impoverished, chronically ill, or institutionalized, an opportunity to see how clowns are made up. The children can choose particular makeup, funny noses, hats, and pants for themselves. They then assume clown identities and act out their individual parts in spontaneous group playlets.

In New Haven, William Carpenter, an actor and professional clown, has initiated such a program for deinstitutionalized retarded and borderline psychotic children and young adults. We joined forces with him and proposed a program for trial in the children's unit of the Connecticut Valley State hospital in Middletown. Larke Nahme-Huang and Amy Bowles Wheaton (now Commissioner of Children and Youth Services for the state) collaborated with us on this effort.

By the time children reached this unit most other resources for psychological help were exhausted. The subjects of this intervention effort were thirty-seven children whose average age was about twelve and who showed a variety of signs of severe emotional distress, impulsivity, and personal disorganization. Autistic children at the unit, a far more specialized group, were not included in the formal study. Children were randomly assigned to one of three groups, a movement-training intervention group, the clown workshop (primarily fantasy play), and a control group. Like the others, the control subjects followed hospital routine, underwent specialized therapies, including psychotherapy, that were already available but simply did not attend either the one-hour weekly movement or clown therapy. The movement training, carried out by skilled therapists, combined elements of physical coordination, motor control and controlled expression, dance, and joy awareness with imagination and fantasy. Stress was placed primarily on the motor coordination aspects of the training.

The clown therapy drew on the resources of the clown workshop, a group trained at the local repertory theater in generating imaginative play for children. This group, led by William Carpenter, had achieved considerable success in reaching inner-city children in the schools. The children were introduced to some adult clowns at a special Clown Carnival run by the group and then allowed to use makeup and role-playing to establish a unique clown identity themselves. Two adult clowns then led them in twos and threes into a room that contained the simplest props: large cardboard boxes, raggedy bits of costume, and so on. The adults gave the children a few hints about creating make-believe games and also provided them with the opportunity to photograph each other and the little scenes they had worked out with props using a Polaroid camera. Finally, as part of the ongoing procedure the children were involved in telling stories, which they dictated or wrote down if they were sufficiently adept with a pencil. Before the beginning of the intervention (which involved only one hour a week and lasted only six weeks), all the children were tested for intelligence, imaginative predisposition (in a combination of the Rorschach and the interviewing procedure already described), and reflectiveness-impulsivity. Samples of the children's behavior during spontaneous play periods were obtained by groups of independent observers, working in pairs, who were blind to the hypothesis of the experiment. The children's behavior was rated for imaginativeness of play; indications of gross positive emotionality; degree of concentration; overt aggressive behavior; and a whole range of moods, such as angry-annoyed, fearful-tense, sad-downhearted, lively-excited; for certain social behavioral patterns, such as cooperativeness with peers, cooperativeness with adults, communication with peers and adults, interaction with peers and adults; and finally, for general body-image awareness.

There were no differences between the three groups in any of the independent variables at the outset of the intervention procedures as a result of the randomization. It should be noted that the average IQ of these groups was 87 and that the level of imaginative play, for example, was extremely low. Of course, we might not expect a great deal of overt imaginative play from children at this age level, but there is ample evidence that, left to their own devices, nine-year-olds still carry on considerable imaginative behavior.

Unfortunately, limited funds prevented carrying this program beyond the six weeks of one-hour-a-week sessions. At the end of this time the children were observed for the following two weeks on at least two occasions during spontaneous free play. Observations of the free-play behavior of children had already been obtained on several occasions by independent raters while the experimental intervention was underway. There were thus three observation points for each child: preintervention, during intervention, and postintervention.

Results indicated a sharp and statistically reliable increase in spontaneous imaginative behavior for both experimental groups. Two weeks after termination of the sessions, however, a reversal occurred in the direction of the control level of imaginative play, although not to the starting point. Clearly, intervention through the more purely imaginative exercises of the clown method and the more body-oriented but still mildly imaginative aspects of perceptual motor training manifests strong effects in the children's generalization of such behavior to their own free-play situations. With the termination of the one-hour-a-week program, however, failure of pattern consolidation was apparent.

The findings for the specific affective state lively-excited showed the same sharp increase for both groups during intervention but dropped off to a level indistinguishable from that of the control group two weeks after termination of sessions. For elated-pleased a similar pattern was found. It is interesting to note that an actual increase in aggressive behavior emerged from the clown training during the period of intervention itself, but this, too, returned to the control level at termination. It would appear that a program like this, at least in its initiation, might stimulate a higher level of overall activity on the part of the children involved, which is manifested in higher spirits, some increased aggression, and a striking increase in spontaneous imagination. Strong trends for the experimental groups to improve in their communication with their peers and in their interaction with adults emerged in the experimental periods. Among the independent variables, imaginative play predisposition correlated significantly with reflectiveness and with positive emotionality. No other relationships of any size and no interaction effects emerged.

This study is but a small beginning in an area that invites more extensive efforts. It is clear that severely emotionally disturbed children do respond to imaginative training exercises and show, along with greater fantasy play, considerably more joy and liveliness. Important social gains, however temporary, were also in evidence. As we reported, *"To witness a severely disturbed, low-verbal child construct a rocketship fantasy and invite a classmate to accompany him in his journey to outerspace—a child who has previously been frightened, rigid and tense—emphasizes the wonderful power of imaginative play."*[20] Perhaps we need a commitment to programs that will initiate such training for the emotionally disturbed and also allow time for extended experience and follow up evaluation of the general usefulness of such imaginative play and clown game procedures with such children.

A more structured short-term psychotherapeutic approach using a Clown Club with early school-age girls has been described by Joan Smith, Richard Walsh, and Mary Richardson working in Peterborough, Canada. Here the focus is more upon the creation of a group fantasy once the children adopt their clown identities. By encouraging a shared story line about how they met and how they will relate to each other, the therapists foster in the children an ongoing play sequence that, from our vantage point, helps them to create new ways of thinking about self and others in an organized fashion. These alternative forms of relating are first practiced in the Clown Club but, with some guidance, can gradually be generalized to their daily life situations.[21]

We can mention a final controlled study conducted in England with seventeen children ranging in age from three to six who were encouraged to engage in make-believe play in ten thirty-minute sessions and followed over several months' time. The children had been institutionalized because of family breakups, illness, or other deleterious conditions. Matched control children from the same setting received institutional attention without the imaginative play training. The training "worked" in the sense that the experimental group showed statistically reliable post-training increments in their spontaneous levels of imaginative play and positive emotionality. The children also showed more creative performance on tests and more skills in story-telling. Of special importance was an increase in "prosocial behaviors," that is, in sharing and cooperation. And, in keeping with earlier research carried out by Ephraim Biblow working with us in a similar experiment, there was a decrement in their levels of overt aggressive actions.[22] Once again one can surmise that the opportunity for imaginative play, by providing new and varied schemas and by increasing a sense of personal power, may reduce the persistently high levels of incongruous material that generate anger. Trying new schemas may also offer guidelines for new approaches to handling obstacles and frustration.

More Extreme Psychopathology

Throughout this volume we have stressed the possibility that imaginative play provides children with a sense of personal power and a feeling of some degree of control over the complex events they encounter. Recently, researchers in psychopathology have been increasingly aware that depression is an identifiable and relatively more frequent source of distress in childhood than had been realized. A major theory about the origins of depression in adults and in children stems from the helplessness concept of Martin Seligman, Lynn Abramson, and Loren Alloy, whose research began at the University of Pennsylvania and is now continuing in a number of settings around the country.[23] A central notion is that depressed individuals attribute unfortunate occurrences or failures to their own inadequacies and generalize these failures to other situations while at the same time explaining their successes as the result of sheer chance. Evidence of this sense of helplessness has been identified in depressed children by Lynn Abramson and Nadine Kaslow.[24]

A team of investigators led by Tiffany Field at the University of Miami's Mailman Center explored the patterns of solitary play and mother-child interaction of groups of five-year-old normal, depressed, and conduct-disordered children.[25] While on the whole the depressed children were not grossly different from the normal children, they did spend significantly less time in fantasy play than the other groups. When observed with their mothers, neither the depressed children nor the adults engaged in very much imaginative play, especially when compared to the time spent in such play by the nondepressed children and their mothers. Indeed, the differences in such play were among the clearest results of this study. We wonder, then, whether the children's depression was simply reflected in reduced make-believe activity or whether possibly the failure of mothers to encourage or stimulate fantasy play may have increased the children's apparent sense of incompetence or helplessness. Further research using imaginative play training as a preventive measure against depression or to relieve an already evident sadness is necessary. Our own hypothesis would be that children whose parents or other caregivers foster imaginative play would later show less of the "global, stable and internal" negative event attributions that prolong helplessness and depression in children.

In Chapter 6 we mentioned Alan Leslie's proposal that the limited capacity for imaginative play in autistic children may reflect a critical brain defect. Still another study carried out at the Mailman Center for Child Development in Miami indicated that autistic preschoolers showed less functional and less generally appropriate toy play as well as less imitation behavior than did comparable normal, speech-impaired, or mentally retarded children.[26] Here, the mother's role as a "teacher" of imaginative skills may be less relevant than it is for depressed children, because the generally unsmiling and socially unresponsive quality of autistic children may discourage even the most imaginatively inclined parents.

Helping Children Learn to Play

The research we have reviewed above suggests that there may be hope for potentially depressed children if they engage in self-healing play, but it remains doubtful whether we can reach the autistic through this avenue. As we have already pointed out, a caregiver's encouragement of pretend play may open the way for children to develop fundamental skills, not only for sheer self-entertainment but also to gain a sense of power and optimism by learning how to manipulate real-world events in symbolic, miniaturized form. Parents can benefit from remembering their own favorite childhood games and using their own creativity to think up age-appropriate approaches that foster fantasy play. In our books, *Partners in Play* and the more recent *Make Believe,* we have sought to provide parents and teachers with concrete games and exercises that entertain children and foster spontaneous make-believe play.[27] Games of size, for example, recognize that for children, "small" may mean weak and vulnerable while "big" means powerful. In a game of "small like a ball, big like a giant," for example, children first roll themselves up and crouch quietly in a corner. Then they gradually unfold themselves, becoming taller and taller until they are on their toes stretching their arms out and taking large steps as they slowly explore the room. They can be encouraged to say, "Small like a ball, tall like a mountain, small like an apple, tall like a tree."

Another even more imaginative exercise is the game "blow me up" using an imaginary "balloon," which, after all, will not burst or blow away. An adult or a peer partner can "puff, puff, puff" while the child becomes the balloon and gradually expands, rising from a curled up position to full height and pretending to float around the room until the "air" is let out and the child collapses in a heap. Once these are mastered, more elaborate games can increase the number of imaginative transformations. Children can try imitating animals "under a sheet" to create different shapes or choose from a "bag of hats" to practice new roles.[28]

Spontaneous Family Healing through Play

We conclude our discussion of play and self-help outside the formal clinical setting with a vivid example recounted by the Israeli psycholinguist, Shlomo Ariel, whose work we mentioned briefly in Chapter 6.[29] In his efforts to study patterns of imaginative play and children's use of language or nonverbal communication during play, he visited a kindergarten in Tel Aviv. The teacher arranged for Ariel to videotape the play of a boy named Joseph in the child's home but had no idea that once the regular taping began a tragic drama would unfold.

Joseph's father revealed that he was leaving the boy's mother, Ada, for another woman. The same thing, it turns out, had happened to Ada when she was a small child. She remained willing, however, to allow weekly videotaping of the play of Joseph and his six-year-old sister, Dalia. In one of these sessions, Joseph cast Dalia and himself as a small prince and princess who were being sent away from the palace by wicked parents. Their mother, obviously distressed by this proposal, assumed the role of the wicked queen and "staged a scene" of confession and bitterness because the king didn't love her and her children misunderstood her. Joseph and his sister, roaming in the wilderness, then pretended to meet a stray horse. At this point, their mother was enlisted to play the animal and what followed was a series of encounters in which mutual support and affective openness evolved between the "horse" and the children. Later on, Ada magically transformed the horse into a "good queen," who gradually encouraged the children to come back to the palace.

Ariel comments wryly that he later learned it was not little Joseph who invented family play therapy after all. Examples can be found in the treatment approaches of a number of leading exponents of the process of family therapy. But Ariel was led to a more systematic development of play therapy in a family group as a specific treatment procedure. What we wish to stress here is that the interaction between Joseph, Dalia, and their mother was a "natural" occurrence in a family subjected to sudden and unexpected stress. The pretend play situations that evolved permitted the children to form a new integration of their schemas about their mother (and, in other games, perhaps their father as well). But it also permitted the mother herself to regain some sense of personal control and competence in relation to her children. On the small stage of pretend play each participant in the larger drama developed a new sense of competence and control and thus fought off the helplessness that could have left them deeply depressed.

Self-Healing in Normal Development

In the 1950s, Lois Barclay Murphy, a great pioneer in child observation research, led a team of investigators who kept thorough records of the daily play of children at the Sarah Lawrence Nursery School. In many cases, they were able to employ psychological tests and extensive home observations to compile a remarkably thorough view of the daily life of the children over several years. In the book *Colin: A Normal Child,* Murphy presents a lively and engaging picture of the emergence of selfhood in a bright and imaginative boy over the three years between two and five.[30] The book includes dozens of examples of Colin's make-believe play at school and at home and also records the fantasies he produced by "dictating" stories.

At the beginning of his first year at school when he was four, he clung to his mother and whined for some time after she left. But gradually he became immersed in group play with puzzles and make-believe games. The next day he dictated a story to his mother that involved a witch who went to the doctor. The doctor said "she had a heart disinfectant. So they called one hundred and fifty doctors and one hundred and thirty wise men, and they cut her open and took her up to God. And God changed her into four ghosts." This fantasy was subsequently associated with more sustained cooperative play, as if somehow Colin had exorcised his extreme dependency on his mother and his fear of the new group.

During the same year Colin became somewhat rambunctious and aggressive at school. Concurrent psychological tests revealed indications of frightening images but also suggested that his fantasies of fighting monsters were then followed by acts of friendliness. After Thanksgiving, Colin seemed to have a set of novel stimuli that he began to assimilate into his play patterns: the Meadow Brook Dairy, lumber freight yards, and Jack Frost's house. For example, he built a lumberyard, which he announced was in Wyoming, in the West. After piling up blocks on a make-believe train he moved them against a wall, placing them in neat rows. He called the train "The Lone Freight." After he finished this game, Colin announced, "I feel so proud of myself. I feel like walking around a little . . . you know what, I'm not going to hit anyone in this school today." Other games, building Jack Frost's house and becoming an "ardent" milk dealer, seemed to reflect his developing sense of strength and traditional male identification. As Murphy notes, "when his self-esteem was high he did not need to attack other children, and, by implication, attacking was a defense against feeling threatened . . . This feeling of power expressed itself in . . . his sense of his ability to defend himself when laughed at, to do constructive things, or aggressive things."

A final example may serve to demonstrate the sense of power and emerging self-confidence Colin achieved through his play, which may well be an apt reflection of the sense of control play provides:

His joy in building and making things expanded into a feeling of omnipotence: "I'm making a big snake. Snake says, 'I'm being made by God on his operating table—' I'm God. I'm making big snakes—I make the world. It's a huge boa constrictor. He's coiling! Isn't he huge! He's a black cobra. I'll take him home and have him bite everyone in my family—even granny and grampy! I'll put him on the terrace and I'll say 'Look at the big black cobra.' And I'll follow 'em." (He laughed delightedly . . .) "I'm God."

He acted out many roles. "I'm a diesel motor digging." (Colin squatted on his knees, moving his arms in rhythmic digging swinging motions with remarkably rhythmic and beautifully coordinated movements.) "Look at the steam shovel moving on his caterpillar wheels."

Colin's fantasy play shows the emergence of an assertive, male-identified, and competent sense of self. This development is also evident in group fantasy play, where Colin's leadership emerged. His early fears of separation and of falling, and his specific fears (for example, of fire) gradually faded as he seemed to work them out in self-healing games. But more important, as Lois Murphy puts it, "he did not fantasize about play but about being, becoming, growing, doing, achieving and what he did was experienced by him as creative work. It was this that made him proud and fortified his confident picture of himself."

What Happens in Play Therapy

The use of play in various forms of psychotherapy with children from the ages of two-and-a-half to twelve or thirteen is now an intrinsic feature of mental health intervention around the world. We do not propose therefore to present a detailed survey of the various approaches, the nuances of difference, or the presumed theoretical underpinnings and conceptual disagreements that characterize the field. Instead, we shall try to focus on the therapeutic uses of imaginative play as they reflect upon our emphasis on the adaptive, self-healing, schema-expanding, and competence-building possibilities of pretending and make-believe.

Psychoanalytic Methods

The use of play in psychotherapy was first described in 1921 by H. Hug-Hellmuth, a psychoanalyst who actually went to children's homes to conduct her sessions.[31] Over the next decade two somewhat contrasting approaches to conducting psychoanalysis with children emerged, both, however, relying heavily on observing children's play in a clinical setting. The method developed by Melanie Klein in Berlin later became an influential force in England not only in child psychoanalysis but also in adult treatment and theory. It is the precursor to the object relations emphasis that is the dominant intellectual feature of psychoanalysis fifty years later in the 1980s.[32] The play therapy procedures worked out by Anna Freud in Vienna and also in England have perhaps had more influence on play therapy *practice* in the United States, although often today the two approaches may be blended in the work of individual child analysts.[33] The Kleinian orientation, as Aaron Esman, a prominent child psychoanalyst at New York Hospital–Cornell Medical Center, has written, "conceived of the child's play as equivalent to the 'free associations' of adult patients. Accordingly, play activities . . . are treated as the primary data on which to base interpretations; further the child's play was to be translated into the presumed language of the unconscious, generally within the framework of the assumed transference configuration."[34]

Examples of Klein's orientation include her statement to a three-and-a-half-year-old boy, after he began a play session by repeatedly making two toy trucks collide, that he was thinking about his parents' sexual relations. Another analyst of this school described how she interpreted the actions of a five-year-old child, who smeared glue on the playroom floor, as wanting "to glue herself . . . to the inside of my body where new babies grew." Next day the child brought in a large red geranium and, pointing to the stem and buds, said, "Do you see? All those babies come out of the stem. This is a present for you." The analyst then went on to note that "now she wanted to give me the penis and all the little babies that come out of it to make up for . . . the mess that she had made of my babies . . . the previous day."[35]

In case examples like the one above, one cannot avoid wondering if the child's presumed preoccupation with babies and penises is her own or simply an attempt to accommodate to the analyst's communications; the child's play may well be an effort to form new schemas in the face of her confusion about the analyst's references. The presumption of an unconscious set of schemas about the birth process, about penises and their absence in girls, and about the transference of the child's preoccupations from home onto the therapist is a central feature of psychoanalytic play therapy. In contrast, the method derived from Anna Freud, while accepting the general proposition that most of the conflicts of childhood are built around fantasies related to oral, anal, phallic, and Oedipal drive-energies, avoids such direct interpretations of unconscious content. Instead, her approach uses play as an entrée to establishing rapport, as a window on the child's conflicts or diagnostic psychopathology, and as a clue to resistances and persisting conflicts. The child analyst interprets such resistances or blockages and seeks to help the child to verbalize difficulties by asking the child for accounts of the meaning of various incidents of play. As Donald Cohen and his collaborators at the Yale Child Study Center have written in describing child analysis: "The goal of the analyst is to understand the child's internal life, to relate this to his behavior inside and outside of the analytic session and, if needed, to try to alter inner or outer functioning through helping the child understand his experiences, feelings, thoughts, and the life he is leading. He offers verbalization, clarification and interpretation in the context of a relationship that includes elements of transference, displacement, and therapeutic alliance."[36]

The art of interpretation in child analysis involves staying within the metaphorical structure introduced by the play theme initiated by the child. Esman exemplifies this principle by describing a six-year-old named Peter, who is playing with cowboys and Indians, flinging the latter around the room wildly. "To have suggested that it appeared that he was expressing his rage against his rigid punitive parents would, at this early stage of the treatment, have induced either bland denial or angry resistance. The principal aim of the moment was to connect the action with a named affect . . . therapeutic tact—and tactics-dictated, then, the comment, 'that cowboy sure looks angry at those Indians.' 'Sure he is,' said Peter. 'They keep taking his things away from him.'"[37] Clearly, such an approach is more cautious than the Kleinian interpretative stance, although the assumed particularized significance of the classic psychosexual stages remains central to psychoanalytic orientations.

Client-Centered Approaches

A third form of play therapy is historically traceable to the work of Otto Rank, one of Sigmund Freud's earliest and closest associates who, in the 1920s, shifted his emphasis from psychosexuality to the greater importance of human differentiation and to the struggle we all experience in expressing individuality yet maintaining intimacy.[38] This conception of an emergent experience of self, and of processes of separation and individuation, is now a key notion in object relations theories, although Rank rarely gets any credit from psychoanalysts, since he withdrew from the Freudian circle (or was expelled from it) early. Rank's point of view eventually influenced Philadelphia mental health workers Jessie Taft and Frederick Allen, directors respectively of the School of Social Work and of the Child Guidance Clinic in that city. Allen's fine, if brief, *Psychother-*

apy with Children, which appeared in 1942, is as wise, valuable, and clear in its presentation of play therapy as any book one might pick up on the subject almost fifty years later.[39]

One finds therein for example, a drily understated reinterpretation of Melanie Klein's case of the boy who banged his trucks together. Allen's position is that one must consider that this boy's mother had just left him with a stranger, had herself gone off with another stranger, and that the boy "now faced a new reality without the support of the old. In using the toys he not only gave evidence of his anger and fear roused by this separation, but more important, he was finding a medium to give some expression and organization to these feelings with a person who could not only understand his need to feel as he did, but who could encourage him to use that medium within the bounds that define . . . this first stage toward a new relationship. The particular form of the play was incidental, even accidental . . . The important point of focus was the child who was responding to this experience and not the particular content of the reaction." This summary contrasts sharply with Klein's, which imposed on the child her assumption (with, we believe, very little evidence) that he was replaying a witnessed or fantasized scene of parental sex.

Actually, Allen's statement encapsulates the fundamental principles of what has come to be known as the "client-centered" approach to play therapy. This widely employed and researched method reflects the influence of the Philadelphia school on Carl Rogers. It was Rogers whose nondirective, later client-centered psychotherapy became internationally influential, and it was his student, Virginia Axline, who became the key figure in developing a form of play therapy that emphasized context, self-actualization, and the expression of feelings but without the psychoanalytic focus on presumed psychosexual content.[40] The work of Clark Moustakas and Louise and Bernard Guerney has moved this approach beyond its first clinical roots. The Guerneys also offer training to parents and nonprofessionals.[41] In Europe, Stefan Schmidtchen of West Germany has represented the client-centered orientation and has also personally carried out or engendered extensive research on the processes of play therapy.[42] The Imagery Interaction Therapy orientation pioneered by E. A. Vermeer and currently reflected in the clinical work and research of Joop Hellendoorn and Ina van Berckelaer-Onnes represents a comparable approach, although with greater emphasis on fostering more vivid imagery in the child through more therapist intervention to provide themes or carefully chosen playthings.[43]

The client-centered approach places its greatest emphasis on the possibility of self-healing through play under conditions in which children feel accepted by a warm and attentive but nonintrusive adult. The opportunity to spend an hour or so in such an atmosphere with a variety of playthings and a kindly adult as an occasional helper allows children to express their persisting dilemmas, to create toy worlds under their own control, to identify their own positive or negative emotions (reflected back nonjudgmentally by the therapist), and gradually to develop new narratives about their lives. Louise Guerney presents the case of C., a girl of eight who was referred because her parents were concerned that she was rejecting her female role. She played almost exclusively with boys and often took risks by hanging around only the biggest, toughest boys.[44] Even on psychological tests the girl showed a rejection of her own gender and an ambivalent identification with powerful male images. She seemed to feel rejected herself, yearning for help but striving to win approval by powerful achievements. Of special concern was this persistent self-rejection.

The origins of the problem were not mysterious. C.'s parents had a younger child, a boy, now three, whose good looks and charm had become a family legend. But the parents were largely oblivious to the impact of their diverted attention. In the therapist's playroom C. at first rejected imaginative play in favor of athletic or competitive games. Gradually, as her attitudes were accepted, she began to explore the "baby toys" and soon started to play out her own needs for succorance and for nurturance of others. She began to enact scenes of weakness and helplessness, feelings she had not permitted herself to show at home or on the playground. As this pattern continued in her play, she sought out boys less and, indeed, was without playmates for a while. But as she tried out new kinds of games (such as playing "house") her external behavior changed, and she soon mingled easily with the neighborhood girls. After just sixteen sessions she was remarkably different, a fact noticed not only by her parents but also by her teachers and her grandparents, whose occasional visits led them to see the change as especially dramatic.

Guerney summarizes the case as follows:

> In the course of less than six months this little girl developed a new concept of herself as a viable, lovable and capable person. She accepted

herself for what she was—an attractive, bright girl. She was able to abandon the self of a superstrong, unfeeling pseudo-boy, which she had constructed for what she must have seen as a crippling deficit—being a girl and thus less able to command attention and respect. Psychoanalytic proponents would probably explain the dynamics in terms of penis envy. Behaviorists would probably be able to identify in family incidents frequent, inappropriate reinforcements for maleness and comparably few reinforcements for age- and sex-appropriate behaviors.[45]

Guerney goes on to describe how this girl "got lost in the shuffle" as her parents built their own egos from the boy's popularity. The parents unwitting but consistent rejection of C.'s unique personality was very clear from the details presented in the family history. Play therapy with an accepting female therapist who tolerated C.'s effort at reconstructing a self through nurturant doll play and playing "house" permitted the child to rearrange her self-schema into one that was more natural, more able to win reinforcement from her ultrafeminine mother and other adults, and more suitable for establishing friendship patterns.

Of course play therapy, whether in the client-centered or analytic form, must impose some limits on the freedom of children's play. As Guerney wisely points out, all kinds of verbalizations, fantasies, and feelings are acceptable, but some limits must be put on behavior. Acts of physical destruction, self-endangerment, or sheer violence are not acceptable. Some therapists have not always understood this principle. A psychologist of our acquaintance became involved in a game with a child in play therapy and permitted the child to tie him to a chair as a captured "bad guy." The child then proceeded to knock over the book shelves in the office, creating a thorough mess, and then left as soon as his hour was up while the therapist struggled to free himself. It is hard to see how such a therapy hour could help the child form any constructive new schemas other than that psychologists are fools and one's own demonic self-concept is a viable script for action.

So far, we have focused on approaches to play therapy with younger children. In the great diversity of case material reflecting various psychoanalytic or client-centered orientations, one can discern a certain confluence of procedures. More emphasis is being placed on the natural unfolding of play; interpretations try to stay closer to directly observable behavior and to the thematic content established by the child. Sensitivity to limited intrusions is shared across schools. There is also a realization that, while a therapist may occasionally and in a subtle way direct a session (as in the case of the child who was given an anatomically correct doll), the major role of the adult is to serve as a "new object," that is, a new kind of adult model who accepts feelings, tolerates and encourages pretend play, and allows the child to explore and experience new self-schemas and scripts. As Wayne Downey, a child psychoanalyst, has written:

Are we relying enough on the health-promoting aspects of play? Paradoxically, to what extent does an overly verbal, interpretative approach become repressive and thwart the child's development of true self-knowledge, self-control, and understanding of self vis-à-vis the world of love objects and others? Winnicott's final words on the subject suggest that in adult as well as in child work we may err in the direction of talking too much in order to undo defense rather than respecting the power of the unfolding, relatively undefended, transitional play process, whether manifest in child's actions or adult's words.[46]

Demonstrating the Efficacy of Play Therapy

Individual case reports, especially those published in journals or in books (like Virginia Axline's "Dibs" or Rudolf Ekstein's "Tommy the Space Child"), are usually examples of effective changes produced presumably by the child's play therapy experience.[47] But how many less successful cases are unpublished? We need more certain evidence of the relative utility of play therapy. Fortunately, a number of controlled studies have compared the outcomes for children treated with play therapy and those for untreated children. A review of seventy-five such controlled studies of various forms of psychotherapy with children (the average age being about nine) was carried out by Rita Casey and Jeffrey Berman of the University of Texas in Austin.[48] They found good evidence that psychotherapy with children (compared to untreated controls) is at least as effective as with adults; and as in adult studies, the more focused the problem and the treatment approach, the better the results. Results comparing play therapies with more behavioral therapies indicated no differences in "effect size," the measure employed in these "meta-analyses" of large numbers of studies. Even more recent research using larger numbers of studies further confirms the indications that psychotherapy with children between the ages of four and twelve is at least as effective (compared to various controls) as adult psychotherapy.[49] A study in England that compared the effect of different types of therapy with different kinds of problem children using two age groups (seven to eight and eleven to twelve) was especially impressive because it examined parent therapy, play therapy, group therapy, and behavior modification.[50] In general, the study concluded that children whose problems involved depression withdrawal, self-doubt, fears, worries, or preoccupations ("internalizers") fared better in therapy than did children whose problem involved "externalizing," that is, delinquency, antisocial or aggressive behavior, running away, and so on.

Our concern here is with the play therapy approach specifically. The data available on such treatment suggest that it is comparably effective to other treatments but especially relevant to younger children. An intriguing demonstration of how play therapy can be applied to enhance the adaptive behavior of four- to six-year-old children in their school settings has been provided by the late Gregory Hannah and Elizabeth Rave of the University of Northern Colorado.[51] These investigators studied nine children, each with different problems ranging from social withdrawal and inattentiveness to aggressive or domineering behavior. By observing and recording the actual frequency of such behaviors prior to the onset of play therapy it was possible to establish a "baseline" assessment of the troublesome behavior to determine if changes occurred. The play therapists were graduate students trained in the client-centered orientation of Axline, Moustakas, and Guerney. Because they used very careful, novel, and sophisticated statistical procedures they could, in effect, use each child as his own control. Great care was taken to be sure that observers and experimenters did not know whether therapy had been initiated or what the nature of the therapy was in order to avoid any chance of biased reporting. One additional child who had a school problem was not offered play therapy until after the experimental period was over in order to identify the pattern of the behaviors in question over time. In this case there was very little variation or change in the frequency of the targeted behavior—"inattentiveness"—across the eleven-week period.

For eight of the nine children in play therapy there were significant improvements in the frequency of problem behavior. For one child, Dru, inattentive behavior declined within a few weeks to zero. As can be seen in Figure 9–1, there was a sharp increase in poor attentiveness ("off-task behavior") about halfway through the eight weeks of therapy and then a sharp decline so that the last four data points are below the baseline average. Inquiry after the treatment

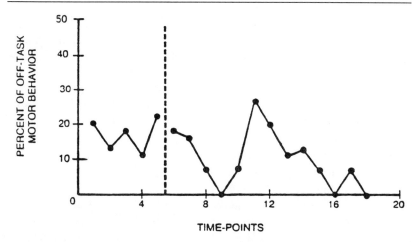

Figure 9–1. A graphic representation of the percentage of time the child Dru showed distractibility before and after the institution of play therapy (vertical dotted line). There is a sharp decrease in "off-task" behavior soon after play therapy starts, then a setback at Time 12, followed by a rapid decline to near zero in the last four weeks. (Reproduced from G. L. Hannah and E. J. Rave, "The Use of Play Therapy to Increase Adaptive Behavior in the Classroom," with permission.)

and observation period uncovered the fact that there had been a serious family quarrel just prior to the upsurge of inattentiveness Dru showed, but that Dru seemed to have recovered quickly and resumed her increased "on task" behaviors soon afterward.

Similar results emerged for seven other children. Some showed improved social interactions with peers, others more effective play with other children without the "bossiness" they had manifested earlier. Of some interest is the finding that the careful recordings of children's actual behavior showed clear improvement, even when the teachers' more general comments failed to indicate such a change. Adult schemas, as the research on memory shows, are conservative and slower to change even in the face of precise evidence that the targeted behavior was sharply reduced once play therapy was initiated.

We have discussed the Hannah and Rave study at some length not only because it demonstrates the potential efficacy of play therapy with relatively normal children in a school setting but also because it highlights the advantages of (1) targeting behaviors that are troublesome and scoring them over baseline periods; (2) using sophisticated "time-series" statistics for evaluating change attributable especially to the intervention rather than to chance variations; and (3) the possible advantages of such procedures for studying accumulations of single cases. Too often, especially in the psychoanalytic literature, therapist anecdotes alone carry the weight of evidence. Yet methods are available that can maintain the variety and uniqueness of the individual case study while still meeting rigorous standards of objective observation and quantitative estimation of changes in behavior, such as social withdrawal or poor attention, that can be forerunners of later, more severe school adjustment problems.

Much work still needs to be done to pin down when play therapy can be most useful—for which types of children and which types of problems—what forms such play therapy must take, and how best to combine it with parent counseling. Indeed, should parents serve more actively as play therapists themselves? Current evidence, summarized in several of the research reviews we have cited, suggests that play therapy may be most effective for children whose problems are more internal, which involve, for example, feelings of sadness, poor attention, social isolation, fear, shame, or guilt. Children who have already developed some skill at imaginative play will certainly do better when offered play therapy opportunities. The famous cases of Virginia Axline's "Dibs," Rudolf Ekstein's "Tommy and the Space Child," or even the adolescent Hannah Green (in real life, Joanne Greenberg) in *I Never Promised You a Rose Garden,* all seem to be youngsters who bring great imaginative skill to the therapy setting. Encouraging children early on to develop their capacity for make-believe play may afford some children opportunities for self-healing. But even if a child develops some adjustment or other neurotic difficulties, imaginative play may help the child to respond more quickly and effectively to various kinds of play intervention.

The Role of the Therapist

We have already described the important role of the parent as a mediator of the confusion and complexity of the child's environment (which includes television). In a sense, the therapist enters the scene as a new mediator when parents or teachers have somehow missed areas where the child remains troubled by persisting ambiguities or incongruities. There is some evidence that underachieving or educationally retarded children can benefit considerably from controlled adult-mediated learning opportunities that build on available cognitive resources. We believe that therapists can play a role similar to those educators who apply Reuven Feuerstein's or Mogens Jensen's methods of mediated cognitive instruction. By substituting for an absent, inadequate, overburdened, or troubled parent the play therapist becomes a key figure who helps the child to identify those features of the complex social milieu that demand attention. In the example we presented at the start of this chapter, the therapist's provision of an anatomically correct doll opened the way for the boy to confront an issue about which he had developed a sense of dread and perplexity. Play therapists provide the child with opportunities for make-believe play and acceptance of that play. They may even offer some instruction or modeling in such behavior. By delineating key life issues, significant people, and ongoing conflicts through play, therapists help the child to construct new schemas, new knowledge structures that will reduce ambiguity, fear, and the other negative affects that result from new experiences that are beyond the child's ability to organize or assimilate.

Moving into the mediator's role requires some caution. As research has shown, while many children need initial encouragement and "plot material," adults must move to the background once a child is well-launched in a play sequence.[52] But the therapist is more than a mediator. An important emotional exchange is critical to the play therapy process. The psychoanalyst, Heinz Kohut, has proposed that the psychotherapist in adult psychoanalysis must become a new "object" the patient can internalize.[53] We take this to mean that the therapist's acceptance, tolerance, and persistent inquiry can become part of the patient's own ongoing thought process. The child forms a new inner sense of self-acceptance, which allows self-scrutiny and curiosity. If the adult's own willingness to listen and to share thoughts and play possibilities is conveyed to the child in a spirit of liveliness and humor, the therapist can open the child to the joys of introspection and controlled fantasy. The therapist's enthusiasm may help change the fearful, despairing, or angry child trapped in a limited world into one who can savor the excitement of reshaping the seemingly "given" world into a new one that is full of possibilities.

10

When Imaginative Play Goes Underground: Fantasy in Middle Childhood

In a *New York Times Magazine* article television producer Bill Boggs recounts his "Farewell to Toyland" on a rainy late summer day when he was twelve and just about to begin the eighth grade. The toy soldiers he regularly lined up for elaborate skirmishes had seen less and less action in recent years, so he organized all his favorites for one "last epic battle." "When the carnage was complete, the cowboys had joined the Indians to capture the Germans, and the Legionnaires, standing tall, were guarding the hospital. The 'Jelly Rider' (a favorite) had been run over by a tank." The young Boggs then wrapped each toy, loaded them all in boxes, and stored them in the basement. He informed his parents that "someday I would give them to my own little boy." The piece goes on to describe his rage toward his parents when, years later, he learns that all the toys, including the "Jelly Rider," had been disposed of. His frantic search to find some relic of his middle childhood play that he can share with his son rounds out this poignant account.[1]

A *New Yorker* magazine profile of the ingenious and subtle magic team of Penn and Teller reports that Teller's parents had provided him with a puppet theater and a "Howdy Doody" Magic set when he was about five. From then on he played at magic constantly. Teller asserts that his magic act strives to produce an experience of change and unexpectedness in the audience comparable to what he used to strive for when, as a child, he set up a "fun house" in his backyard. It consisted of boards, planks, and boxes arranged to produce unanticipated movement or loss of balance as one progressed through the sequence. "And then I would get kids who lived on my street to come in and walk through it. And I would be right there to catch them if they fell . . . But in my head what was happening was they were going into a fun house in an amusement park—a haunted house that was pretty scary." Recounting this incident, Teller's eyes well up with tears. "You start off at the beginning, and you come out and you feel like you've been someplace. I don't know why I get all weepy over that."[2]

Both of these memories from middle childhood reflect the fact that imaginative play persists well beyond the usual "cut-off" age of six or seven, even though it becomes increasingly internalized into private thought—Teller's fun-house fantasy. Our joy in fantasy, the need to keep alive the fun of make-believe, is reflected in the nostalgia and pathos that characterize both of these anecdotes.

Finally, a brief quotation from the writers Jon and Rumer Godden's account of their upbringing in India perhaps seventy years ago. Describing their make-believe games, they point out that when their parents inquired what they were playing, they often camouflaged the topic behind a cliché like "Mothers and Fathers" or "Shops." They go on, "Yet if we had told what we were playing no one would have been much the wiser, because our plays were like icebergs, only three-tenths seen, the rest hidden, inside ourselves. It was what we thought into our play that made its spell."[3]

In middle childhood overt play is gradually and subtly transformed into private thought. It does not disappear, but a deeper level of inner experience becomes central to the nature of the child.

What Happens to the Make-Believe Games of Yesteryear?

One of the mysteries of human development involves the transformation of children's play from a behavior expressed in overt speech and action into one that flowers and expands privately through interior monologue, daydreaming, or fantasy. In a remarkable book written in the Soviet Union in the late 1920s that reflects the influences of Freud, early Piaget, and Vygotsky, the great A. R. Luria described a series of observations of children's fantasy play.[4] At first, as Piaget had already reported, the children talk out their thoughts and manifest them in the visible actions of the pretend game. By early school age they demonstrate some restraint: a battle scene is reflected in a sketchy drawing of a cannon but there is still much jumping around and sound effects. By middle childhood, the children draw with only minimal verbalization: the make-believe now goes on privately through imagery and covert speech.

Curiously enough, the fate of fantasy play and imagination in middle childhood was of surprisingly little interest to either Freud or Piaget. For psychoanalysis the great climactic drama of development is enacted in the Oedipal period between the ages of five and seven; modern revisionism in the form of object relations theory has merely shifted the critical stages to even earlier phases of babyhood in what Mitchell has called the "developmental tilt."[5] In the classic psychoanalytic conception, the resolution of the Oedipus complex was reflected in identification with the same-sex parent, the internalization of parental figures as ego ideals and punitive superegos associated with increased delaying capacities, the crystallization of the defense mechanisms, and the capacity for self-restraint.[6] Research support for the connection between this internalization process and heightened imaginative tendencies was adduced from the fact that it was only after age seven or so that children responded to the Rorschach inkblots by producing associations involving images of humans in motion. These so-called M responses are known to correlate with self-restraint on the one hand and imaginativeness on the other.[7] Despite the intriguing developmental implications of this link between flowering imagination and heightened powers of self-restraint or behavioral control, to this day many psychoanalysts persist in referring to middle childhood as the "latency period," a reference to the presumed repression of psychosexual urges until these are forcefully revived by the biological changes of puberty and early adolescence.

For Piaget as well, the great elaboration of fantasy that occurs with internalization in middle childhood evoked little interest, as Inge Bretherton and Brian Sutton-Smith have separately noted.[8] Referring to the fading away of overt symbolic play, Piaget wrote: "the more the child adapts himself to the natural and social world the less he indulges in symbolic distortions and transpositions, because instead of assimilating the external world to the ego he progressively subordinates the ego to reality."[9]

We concur with Bretherton that Piaget's view derives from his great mission, to understand the sources of orderly logical and scientific thought, what he called concrete and formal operations. But today new models of intelligent thought suggest that the storylike narrative forms (what Bretherton, following Piaget, calls "figurative thought") and playlike styles of assimilation may be critical in helping children *and* adults to create the schemas, scripts, and prototypes that are as central to adaptive thought as Aristotelian logic. We will propose here that, for better or worse, our impulse for make-believe and pretending, for role-enactment and fantasy, scarcely fades away at all. The constraints imposed by society, along with increasing brain complexity and cognitive abilities, make it possible to miniaturize our floor games into images, silent self-talk, and, gradually, an elaborate stream of consciousness that meanders along with an inner "voice-over," commenting wrily on new experiences, reflecting on the past, and predicting the future during wakefulness and sleep.

While children certainly tend to "shut up" rather abruptly once they start first grade, especially under the stress of parental and teacher admonitions, they continue to take advantage of opportunities to engage in make-believe play during breaks and recreation periods, on the way home from school, and, whenever possible, during their free time. Undoubtedly some of the impulses toward overt play have been displaced by television-viewing, which substitutes an externally generated make-believe world for one of children's own creation. But even during pick-up athletic games one can observe children of seven to nine or so pretending to be sports announcers, calling out the sequence of plays and throwing in some local color with a few humorous commercial announcements. Various societies have sought to channel these middle-childhood story or pretend game tendencies by providing children with uniformed organizations such as the Brownies or Cub Scouts, or, more ominously, the *Komsomol* or the Nazi Youth.

For large groups of unaffiliated children, peer-generated clubs and later gangs (usually sexually segregated), which only occasionally evolve into quasi-criminal groups, become contexts for expressing make-believe tendencies.[10] In the early 1930s in parts of New York City, boys between the ages of nine and twelve would form street "gangs," arming themselves with gun-shaped corner pieces from wooden orange crates with rubber bands attached to project square cardboard "bullets." Gang members would be assigned specific roles, from leadership positions to front-line foot-soldier, messenger, or spy. One of us (JLS), the youngest and the "new kid on the block," was designated a scout to spy on the doings of the Sixth Street gang and to report back to the Fifth Street boys. Indeed, a negotiated alliance between the Fifth and Seventh Street kids against the Sixth Streeters remains a positive early memory in that Brooklyn neighborhood. The excitement of being a secret scout inspired a fantasy indulged in during school hours in the early school grades and resumed years later during the long marches of military training in World War II, which eventuated, curiously enough, in an actual assignment as a Special Agent in Military Intelligence. Was a later career in clinical psychology and psychoanalysis already prefigured in these middle-childhood and late adolescent military intelligence fantasies?

In this chapter we will explore the vicissitudes of imaginative play through the relatively neglected period of middle childhood. We propose that it is during these years, as boys and girls begin school, learn reading and arithmetic, are exposed to the formal study of literature, history, geography, and science, the discipline of school, and greater freedom to play with peers away from direct adult supervision, that fantasy and daydreaming replace material-, space-, and time-limited make-believe games. But new outlets for even overt expressions of fantasy do emerge in the shape of board games, computer games, video games, and, as we shall see, in opportunities to participate in creative drama or theatrical productions at school. As new horizons open in every direction, unconstrained by reality or an accurate view of actual possibilities, the realm of fantasy becomes a central feature of experience. When Erikson termed this period the "stage of industry," he certainly captured a critical aspect of these middle-childhood years. But one could well add that the ages from seven to thirteen also represent a period of accelerated growth and differentiation in the child's fantasy capacities and perhaps also the most critical period in which self-awareness, beliefs about self and others, and a host of wishes begin to crystallize. We should forever banish such terminology as the "latency-aged" child!

A General Perspective on Middle Childhood

We can identify a dramatic deceleration in sheer physical growth between the ages of five and eleven for girls and five and almost fifteen for boys.[11] Children stay small and cute for almost six years—more than half their childhood life span—before subtle changes like the full growth of the pisiformae wrist bones (beginning around age nine for girls and age eleven or twelve for boys) signal the onset of puberty, with its massive growth spurts, first for girls and two years later for boys. The differences between the sexes in physical strength and agility are relatively minor during this period except for those skills that are differentially encouraged by society. In contrast to sheer size differences, these skills show a steady increment for both boys and girls during this period.[12] This is also the time when parents and teachers—and soon after, same-sex peer groups—begin to heighten children's awareness of participant sports, gymnastics, and dance skills. In addition, children become increasingly aware of the external popular cultural framework of observer sports, pop music, movies, and television, and their celebrated stars. At age eight when boys begin Little League, they seem somewhat dazed and confused by what their often tense and overeager fathers want them to do out on the big grass diamond. Within a few years (especially with the regular availability of televised ball games, which provide models) they know the rules well and carry themselves with all the gum-chewing grace of professional athletes even though they still can rarely hit the ball solidly.

In the schematic diagram of the life cycle presented in Table 2-1 (Chapter 2) it is apparent that during this period, children demonstrate a greatly accelerated, conscious effort to learn. Erikson has characterized it as the period of industry versus inferiority, but it is also one during which children acquire those social skills that permit them to become part of a same-sex peer group and to feel that they are members of several broader groups as well, whether religious, ethnic, or national, or even pop cultural, such as Red Sox fans or followers of Michael Jackson. Because school as a disciplined, regularized setting becomes the focus and turning point, the child who does not acquire some reasonable degree of reading skill within the first three to five grades is in effect cut off from the entire system. For many such children (usually boys) school simply becomes a house of detention that has no intrinsic meaning other than as a place where they may hope to find some comparable semiliterate peers who can establish a separate subculture all too often built around truancy, substance abuse, and mild antisocial behavior.

Some of Piaget's most stimulating research focused on the critical emergence, beginning around age seven, of concrete operations, that is, as we have noted, the ability to grasp (even if the principle cannot yet be verbalized) that distorted or spatially transposed shapes remain what they were originally; that ten M & Ms still amount to the same quantity whether they are in a closely or widely spaced row. This concept of conservation reflects a new mental capacity that becomes possible during this period.[13] Numerous experiments demonstrate how seven-year-olds differ from five-year-olds in their ability to conserve number, length, solid substance, weight, liquid amount, area, and so on. For the child who has attained the level of concrete operational thought, appearance becomes less important than some more general category. Indeed, in keeping with the emerging complexity of schematic thought, children of school age are more likely to make errors in identifying whether a picture has been shown to them before if the picture falls into the same category (fruits or animals, for example) as some that actually have been presented earlier. Such "false positives" are less likely for preschoolers, for whom an earlier picture of a banana is just that, not a member of a special class of edibles, and a later picture of an orange is a new picture, unconnected with the banana.[14]

Concrete operational thought is a milestone for the middle-childhood period, but it still depends heavily on the physical presence of the stimuli in problems. It is generally not until adolescence that young people can demonstrate formal operational thought, that is, sustain an abstract representation of a series of hypothetical objects or numbers and perform logical operations on them. For most purposes adults function on the concrete operational level most of the time, and a significant percentage, perhaps as many as 40 percent of adults, cannot demonstrate the capacity to engage in hypothetical-deductive thought.[15] Most of what we have to think about and many of the daily chores and tasks we confront can be addressed with the fundamental intellectual capacities that have emerged in middle childhood. What makes ordinary adult thought and action generally more effective than that of children between seven and twelve or thirteen is wisdom, sometimes called crystallized intelligence, the accumulation of a much greater array of organized experiences that highlight both the possibilities and the constraints of a given course of action.

As we have suggested, Piaget's goal was the study of the sources of logical thought, abstract moral principles, the principles of cause and effect, and mathematical or scientific reasoning. Even Piaget and Inhelder's great study, *Mental Imagery in the Child,* focuses primarily on images of physical objects, geometric shapes, rotations, and anticipatory images of changed spatial relations, all in the service of the proposition that images, however helpful as memory cues, are ultimately subject to logical operations if they are to serve as knowledge.[16] The study makes no reference to human representations, memories of relationships, or anticipations of future relationships or adventures, those images that are so central to psychoanalytic theory and to all ordinary human fantasies and daydreams.

For the child now confronting the discipline of school and the need to concentrate attention on phonemics in order to read or, increasingly, to employ concrete operational skills just to get by in the classroom, playing at make-believe seems superfluous and often embarrassing. Yet the urge remains, and perhaps for the adaptive reason we suggested earlier. Story-telling and pretending are sources of simple pleasure, but they also turn out to be useful communication tools for engaging the interest of teachers and peers. And the gradual miniaturization and internalization of events in stories provide a sense of control.[17] Even overt make-believe play behaviors seem to have value in broadening memory and thinking skills.

Two recent studies demonstrate that thematic or fantasy play may actually enhance memory and the ability to contemplate impossible or absurd situations in the interests of logical thought. In England, Dias and Harris of Oxford University explored six-year-old children's capacity for following logical statements even when the concrete terms were absurdities according to their actual world knowledge. When material was presented to these children, they were much more accurate in dealing with it within a make-believe context than when they confronted the syllogisms in purely verbal form. It appears that, by establishing a context of "what if," or a playful approach to the improbable, make-believe play actually permitted more effective understanding—as if by turning situations on their heads the children could increasingly adopt the metarepresentational mode Alan Leslie has emphasized as critical for effective socialized thought (see Chapter 6).[18]

In the United States, Silvern and colleagues looked at children's story memory after their exposure either to make-believe play or to the observation of such play. The five- and six-year-olds in their large sample showed better recall of nonenacted stories after make-believe play exposure. A second study looked at two kinds of make-believe intervention with children aged seven to thirteen. Thematic play continued to facilitate recall of nonenacted story content, but there was some indication that more directive guidance by teachers in the make-believe play was more useful for children seeking to recall an unfamiliar story. A more indirect but facilitative approach to children's imaginative play was more useful in helping them recall more familiar story material.[19]

What we are suggesting is that children's impulse to continue make-believe play in middle childhood represents more than the mere persistence of the preoperational accommodation-assimilation cycle into the concrete operations period. Rather, without completely realizing it, children may actually find that their taste for pretending actually helps them to master school content, to confront the novelty of the school setting, and to remember and think more clearly than their peers who have already put aside such "childish things." The Israeli psychologist and psychoanalyst C. Frankenstein has argued that fantasy may be regarded as a "legitimate partner of abstract thought." It frees the child living in an externalized world to surmount what he terms the "illusion" that what we see or know is a given. "Fantasy not only leads to the permanent discovery of new relations [but] also creates the experience of values, because every connotation which has been imagined transcends in its value the object to which it is related."[20]

What the late educational psychologist Herschel Thornburg called the "bubblegum years" also include the beginnings of persisting peer-group formations. Initially, school structures put children into particular seating arrangements, reading or spelling teams, and soon enough intellectually graded "streams," all of which provide opportunities for communal and friendship group identifications. Such groups, while first structured around school matters, expand as children talk about their families, their possessions, the TV shows they've watched, the latest pop music records they've heard, or their music video idols. The research of William and Claire McGuire of Yale University has shown that during these early school years children begin to form their self-concept largely around the differences they recognize between themselves and other children.[21] Some of these differences may simply reflect national, racial, or ethnic background, but others deal with special skills, such as the comedian Teller's early magic tricks, or with special possessions, such as baseball cards or autographed photos of pop singers. One of us (JLS) was introduced by a cousin to the adventure books of Edgar Rice Burroughs, which led to his telling these stories to the other boys while walking home from school or standing around the front stoops of neighborhood apartment houses. As a result, the scrawny storyteller was nicknamed "Tarzan," which was very positive reinforcement—not for emulating the Burroughs character's physical achievements but for further reading and, soon enough, writing. We would propose that, while certainly some elements of a sense of self, especially feelings of being loved or lovable and basic trust and optimism, may begin in the preschool years, it is in middle childhood that organized beliefs about self become crystallized. Such self-schemas form around school achievements or failures, early athletic or artistic successes, and group reinforcement of certain unique qualities. But these beliefs also serve as the starting point for elaborate fantasies that often persist throughout a lifetime. Such fantasies may be so strongly held they become the basis for the psychoanalytic concept of transference; or, although they are recognized as unattainable or childish, they may persist as playful recollections or reflections of lost innocence.

Sharing make-believe play and various forms of story-telling becomes a kind of cement that enhances the formation of early peer groups in middle childhood. Group games of cowboys, pirates, or romantic encounters or rescues are still in evidence during these years. With the advent of television, however, at least in America, much of this play has shifted to vicarious recounting of episodes from sitcoms, afternoon soap operas, or adventure shows. A scene in *Small Change,* a fine French film about children at this age level, depicts in touching fashion how important television-viewing and story-telling are for the child. One of the characters is a boy from a somewhat disorganized, poverty-stricken family living in a squatters' shack in what looks like a junkyard. Naturally the family has no television set. As he walks to school one morning he sidles over near some other kids who are chattering away about the latest episode of the American detective series, "Kojak," which they had watched the night before. Further along on his route he encounters another group and, mixing in, he says, "Say, wasn't that something on 'Kojak' last night?" and recounts the episode.[22]

Continuing Outlets for Make-Believe Play

Board Games, Computer Games, and Video Games

We have already referred to the developmental sequence proposed by Piaget, that is, the shift from sensory-motor play to mastery play to symbolic play and finally to games with rules. Certainly some time after the age of six or seven, many children become increasingly capable of using their capacity for concrete operational thought in the ordering and sequential performances necessary to play board games. Such games represent in miniaturized form the outdoor athletic games with rules they are also learning, and are at the same time a way to sustain pretend play in forms acceptable to the adult world. Even the most rule-governed traditional games—checkers, chess, playing cards, backgammon, Clue, Monopoly, and Stratego—all contain a fanciful element of fairy tale or myth. The king in checkers, the hierarchy of king, queen, knight, bishop, castle and lowly pawn in chess, and the king, queen, and princely jack in cards reflect a vestigial story-telling element. Twentieth-century board games are even more obvious in propounding military or entrepreneurial story-telling along with their increasingly complex rules. But within the past twenty years, new variants of rule games have appeared that not only attract children in this middle-childhood group but have rapidly come to dominate the field. These are computer games, and especially, video games.

Geoffrey and Elizabeth Loftus, cognitive psychologists at the University of Washington, have traced the origins of video games to their earliest prototypes, war and athletic contests, and to their most recent forebears, the mechanical arcade games that mirror sports and war scenes, gambling, gypsy fortune-telling, and the much more recent gamelike products of digital computers.[23] The Loftuses have analyzed how the tremendous attraction of video games can be understood using psychological principles ranging from B. F. Skinner's schedules of reinforcement to the cognitive dissonance studies of social psychologists. Psychologists Daniel Kahnemann and Amos Tversky have proposed a theory of "regret": a very recent specific cause of failure evokes greater distress than a long chain of mistakes. Thus, a video game like Pac-Man (named after the Japanese *pacu-pacu* meaning "to gobble") becomes an obsession because failure is specifically traceable to the last move and not to any earlier misplays.[24] The Loftuses and Patricia Greenfield of UCLA (who has also written on video games, stressing their potential as teaching and learning devices) draw extensively on the seminal research of Thomas Malone in a Stanford University dissertation.[25] Malone sought to develop various versions of computer-generated video games to determine what components were most appealing to boys, to girls, and to children in general. He identified challenge, curiosity, and fantasy as the critical ingredients of video games and the elements of personal instrumentality and feedback as the underlying features responsible for the special appeal of both video and computer games. The fantasy component is present in imagining physical characteristics, such as what Pac-Man is eating, but more especially in identifying with a character, such as the ruler of a country or the rescuer of a maiden. In the five or six years since the publication of these studies, the arcade market and the games they described have been dramatically superseded by yet another new generation of video games, the Nintendo type. These are far more sophisticated in their level of complexity and in their "realistic" depiction of characters (in contrast to the minimal representation of Pac-Man). Their varied and elaborate fantasy and narrative lines bring them closer in form to "interactive" TV shows like "Captain Power," but their much greater degree of physical and intellectual involvement is far more appealing than the more passive experience of watching interactive TV.[26]

Although the wider reaches of pretending are inevitably constrained by games with rules, it is apparent that some children at least will persist in introducing additional components of imaginativeness into such games. A seven-year-old girl we know has become intrigued with the game Clue, which she plays fairly often with her family and babysitters. She links the adventure of crime solution in this game (which combines chance, fantasy, and a capacity for logical, analytic thought) to her regular viewing of a popular and, despite its title, relatively nonviolent Sunday-night TV program, "Murder She Wrote." When she plays Clue she becomes Jessica Fletcher, the writer-detective heroine of the TV show, solving yet another weekly mystery. This fantasy identification is made easier by the fact that both her parents are writers and may be seen at any time working at their word processors, just as Jessica is often at her typewriter.

Back in later middle childhood, one of us (JLS) was given a baseball board game in a stadiumlike box, which involved some motor skills to simulate the pitching, catching, and hitting of a ball game. This two-person game soon attracted the interest of several neighborhood boys. A league was formed using favorite teams and rosters of players. Since New York City then sustained three major league clubs, the Yankees, the Dodgers, and the Giants, these entrants were inevitable, but to the dismay of the others one boy also insisted on creating an entirely new team made up of exotic fantasy characters, apparently a continuation of his own earlier fantasy play. Games were accompanied by elaborate simulations of radio announcers' play-by-play descriptions, which included all their "rooting," hyperbole, and small talk between plays. In typical baseball fashion, extensive statistics were maintained for the imagined players and the team performances. When the season changed to football, the group created a new board game complete with a drawn gridiron, charts of possible outcomes for plays like Off-Tackle, End Run, Punt, or Pass (short or long), a spinner to determine the chart numbers to consult, and a new cast of teams and players. One of the boys invented a superstar runner with the odd name of Pheneffson, who, despite the disdain of the other boys, seemed nevertheless to "run" very well indeed whenever his plays were called and the spinner set in motion. Thirty years later, newspapers and news magazines have reported on a fad among young businessmen and professionals who play more computerized versions of these sports board games in almost compulsive fashion during lunch breaks.

Sometimes a spontaneous fantasy game can be organized into a game with rules. We both remember observing one of our own boys on a fine autumn day trying to catch leaves as they floated gently from a tall tulip tree. In almost balletlike fashion he leaped, dived, and stretched to catch one after another. In about an hour, however, he had organized some other neighborhood children into a leaf-catching game that had rules and scores. The whole group now dashed madly around the yard pursuing drifting leaves, each child, having assumed some sports hero identity, eager to garner as many points as possible while our son kept score.

The mix of games with rules and fantasy raises a concern that has become the focus of some controversy and has even reached the halls of Congress. As Loftus and Loftus have pointed out, many of the games of middle childhood stem from simulations of warfare and aggression. It would be absurd to assume that players of chess, Stratego, or very complicated computer games like Wizard would be prone to overt aggression. What most data suggest, however, is that the more realistically violent the material appears in game form, the more likely children are to engage in overt imitation. Chess, computer games, or fairly complicated board games require far more thought that involves concrete and formal operations, logic, and analysis. Watching violent television or playing most video games, with their repeated messages that violence solves most conflicts, presents more serious problems. The data from a few studies suggest that video games in which children "shoot" targets on the screen can be associated with greater subsequent aggressive behavior, much as do the data from studies of children who watch violent television.[27] It is too soon to assess the long-term effects of the Nintendo video games or of interactive TV shows in which children are, in effect, practicing shooting reactions over and over against victims who simply disappear and clearly do not suffer. While basically hopeful that video games can be put to good use for educational purposes, Geoffrey and Elizabeth Loftus admit their dismay that the social learning from most video games may promote violence. Patricia Greenfield's review of the video game literature, while also optimistic about the potential value of the combination of interaction and computerized logic in the nonviolent games, deplores the potential risks of increased violence among children who are ultimately being systematically reinforced to aim and shoot all day long.

We once had the occasion to attend hearings of the U.S. Congressional Subcommittee on Telecommunications. A representative of a major toy company, which was marketing a toy that could be beamed at the television set and could presumably shoot the "bad guys" on the "Captain Power" science fiction program (also sponsored by the company), presented testimony. He argued that interactive TV broke away from passive viewing and gave children a greater sense of involvement. While those social scientists who, like ourselves, were called on to testify, agreed that interactive processes, especially with computer teaching programs, could be very useful as aids to classroom teaching, the "Captain Power" model (rated by the National Council on Television Violence as the most violent of children's shows then being aired) simply trained the child in simulated shooting. To the embarrassment of the congressional committee, the company spokesman switched on a tape of the show and bounded around the room, pointing his weaponlike toy at the set and firing away in response to the cues provided in the adventure story.

The potential value of harnessing the story-telling and fantasy interest of the elementary school child or even the adolescent for learning through computerized games is well documented in the studies of Greenfield and the Loftuses. The increasing levels of challenge built into these games provides the element of difficulty and curiosity that sustains interest, along with the storyline and fantasy. Naturally, such characteristics can be addictive, although there is also evidence that playing stops once the player has mastered all the levels available in a given game.[28] Greenfield cites some pioneering work that combines fantasy and intellectual challenge with basic information to teach the periodic table of chemical elements. James Levin and Yaacov Kareev have proposed such a game:

> We personify elements as people having characteristics analogous to their namesake elements . . . [t]he muscle men Chlorine, Fluorine and Iodine, the casanovas Lithium, Sodium and Potassium, the super rich Platinum, Gold, Silver and Copper. A goal in this game might be to rescue Silver who is being held hostage by the seductive Chlorine (the compound silver chloride, used in photographic paper) . . . the player could use a magic power (free electrons) to sprinkle over Silver to reduce his attraction to Chlorine, so that he can get free . . . Along the

way the player would have to avoid the dangerous Arsenic and Plutonium, distracting Arsenic with Gallium, or using Lead as a shield from
Plutonium's rays.[29]

As Greenfield points out, the obvious value of using board games
and computer games to harness children's love of pretending and
story-telling for educational purposes has distinct advantages in
drawing them into mastering the necessary substantive knowledge
and relevant skills for processing scientific information. What is
more problematic, however, as she also points out, is whether there
are some risks as well. The video game emphasis on rapid motor
performance minimizes reflection and organized thought. Computer
games, while more reflective and logical, may lead children to expect too much order from the rather messy social world we all inhabit.

Creative Dramatic Play

Another expression of children's fantasy interest in middle childhood, actual dramatic play or theaterlike performance, comes closer
to mimicking the orderly and logical properties of rule games and
may be useful in helping to develop social imagination and actual
interpersonal skills.

The use of amateur theatricals as a form of entertainment, even
for young adults, has been well-documented in histories of the royal
counts of Renaissance France and, later, in accounts of life in the
large and comfortable country homes of the English gentry.[30] Jane
Austen's *Mansfield Park*, published in 1814, reaches its climax when
the gentle heroine, Fanny, resists the efforts of more wayward young
people who seek to involve her in their production of a scandalous
play while the kindly but very proper master of Mansfield Park is
away on a trip. In more recent times, the transition from the make-
believe play of the preschooler to more structured theatricals is
evident in the makeshift efforts of children in middle childhood to
set up little playlets. Both of us recall participating in such performances as children in backyards or inside during inclement
weather. In one case, a series of Sherlock Holmes episodes was produced for the benefit of younger siblings and neighborhood children.
The boy who actually owned a deerstalker cap and had an aquiline
nose always got to play the great detective; the other children in the
troupe were relegated to being Dr. Watson, Professor Moriarity,

various clients, and the Hound of the Baskervilles! No script was employed. Rather the stories were improvised along the lines of one of the Arther Conan Doyle plots as read or, more likely, heard on radio or seen in film.

Sometimes such games are elaborated into ongoing play. Acted out in basements, in rocky sections of public parks, or on beaches they reflect a somewhat greater complexity and sophistication than the make-believe of the preschooler but sustain some of the same delight. As cognitive skill, and thus the capacity for rule development, increases such play takes on a more literary form but still maintains the elements of war, conflict, chase, and capture that were evident in earlier childhood. Two variants of role-playing games that have spread nationally in recent years are Lazer Tag (also known as Gotcha) and Dungeons and Dragons. The former, essentially a war game between competitive teams, has drawn heavily on movie, television, comic book, and novelistic accounts of espionage (satirized in *Mad* magazine's cartoon series "Spy versus Spy"). Extending to college students who use laserlike pistols or weapons that project colored dyes to "shoot" their opponents, this game has been much criticized, not only for its excessive emphasis on warfare and violence as a problem-solving device but also because of evidence that occasionally, players engage in direct and all-too-real violence or may themselves become victims.[31] In Rancho Cucamongo, California, a group of teenagers playing Lazer Tag stimulated a call to the police from someone who believed a real gun-fight was occurring. When one of the players leaped out from behind a bush and fired his Lazer Tag gun at a deputy sheriff, the officer had no choice but to respond out of fear for his own safety by shooting his own very real weapon and killing the boy.

Dungeons and Dragons is a much more elaborate game apparently inspired by J. R. R. Tolkien's *Lord of the Rings* and the Sword and Sorcery novels and magazines that attract a somewhat more literate group of children in middle childhood and early adolescence. Available as a board game that leads to elaborate, overt make-believe play, and also attractive to computer-literate children who play adventure and wizardlike computer games, Dungeons and Dragons has developed some features of cultism. Although its fairy-tale quality has some appeal in middle childhood, its complex hier-archical structure, secrecy, suggestions of lurid sexuality, and perhaps even satanic qualities have made it the object of intense criticism by Fundamentalist Christians and antiwar toy or television groups like those led by the psychiatrist Thomas Radecki.[32] Since its more "sinister" elements are associated with adolescent or young adult players, we will return to this game in Chapter 11.

Most of the dramatic play of middle childhood is more benign, casual, and spontaneous. Sensitive teachers have generally recognized the great value of these play tendencies and have harnessed children's energy by using playlets to teach lessons about history, geography, and current events. Actually moving well beyond such focused efforts are those educators who feel that dramatic play can be a critical device for a great variety of educational and mental health functions. We will mention just a few examples, since there are already a number of significant textbooks in the field.[33]

Winifred Ward, a wonderful classroom storyteller, is often considered the key figure in the past half-century in spreading the message that good teaching and imaginative or sociodramatic play go hand in hand. She wrote that "drama comes in the door of every school with the child."[34] For Ward, listening to stories was a start, but the real opportunities for developing imagination, social skills, and approaches to problem-solving came through improvised drama, writing, and acting in playlets and eventually trying out more formal roles. Nellie McCaslin, the author of a major textbook on drama in the classroom, extends these benefits to include heightened social awareness, an opportunity for acceptable emotional expressiveness, and improved speech pronunciation and usage.

Programs that engage children's natural inclination to pretend usually begin with rhythm and movement, improvisation, and mime and gradually move to simple exercises that foster self-expression and the communication of emotions. Great sensitivity to group interaction is necessary in order to sustain a general sense of participation and to avoid isolating and scapegoating those children who are shy or who lack pretend play skills, perhaps because of inexperience. Today we recognize that the values of caring, sharing, concern for the weak and disadvantaged, and responsibility are important features of a full curriculum. The creative educator seeks to foster the internalization of these values at two levels: through the content of the plays the children enact and through their actual participation in writing the play, assigning parts, rehearsing, preparing scenery, helping each other learn lines, and building simple sets or props. There is something for everybody in the process and since the central focus is story-telling, it draws on earlier make-believe experience.[35]

Helane Rosenberg, working with her group at Rutgers University, has produced a delightful and practical volume on stimulating creativity and imagination in the schoolroom. The book includes dozens of simple, concrete procedures for engaging children's attention and generating imaginative activity in a playful but ultimately educational fashion.[36] She proposes that dramatic play can enhance on the one hand, imagery and related internal capacities and on the other, overt social and behavioral skills. Through the interactive process the child develops a new sense of an inner self, a heightened awareness of autonomous skills, and a sense of connectedness. Dramatic play, by enriching inner experience and also by fostering social interaction, can help the seven- to twelve-year-old confront and resolve the inherent human tension between connection and autonomy (see Figure 2-2).

The Rutgers Imagination method Rosenberg outlines involves three major aspects:

1. Participants plan, play, and evaluate using their ability to imagine, enact, and reflect.
2. The tools include images, scripts, and modest props produced by the participants.
3. A sense of organization or at least some formal structure (circular, hierarchical, or linear) sustains the exercises, often with the limited but clear guidance of the instructor.

Extensive use is made of individually constructed props, of photographs that are easily available from family albums, and of paintings and drawings produced by the children themselves. Children not only act—they write, design, direct, and criticize. Once again, children's natural inclination to pretend and their joy in storytelling are subtly and effectively enlisted for exercises that enhance their self-esteem and social adaptiveness.

Psychotherapeutic Applications of Board Games in Middle Childhood

The principles of dramatic play used in the schools for educational or mental health purposes apply equally well to the play therapy situation. We have already described some ways in which overt play has been applied in psychotherapy. The continuation of make-believe games into middle childhood has also served as the basis for a form of psychotherapy that is employed mainly with adults: Jacob L. Moreno's Psychodrama. This method involves the development of dramatic situations in which the patient enacts confrontations with various family members or other key life figures. Other patients or confederates of the therapist serve as "auxiliary egos" and are cast as fathers, mothers, or siblings. At various points the target patients in the playlet are expected to "reverse roles" and play their parents or spouses while auxiliaries play them. This method enhances empathy for others and helps identify personal defenses or obfuscations. It can also help teach new ways of relating. Although psychodrama continues as a separate form of therapy with slightly cultic adherents and organizations, its success is attested by how thoroughly it has been incorporated into much current psychotherapeutic practice, from Kelly's Role Repertory approach to Transactional Analysis, Gestalt therapy, and the cognitive behavioral methods of treating phobias and problems of assertiveness.

Moreno's own account of the origins of this approach makes it clear that they reflected his middle-childhood play experiences. In addition to his great success as a neighborhood storyteller for the other children, a genuine "Pied Piper" as he designates himself, he also initiated dramatic games: "One Sunday afternoon . . . I and some of the neighbor's children decided to play at 'God' . . . the first thing was to build our HEAVEN . . . we collected every chair and piled them up . . . until they reached to the ceiling. I now mounted my heavenly throne . . . mine 'the kingdom, the power and the glory'—while my angels 'flew' around me singing. Suddenly one of the children called out 'why don't you fly too?' Whereupon I stretched out my arms—and one second later lay on the floor with a broken arm. So ended my first psychodrama."[37]

Anyone who had the privilege of observing Moreno conducting a workshop on Psychodrama can attest to the fact that this early experience did not completely dampen his God-like identification. With his shock of wild hair, his Hungarian accent, and his broad gestures, he dominated the sessions. Though he resembled the movie stereotype of the mad psychiatrist—a real-life Dr. Caligari or Dr. Mabuse—he was also brilliant, perceptive, and imaginative, as his psychodrama or sociodrama therapies demonstrate. His invention of the sociometric method for measuring the social structure of children's groupings has been a major contribution to the study of peer relations in middle childhood.

Moreno applied his methods to his family to resolve disputes around the dining-room table and in particular situations, such as helping his son Jonathan, aged twelve, overcome his fear of going out on a date. While Jonathan later rebelled against these applications of role-playing and role reversal, it is reported that he eventually came to recognize their usefulness and as an adult employs them moderately in his own family.[38]

In the past twenty years psychotherapists working with children in the nine- to twelve-year-old age group have recognized that many are no longer comfortable with overt role playing and yet cannot articulate their problems or dilemmas using the verbal methods of adult psychotherapy. Board games provide opportunities for these children to combine their newfound capacity for rule games with the intrinsic appeal of narrative or fantasy. Pioneered by child psychiatrists such as Richard Gardner and Nathan Kritzberg, a small and useful industry of therapeutic board games has evolved to the point that Charles Schaefer and Steven Reid have recently edited a volume describing many of them.[39] A list of available games has been assembled by Diane Frey, who categorizes them into three general groups: games fostering more effective interpersonal communication; those focused on special problems like children of divorce; and those that are designed to introduce children to particular therapeutic approaches, such as transactional therapy or rational-emotive therapy.[40] Some of the names are clearly suggestive and reflect the make-believe elements that underlie them: Imagine; Social Security; Talking, Feeling, Doing; Tisket, Tasket; and the Changing Family Game. Most of these games involve moving around a board and landing on spaces that require the player to draw a message card. They usually also use symbolic tokens. In Imagine players pick up cards that say things like, "Pretend you could take a ride on the flying horse. What happened?" "If someone called you up on the amazing telephone, who would it be?" Kritzberg's Tisket, Tasket is linked to an elaborate theory that draws on developmental psychology and psychoanalytic principles. It involves both competitiveness (the acquisition of tokens and chips) and the reinforcement principles for more elaborate, self-revealing story-telling.

Connie Behrens has described her Problem-Solving Game as having evolved from her therapeutic interaction with a nine-year-old boy named Trent. Confronted with this boy, who was rigid and withholding, she tried reversing roles, telling him that *she* had a problem. He played therapist and she then revealed that her problem was how to help him. His response was to perch himself high on a "throne" and then ask Behrens to bring him rubber animals and dinosaurs. For each he asked Behrens to make up a problem which he then sought to answer. She wisely presented his specific difficulties as "their" problems and he sought solutions. This approach enhanced the rapport between the two, and he gradually improved at school and at home. The problem-solving board game involves several children who respond to colored cards that are worth different points with solutions to problems such as shyness, aggression, fearfulness, confusion, anger, physical handicaps, and so on. Cards also reflect adult figures who need help. The therapist gradually personalizes the situation so that the players bring the problems and solutions more into relationship with themselves and are willing to share these with each other.[41]

Richard Gardner's Talking, Feeling, Doing game uses different categories of cards for (1) primarily cognitive answers; (2) emotional answers; or (3) overt action or role-playing. The cards vary in anxiety level and rewards are given for answers. The therapist also plays but gears answers to the problem areas of the child. Gardner tries to be very honest and self-revelatory because he believes this will enhance the bond between himself and the child. In keeping with the principles he laid out in his early Mutual Story Telling approach, he also strives to present stories that provide alternative solutions to the more confused or self-defeating responses he obtains from the children.[42] The art of techniques like Kritzberg's and Gardner's is to present psychologically useful approaches geared to the child's level of comprehension and therapeutic stage without seeming to moralize. These board games, they believe, call for professional training and are not for casual family use.

While there is as yet little systematic research evaluating the therapeutic value of particular board games for disturbed children, the possibilities seem self-evident. The therapist has the opportunity to marshall the tremendous fascination of the middle-childhood period through a combination of fantasy and concrete operational thought. Elaine Blechman and her colleagues have even integrated board games of this type with computer games for family therapy and for couples counseling with adults. This is a clever notion indeed, since board and computer games have become ways in which seven- to twelve-year-olds and their parents can share the human fascination with pretending. In fact, in one of the few controlled research evaluations of various methods of reducing aggression in boys at this age level, Eric Dubow, L. Rowell Huesmann, and

Leonard Eron reported the clear advantage of game playing of this type in producing results that lasted for at least six months.[43]

The Internalization of Make-Believe Play

Overt make-believe play does not really fade away during the early school-age years; it simply becomes harder to observe because it occurs privately in a child's room or becomes incorporated into the ebb and flow of after-school street play. Gender and social class differences now become more prominent determinants of how children use their time, what kinds of play seem open to them, and what strictures are imposed on their recreation. Elliot Medrich and a team of investigators from the University of California at Berkeley spent more than five years observing children's out-of-school activities in relatively distinct neighborhoods in the city of Oakland. Socioeconomic status differences among the families of the children were significant elements in the children's activities, although more in terms of the family's "life-circumstance perspective" than in the more traditional scoring categories of parental income, education, or housing. Time restrictions and expectations were the major ways these differences were manifested, with the more well off African-American, white, and Asian families imposing more time restrictions or household chore expectations on their children. Girls were also confronted with more rules about television-watching, outdoor play, and late hours and were frequently expected to cook and to oversee younger siblings, all activities that socialized them earlier and more firmly into a "clock consciousness."[44]

Observations and interviews with the hundreds of children who made up the Oakland sample indicated that while only about 5 percent admitted to "role-playing" games when alone, these numbers vary across ethnic groups, with white and Asian children generally reporting the highest percentage of fantasylike games. Unfortunately, the study did not permit observation of the ways make-believe elements may have been introduced even into skateboarding or athletic activities or into hobby or board game play. The nature of their physical settings seems an especially strong determinant of the kinds of play possible for many of these children.[45]

Studies of imaginative play that have been carried out on a smaller scale are often more revealing because they allow for regular observations over time. In the period between ages five and seven the shift toward greater conservational capacities and concrete operational thought is evident in the greater narrative complexity in the play of the older children and their greater use of metaphor and categorization.[46] David Forbes and Gary Yablick of the Harvard School of Education arranged for teams of raters to score the play behavior of groups of five- and seven-year-olds over a twelve-day period and found that while the younger children focused on settings and objects, the older groups were more interested in the characters in the games, their role appropriateness, and their consistency.[47] Variations in the play complexity of fourth graders were further studied by David Sleet of San Diego State University. He observed that boys' games showed more elaboration and social differentiation than girls' play, and that inner-city children in general preferred more socially complicated games than did rural children. Sleet proposed that more opportunities for group and team play may have led the inner-city boys to choose more hierarchically structured play themes, while more isolated rural children continued to choose games that involved more limited structures.[48]

The persistence of interest in make-believe play in early school-age children has often been used as a focus for further training in cognitive growth or for diagnostic purposes.[49] In Richmond, Virginia, Andrew Newcomb and Judith Meister employed observations of free play between pairs of unacquainted children to identify the special qualities manifested by those children who had earlier been identified as high in popularity and social effectiveness. These children were much more likely than other groups to initiate play through personal greetings and introductions and to lay out the terms of play or provide information about the game at the outset.[50] Brenda Engel's observations of the conversations of seven-year-olds during play revealed their attitudes about war and nuclear weapons, and their own personal insecurities or happiness.[51] Role assignments such as teacher or learner, manager or employee, helper or victim continue to be central issues for seven- to nine-year-old sibling-pairs, with the older children regularly taking the more dominant position.[52]

Observations of children telling stories during play, dealing with bean bag chairs in group situations, or interacting with their mothers during play all call attention to recurrent themes involving a persistent hope for a lasting relationship or power and autonomy.[53] Generally, it appears that girls continue more nurturant play and include more prosocial or helping behaviors in their stories, but they also reflect more fear of bodily injury than boys, who persist in more adventurous and varied around-the-world themes.[54] Finally, in an intriguing if perhaps flawed study a group of investigators from the City College of New York sought to test Bruno Bettelheim's proposal that fairy tales, by touching on profound themes in a child's psychic life, may actually have a greater impact than other more realistic stories or television fare.[55] In two experiments, one with urban ghetto children ages nine to eleven and the other with suburban six-year-olds, they found that, compared to children who either heard a "trivial" story or saw a cartoon, children who listened to a fairy tale subsequently played quietly in a rather self-reflective manner, as if they had been deeply involved. Whether a modern age-appropriate children's story would have had a similar effect on play should probably also have been tested.

Perhaps reading plays a crucial role (along with the constraints on overt play imposed by school) in the enhancement of the child's private fantasy world. Reading necessitates an effort by the child not only to sound out words but also to try to imagine the situations depicted by their syntactic combinations. As children read they become more and more absorbed in the story line, whether fictional or historical. Even arithmetic problems about buying apples and getting the right change call for some envisioning of events. Listening to poetry or to pop song lyrics (without the benefit of the lurid images of music videos) may also evoke particular mental representations or story lines. A child hearing a traditional English ballad about how, after poor Edward was found murdered, the people "laid him on the green" might misunderstand and conjure up an image of a "Lady Mondegrene," who is then given a new life in a series of private fantasies. Such a transformation recalls our friend, mentioned in Chapter 5, whose childish interpretation of ultraviolet ray led her to create imaginary playmates named Ultra, Violet, and Ray. Gradually the child makes more use of private self-narration, anticipated adventures, and private story-telling.

But many puzzles persist. Can we show that children who demonstrate richer and more elaborate make-believe games in the preschool or early school-age period actually do have more complex inner lives as nine-year-olds or as adolescents? We may believe this to be likely, as our general emphasis suggests, but the basic longitudinal research is lacking. And how can we tell whether reading does indeed stimulate imaginative flexibility? Despite thousands of studies of the reading process surprisingly little attention has been paid to how we encode the stories we decipher from print and how we relate them to ongoing images or to established schemas in ways that deepen previous fantasies or promote new ones. With the current, unfortunately high rate of illiteracy in America are we prepared to say that imagination is limited or impoverished in those who are unable to read? After all, traditional oral cultures have maintained mythological and historical narratives over centuries. Finally, how can we even estimate the patterns of inner experience or fantasy that characterize middle childhood?

For this last question we do have the beginning of an answer. Erica Rosenfeld, Rowell Huesmann, Leonard Eron, and Judith V. Torney-Purta brought together a team of investigators from the University of Illinois in Chicago who were ultimately interested in relating children's fantasy patterns to the effects of television-viewing.[56] They first asked whether a questionnaire measure that was reliable and valid could be devised to estimate styles of make-believe play and fantasy. Such a measure would have to estimate not only the *content* (such as themes of romance or adventure) but also the *emotionality* (sadness, fear, or joy) and the *structure* (persistence, involvement, or fragmentation) of daydreaming. Next, one would need to show that such a questionnaire and its subscales could be reliably associated with other estimates of fantasy or creativity. How similar would children's daydream patterns be to those of adults? What role would gender and age play in the organization of daydreaming styles?

Following preliminary trials the group devised a forty-five item questionnaire understandable when read to first-grade children and within the reading capacity of older children. Questionnaire items were derived in part from the Singer-Antrobus Imaginal Processes Inventory, a set of scales used with adults,[57] and included such items as "Do you have a special daydream that you like to think about over and over?" (an item tapping Absorption in Fantasy), "Do you sometimes have daydreams about hitting or hurting somebody that you don't like?" (Aggression scale), or "Sometimes when you play pretend things do you feel so happy that you don't ever want the game to end?" (Vividness, Fanciful scales).

Eventually these scales were administered to 713 children between the ages of six and nine in the first and third grades of the Oak Park School, located in an area ranking at the midpoint of Chicago suburban schools in family income levels. A year later the questionnaire was again administered to 540 children from this original sample. The administration began with a simple explanation of daydreaming as a form of make-believe play in thought.

Considering the ages of this group the data indicated a surprisingly good internal consistency for the scales of the test and quite respectable one month or one year test-retest reliabilities. That is, children did not answer randomly and they showed a good tendency to demonstrate the same patterns when they retook the test a month or a year later. By various statistical procedures the researchers identified three underlying patterns or factors that characterized children's responses. These were labeled Dysphoric or Unpleasant and Aggressive Style (Factor I), Fanciful-Intense Style (Factor II), and the Active-Intellectual Style (Factor III). Such styles bear considerable resemblance to the three factors that are consistently found for adults' daydreams.[58] These patterns also proved to be correlated with the children's responses to the Fantasy Predisposition interview we had used in earlier research and with a measure devised by the Chicago group called "Tell-Me-a-Daydream." In general, questionnaire answers and especially the Fanciful daydreaming scale do hang together with the children's responses to different ways of estimating fantasy tendencies. Differences across age levels indicate that younger children are characterized more by Fanciful, Intellectual, and Scary Fantasy scales, while older children score higher on the Aggressive and Absorption scales. The younger children were more likely to report night dreams influenced by television. Gender differences mainly reflected the boys' greater Heroic fantasies while the girls in general showed not only more Fanciful Fantasy but also more Scary and Dysphoric patterns. There were no gender differences in frequency.

The parallels between this study's findings and the far more numerous adult studies on daydreaming suggest that by about nine years of age, or smack in middle childhood, the general structural characteristics of children's imaginativeness are indeed comparable to adult patterns. The internalization process is well-nigh complete. Children at the younger ages do show fewer of the aggressive fantasies that are reported a few years later by the third graders and that are quite prominent in adults. Nor do any of the younger children show the guilty fantasies that, together with aggression, form the adult factor of dysphoric daydreaming. Age and experience seem especially likely to expose children to more failures and frustrations, and by late adolescence the guilty, fear of failure, and aggressive fantasies are all apparent according to various studies available in the literature.[59]

The emergence of the possibility of a rich and varied inner life by middle childhood suggests a number of significant implications for personality variations and for needed research. In effect, the child now has available an entirely new dimension of experience in which wishes, fears, doubts, and frustrations can be dramatized as *possibilities,* as, to use Freud's phrase, "experimental action."[60] On this private stage the child can play out desires that, if expressed overtly, might have dire consequences. Freud also added, however, the notion that such wishful fantasy also discharged small quantities of energy, thus reducing the pressure of the presumed drive. This latter hypothesis has served as the foundation for the theory of "catharsis" still popular among some mental health workers and even childhood educators. Presumably, fantasizing about a strong basic impulse such as aggression or sexuality should at least for a while reduce the tendency to turn such a wish into action. The principle of partial discharge has served as a basis for arguing that aggressive play or fantasy is adaptive in minimizing overt aggression. Watching violent films, wrestling, or prizefights should reduce the viewer's likelihood of engaging in overt assaults on others because basic drive energies are partially discharged vicariously.

One could pass lightly over this catharsis theory, which has been discredited by literally dozens of experimental studies, were it not for the fact that the notion continues to be promulgated by defenders of televised violence and even by some child educators. The ABC network's "20/20" magazine program on May 26, 1989, allotted considerable time to an operator of daycare centers in California who actively trains preschoolers and children of eight and nine to engage in fighting with plastic bats and elongated cushionlike "pushers." He encouraged child viewers to cheer and pound the floor like fans at a wrestling match while boys and girls pummeled away at each other with considerable ferocity. Everything we know from psychological research on how children learn through imitation suggests that such training can only increase the likelihood of subsequent aggressive behavior, not just in play but in other social encounters.[61] In view of the strong evidence of potential harm to the children and more generally to the society exposed to such a theory of child care, we believe that anyone who teaches violent play is under obligation to demonstrate systematically that the children exposed to his program are happier and healthier and, indeed, not prone to undue subsequent aggressive behavior, if he is to be allowed to stay in business.

Rowell Huesmann and Leonard Eron of the Chicago group we mentioned earlier have devoted many years to examining the consequences for children in middle childhood of exposure to violent television content that then becomes part of their fantasy lives.[62] Their work, which includes in one major study a twenty-year follow-up of children whose television viewing was first noted when they were ten-year-olds, has consistently found significant correlations between the viewing of violent shows and later aggressive behavior. They obtained similar results in a shorter term follow-up of the Oak Park children. Our own research involving several different studies of preschoolers or early school-age children has also yielded evidence of comparable links between heavy television-viewing, especially of the more violent adult action-adventure programs or violent cartoons, and overt aggressive actions by children.[63] Of particular relevance for our discussion of fantasies in middle childhood are the findings reported by Huesmann summarizing studies conducted in five countries, Australia, Finland, Poland, Israel, and the United States, all using the methods developed for the Oak Park children. The data show strong indications that both heroic-adventure fantasies and aggressive fantasies are generally associated with overt aggression for both boys and girls. Huesmann writes:

> According to our model, once a script for aggressive behavior is stored, whether or not it is ever retrieved may depend on whether it is rehearsed. One form of rehearsal is daydreaming . . . greater aggressive behavior and more TV violence viewing were associated with more frequent aggressive and heroic daydreams in most countries. The strength of the relationship varies greatly across samples, but overall the results are consistent with the theory that violent TV (and violent behavior) may stimulate violent fantasies, and violent fantasies may increase the likelihood of violent behavior. Certainly, these data contradict the theory that aggressive fantasies stimulated by aggressive TV might act as a catharsis and reduce the likelihood of aggressive behavior.[64]

While heroic and aggressive fantasies, especially the former, are particularly characteristic of boys in middle childhood, who are also generally more aggressive than girls, an additional factor to be considered is the extent to which children have developed a varied and complex inner life. A body of research literature suggests that aggressive fantasy is more likely to be translated into overt action when it is a predominant, central focus of most ongoing thought and when it is nakedly aggressive, with no sense of its consequences or moral implications and with no attention to the possibility of suffering for the victim or punishment for the fantasizer. Studies with children and adolescents indicate that those with more fantasy tendencies in general and those who report aggressive fantasies that also reflect awareness of the possible implications of violence are less likely to show overt aggressive behavior.[65] A very careful study carried out by Ephraim Biblow at the City College of New York examined how nine- and ten-year-olds who were either very high scorers on two measures of general fantasy tendencies or who showed little predisposition for fantasy differed in their aggressive responses before and after a frustrating situation. The measures of fantasy included the Rorschach inkblot human movement (M) scores and a "just suppose" series of questions. Because Biblow was interested in testing the catharsis theory, following a frustrating situation, subgroups of children were assigned to conditions involving watching either an aggressive film or a nonaggressive film or simply engaging in a neutral, easy problem-solving activity that was sufficiently demanding to minimize the opportunity for much free fantasy. Again, no evidence was found in support of the catharsis theory. Rather, the more imaginative children (both boys and girls) showed significant reductions in aggression following both types of film while the low-fantasy children increased in aggression only following the aggressive film. The high fantasy children had initially been less aggressive than the low fantasy group, and they responded to both types of film-viewing with decreases in anger and with increases in fearfulness, sadness, and shame; the low fantasy children showed only an increase in anger following the aggressive film.

Biblow suggests that a rich, complex fantasy life prepares children for a greater variety of options and that any vicarious stimulation after frustration will result in complex emotions. Significantly, all the low fantasy children who saw the aggressive film became more angry and their aggressive behavior increased. No effects either way were produced for the control group, as expected. In general, these results point up the importance of carefully considering varieties of fantasy and their uses by children and suggest that the catharsis drive reduction model is not a useful one. Imaginative children can use a variety of vicarious fantasy experiences to moderate their anger, while children who lack these inclinations are not only basically more aggressive but may show an increase in anger and aggression following exposure to a violent film.[66]

The ways in which fantasy predisposition, age, and exposure to different models influence children's subsequent imaginative productions were examined in a complex investigation of children aged ten to fourteen by Sybil Gottlieb, also of the City College of New York.[67] She used the same measures as Biblow for estimating fantasy richness and complexity. Children watched abstract, non-representational films by the artist, Norman McLaren, under conditions in which different kinds of response to the ambiguous content were modeled by a teacher. They were subsequently asked to write what they thought the film was about. While almost none of the children copied the ideas of the model directly, the younger age group produced imaginative productions that reflected the general influence of the model. The older children reacted more in terms of their own imaginative predisposition, with the more fantasy-prone group showing richer and more vivid story-telling, irrespective of whether they had been subjected to a realistic or fantasy model condition after viewing the abstract film. The following is an example of the response of a low fantasy child, aged twelve:

> The film dealt with balls dancing around each other. The movement of the balls was set to music. It did not impress me. It made me feel sleepy. The tone of the music did nothing but make me sleepy.

In contrast, here is the response to the same film of a child who scored high in fantasy-predisposition:

> Once there was a lonely person. He never played with his friends because they didn't like him. He watched all his friends play all day long. They would make beautiful trees come out of the ground and flowers too. He was lonely because he was odd. He just sat and watched. One day when he was watching he felt something strange. All of a sudden he was just like his friends. He would play and play. From then on he lived happily ever after.[68]

Gottlieb also found strong indications that fantasy themes changed markedly from middle childhood through puberty and early adolescence. The younger children's fantasies were much more likely to involve team or group adventure stories, while the older children's productions more often involved individual opposite-sex romances, vocation plans, or achievement. While the younger children emphasized exploration, invasions, and athletic contests, the older children told stories in response to the nonrepresentational films that involved mating, the creation of life, the origin of new discoveries, and the meaning of existence. We can trace this critical shift to the concerns of adolescence and the growing importance of the problems of personal identity and intimacy as we move from the ten- to the fourteen-year-old.

The Implications of Internalized Fantasy

We want to pause now in our review of formal research data to reflect and perhaps to speculate a little on the nature of thought and imagination in middle childhood. While some overt floor play persists, as Bill Boggs's reminiscences about his toy soldiers indicate, and while, as we have discussed, imaginative play may find an outlet in board games, computer games, video games, and amateur theatricals, middle childhood and early adolescence are the great periods of extended internal fantasy. Children can begin to speculate about dozens of alternative lives, about adventure and romance, about heroism, and (especially with the increasing sexual openness of novels, comic books, films, and television) even about various kinds of sexual encounters. Latency indeed! While the seven- to eleven-year-old may not yet be certain about sexual processes and may not yet experience clear bodily signals, fantasies about some kind of intimacy begin to flower. With puberty, self-touching and masturbation are experimentally tried and the extensive fantasies associated with such activities begin to take shape. Clinical experience in the absence of more formal research must be relied on here, but it does seem very likely that specific "appetites" for sexual encounters, for a specific kind of partner, and for the circumstances and activities of sexuality become increasingly crystallized. We believe that the origins of particular kinds of sexual expression, whether normal or deviant, heterosexual or homosexual, or involving particular kinds of role playing—sadistic or masochistic, promiscuous or monogamous—are largely traceable to this special time. Often, almost by chance, the child's reading, TV-watching, and fantasies about the nature of intimacy are suddenly associated with sexual stirrings. The conditioned pairing of a particular fantasy with the experience of arousal may form the basis for sexual anticipation that then becomes further reinforced by actual masturbation.

For the child moving from middle childhood into puberty and the onset of sexual arousal without, as a rule, any direct experience of physical intimacy, images drawn from life may of course predominate. We would speculate that the so-called Oedipal fantasies, usually assigned to the preschool period, may actually flourish more in middle childhood or puberty, especially if some quasi-seductive or flirtatious behavior (not to mention occasional actual incest) by a parent, other familial adult, or sibling has occurred already. Much of this behavior may be relatively "innocent," perceived as "teasing" by the older person. It may be worked into quasi-theatrical play, as in the case of older sisters or cousins who, in need of a male "lead" enlist a ten-year-old boy to participate in a romantic dramatization in which some kissing is involved. For the boy, such an episode may be a source of fantasizing about intimacy and if, not long after, sexual arousal begins, fantasies may focus on the theme of the play enacted or on one of the older "actresses." Oedipal fantasies about parental figures may be especially embarrassing and in the interest of inhibiting or repressing such fantasies the child or very early adolescent may go to the opposite extreme, seizing on a figure from comic books or movies (or, for more affluent children, a servant from a different social class or ethnic background) who represents a sharp contrast. The new figure becomes a focus of fantasies in masturbation or (to use a phrase reported by English school girls) "keeping warm in bed."

While research on the fantasy life of children in middle childhood and puberty is very sparse, especially in relation to sexual fantasy, we have some suggestions from retrospective data that are somewhat relevant. Working with one of us at the City University of New York, Barbara Hariton explored the sexual fantasies of married women. A significant subgroup reported that during the sexual act itself they experienced fantasies of being dominated or forced, of being harem wives or prostitutes, and that these images were arousing and sometimes seemed to ensure orgasm. Further inquiry brought out memories from early adolescence, when these rather strictly, religiously reared girls had developed such seemingly masochistic fantasies in order to give them "license" to masturbate or to enjoy arousal without associated guilt feelings.[69] In yet another study with male seventeen- and eighteen-year-old Yale College freshmen, Anthony Campagna was able to identify four styles of fantasy that occurred during masturbation. Students who claimed some degree of "mature" sexual activity tended to fantasize a reasonably detailed encounter with someone who had been or could become a sexual partner. A second pattern, more characteristic of youngsters with minimal sexual experience (and thus in a sense closer to the child's circumstances) involved elaborate storylike fantasies in which the details of the sexual act were somewhat less specific but were the culmination of an adventurous encounter (not too different from the women's reports in the Hariton study, although without as much of the "forced" element). A third pattern involved sexual daydreams that included a spectrum of more unusual or statistically less typical encounters or sexual acts, including homosexuality. A final pattern seemed to reflect fragmented fantasy or almost a failure of fantasy, focusing on images of body parts, breasts, and behinds, but revealing no articulated image of a complete woman or of any storylike encounter. This last pattern, if a dominant one, was more typical of students who showed evidence, on other measures, of significant emotional disturbance.[70] One cannot help but wonder if certain literary or artistic representations may occasionally reflect memories of such fragmented fantasies; for example, Philip Roth's novel, *The Breast,* a take-off on Kafka's *Metamorphosis,* in which a professor turns into a giant breast, or Woody Allen's film, *Everything You Always Wanted to Know About Sex but Were Afraid to Ask,* in which a giant predatory breast is at large in the streets.[71]

It is not our intention to overemphasize the role of sexual fantasy in middle childhood. Rather, we are using this particular type of daydream to point out the exploratory characteristics of childhood imagination during this period. Such fantasies may become embedded in a broader pattern of self-entertainment through private storytelling using images and monologues. Thus, some people may simply emerge from middle childhood as general fantasizers for whom "anything goes" in the realm of private make-believe but who also have some sense of what kinds of fantasies can be acted on or taken seriously. The Roman dramatist Terence's saying, "I count nothing human foreign to me," is reflected in the creative efforts of poets, writers, filmmakers, and playwrights, who translate into words and visible images the most far-fetched of our human fantasies. The positive daydreamer, so scored by the adult version of the Imaginal Processes Inventory, or what Steven Lynn and Judith Rhue have called the "fantasy prone personality," may represent such a cognitive style.[72]

But as children explore possible futures through their fantasies in middle childhood and early adolescence, they do begin to make some choices. When he was at the University of Kansas, Michael Storms developed a theory about how boys and girls begin to settle on whether they will incline toward a homoerotic or heteroerotic sexual orientation. During middle childhood, as part of what society expects and as a means of solidifying their gender identification, boys play largely with boys, girls with girls. As puberty begins, children enter what the American psychiatrist Harry Stack Sullivan has called the "juvenile" phase of development (see Table 2-1). Here they are seeking for and learning about intimacy and friendship, how to relate not just to a "gang of kids" but to one or two special ones. Their fantasies may involve some expectations about special relationships with these actual or possible friends, as the research of Purdue University's Thomas Berndt also suggests.[73] If, in keeping with normal variations in the onset of puberty, they become more sexually attuned and responsive very early in the cycle, they may begin to experience sexual interest and have fantasies about same-sex figures, and such daydreams may be further reinforced by sexual arousal, actual sex play initiated by another same-sex person, or masturbation. If sexual activity and bodily changes appear a bit later, when sexual mixing is already expected, then fantasies may adopt the general social expectation already reflected in TV, fiction, or ordinary family communication about a heterosexual choice. We believe that fantasy plays an important mediating role here, but really careful research on sexual "object" choice and middle-childhood fantasy still remains to be done.

As our earlier example of the "spy" fantasy indicated, even some vocational choices may be prefigured early. In that case, another concurrent middle-childhood fantasy revolved around Sherlock Holmes, a highly intellectual detective. From military intelligence agent and detective to psychoanalyst is not so great a leap—a number of observers of the profession have called attention to the detective fantasy at the root of much of Freud's orientation to psychotherapy and that of his followers.[74] The magician Teller's childhood fun house fantasy and magic tricks also eventuated in a vocational goal. Goethe's early play with puppet theaters certainly foreshadowed his later choices as a dramatist and as a theatrical manager. In addition, his middle-childhood fantasy of having seven siblings in far-flung regions, with whom he communicated, also seems a subtle anticipation of his later willingness to become a government administrator for the Duchy of Weimar and a cosmopolitan "citizen of the world" with an international correspondence.[75]

The far-flung fantasies of middle childhood reflect, we believe, a genuine treasure trove for more extended research and clinical analysis. It should be clear that, although we suggest that this great source of imaginativeness rests on a foundation developed in the pretending and make-believe of early childhood, the child's new internalized capacity for elaborate imagery during this stage of development takes on a life of its own. It remains to be seen whether we are correct in our suggestion that because psychoanalysts seek the sources of the fantasies they hear from their adult patients in earlier and earlier experiences in the life cycle, they are overlooking the great riches to be explored in the memories of middle-childhood daydreams and beliefs. Certainly we hope that behavioral researchers will turn more attention to this age group and look for ways of tapping the fantasies of children during this period as major clues to the origins of attitudes about self, goals, and imagination itself. This may well be the phase of childhood during which conflicts are internalized and most of the foundations of neurotic patterns are formed. The optimism, the illusions of control, and the beliefs that we can be heroic and courageous, friendly and wholesome, also seem to crystallize during this period.[76] Along with many of the plagues and evils released from the Pandora's box of our fantasies in middle childhood, many of us also assimilate the hope that lies buried there. This hope sustains us in defeat, illness, and frustration so that we keep trying and often succeed in creating new realities.

11

Toward the Creative Adult

The Idea

For us, too, there was a wish to possess
Something beyond the world we knew, beyond ourselves,
Beyond our power to imagine, something nevertheless
In which we might see ourselves; and this desire
Came always in passing, in waning light, and in such cold
That ice on the valley's lakes cracked and rolled,
And blowing snow covered what earth we saw,
And scenes from the past, when they surfaced again,
Looked not as they had but ghostly and white
Among false curves and hidden erasures;
And never once did we feel we were close
Until the night wind said, "Why do this,
Especially now? Go back to the place you belong";
And there appeared, with its windows glowing, small,
In the distance, in the frozen reaches, a cabin;
And we stood before it, amazed at its being there,
And would have gone forward and opened the door,
And stepped into the glow and warmed ourselves there,
But that it was ours by not being ours,
And should remain empty. That was the idea.

—Mark Strand

We have come a long way from the earliest beginnings of make-believe and pretend play in childhood. Seen from a life-span perspective, human consciousness is manifest initially as a single stream in which the child's thought and play are chiefly expressed in overt action and in those short sentences or sound effects that reflect the effort to create narrative. By middle childhood this widening stream divides: a narrower but persisting rivulet continues on in public forms of play and make-believe, but an increasingly broadening watercourse parallels it, representing the great stream of private thought first recognized by William James as a basic psychological phenomenon.

As the child moves into adolescence, make-believe play certainly becomes a less prominent part of life, but it continues to be manifested in computer and video games and often in more formal school or after-school activities such as drama, ballet, or amateur film-making. But from adolescence on, most expressions of human play-fulness and most continuing efforts at assimilating new experience occur in the private realm of thought. For the untried adolescent, a vast horizon of possibilities stretches ahead and fantasy thinking ranges widely. By early adulthood, however, many of these options have been foreclosed. Fantasy persists but may become more constricted and "realistic" as one struggles to sustain a decent job, establish and care for a family, and carve out a secure niche in a particular society. There may also be great variation in how much each individual values the capacity for private playfulness, for leaps of faith, for even modest thoughts about "what if" or "what might be." Mark Strand's poem suggests the enormous, if sometimes subtle, attraction of finding and exploring the possible, the rooms of our future, so fraught with interest that we cannot bear to "settle in" and give up further opportunities for mental travel. In this chapter we explore make-believe play into adolescence and adulthood and then consider the broadening and deepening stream of private human consciousness.

Some Characteristics of Adolescence

Edith Cobb has described middle childhood as a "period in which latent and subliminally experienced images are active but unformulated, awaiting 'release' into the wholeness of culturally meaningful expression."[1] Cobb believed that the early adolescent period remains the "basic phase of development of human levels of dynamic thought during the whole life." In Chapter 10 we suggested that six-to thirteen-year-olds are using their imaginations to carry them into a "deepening world image"—the child is, "in fact, in love with the whole universe."[2] Although play may have gone "underground," we hypothesized that it continued to be a source of pleasure and served as a precursor of the tasks of late adolescence: mastery, the understanding and control of the physical world, and entry into a broader social milieu. During this "stormy" time, the adolescent, in Erikson's words, "looks for an opportunity to decide with free assent on one of the available or unavoidable avenues of duty and service, and at the same time is mortally afraid of being forced into activities in which he would feel exposed to ridicule or self-doubt."[3] Erikson believed that young children's sense of what they could become is unlimited, but that adolescents are constrained by their peers and by their elders, who they trust will give "imaginative, if not illusory," scope to their aspirations. Gifted adolescents may easily fit into the technological occupations and demands of a complex society, but many young people also want to identify themselves with an ideology that offers something beyond vocational satisfaction.

Sadly enough, there are young people who feel estranged, like Chato, a character in "The Somebody," a short story by Danny Santiago. Chato, or Catface, reared in an impoverished neighborhood, quits school one day and goes to work as a "writer"—writing his name and street, "Shamrock," on fences, buildings, the walls of stores and bars, even the white columns of a funeral home. Chato's father wants him to become a lawyer to defend the Mexican people in Los Angeles or a doctor, but Chato decides instead to leave home. His neighborhood has deteriorated, school is a problem for him, and his friends have moved away. Without his gang, he has no unique identity. All Chato needs, he says, "is plenty of chalk and crayons— give me a couple of months and I'll be famous all over town . . . of course they'll try to stop me . . . But I'll be real mysterious, all they'll know is just my name, signed like I always sign it, Chato De Shamrock with rays shooting out from the Holy Cross."[4] In this pathetic, but tangible way, Chato tries to make the world aware of his existence and finds an identity in his "fame."

For some young people, writing poetry or short stories, painting, photography, and other similar activities may provide an outlet for feelings of loneliness and alienation, or, on the other side of the coin, of joy, or love. Many adolescents are excited about their career plans, or their involvement in social or political causes. Some volunteer as Big Brothers, Big Sisters, or Candy Stripers, join 4-H Clubs or Scouting, or apply themselves in earnest to mastering some form of athletics. Creative expression may be reflected in a serious science project or in more frivolous experiments with outrageous hair styles (punk haircuts with shaved designs), nail polish (each fingernail a different color), makeup (weird shades of lipstick and mascara), and strange clothing (sometimes torn or purposely patched). Youthful exuberance, however, coupled with boredom, a failure to channel energies into socially acceptable acts, a disregard for morality, and the anonymity provided by a gang may erupt into violence, like the "wilding" attack on the Central Park jogger in New York City in the spring of 1989 and other less well publicized acts of destruction or vandalism.

Creativity and Imagination

But for those adolescents—and adults—who maintain a playful, creative spirit, there are many positive outlets. As Teresa Amabile states, "in contrast to popular views of creativity as an all-or-nothing entity, [my] perspective proposes that it is at least theoretically possible for anyone with normal cognitive abilities to be creative to some degree in some domain of endeavor."[5] She notes that there has been little research on the social psychology of creativity, that is, on which social and environmental factors interact with personality and cognitive abilities. Our own thinking, like that of many of the studies we have cited, supports Amabile's notion that for imagination to blossom, in addition to intrinsic motivation, the creative individual must be consistently reinforced by external factors. By praising something a child has made (a turreted sand castle or a finger painting of a cat or a rainstorm), adults offer both encouragement and recognition.

The creative thinking process has been described in various ways by people in the field: as preparation, incubation, illumination, and verification; as preparation, production, evolution, and implementation; and as problem or task presentation, preparation, response generation, response validation, and outcome.[6] But are creativity and imagination the same? Imagination seems freer and broader, since our thoughts may remain as private and as fanciful as we may want them to be, with no constraints. Imagination may take the form of visual imagery with no obvious outcome other than the pleasure it affords us. The child who does not give us evidence of this ability through play, or later, through science projects, art, writing, or other forms of activity, may indeed have a rich inner life, but without an end product we have no way of knowing it.

The Lifetime Creativity Scales (LCS), a research tool developed by Ruth Richards and Dennis Kinney, consist of items that identify creativity in adults, ordinary people who demonstrate originality in their work and leisure activities over time.[7] A person who designs a house, launches an advertising campaign, or is an imaginative cook may be classified as creative on a scale of creativity with progressive levels from "not significant" to "exceptional." Peak innovation as well as moderate levels of innovation can also be assessed. Based on a lifetime study of 461 adults, about 60 percent of people fall into categories of moderate to some creativity, while fewer than 1 percent have exceptional creativity.[8] What is relevant to our interest in imagination and fantasy is their finding that there are strong correlations between creativity in adults and childhood creativity and fantasy production.[9]

The research of David Harrington, Jack Block, and Jeanne Block, although not with adults, indicates that children who were imaginative and sensitive to task constraints at ages four and five were rated high in creativity at age eleven.[10] The authors claim that over a six- or seven-year time span children tended to "maintain their relative levels of relevant intellectual skills throughout this period of profound cognitive development."[11] The traits of curiosity, ego resilience, and self-confidence were continuous across time, and, the authors argue, may have been the result of environmental factors. This supports Amabile's position that social and environmental conditions contribute to creativity. Harrington and colleagues make the point that parents who provided their children with environments conducive to divergent thinking and intellectual playfulness in early childhood may continue to do so six or seven years later. We wonder if these children would manifest the same creative cognitive and personality traits into late adolescence and adulthood.

We do have some evidence that at least the imaginary companions of childhood may have a bearing on adolescent creativity. Using a sample of 800 high school students, Charles Schaefer found that those students who produced creative works in literary genres reported a greater incidence of imaginary companions in childhood than did matched less creative controls.[12] The criteria for assessing creative achievement included two standardized tests of creative thinking as well as teachers' evaluations. The sample was selected from schools that provided opportunities for creative activities and as a whole were superior in terms of academic achievement. The finding is compelling but leaves open the question of other unknown variables in childhood that might also have contributed to the higher creativity scores.

In order to stimulate creativity and imagination in adolescents, the Georgia Future Problem-Solving Program has been instituted in Georgia and nationally.[13] National competitions are held to encourage the best ideas for creative problem-solving focusing on school and community issues. This program was inspired by the work of Paul Torrance, a leader in the field of creativity.

Creativity, then, is manifest through products or actions. We can tentatively conclude that imagination and, earlier, the predisposition to pretend and make-believe play may well be necessary ingredients in stimulating and developing divergent thought. But the production of a socially defined creative product, whether it takes the form of an artistic, scientific, or business achievement, calls for specific skills and knowledge, high motivation and effort, and the capacity for a playful consideration of many possibilities. Imagination is fun in its own right whether or not it contributes to a public product.

Natural Continuations of Make-Believe

The Georgia program is geared to adolescent problem-solving. Other adolescents may use their energies in what folklorists call the "legend trip."[14] This is a widespread phenomenon involving haunted houses, mysterious caves, spooky bridges, or other community sites that attract adolescents at night, who come in order to experience terror but to survive and tell about it.

According to Elizabeth Bird, the "legend trip" centers "around stories or legends shared among people who travel to a particular place."[15] Although some suggest that people disseminate such legends because they express and dramatize cultural values, fears, and concerns, Bird regards the legend trip as "essentially play, involving not only story-telling, but also doing particular things. The emotional power of the experience derives from a combination of setting, narratives, and actions, all of which are interdependent."[16] Focusing on one site, the Black Angel, a monument in Oakland Cemetery in Iowa City, Bird substantiates her argument by presenting various interpretations of what the angel signifies and then describes how adolescents use the trip. Generally, young people, including college students, visit the angel at night, sometimes after viewing a horror film, going in mixed or all male groups. Rarely do females go alone. They tell frightening stories, may use alcohol or drugs, and then challenge each other to certain actions, such as kissing, defacing, or insulting the statue. After everyone is thoroughly frightened, the group leaves, sometimes for more partying or a post-trip discussion. In the light of day, the legends as well as the experiences seem laughable, but the darkness, the group phenomenon, and alcohol and drugs lend a scary element. The angel, according to Bird, "provides a setting for young people to play, exploring their fears in a make-believe world that at least while the game continues, may seem very real."[17]

In the film, *Dead Poet's Society,* a group of sixteen- and seventeen-year-olds also "play," but their experiences are a mixture of positive and negative. They meet at night in a cave near their boarding school to read poetry and experiment with smoking pipes and drinking alcohol. One member, adopting the name Nwanda, puts on "war paint" to transform himself into a more primitive and powerful person. In the dim, dank cave, the boys' inhibitions are suspended and imagination soars. Together in this mysterious place, the boys indulge themselves in romantic illusion.

So far, we have perhaps overemphasized the more romantic, idealized forms of imaginative play. Within reasonable limits it can be an uplifting, moderating human activity that enhances adjustment in social behavior and, in concert with logical or paradigmatic thought, makes for intelligent functioning. This view may be regarded, in Nietzsche's famous term, as an "Apollonian" conception. But Brian Sutton-Smith has astutely called attention to another facet of play manifested by teenagers, especially boys, which takes a more sinister and, as in the legend trip, a more risky and often antisocial turn. This kind of play, which is exemplified in activities that go well beyond the frame of pretend narratives, may be characterized by Nietzsche's term "Dionysian" (or, in the phrase of comedian Steve Martin, "wild and crazy"). As Sutton-Smith writes, "Those who deal with children in the contained worlds of nursery schools and laboratories can think of their play largely in terms of pretense and fantasy, while those who deal with them in high schools . . . must deal with the constant insurgence of obscene play, humor, pranks, graffiti, verbal dueling, insults, slang, mooning, cruising, necking, drinking, mocking laughter and sexual exploits."[18] Other young people may turn to horror films and rock music for escape and thrills. A study correlating the consumption of movies, books, and music with the fantasy lives of adults, for example, found that males who were heavy viewers of horror films and favored rock music reported more hostile-guilty-failure fantasies as measured by the Imaginal Processes Inventory.[19] It is difficult to determine in a correlational study whether the media engendered such fantasies or whether these males chose those particular forms of entertainment because their fantasies were of such a dysphoric nature.

The game Dungeons and Dragons, in which the players can actually use their own fantasies to complete the moves, appeals to adolescents as well as adults. In a socially acceptable way, they can express fantasies of aggression without physical harm to others.

Some critics have complained that the board game, the reported college cults, and the TV program based on the game have caused copycat episodes of violence in real life. It would be difficult to prove that either the game or the program alone could be responsible for such actions. Surely a person who uses the context of a game to carry out a destructive act is already predisposed to such behavior by other life factors.

But make-believe adventure play is not limited to adolescents. Some adults reenact historic battles using toy soldiers. These mock wars are accurately executed by two or more players, often history buffs who keep in touch with other afficionados around the country. The love of past eras is also expressed through the imaginative play of members of the Society for Creative Anachronism, a national organization dedicated to reliving the experiences of knights and ladies in the Middle Ages. Members assume medieval or Renaissance names and move up the ranks, through special ceremonies, from lowly serf to lord and lady. They wear costumes at their more formal fairs and try to replicate the ancient games that were played and the food that was prepared. The banquets resemble the feasts our imaginations believe a knight would have hosted in the inner courtyard of his castle. We actually visited one such festival and were delighted by the scene before us: Pennants surrounded a large field; octagonal tents were erected with colorful flags atop each. One area was designated for combat and there, "knights" with lances took part in mock-battles with each other. People of all ages were in costume and for a brief while, reality was suspended while the players lived the lives of King Arthur, the fair Elaine, Lancelot, and Queen Guinevere.

Other clubs, such as the Baker Street Irregulars (dedicated to the fictional detective, Sherlock Holmes), exist to bring together people who enjoy a common interest, here discussing the clever plots of Holmes's cases and the masterful way he reached his conclusions. These clubs perpetuate childhood or adolescent interests. With others to share one's pleasures, memories of childhood play are kept alive and imaginations remain fertile.

Wearing costumes, or changing into make-believe characters under the auspices of a particular group or club, or acting in theatrical productions have always been among the ways that adults continue the playful spirit of childhood. We all want to maintain the ability to pretend, to escape perhaps from the more mundane or annoying tasks of everyday life or from vocations that seem pedestrian and unfulfilling. Robert Frost, in a poem written when he was in his seventies, reminisces about childhood:

> First there's the children's
> house of make-believe.
> Some shattered dishes underneath a pine,
> The playthings in the play-
> house of the children.
> Weep for what little things
> could make them glad.[20]

We can recapture some of that joy through our board games. Chess, for example, a stylized form of combat, can be a highly abstract mental contest that demands intense concentration. Even if one player succeeds in capturing the opponent's king, a tone of playful camaraderie can prevail. Costuming ourselves as mummers in a Philadelphia parade, participating in a Mardi Gras festival, or attending a Beaux Arts ball provides us with the opportunity to replay the dress-up games of childhood and the license to release the inhibitions held in check by our conventional wardrobes. The custom of "charivari," dating back before the sixteenth century, called for villagers to don outlandish and sometimes ghoulish costumes and perform a mock serenade to newly married couples on their wedding night. A scene in the extraordinary film, *The Return of Martin Guerre,* portrays this custom in a small French village and suggests that such taunting is permissible if done in disguise and with a playful spirit.

Fraternal organizations such as the Knights of Columbus, the Knights of Pythias, and the Freemasons no longer bind people together according to specific crafts as the medieval guilds did. Rather, secret rituals, symbols, and allegories unite members, as does the group's purpose, which often emphasizes benevolence. Some lodges offer rings and other adornments to their members so that membership can be made public. Others have secret handclasps and passwords, not unlike those in children's secret clubs.

Play for the adult, as Eugen Fink describes it, is "activity and creativity—and yet it is close to external things. Play interrupts the continuity and purposive structure of our lives; it remains at a distance from our usual mode of existence. But while seeming to be unrelated to our normal life, it relates to it in a very meaningful way."[21] Examples of play that fit this description are two traditional events—the Morris, a dance festival that takes place every year in

England from May until the end of summer, and the Palio, the violent horseback race that is run every July and August in the Piazza del Campo, the main square of Siena, Italy, in which both jockeys and officials wear Renaissance attire.

Currently, there are about five hundred Morris dancing groups in England. The dancing itself dates back to the Middle Ages and may even go back much further.[22] The dancers, usually male, wear assorted and sometimes bizarre costumes, depending on which team they belong to, that often include colored ribbons and bells. The dancing can go on for hours and is accompanied by much visiting of local pubs and ale consumption. The various dances, a form of ritual play, represent everyday concerns of rural people—fertility, good crops, mock combat. Morris dancing provides the villagers an opportunity for some boisterous escapades that sometimes end in a free-for-all. The tradition may also be found in the United States— in New Haven, Connecticut, for example, where summer visitors may see a troupe of Morris dancers in full costume rehearsing in the street, and in Cambridge, Massachusetts, and other cities where seasonal "Revels" include Morris dancing, song, mumming, and other forms of ritual and traditional celebration.

The Palio horse race in Siena, which also dates back to the Middle Ages, has political and social overtones.[23] The entrants in the race are the various city districts, each bearing a name (such as Eagle, Dragon, She-Wolf, Unicorn). Horses are led into the churches and blessed before the race; jockeys are kept practically under guard to prevent any rival district from bribing them to lose. A huge procession marches around the arena before the race begins. People dressed in splendid robes and carrying the insignia of the participating districts pass by the crowds of spectators. Religious symbols, candles, and usually a statue of the Virgin Mary as well as political banners (the town has had communist or socialist mayors for years) are also carried along as the crowds cheer their favorites. Trial heats are run for several days before the actual race and all Siena remains in a festive mood, even long afterward. The winner of the main event receives the "Palio" or banner, which is proudly displayed. Singing is an important part of the festivities, and groups of people stroll through the city singing songs with "lyrics rich in self-praise and insults to their enemies."[24] The general atmosphere of fun, intrigue, and violence on the field are all a part of tradition that some believe supplanted the warfare between the Italian city-states during the sixteenth century. For tourists the pageantry is unforgettable. The first Palio we attended left us exhausted by the noise of the vendors and souvenir hawkers, the continuous roar of the crowd, and the heat of the July day. But as we watched we were transfixed, carried back in time to the medieval city.

Puppet shows featuring almost life-size puppets represent another form of adult play. One group in Connecticut, sustaining an old Sicilian tradition, has for many years used elaborately dressed puppets to reenact the battles waged by the knights of Charlemagne against the Saracens invading southern Europe. Every July in Glover, Vermont, the Bread and Puppet Theater presents the Domestic Resurrection Circus. People from around the world gather to watch and to perform using puppets that are as small as a finger and as large as nine feet tall. One puppeteer has commented that puppets help him to forget the stress and strain of his job; through puppetry, he feels that he can express his personality.[25] Peter Schumann, who trained as a sculptor and dancer in Munich, founded the Bread and Puppet Theater in New York City. He claims that the themes of the Circus are philosophical but the pageant that follows it is more mystical. It consists of giant puppets who "dance over grassy ridges, emerge from behind green hills, disappear into pine forests and stand glowing in the rays of the setting sun."[26] The adults who participate relish the opportunity to design the puppets' features and clothing and to manipulate them during the performances. The puppets can be as fanciful as imagination permits, and they provide an entry into the circus cycle of drama, dance, farce, and political satire.

John Ludwig, the creator of the "Heaven-Hell Tour" produced at the Center for Puppetry Arts in Atlanta, Georgia, believes that puppets can heighten the imagination because they resemble real people, yet with a certain quality of make-believe.[27] His show is a combination of music, dancing, and singing highlighted by enormous puppets of various sizes and shapes that float over the audience and create an eerie atmosphere.

There are other ways adults can keep childhood pleasures alive. If one is as gifted as Gad Ya'acubi, the Communications Minister of Israel, writing stories drawn from childhood memories can be both satisfying and an excellent outlet for a playful spirit in a busy political life.[28] One can also become a maestro and conduct an imaginary orchestra. A company called the North American School of the Artsy and Somewhat Musically Inclined offers a complete conductor's kit that includes a cork-handled wood baton, a cassette of baroque music, a "Master's degree" from the "supposititious" school, and paper doll musicians. And they guarantee, "no experience needed."[29]

Adult dressing up and make-believe can take a more sinister turn, as the white robes and bizarre titles of Ku Klux Klan members unfortunately attest. A recent anthropological study of witchcraft and ritual magic in contemporary England carried out by an American researcher who became a participant-observer elucidates the powerful pull of communion in expressing one's more unusual fantasies.[30] T. M. Luhrmann has reported that, despite her best efforts at scientific detachment, she found herself becoming more and more caught up in the magical robes, incantations to Hecate, the ancient Greek goddess of the underworld, and the electrifying symbolism.

While Luhrmann did not directly observe "evil" practices of the type depicted in some horror films, she had reason to believe they might exist. Her interviews with participants revealed that they were often persons with a history of elaborate childhood fantasy and a taste for the Sword and Sorcery genre in reading. Often their experiences with traditional religion had been disappointing, and they had developed an oppositional reaction-formation against establishment beliefs and practices. Such individualistic, vivid fantasies, which turned against the more widespread conventional social behavior of their peers, left these people feeling even more isolated. Pride in one's own unique beliefs is not enough to overcome the human yearning for affiliation and communion (see our discussion of Figure 2-2). The thrill of discovering that others share these fantasies, this yearning to play at make-believe magic, accounts for the formation and persistence of the witches' and warlocks' covens that Luhrmann penetrated. This oppositional streak is also evident in Satan-worshipping religious groups, some presumably secret and dangerous cults but others assuming a quasi-establishment status. A directory provided to hotel guests in San Francisco lists opportunities for religious observance that include Catholic, Episcopalian, Presbyterian, Jewish, Seventh Day Adventist—and the Church of Satan!

Perhaps children's make-believe never really does go underground after all. The great students of adult games, Johan Huizinga and Roger Caillois, have documented the widespread role of competitive and rules play in civilization.[31] The anthropologist Clifford Geertz, in his masterful study of Balinese cock-fighting, has tried to show that this bloody sport, practiced by so benign and esthetic a people, is not just a rules game on which to bet but rather a kind of fantasy about the hierarchical structure of Balinese life: "Its function, if you want to call it that, is interpretive: it is a Balinese reading of Balinese experience; a story they tell themselves about themselves."[32] From the perspective of these scholars, all games thus take on a make-believe quality as elaborations of a more private fantasy. Mikhail Bakhtin, the Russian pioneer of research on the narrative mode of experience, has also written eloquently on the range of human game-playing, reviewing, for example, the vast compilation of play activities provided by Rabelais in *Gargantua and Pantagruel* (217 in the original edition).[33] To document further the profound role of all the types of play that characterize human societies would take us far afield from our emphasis on the simpler make-believe games. What should be clear is our hypothesis that the floor play of toddlers and preschoolers reflects a human need that does not fade with age but takes on new forms and, responsive to the task-demands of each age level in a culture, reemerges in adulthood in ever more intriguing patterns.

Adolescents and Adult Fantasy

We have dealt at some length with overt expressions of pretend and make-believe play because they have often been minimized by developmental researchers who, influenced by Piaget, have focused on directed, logical cognitive processes in the adult. In middle childhood, however, the social constraints of school attendance, combined with newly emergent cognitive capacities, lead as we have seen to the internalization of speech and overt play. This capacity for private play in the form of fantasy and imagery exploration is flourishing by puberty and may well reach its peak in adolescence.[34] Through TV, reading, music, education, and peer interaction as well as a greater awareness of parental occupation young people between the ages of thirteen and nineteen envision a vast range of possible futures and possible selves, with only limited constraints. The more unrealistic adventure scenarios of middle childhood may yield to a flood of romantic and sexual daydreams (as the research of Sybil Gottlieb and others suggests);[35] various vocational, athletic, travel, artistic, glamorous, and wealthy life-style fantasies thrive. Idealistic hopes of changing one's life, whether by escaping from the constraints of family and social group or embracing new careers or social activism, can be entertained at length without clear contradiction. Mark Twain wryly commented that at fourteen he thought his father to be utterly ignorant but by twenty-one he was amazed at how much the old man had learned in that short time. For the teenager hope abounds. The demands of students in China for a vaguely defined democracy reflect such a spirit of free-floating imagery, yet youthful hopes were quickly crushed by an aged oligarchy whose leaders were willing to pay a harsh price to sustain a unified, economically viable nation of one billion people.

While research suggests that daydreaming peaks in adolescence and that adult thought takes on a more chore-oriented, workaday quality by the twenties and thirties, surveys of adults' inner experience continue to reflect a good deal of playlike or speculative fantasy.[36] Questionnaire and experimental thought-sampling studies make it clear that most adult thought is not organized around logical, planful sequences. The narrative mode of thought so deftly characterized by Jerome Bruner is more often the rule in naturally occurring mentation, while those formal logical operations necessary to describe or solve problems are the exceptions, even in the ongoing thought of scientists and mathematicians.[37] Reporting on his samplings of the thoughts of surgeons during operations, Mihalyi Csikszentmihalyi of the University of Chicago noted how often, when not actually engaging in a specific surgical procedure, they drifted into very private daydreams of sexual, financial, or professional achievements.[38]

What we are suggesting is that, for most people, the make-believe of childhood, with its elements of freedom from the constraints of physical structures and time- or person-boundedness, lives on in the privacy of thought. Indeed, as William James long ago suggested, the stream of consciousness and the sense of self are closely intertwined; mentation is not just there somewhere "in one's head." Rather, one experiences thinking as "my thoughts."[39] The possessionlike quality of one's images, wishes, expectations, and beliefs becomes a closely guarded feature of one's sense of individuality and uniqueness. Even if we do not accept Julian Jaynes's proposal that the evolutionary emergence of biologically differentiated left and right cerebral hemispheres occurred about thirty-five hundred years ago, we can still acknowledge his insight that pretense, deception, lying, or simply guarding the separateness of one's memories is a major development in the child's cognitive capacities. When the prophet Jeremiah wrote his poetic, "If I forget thee, O Jerusalem," which reflects the memories and yearnings of the Hebrews transported to Babylon after the destruction of their Temple, he captured the importance of thought as a liberating element even in exile and bondage. In the same way, the Italians, exiles in their own land, which was under the sway of Austria, responded with great passion during the first performances of the opera *Nabucco* in 1842, when the exiled Hebrews on the stage sang the Italian paraphrase of Jeremiah's words, "Va Pensiero,"* to Giuseppe Verdi's deeply moving melody.

If thought is so private, how can we study it scientifically? Ultimately, we must rely on what people tell us. There are increasingly refined methods for sampling and evaluating these accounts that discourage people from simply telling us what they believe we would like to hear.[41] One major approach involves straightforwardly asking groups of people to respond to questionnaires in which they can report on the frequency of particular forms of thought or specific daydreams and on the vividness or realitylike quality of their inner experience. The Imaginal Processes Inventory, which was the basis for the Children's Fantasy Questionnaire used by Rosenfeld and Huesmann (see Chapter 10), is one such instrument. Despite some obvious limitations, these questionnaires do seem to provide reasonably consistent reports from groups; they also indicate that those who score in particular ways on the relevant scales often behave under other circumstances in a manner consistent with their questionnaire responses.[42]

Another approach is to attempt to capture private thought as it occurs. Here, Sigmund Freud was a pioneer. He first asked patients to report their images, one after another, and then later asked for the verbal free associations that are the basis for the psychoanalytic process.[43] While much has been learned through this method, its embeddedness in a clinical psychotherapeutic situation prevents the analyst from trying to study the properties of thought and imagery under scientifically controlled circumstances; one must concentrate on helping the client not on studying the abstract question of thought.[44] An alternative that can meet reasonable scientific standards involves normal volunteer participants, who report their thoughts under controlled laboratory conditions. They simply talk aloud, uninterrupted, for an extended period or report their thoughts

---

* "Fly, thought, on golden wings and light upon the hills and banks where the sweet breezes of our native land blow soft and fragrant."[40]

when interrupted while performing more or less demanding perceptual-motor or creative tasks.[45] In an experiment of this type, individuals were seated in light- and sound-proof booths listening through earphones to a series of rapidly presented "beeps" and pressing buttons whenever one was louder or higher in pitch than the one before. By interrupting these people every fifteen seconds and asking them to indicate whether they had experienced any Task Unrelated Thought or Imagery (TUITs) during the fifteen or so "signal detections" they had just completed, it becomes possible to estimate how much of our thought is a break from directed, chore-related mentation and what forms and contents predominate in thought under particular circumstances. John Antrobus of the City University of New York, working with various colleagues, has shown that TUITs constitute a majority of most people's thoughts when they spend an hour a day for as long as eleven days detecting signals in the laboratory. These experiments also indicate that TUITs vary as a function of the regular daily biological cycle; they increase when the experimenter and the participant are of opposite sexes (especially when women are the subjects) and following unresolved activities, emotionally distressing films, or when startling news is overheard on the radio just prior to entering the signal detection booth. Individuals who report a great deal of daydreaming on a questionnaire are also more likely to report such task-irrelevant thought when interrupted regularly during a forty-five minute period of detecting auditory signals.[46]

An expansion of these thought-sampling methods has emerged in the past fifteen years with the use of the "beepers," or paging devices, that signal physicians to call their answering service. Study participants carry such devices around in their pockets or purses and when they hear the beep must immediately record their thoughts and other activities on handy cards. Such methods have the advantage of being less artificial than laboratory studies but are of course harder to control.

Finally, there are other kinds of experiments that study the physiological concomitants of ongoing thought, examine the ways in which daydreaming or imagery influence subsequent behavior, or seek to estimate the determinants of the particular contents of thought samples from prior experiences, such as conflict with parents, physical activity, or various kinds of social interaction.[47]

What can we conclude about ordinary waking consciousness using the questionnaire, thought-sampling, and laboratory approaches? It seems clear that a great deal of ordinary thought is not directly focused on the task at hand. This does not mean that those shifts of focus while one is bathing the baby, mowing the lawn, or driving to work necessarily yield unproductive thoughts. Even playful fantasies, which make up a sizable percentage of many individuals' stream of thought, are often expressions of some long-term effort to cope with issues in one's life, whether by sheer escape or by gradually zeroing in from absurd possibilities to a solution. Studies of large numbers of people using the Imaginal Processes Inventory or its short form have identified three major underlying patterns that are characteristic of thoughts other than those directed at a specific immediate chore, such as paying bills or solving math problems. People vary systematically in the frequency with which they demonstrate high scores on one, two, or all of these dimensions. One pattern reflects an ability to focus attention on and sustain interest in one's mental activity. Some people regularly show what is called Poor Attentional Control: they are easily bored and distracted; their minds wander so that they cannot sustain an extended fantasy. Such individuals' fantasies are often of a fearful kind, and they also show more anxiety on other measures. In contrast, at the other pole are those who are singularly organized, directed, and lucid in thought.

Two other independent patterns can also be identified. One is characterized by a consistently negative emotionality and by daydreams that involve guilt, hostility, and fear of failure as well as striving for achievement. The other pattern, which clearly emerged in the Rosenfeld and Huesmann studies with nine-year-olds, reflects a playful, fanciful, positively toned emotionality in fantasy, a clear continuation of the happier make-believe of the preschooler. These two patterns, the Guilty-Dysphoric and the Positive-Constructive, are not opposites but independent factors; we all score higher or lower on one type or the other. Several studies by Steven Starker of the Portland Veterans Medical Centers (VMC) in Oregon have shown that people who score higher on the scales measuring the Dysphoric pattern also show a tendency to recall "bad" dreams. Vietnam veterans who were subjected to severe stress during that war show more inclination toward such guilty, hostile, or fear-of-failure fantasies.[48] Most people show at least some tendency to reflect more positive-playful fantasies as part of their ongoing thought unless they are severely depressed.

Whatever the emotional tone of their fantasies, those who report a good deal of daydreaming do seem in general to be characterized by a considerable interest in narrative and imagery, by better recall of night dreams, and also by a greater ability to enter states of intense absorption in reading, films, or music. There are also suggestions that fantasy-prone people may be more hypnotizable, provided they do not use their imaginativeness to resist because of a distaste for loss of control. Josephine Hilgard's important research on such individuals found that the hypnotizable respondents remembered more daydreaming and imaginary playmates from their childhood days. The connection between one's early make-believe play, one's ability to immerse oneself deeply in a film or book, and one's willingness to enter into the contract with the hypnotist and play along in the temporary pretend world of trance is intriguing and merits far more careful research study.[49]

In his last great work, Piaget finally addressed the issue of the origins of possibility in the accommodation-assimilation cycle and demonstrated that possibility was a key feature in the development of adaptive thought and behavior.[50] Once-maligned,* daydreaming is a central feature of naturally occurring thought and, we propose, serves a function for the adult that is comparable to the child's make-believe exploration. Adult thought reflects a striving through possibility to entertain oneself but even more to create new schemas and scripts, new avenues of thought and behavior. We often become prisoners of our fantasies or our metaphorical leaps, but we can also use them to sustain us in misfortune or to help us to persist in finishing tasks. In her great novel, *Middlemarch,* George Eliot describes the pedantic Angelican minister and scholar, Casaubon, as someone who "had imagined that his long studious bachelorhood had stored up for him a compound interest of enjoyment, and that large drafts on his affections would not fail to be honored, for we all of us, grave or light, get our thoughts entangled in metaphors and act fatally on the strength of them."[52]

Casaubon's scholarliness attracted Dorothea Brooke, the spirited and romantic heroine of the novel, and it appeared that his metaphor had paid off. But being a one-metaphor man with no tenderness, humanity, or social skills to sustain a relationship, things went sour before long. The more imaginative Dorothea, whose fantasy life was fraught with possibility, ultimately helped others and won their friendship and love for herself.

---

* Early American tests of personality classified self-reports of daydreaming as "neurotic."[51]

The normal stream of consciousness, we suggest, consists of short sequences of directed thought, either verbal or represented in images (visual, auditory, or kinesthetic ones especially) geared to carrying out an immediate task but sustained for most people only briefly. Much of the time we drift off into bursts of memory or into sequences of "what if" or "suppose," often themselves interrupted as we force ourselves back to the task but sometimes so sustained that we temporarily lose track of our prior goal or our surroundings. Saul Bellow catches this experience masterfully in the interior monologues of the protagonists of his novels. Recordings of people who are asked to talk continuously or to give thought samples over a period of time demonstrate similar patterns. *Sampling Normal and Schizophrenic Inner Experience* by Russell Hurlburt of the University of Nevada at Las Vegas provides actual texts of the stream-of-consciousness thoughts of normal, depressed, and schizophrenic individuals. Normal thought includes the playful "as if" sequences that we see as long-term continuations of make-believe play. Although transcripts of the thought of "ordinary" people generally lack the great variety of literary or artistic allusions one finds in the musing of fictional characters like Joyce's Stephen Dedalus or Bellows's Mr. Sammler, they still reflect a more flexible and even daring "life space" than one might surmise in ordinary conversation.[53]

Most people acknowledge that their nocturnal dreams are more interesting and varied, more playful or menacing than their waking thoughts. Research in sleep laboratories where recordings of an individual's mentation throughout the night can be obtained during regular awakenings reveals that ordinary people's dreams are not nearly so wide-ranging or mystical as popular dream books would suggest. Yet because of the reduced ability to process information from the external environment during sleep (especially during the so-called Stage-1 EEG-Rapid Eye Movement phase of sleep) the sleeper confronts a sequence of visual imagery material from his long-term memory in an almost random order on awakening from a dream. Such material can be dealt with chiefly through the capacity for narrative formation. What little systematic data we have comparing the waking and sleeping thought streams suggests that if we subtract the on-task logical thought that characterizes waking thought and is infrequent during sleep, we find a continuity in structure and content. John Antrobus had judges rate samples of study participants' thought reports, which were obtained while they were awake but in restful, relatively stimulation-free environments. These ratings were then compared to reports obtained from nocturnal sleep awakening during State-1 REM periods. Independent judges could not really say which reports were "dreams." If anything, they more often chose the waking-state (under reduced stimulation) reports as more dreamlike than the actual nocturnal reports.[54]

Waking thought is thus much more often intriguing, varied, and playful or potentially creative than most people realize. For many of us, the bustle of going about our daily business precludes our noticing, labeling, or encoding for later memory retrieval the many fanciful thoughts that flit into our consciousness during the day. Some individuals, Jung's introverts, artists, and writers or esthetically sensitive persons do take the time to "loaf and invite their souls," as Walt Whitman put it. But many people, unless encouraged, fail to take note of the richness of normal imagery or to pursue a fleeting allusion. As Wordsworth wrote, "The world is too much with us; late and soon, / Getting and spending, we lay waste our powers." Perhaps we need to look more closely at the potential advantages for enjoyable *and* practical living that may accrue if we recognize our continuing capacity to pretend, imagine, and involve ourselves in mental play—the legacy of the exploratory excitement of childhood.

Creativity in Adulthood

Research into what goes on in the various forms of adult psychotherapy that have emerged in this century suggests that most approaches to symptom relief and personality change draw on the patient's capacity for imagery and narrative thought. These methods implicitly train people to enhance these mental skills.[55] In his recent books on the psychoanalytic method, *Narrative Truth and Historical Truth* and *The Freudian Metaphor*, Donald Spence of Rutgers University seems to be saying that this form of psychotherapy, and possibly others linked to overarching theories, may be "working" because therapist and patient unwittingly collude in an elaborate pretend game in which they construct a mutually agreed-upon story about the patient's life and relationships and even about their own relationship.[56] Such a position need not be viewed as trivializing the method. Rather, it points up further that Piaget's dialectic of assimilation-accommodation, with symbolic play as a central tool, is a never-ending dynamic in personal growth throughout the life span.

One feature of our human capacity for pretending or imaging is our ability to create at least temporary alternative environments in which we can play out with impunity a variety of potential scenarios. Writing in the 1660s, Thomas Hobbes stressed the power of imagination to extrapolate memory to explore future events. One can employ this process either to examine the moral implications of various actions or to create new works of science or literature. In essays written in the early 1700s, Gottfried Wilhelm Leibniz also described how we form a sense of identity through imagination, which then unites our past experiences with intended actions or wishes about future events. One might indeed suffer in memory the insults, checks, or frustrated efforts of the past, but one might also seek to reshape these through vengeance, retribution, recompense, or constructive action. For Leibniz, imagination was apparently closely tied to both *suffering* and *becoming,* an anticipation of existentialism.[57]

That we can shift into a temporary alternative realm in our thoughts is clear enough to any absent-minded professor who, absorbed in thinking about the meaning of an obscure ancient text, walks past his own apartment door and then cannot understand why his key does not open the door at which his "automatic pilot" has landed him. Research has demonstrated that absorption in thought, like the absorption in a hypnotic trance, leads to actual failure to process external cues.[58] Fortunately, our environment usually provides enough redundancy so that we can move mentally to another place and return without missing a "beat" or seriously inconveniencing ourselves or others.

Actually, being a good listener to another person's story requires temporarily entering into that person's mental framework and making believe we are in that other place. Psychotherapists call this "empathic" listening; one tries to envision the people or places being described and to feel what the narrator or the others in the story might have felt. At the same time, one must guard against taking an allusion that touches on one's own worries and becoming so absorbed in one's own personal memories that one no longer hears the narrator's story—an example of psychoanalytic countertransference.

We can briefly outline a number of ways in which various psychotherapies use imagery and fantasy to enhance self-awareness and personality change. These include first, simply being aware of imagination and practicing using it. Keeping track of fantasies or maintaining diaries of dreams is usually in itself a revelation of how much internal make-believe and potential creativity we ignore. Or we can consciously use imagery to discover things about ourselves. As we noted in Chapter 7, the psychologist Richard de Mille has developed a series of imagery exercises, charmingly titled *Put Your Mother on the Ceiling*, designed to help children and adults rethink their relationships.[59] The Los Angeles psychotherapist and pioneer in imagery methods, Joseph Shorr, assigns patients tasks: Imagine the distance you prefer people to stay away from you in ordinary situations . . . now draw an imaginary line around you to show how close you allow others to come toward you comfortably.[60]

Imagery is extensively used in helping people to relax by pretending they are in a peaceful, nonthreatening environment. It also forms an important feature of the most effective behavioral approaches to overcoming irrational fears or discontinuing embarrassing, or even illegal, compulsive behaviors (usually by imagining a really noxious or nauseating image while thinking about the unwanted behavior). Studies of pain indicate that making up a mental story of being in another place at another time is one of the most effective procedures in achieving relief. Changing one's mood by imagining a humorous outcome or picturing a beautiful alternative setting has also been shown to be effective at least temporarily, even with individuals hospitalized for depression.

All these applications of our capacity for pretending and imagining can be employed with care by ordinary people outside therapeutic situations. Recently, athletes have increasingly been using mental practice as a part of their training. While clearly no substitute for the necessary physical practice, additional fantasy runthroughs of a particular course or competitive event seem to give an edge to those athletes who use these methods.[61]

In her reminiscences, the great choreographer of modern dance, Martha Graham, describes her conscious use of narrative thought and imagery as a means of coping with fear. She and her dance troupe were traveling on a small plane over the mountains of Iran on the way to a performance in Teheran. They ran into a fierce snow storm, so blinding that she felt as if she were in one of those glass balls one shakes to create a snow storm. The plane was forced to turn back. In her terror Miss Graham suddenly shifted her thoughts to the choreography for her famous "Errand into the Maze," an abstract impression of the Greek legend of Theseus, Ariadne, and the Minotaur. She ran through the sequence of dance movements for the whole piece three times and even before they landed safely she was feeling much more peaceful and relaxed.[62]

Mental playfulness need not have quite so specific a purpose. It can be simple self-entertainment, making up pleasant adventures to while away a long wait at an airport or bus terminal. Anecdotal accounts from prisoners indicate that some sustained themselves during their imprisonment by taking fantasy trips or writing mental novels. The Uruguayan playwright, Mauricio Rosencof, spent more than twelve years imprisoned in closet-sized cells in military arsenals. He survived, he said, by "dreaming . . . Imagination. Taking long walks with my daughter. Sometimes . . . I'd stretch myself out for a sunbath on the beach . . . I'd get hot and go off to get a nice, cold drink. Then the problem became hiding the bottle, because the cell was searched daily . . . Hiding objects I acquired in my fantasies became quite a chore."[63]

Such methods of maintaining sanity or resisting brainwashing are not uncommon among those held hostage by kidnappers or otherwise imprisoned. But at a more mundane level, a fantasy game can also sustain and enrich a simple life. In a letter we received many years ago, an old woman confined to her house because she was caring for an even older bed-ridden relative described how she freed herself from the monotony of her daily routine. She mentioned her daily imaginary trips, which she allowed herself for an hour each afternoon as she sat in her armchair:

> [I] picture myself living in a villa in Florence, Italy. I see the pink-roofed houses, the geraniums in the window boxes and in the clay pots along the path. I may work in the garden for a while amid the singing of the birds. Sometimes I walk down the hill to the street and cross the Arno River by the Ponte Vecchio and head up the hill to the Pitti Palace. I stroll through cool galleries looking at the paintings and at the lovely views of the city one gets from the palace windows. Then I meander slowly up through the Boboli Gardens to the Porcelain Museum and the panoramic view of the whole city and the Tuscan hills one gets there.

Here, then, we see the persistence of playfulness into old age. Memory and creativity are the wings that allow this woman to soar away from a humdrum life.

And this brings us to our final perspective on how the child's fantasy play can serve the adult. Creativity need not be the generation of a masterpiece, a marble *David,* a Symphony in C-minor, or a *War and Peace.* The products of genius depend upon complex processes that combine high levels of particular skills and a willingness to use imagination, to entertain contrary possibilities, to engage in what Albert Rothenberg terms Janusian thinking.[64] The physical, verbal, musical, or mathematical skills of artists and thinkers like Michelangelo, Tolstoy, Beethoven, or Einstein are not given to everyone. But we do possess that same potential for playfulness, for trying out possible lives, that is the foundation for humbler but personally meaningful creativity. Our willingness to suspend disbelief temporarily can help us to enter deeply into aesthetic experience, to be "lost in a book" as Victor Nell's work has demonstrated, to find endless entertainment in reading history and in imagining how we would survive in the Paris of 1789, the United States of 1863, or the world of 2050.[65] Sometimes our fantasies will result in creative products of great value to us if not to the marketplace. The teacher who engages her pupils in a short play that suddenly brings home to them the issues of American history may be celebrated only in the memories of some of her pupils. Our own mothers, who by world standards have lived rather ordinary lives, were both unusually adept at finding interesting things for their children to do on rainy summer days—parades with kitchen pot drums or pretend picnics on the rug. We remember.

We began this book by listening to people's childhood memories. Perhaps it is fitting then that we close with our own, remembering mommas who showed their creativity in playful interactions with their children; tolerating our flights of imagination and fantasy, telling and reading us stories, and sharing their own sense of humor and whimsical fun. We also quoted from a poem by Rainer Maria Rilke to point the way toward the great role of children's imaginative play in the origins of human consciousness. Let us close then with still another Rilke poem drawn from a late fragment.[66] Although Rilke is speaking of poetry, we would propose that his words apply to the very nature of the imaginative process in each of us, our inherent capacity for pretend and make-believe, which opens the way for creativity in even the humblest lives.

> As long as you catch what you yourself threw into the air,
>   all is mere skill and petty gain;
> only when you unexpectedly become the catcher of the ball
> that the Goddess, your eternal playmate,
> threw toward you, toward the center of your being
> in a precisely calculated curve, in one of those arcs
> reminiscent of God building bridges;
> only then is being able to catch the ball an ability
>   to be cherished—

not yours but a world's. And if you
were to have that strength and courage to return the throw,
nay, even more miraculous, . . . if you had forgotten about
  strength and courage
and had already thrown . . . as the year
throws birds, the migrating flock
that an older warmth flings
across seas to a younger—only
through your daring is your play genuine.
You neither make throwing easier nor harder
for yourself. From your hand issues
the meteor and races towards its place in the heavens.

Notes

1. Memories of Childhood Play

1. Edith Cobb, *The Ecology of Imagination in Childhood* (New York: Columbia University Press, 1977), p. 3.
2. Richard Wright, *Black Boy: A Record of Childhood and Youth* (New York: Harper, 1945), p. 40.
3. Louis Untermeyer, ed., *The Poetry and Prose of Walt Whitman* (New York: Simon and Schuster, 1949), pp. 346–348.
4. Elspeth Huxley, *The Flame Trees of Thika: Memories of an African Childhood* (London: Chatto and Windus, 1959), p. 129.
5. Sarah Shears, *A Village Girl* (New York: Simon and Schuster, 1971), p. 73.
6. Peter Abrahams, *Tell Freedom: Memories of Africa* (New York: Knopf, 1954), p. 43.
7. John Van Druten, *The Widening Circle* (London: William Heinemann, 1957), p. 142.
8. Leo Tolstoy, *Childhood, Boyhood and Youth* (New York: Washington Square Press, 1967), p. 30.
9. Selma Lagerlof, *Memories of My Childhood: Further Years at Marbacka* (Garden City, N.Y.: Doubleday, 1934), p. 35.
10. Huxley, *Flame Trees*, pp. 99–100.
11. Chiang Yee, *A Chinese Childhood* (New York: Day, 1953), p. 49.
12. Dina Feitelson has described these same factors in her work with children in Israel. See "Imaginative Play and the Educational Process," in *Proceedings of the International Year of the Child Advocacy*, ed. S. L. Katz, Yale Child Study Center (New Haven: Yale University Press, 1979), pp. 185–197.
13. Vladimir Nabokov, *Speak, Memory: A Memoir* (London: Gollanz, 1951), p. 36.
14. Nabokov, *Speak, Memory*, p. 86.
15. Nabokov, *Speak, Memory*, p. 96.
16. Nabokov, *Speak, Memory*, p. 36.
17. Nabokov, *Speak, Memory*, p. 40.
18. Delmont Morrison and Shirley L. Morrison, "The Development of Romantic Ideation and J. M. Barrie's Image of the Lost Boy," in *Organizing Early Experience: Imagination and Cognition in Childhood*, ed. Delmont Morrison (Amityville: Baywood, 1988), pp. 226–241.

19. Morrison and Morrison, "Development of Romantic Ideation," p. 233.
20. Cynthia G. Wolff, *A Feast of Words* (New York: Oxford University Press, 1977), p. 28.
21. George H. Lewes, *The Life of Goethe* (New York: Frederick Ungar, 1965), pp. 13–14.
22. Lewes, *Goethe*, p. 7.
23. Ronald Hingley, *Chekov* (Liverpool: Tinling, 1966), p. 16.
24. Hingley, *Chekov*, p. 16.
25. Hingley, *Chekov*, p. 20.
26. George B. Shaw, *Shaw: An Autobiography, 1856–1898*. Selected from his writings by Stanley Weintraub. (New York: Weybright and Talley, 1969), p. 20.
27. Shaw, *Shaw: An Autobiography*, p. 24.
28. Shaw, *Shaw: An Autobiography*, p. 36.
29. Gardner B. Taplin, *The Life of Elizabeth Barrett Browning* (New Haven: Yale University Press, 1957), p. 22.
30. Taplin, *Elizabeth Barrett Browning*, p. 9.
31. Henri Troyat, *Tolstoi* (Garden City, N.Y.: Doubleday, 1967), p. 16.
32. Troyat, *Tolstoi*, p. 19.
33. A. A. Milne, *Autobiography* (New York: Dutton, 1939), p. 53.
34. Milne, *Autobiography*, p. 46.
35. Milne, *Autobiography*, p. 135.
36. Milne, *Autobiography*, p. 133.
37. Milne, *Autobiography*, p. 40.
38. Milne, *Autobiography*, p. 283.
39. Vyvyan Holland, *Son of Oscar Wilde* (London: Hart-Davis, 1954), p. 41.
40. E. C. Gaskell, *The Life of Charlotte Brontë* (Edinburgh: John Grant, 1924), p. 36.
41. Gaskell, *Charlotte Brontë*, p. 44.
42. F. E. Ratchford, *The Brontës' Web of Childhood* (New York: Russell and Russell, 1964), pp. 6, 8.
43. Shears, *Village Girl*, p. 54.
44. Nabokov, *Speak, Memory*, pp. 81–82.
45. Helen T. Flexner, *A Quaker Childhood* (New Haven: Yale University Press, 1940), p. 19.
46. Samuel Chotzinoff, *A Lost Paradise* (New York: Knopf, 1955), pp. 71, 88.
47. Nabokov, *Speak, Memory*, p. 23.
48. Wolff, *Feast of Words*, p. 43.
49. Wolff, *Feast of Words*, p. 44.
50. Wolff, *Feast of Words*, p. 33; George Sand, *Histoire de ma Vie*, quoted in Sian Miles, ed., Introduction to *Marianne* (New York: Carroll and Graf, 1988), pp. 1–2.
51. Erich Kastner, *When I Was a Little Boy* (London: Jonathan Cape, 1959), p. 59.
52. Kastner, *When I Was a Little Boy*, p. 60.
53. Wright, *Black Boy*, p. 33.

54. Lillian Hellman, *An Unfinished Woman* (New York: Bantam Books, 1969), pp. 7–8.
55. Shaw, *Shaw: An Autobiography,* pp. 45–47.
56. Kastner, *When I Was a Little Boy,* p. 85.
57. Maurice Baring, *The Puppet Show of Memory* (London: William Heineman, 1922), p. 1.
58. Wolff, *Feast of Words,* p. 29.
59. Margaret Mead, *Blackberry Winter: My Earlier Years* (New York: William Morrow, 1972), p. 72.
60. Sigrid Undset, *The Longest Years* (New York: Knopf, 1935), p. 66.
61. Holland, *Son of Oscar Wilde,* p. 41.
62. Nabokov, *Speak, Memory,* p. 28.
63. Robert Lindsey, "Francis Ford Coppola, Promises to Keep," *New York Times Magazine,* July 24, 1988, pp. 23, 26.
64. Baring, *Puppet Show,* p. 36.
65. Baring, *Puppet Show,* p. 8.
66. Kastner, *When I Was a Little Boy,* p. 61.

2. Imagination

1. Kurt Goldstein, *Human Nature in the Light of Psychopathology* (Cambridge, Mass.: Harvard University Press, 1940).
2. Sigmund Freud, "Formulations Regarding the Two Principles of Mental Functioning," in *The Complete Psychological Works of Sigmund Freud,* vol. 12 (London: Hogarth Press, 1911; 1962).
3. Kurt Lewin, *A Dynamic Theory of Personality* (New York: McGraw-Hill, 1935); L. S. Vygotsky, "Play and Its Role in the Mental Development of the Child," *Soviet Psychology* 12 (1966): 62–67; Jean Piaget, *Play, Dreams and Imitation in Childhood* (New York: Norton, 1962).
4. Freud, "Formulations Regarding Two Principles of Mental Functioning."
5. Ernst Kris, "On Preconscious Mental Processes," in *Organization and Pathology of Thought,* ed. David Rapaport (New York: Columbia University Press, 1951).
6. Jerome Bruner, *Actual Minds, Possible Worlds* (Cambridge, Mass.: Harvard University Press, 1986), p. 11; For broader historical reviews of how the imagination has been identified and treated in works of philosophy and literature see James Engell, *The Creative Imagination: Enlightenment to Romanticism* (Cambridge, Mass.: Harvard University Press, 1981); Jerome L. Singer, "Towards the Scientific Study of Imagination," *Imagination, Cognition and Personality* 1 (1981–1982): 5–28.
7. Peter K. Smith, "Does Play Matter? Functional and Evolutionary Aspects of Animal and Human Play," *Behavioral and Brain Sciences* 5 (1976): 139–184.
8. Brian Vandenberg, "Play, Myth and Hope," in *Play, Play Therapy, Play Research,* ed. Rimmert van der Kooij and Joop Hellendoorn (Lisse, The Netherlands: Swets and Zeitlinger, 1986).

9. Stephen Mitchell, "Object Relations Theories and the Developmental Tilt," *Contemporary Psychoanalysis* 20 (1984): 473–499.

10. Mechthild Papousek, Hanus Papousek, and Betty Harris, "The Emergence of Play in Parent-Infant Interactions," in *Curiosity, Imagination and Play*, ed. Dietmar Gorlitz and Joachim Wohlwill (Hillsdale, N.J.: Erlbaum, 1987).

11. R. B. Zajonc, "Feeling and Thinking: Preferences Need No Inferences," *American Psychologist* 35 (1980): 151–175.

12. Silvan S. Tomkins, *Affect, Imagery, Consciousness*, 2 vols. (New York: Springer, 1962; 1963); Carroll E. Izard, ed., *Human Emotions* (New York: Plenum, 1977); Paul Ekman, W. V. Friesen, and P. C. Ellsworth, *Emotion in the Human Face: Guidelines for Research and an Integration of Findings*, rev. ed. (Cambridge, Mass.: Cambridge University Press, 1982); Hans Kreitler and Shulamith Kreitler, *Cognitive Orientation and Behavior* (New York: Springer, 1976).

13. Tomkins, *Affect, Imagery, Consciousness*.

14. Jerome L. Singer, *Imagery and Daydreaming Methods in Psychotherapy and Behavior Modification* (New York: Academic Press, 1974).

15. Tomkins, *Affect, Imagery, Consciousness*.

16. Gordon Bower, "The Architecture of Cognition, Mental Imagery, and Associative Learning," in *Cognition in Learning and Memory*, ed. W. L. Gregg (New York: Wiley, 1972); John R. Anderson, *The Architecture of Cognition* (Cambridge, Mass.: Harvard University Press, 1983).

17. George Mandler, *Mind and Body* (New York: Norton, 1984).

18. David Bakan, *The Duality of Human Existence* (Chicago: Rand McNally, 1966); Andras Angyal, *Neurosis and Treatment: A Holistic Theory* (New York: Wiley, 1965); Otto Rank, *Will Therapy and Truth and Reality* (New York: Knopf, 1945); Carl C. Jung, *Psychological Types* (New York: Pantheon, 1971).

19. Sigmund Freud, "Beyond the Pleasure Principle," in *The Complete Psychological Works of Sigmund Freud*, vol. 18 (London: Hogarth Press, 1920; 1962); Sigmund Freud, "Civilization and Its Discontents," in *The Complete Psychological Works of Sigmund Freud*, vol. 21 (London: Hogarth, 1930; 1962); Louis Breger, *Freud's Unfinished Journey* (London: Routledge and Kegan Paul, 1981); Sidney J. Blatt, "Interpersonal Relatedness and Self-Definition: Two Personality Configurations and Their Implications for Psychopathology and Psychotherapy," in *Repression and Dissociation*, ed. Jerome L. Singer (Chicago: University of Chicago Press, 1990); George Bonanno and Jerome L. Singer, "Repressive Personality Style: Theoretical and Methodological Implications for Health and Pathology," in Singer, *Repression and Dissociation*.

20. Jean Piaget, *Play, Dreams and Imitation in Childhood* (New York: Norton, 1962).

21. David Rapaport, "The Structure of Psychoanalytic Theory: A Systematizing Attempt," *Psychological Issues*, vol. 6 (New York: International Universities Press, 1960).

22. Piaget, *Play, Dreams and Imitation in Childhood*.

23. Philippe Ariès, *Centuries of Childhood* (New York: Vintage Books, 1960).

24. Yvonne Kapp, *Eleanor Marx: The Crowded Years, 1884–1898* (New York: Pantheon, 1976); R. Carlson, "Exemplary Lives: The Uses of Psychobiography for Theory Development," *Journal of Personality* 56 (1988): 105–138.

25. Erik H. Erikson, *Childhood and Society* (New York: Norton, 1962); C. E. Franz, and K. M. White, "Individuation and Attachment in Personality Development: Extending Erikson's Theory," *Journal of Personality* 53 (1985): 224–256.

26. Harry S. Sullivan, *The Interpersonal Theory of Psychiatry* (New York: Norton, 1953); Thomas Berndt, "Developmental Changes in Conformity to Peers or Parents," *Developmental Psychology* 15 (1979): 608–616; Thomas Berndt, "Age Changes and Changes over Time in Prosocial Intentions and Behavior between Friends," *Developmental Psychology* 17 (1981): 408–416; Erik H. Erikson, *The Life Cycle Completed* (New York: Norton, 1962).

27. Erikson, *Childhood and Society.*

28. R. J. Havighurst, *Human Development and Education* (New York: Longmans and Green, 1953); C. Tryon and J. Lillienthal, *Fostering Mental Health in Our Schools* (Washington, D.C.: National Education Association, 1950).

29. Joan Erikson and Erik Erikson, "Wisdom in Old Age," in Joan Erikson, *Wisdom and the Senses* (New York: Norton, 1988).

30. Charles Darwin, *The Expression of Emotion in Man and Animals* (Chicago: University of Chicago Press, 1872; 1965).

31. Karl Groos, *The Play of Animals* (New York: Appleton, 1898); Karl Groos, *The Play of Man* (New York: Appleton, 1901); Johan Huizinga, *Homo Ludens* (Boston: Beacon, 1950).

32. Owen Aldis, *Play Fighting* (New York: Academic Press, 1985); Robert Fagen, *Animal Play Behavior* (New York: Oxford University Press, 1981); Helen Schwartzman, *Transformations* (New York: Plenum, 1978).

33. Eric Klinger, *Structure and Functions of Fantasy* (New York: Wiley, 1971).

34. Smith, "Does Play Matter?"

35. Mihalyi Csikszentmihalyi, "Does Being Human Matter? On Some Interpretive Problems of Comparative Ludology." *Behavioral and Brain Sciences* 5 (1982): 160; Michael Lewis, "Play as Whimsy," *Behavioral and Brain Sciences* 5 (1982): 166; Brian Sutton-Smith, "The Epistemology of the Play Theorist," *Behavioral and Brain Sciences* 5 (1982): 170–171; Brian Vandenberg, "The Essentials of Play?," *Behavioral and Brain Sciences* 5 (1982): 171–172.

36. Freud, "Beyond the Pleasure Principle."

37. Piaget, *Play, Dreams and Imitation in Childhood.*

38. Brian Sutton-Smith, "Piaget on Play: A Critique," *Psychological Review* 73 (1966): 104–110; Inge Bretherton, "Representing the Social

World," in *Symbolic Play: Reality and Fantasy,* ed. Inge Bretherton (Orlando: Academic Press, 1984), pp. 3–41.

39. Piaget, *Play, Dreams and Imitation in Childhood,* p. 145.

40. Brian Sutton-Smith, "The Metaphor of Games in Social Science Research," in van der Kooij and Hellendoorn, *Play, Play Therapy, Play Research,* pp. 35–63.

41. Sutton-Smith, "The Metaphor of Games." For a thoughtful view of the more sinister, sordid, or risk-taking forms of play among older children—such as drag-racing, quasi-violent group games, or dangerous "deep play"—see Brian Sutton-Smith and Diane Kelly-Byrne, "The Idealization of Play," *Play in Animals and Humans,* ed. P. K. Smith (London: Basil Blackwell, 1984), pp. 305–321.

3. The Beginnings of Pretending and Baby Play

1. Selma Fraiberg, "Shake off Slumber and Beware," in *Interdiscipline,* ed. Edward Quinn, Robert Lilienfeld, and Rodman Hill (New York: Macmillan, 1972), p. 46.

2. Enid Bagnold, "The Door of Life," in *Child Development through Literature,* ed. Elliott Landau, Sherrie Epstein, and Ann Stone (Englewood Cliffs, N.J.: Prentice-Hall, 1972), p. 6.

3. Christina Arco and Kathleen McCluskey, "A Change of Pace: An Investigation of the Salience of Maternal Temporal Style in Mother-Infant Play," *Child Development* 52 (1981): 941–944.

4. Diana Shmukler, "Imaginative Play: Its Implication for the Process of Education," in *Imagery and the Educational Process,* ed. Anees Sheik (New York: Baywood, 1984). For data from Japan bearing on this area see also Tamaki Takahashi, "Verbal and Non-Verbal Communication in Mother-Child Relationship," *Hiyoshi Report,* no. 12 (1985): 11–24, published by the Department of General Arts and Literature, Japanese Women's University, Tokyo (in English); Tamaki Takahashi, *Imagination and Reality: The Child's World of Pretend Play* (Tokyo: Doshin, 1989) (in Japanese).

5. Owen Aldis, *Play Fighting* (New York: Academic Press, 1975).

6. William Booth, "The Social Lives of Dolphins," *Science* 240 (1988): 1273–74.

7. Rita Reif, "Archaic Smiles Have Persisted for 2000 Years," *New York Times,* June 19, 1988, p. 36.

8. Robert Hecht and Andrea Hecht, eds., *Greek and Etruscan Art of the Archaic Period* (New York: Atlantic Antiquities, 1988), p. 31.

9. Cornelius Vermeule, "Archaic Art," in Hecht and Hecht, *Greek and Etruscan Art,* pp. vi–vii.

10. J. Eric Thompson, *The Rise and Fall of Mayan Civilization* (Norman: University of Oklahoma Press, 1970), p. 204.

11. Philip Lieberman, "Voice in the Wilderness," *Sciences,* July–August, 1988, p. 23.

12. R. Thompson, D. W. Leger, J. A. Walker, and C. P. Gurbin, "Infant Cries as Graded or Discrete Socioemotional Signals," in *Emotional Expression in Infants: New Perspective on an Old Controversy,* H. Oster (Chair) (Symposium conducted at the International Conference on Infant Studies, Washington, D.C., April, 1988).

13. Carroll Izard, ed., *Human Emotions* (New York: Plenum, 1977); S. S. Jones and T. Raag, "Smile Production in Older Infants: The Importance of a Social Recipient for the Facial Signal," *Child Development* 60 (1989): 811–818.

14. Carol Z. Malatesta, Clayton Culver, Johanna R. Tesman, and Beth Shepard, *The Development of Emotion Expression during the First Two Years of Life,* Monographs of the Society for Research in Child Development, vol. 54, nos. 1–2 (Chicago: Society for Research in Child Development, 1989).

15. Michael Lamb, Mast Frodi, Carl-Philip Huang, and Ann Frodi, "Effects of Paternal Involvement on Infant Preferences for Mothers and Fathers," *Child Development* 54 (1983): 450–458.

16. Catherine Garvey, *Play* (Cambridge, Mass.: Harvard University Press, 1977), pp. 21, 63.

17. Andrew Meltzoff and M. Keith Moore, "Newborn Infants Imitate Adult Facial Gestures," *Child Development* 54 (1983): 702–709.

18. Jean Koepke, M. Hamm, M. Legerstee, and M. Russell, "Neonatal Imitation: Two Failures to Replicate," *Infant Behavior and Development* 6 (1983): 97–102.

19. Andrew Meltzoff, "Infant Imitation and Memory: Nine-Month-Olds in Immediate and Deferred Tests," *Child Development* 59 (1988): 217–225.

20. Jean Piaget, *Play, Dreams and Imitation in Childhood* (New York: Norton, 1962), p. 29.

21. Craig Stenberg, Joseph Campos, and Robert Enide, "The Facial Expression of Anger in Seven-Month-Old Infants," *Child Development* 54 (1983): 178–184.

22. Alan Sroufe, "Socioemotional Development," in *Handbook of Infant Development,* ed. Joy D. Osofsky (New York: Wiley, 1979).

23. Charlotte Bühler, *The First Years of Life* (New York: Day, 1930). For a more recent study with older children see C. Hoffner and D. M. Badzinski, "Children's Integration of Facial and Situational Cues to Emotion," *Child Development* 60 (1989): 411–422.

24. Irina Skariatina, *Little Era in Old Russia* (Indianapolis: Bobbs-Merrill, 1934), p. 39.

25. Albert Caron, Rose Caron, and Darla MacLean, "Infant Discrimination of Naturalistic Emotional Expression: The Role of Face and Voice," *Child Development* 59 (1988): 615.

26. Anat Ninio and Nurith Rinott, "Fathers' Involvement in the Care of Their Infants and Their Attributions of Cognitive Competence to Infants," *Child Development* 59 (1988): 656; Garvey, *Play,* p. 65.

27. Ruth Weir, *Language in the Crib* (The Hague: Mouton, 1962).

28. Jerome Bruner, *Child Talk* (New York: Norton, 1983), p. 47.

29. Linda Acredolo and Susan Goodwyn, "Symbolic Gesturing in Normal Infants," *Child Development* 59 (1988): 450.
30. Elise Masur, "Mothers' Responses to Infants' Object-Related Gestures: Influences on Lexical Development," *Journal of Child Language* 9 (1982): 23–30.
31. Joyce Carey, "Spring Song," in Landau, Epstein, and Stone, *Child Development through Literature,* pp. 176–177.
32. Mabel Rice and Linda Woodsmall, "Lessons from Television: Children's Word Learning When Viewing," *Child Development* 59 (1988): 426.
33. Stella Vosniadou, "Children and Metaphors," *Child Development* 58 (1987): 871.
34. Vosniadou, "Children and Metaphors," p. 875.
35. John Waggoner, Miriam Messe, and David Palermo, "Grasping the Meaning of Metaphor: Story Recall and Comprehension," *Child Development* 56 (1985): 1156–66.
36. Jean Piaget, *The Language and Thought of the Child* (New York: World Publishing, 1955), p. 26.
37. Piaget, *Language and Thought,* p. 59.
38. Catherine S. Tamis-LeMonda and Marc H. Bornstein, "Habituation and Maternal Encouragement of Attention in Infancy as Predictors of Toddler Language, Play, and Representational Competence," *Child Development* 60 (1989): 738–751.
39. Aldous Huxley, "Brave New World," in Landau, Epstein, and Stone, *Child Development through Literature,* pp. 22–29.
40. Huxley, "Brave New World," p. 23.

4. The High Season of Imaginative Play

1. Terrence Rafferty, "The Current Cinema: All Sizes," *New Yorker,* August 8, 1988, p. 77.
2. Jerome L. Singer and Dorothy G. Singer, *Television, Imagination, and Aggression: A Study of Preschoolers* (Hillsdale, N.J.: Erlbaum, 1981).
3. Erik H. Erikson, *Identity, Youth and Crisis* (New York: Norton, 1968), p. 116.
4. Daniel Goleman, "Erikson, in His Own Old Age, Expands His View of Life," *New York Times,* June 14, 1988, p. C1.
5. Larry Fenson and Robert E. Schell, "The Origins of Exploratory Play," *Early Childhood Development and Care* 19 (1985): 14.
6. Jean Piaget, *Play, Dreams and Imitation in Childhood* (New York: Norton, 1962).
7. Greta G. Fein, "Pretend Play in Childhood: An Integrative Review," *Child Development* 52 (1981): 1095–1118.
8. Edith Cobb, *The Ecology of Imagination in Childhood* (New York: Columbia University Press, 1977), p. 29.
9. Piaget, *Play, Dreams and Imitation in Childhood.*
10. Dorothy G. Singer and Tracey Revenson, *A Piaget Primer: How a Child*

Thinks (New York: International Universities Press and New American Library, 1978).

11. Dorothy G. Singer and Barbara Kornfield, "Conserving and Consuming, a Developmental Study of Abstract and Action Choices," *Developmental Psychology* 8 (1973): 314.
12. Piaget, *Play, Dreams and Imitation in Childhood,* p. 87.
13. Piaget, *Play, Dreams and Imitation in Childhood,* p. 132.
14. Piaget, *Play, Dreams and Imitation in Childhood,* p. 151.
15. Judith Van Hoorn, "Games that Babies and Mothers Play," in *Looking at Children's Play,* ed. Patricia Monighan-Nourot, Barbara Scales, Judith Van Hoorn, and Millie Almy (New York: Teachers College Press, 1987), pp. 38–62.
16. Singer and Singer, *Television, Imagination, and Aggression,* p. 60.
17. Greta G. Fein, "Pretend Play: Creativity and Consciousness," in *Curiosity, Imagination, and Play,* ed. Dietmar Gorlitz and Joachim Wohlwill (Hillsdale, N.J.: Erlbaum, 1987), p. 300.
18. Jennifer A. Connolly, Anna B. Doyle, and Erica Reznick, "Social Pretend Play and Social Interaction in Preschoolers," *Journal of Applied Developmental Psychology* 9 (1988): 301–313.
19. Roni Tower, "Preschoolers' Imaginativeness: Subtypes, Correlates, and Maladaptive Extremes," *Imagination, Cognition and Personality* 4 (1984–1985): 349–364.
20. Tiffany M. Field and Tedra A. Walden, "Production and Discrimination of Facial Expressions by Preschool Children," *Child Development* 53 (1982): 1299–1311.
21. Gary W. Ladd, Joseph M. Price, and Craig H. Hart, "Predicting Preschoolers' Past Status from Their Playground Behaviors," *Child Development* 59 (1988): 991.
22. Carollee Howes, "Sharing Fantasy: Social Pretend Play in Toddlers," *Child Development* 56 (1985): 1253–58.
23. Catherine Garvey and Rita Berndt, "The Organization of Pretend Play" (Paper presented at the Symposium on Structure in Play and Fantasy, American Psychological Association, Chicago, September 1985).
24. Connolly, Doyle, and Reznick, "Social Pretend Play."
25. Carollee Howes, *Peer Interaction in Young Children,* Monographs of the Society for Research in Child Development, vol. 53, no. 1 (Chicago: Society for Research in Child Development, 1988), p. 4.
26. Singer and Singer, *Television, Imagination, and Aggression.*
27. Dennis P. Wolf, Jayne Rygh, and Jennifer Altshuler, "Agency and Experience: Actions and States in Play Narratives," in *Symbolic Play,* ed. Inge Bretherton (Orlando: Academic Press, 1984), p. 214.
28. Wolf, Rygh, and Altshuler, "Agency and Experience."
29. Dennis P. Wolf and Sharon H. Grollman, "Ways of Playing: Individual Differences in Imaginative Style," *Contributions to Human Development* 6 (1982): 46–63.
30. Wolf and Grollman, "Ways of Playing," p. 52.
31. Wolf and Grollman, "Ways of Playing," p. 55.

32. Wolf and Grollman, "Ways of Playing," p. 59.
33. Tower, "Preschoolers' Imaginativeness," p. 362.
34. C. A. Seavey, P. A. Katz, and S. R. Zalk, "Baby X: The Effect of Gender Labels on Adult Responses to Infants," *Sex Roles* 1 (1975): 103–109.
35. B. I. Fagot, "Sex Differences in Toddler's Behavior and Parental Reaction," *Developmental Psychology* 10 (1974): 554–558.
36. Nancy J. Bell and William Carver, "A Reevaluation of Gender Label Effects: Expectant Mothers' Responses to Infants," *Child Development* 51 (1980): 927.
37. Wolf, Rygh, and Altshuler, "Agency and Experience."
38. Wolf, Rygh, and Altshuler, "Agency and Experience," p. 208.
39. Wolf, Rygh, and Altshuler, "Agency and Experience," p. 209.
40. Jack Block, "Assimilation, Accommodation, and the Dynamics of Personality Development," *Child Development* 53 (1982): 281–295.
41. Block, "Assimilation," p. 293.
42. Singer and Singer, *Television, Imagination, and Aggression.*
43. Lois W. Hoffman, "Changes in Family Roles, Socialization, and Sex Differences," *American Psychologist* 32 (1977): 644–657.
44. Corinne Hutt and Reena Bhavnani, "Predictions from Play," in *Play,* ed. Jerome S. Bruner, Alison Jolly, and Kathy Sylva (New York: Basic, 1976), pp. 217–219.
45. D. L. Singer and Judith Rummo, "Ideational Creativity and Behavioral Style in Kindergarten Aged Children," *Developmental Psychology* 8 (1973): 154–161.
46. Hutt and Bhavnani, "Predictions from Play," p. 219.
47. Singer and Singer, *Television, Imagination, and Aggression.*
48. G. V. Prosser, C. Hutt, S. J. Hutt, K. J. Mahindadasa, and M. D. J. Goonetilleke, "Children's Play in Sri Lanka: A Cross-Cultural Study," *British Journal of Developmental Psychology* 4 (1986): 179–186.
49. Richard A. Martin, "Babies Rattles from 2600 B.C. and Other Ancient Toys," *Field Museum News* 8 (August 1937): 5. Reprinted in *A Children's Games Anthology,* ed. Brian Sutton-Smith (New York: Arno Press, 1976), p. 79.
50. Sutton-Smith, *A Children's Games Anthology.*
51. Bernard Mergen, "Toys," in *Children's Play: Past, Present and Future,* ed. Brian Sutton-Smith (Philadelphia: Please Touch Museum, 1985), pp. 12–13.
52. Mary Ann Pulaski, "Toys and Imaginative Play" in *The Child's World of Make-Believe,* ed. Jerome L. Singer (New York: Academic Press, 1973), pp. 74–103.
53. Jennifer A. Connolly, Anna B. Doyle, and Erica Reznick, "Social Pretend Play and Social Interaction in Preschoolers."
54. Pulaski,, *Toys and Imaginative Play,* p. 101.
55. Singer and Singer, *Television, Imagination, and Aggression.*
56. Vonnie C. McLoyd, "The Effects of the Structure of Play Objects on the Pretend Play of Low-Income Preschool Children," *Child Development* 54 (1983): 626–635.

57. McLoyd, "The Effects of the Structure of Play Objects," p. 633.
58. C. G. Schau, L. Kahn, and J. H. Diepold, "The Relationship of Parental Expectations and Preschool Children's Verbal Sex Typing to Their Sex-Typed Toy Play Behavior," *Child Development* 51 (1980): 266–270.
59. Yvonne Caldera, Aletha Huston, and Marion O'Brien, "Social Interactions and Play Patterns of Parents and Toddlers with Feminine, Masculine and Neutral Toys," *Child Development* 60 (1989): 70–76.
60. Nancy Eisenberg, Kelly Tryon, and Ellen Cameron, "The Relation of Preschoolers' Peer Interaction to Their Sex-Typed Toy Choices," *Child Development* 55 (1984): 1044–50.
61. Eisenberg, Tryon, and Cameron, "Relation of Preschoolers' Peer Interaction," p. 1049.
62. Rena L. Repetti, "Determinants of Children's Sex Stereotyping: Parental Sex-Role Traits and Television Viewing," *Personality and Social Psychology Bulletin* 10 (1984): 457–468.
63. Brian Sutton-Smith, "Novel Responses to Toys," *Merrill-Palmer Quarterly* 14 (1968): 151–158.
64. Erica F. Rosenfeld, "The Relationship of Sex-Typed Toys to the Development of Competency and Sex-Role Identification" (Paper presented at the meeting of the Society for Research in Child Development, Denver, April 1975).
65. James E. Johnson and Joan Ershler, "Developmental Trends in Preschool Play as a Function of Classroom Program and Child Gender," *Child Development* 52 (1981): 995–1004.
66. Zolinda Stoneman, Gene H. Brady, and Carol MacKinnon, "Naturalistic Observation of Children's Activities and Roles While Playing with Their Siblings and Friends," *Child Development* 55 (1984): 617–627.

5. Imaginary Playmates and Imaginary Worlds

1. Sigmund Freud, "The Future of an Illusion," in *The Complete Psychological Works of Sigmund Freud*, vol. 21 (London: Hogarth Press, 1927; 1962).
2. Philips Stevens, Jr., "The Appeal of the Occult: Some Thoughts on History, Religion, and Science," *The Skeptical Inquirer* 12 (1988): 379.
3. D. W. Winnicott, "Transitional Objects and Transitional Phenomena," *International Journal of Psychoanalysis* 34 (1953): 89–97.
4. M. Tolpin, "On the Beginnings of a Cohesive Self," *Psychoanalytic Study of the Child* 26 (1971): 316–352.
5. David R. Metcalf and René Spitz, "The Transitional Object: Critical Developmental Period and Organizer of the Psyche," in *Between Reality and Fantasy*, ed. S. A. Grolnick, L. Barkin, and W. Muensterberger (New York: Jason Aronson, 1978), pp. 97–108.
6. C. J. Litt, "Theories of Transitional Object Attachment: An Overview," *International Journal of Behavioral Development* 9 (1986): 383–399.

7. Helen B. Schwartzman, *Transformations: The Anthology of Children's Play* (New York: Plenum, 1978).
8. Litt, "Theories of Transitional Object Attachment."
9. Mark Twain, *The Autobiography of Mark Twain,* ed. Charles Neider (New York: Harper and Row, 1959).
10. Mark Twain, *The Mysterious Stranger* (New York: Harper and Row, 1922).
11. C. Vostrovsky, "A Study of Imaginary Companions," *Education* 15 (1895): 383.
12. Jean Piaget, *Play, Dreams and Imitation in Childhood* (New York: Norton, 1962).
13. Martin Manosevitz, Norman M. Prentice, and F. Wilson, "Individual and Family Correlates of Imaginary Companions in Preschool Children," *Developmental Psychology* 8 (1973): 72–79.
14. Jerome L. Singer and B. F. Streiner, "Imaginative Content in the Dreams and Fantasy Play of Blind and Sighted Children," *Perceptual and Motor Skills* 22 (1966): 475–482.
15. Dorothy G. Singer and M. L. Lenahan, "Imagination Content in the Dreams of Deaf Children," *American Annals of the Deaf* (February 1976): 44–48.
16. V. K. Masih, "Imaginary Play Companions of Children," in *Piagetian Theory and the Helping Professions,* vol. 1, ed. R. Weizman, R. Brown, P. Levinson, and P. Taylor (Los Angeles: University of Southern California Press, 1978).
17. J. U. Somers and T. D. Yawkey, "Imaginary Play Companions: Contributions of Creative and Intellectual Abilities of Young Children," *Journal of Creative Behavior* 18 (1984): 88; J. R. Meyer and S. Tuber, "Intrapsychic and Behavioral Correlates of the Phenomenon of Imaginary Companions in Young Children," *Psychoanalytic Psychology* 6 (1989): 151–168; Mary Watkins, *Invisible Guests: The Development of Imaginal Dialogues* (Hillsdale, N.J.: Analytic Press, 1986).
18. Jerome L. Singer and Dorothy G. Singer, *Television, Imagination, and Aggression: A Study of Preschoolers* (Hillsdale, N.J.: Erlbaum, 1981).
19. A. T. Jersild, F. V. Markey, and C. L. Jersild, *Children's Fears, Dreams, Wishes* (New York: Teachers College Press, 1933).
20. L. B. Ames and J. Learned, "Imaginary Companions and Related Phenomena," *Journal of Genetic Psychology* 69 (1946): 147–167.
21. A. T. Jersild, *Child Psychology* (Englewood Cliffs, N.J.: Prentice-Hall, 1968).
22. Manosevitz, Prentice, and Wilson, "Individual and Family Correlates of Imaginary Companions."
23. Brian Sutton-Smith, *The Folkgames of Children* (Austin: University of Texas Press, 1972).
24. L. Rowell Huesmann and Leonard D. Eron, eds., *Television and the Aggressive Child: A Cross-National Study* (Hillsdale, N.J.: Erlbaum, 1986).

25. Manosevitz, Prentice, and Wilson, "Individual and Family Correlates of Imaginary Companions."
26. Otto F. Kernberg, *Object Relations Theory and Clinical Psychoanalysis* (New York: Jason Aronson, 1976).
27. Selma Fraiberg, *The Magic Years* (New York: Scribner and Sons, 1959).
28. Bruce R. Klein, "A Child's Imaginary Companion: A Transitional Self," *Clinical Social Work Journal* 13 (1985): 272–282.
29. Steven J. Lynn and Judith W. Rhue, "Fantasy Proneness: Hypnosis, Developmental Antecedents, and Psychopathology," *American Psychologist* 43 (1988): 35–44.
30. T. D. Yawkey and M. L. Yawkey, "Assessing Young Children for Imaginativeness through Oral Reporting: Preliminary Results" (Paper presented at the International Conference on Play and Play Environments: Research and Its Applications to Play Settings, The University of Texas, Austin, 1983).
31. Klein, "A Child's Imaginary Companion."
32. Leo Tolstoy, *Childhood, Boyhood and Youth* (New York: Washington Square Press, 1967).
33. R. Bensen and D. Pryor, "When Friends Fall Out: Developmental Interference with the Function of Some Imaginary Companions," *Journal of the American Psychoanalytic Association* 21 (1973): 457–473.
34. Klein, "A Child's Imaginary Companion," p. 276.
35. Marc Gershowitz, "Fantasy Behaviors of Clinic Referred Children in Play Environments with College Undergraduates" (Ph.D. diss., Michigan State University, 1974); Diana Shmukler, "Mother-Child Interaction and Its Relationship to the Predisposition of Imaginative Play," *Genetic Psychology Monographs* 104 (1981): 215–235.
36. Richard B. Sapir, *The Far Arena* (New York: Seaview Books, 1978).
37. C. E. Schaefer, Imaginary Companions and Creative Adolescents, *Developmental Psychology* 1 (1969): 747–749.
38. J. W. von Goethe, *Faust,* trans. W. P. Andrews, ed. G. M. Priest and K. E. Weston (Princeton: Princeton University Press, 1929); Thomas Mann, *Doctor Faustus: The Life of the German Composer, Adrian Leverkuhn, as Told by a Friend,* trans. H. T. Lowe-Porter (New York: Knopf, 1984).
39. Maurice Baring, *The Puppet Show of Memory* (London: William Heinemann, 1922), p. 37.
40. Stephen Mackeith, "Paracosms and the Development of Fantasy in Childhood," *Imagination, Cognition and Personality* 2 (1982–1983): 261–268; Robert Silvey and Stephen Mackeith, "The Paracosm: A Special Form of Fantasy," in *Ongoing Early Experience: Imagination and Cognition in Childhood,* ed. Delmont C. Morrison (Amityville, N.Y.: Baywood, 1988), pp. 173–197.
41. Tolstoy, *Childhood, Boyhood and Youth,* p. 16.
42. Mackeith, "Paracosms and the Development of Fantasy in Childhood"; Silvey and Mackeith, "The Paracosm: A Special Form of Fantasy."

43. F. E. Ratchford, *The Brontës' Web of Childhood* (New York: Russell and Russell, 1964).

44. Mackeith, "Paracosms and the Development of Fantasy in Childhood," p. 195; Silvey and Mackeith, "The Paracosm: A Special Form of Fantasy."

45. Hannah Green, *I Never Promised You a Rose Garden* (New York: Signet, 1964).

46. Robert Lindner, *The Fifty-Minute Hour* (New York: Bantam Books, 1955).

6. Cognitive and Emotional Growth through Play

1. Sigmund Freud, "Beyond the Pleasure Principle," in *The Complete Psychological Works of Sigmund Freud,* vol. 18 (London: Hogarth Press, 1920; 1962), pp. 15–16.

2. Inge Bretherton, "Representing the Social World in Symbolic Play: Reality and Fantasy," in *Symbolic Play,* ed. Inge Bretherton (Orlando: Academic Press, 1984), pp. 1–41.

3. Ernst G. Schachtel, *Metamorphosis* (New York: Basic Books, 1959).

4. Kurt Lewin, "Environmental Forces in Child Behavior and Development," in *A Dynamic Theory of Personality,* ed. Kurt Lewin (New York: McGraw-Hill, 1935), pp. 66–113.

5. Schachtel, *Metamorphosis,* p. 265.

6. David A. Caruso, "Play and Learning in Infancy: Research and Implications," *Young Children* 43 (1988): 63–70.

7. Jay Belsky and Robert Most, "From Exploration to Play: A Cross-Sectional Study of Infant Free Play Behavior," *Developmental Psychology* 17 (1981): 630–639.

8. Caruso, "Play and Learning in Infancy," p. 65.

9. Julian Jaynes, *The Origins of Consciousness in the Breakdown of the Bicameral Mind* (Boston: Houghton Mifflin, 1977).

10. Alan M. Leslie, "Pretense and Representation: The Origins of "Theory of Mind," *Psychological Review* 94 (1987): 412, 422.

11. S. Baron-Cohen, Alan M. Leslie and Uta Frith, "Mechanical, Behavioral and Intentional Understanding of Picture Stories in Autistic Children," *British Journal of Developmental Psychology* 4 (1986): 113–125; H. Wimmer and J. Perner, "Beliefs about Beliefs: Representation and Constraining Function of Wrong Beliefs in Young Children's Understanding of Deception," *Cognition* 13 (1983): 103–128.

12. Leslie, "Pretense and Representation"; L. Nahme-Huang, Dorothy G. Singer, Jerome L. Singer, and A. B. Wheaton, "Imaginative Play Training and Perceptual-Motor Interventions with Emotionally Disturbed Hospitalized Children," *American Journal of Orthopsychiatry* 47 (1977): 238–249; Sandra Blakeslee, "Crack's Toll Among Babies: A Joyless View, Even of Toys," *New York Times,* September 12, 1989, pp. 1, 24.

13. Brian Sutton-Smith, "Piaget on Play: A Critique," *Psychological Review* 73 (1966): 104–110; Bretherton, "Representing the Social World in

Symbolic Play"; Jean Piaget, *Play, Dreams and Imitation in Childhood* (New York: Norton, 1962).

14. Bretherton, "Representing the Social World in Symbolic Play."
15. Katherine Nelson and Susan Seidman, "Playing with Scripts," in Bretherton *Symbolic Play*, pp. 45–71; M. W. Kreye, "Conceptual Organization in the Play of Preschool Children: Effects of Meaning, Context, and Mother-Child Interaction," in Bretherton, *Symbolic Play*, pp. 299–336.
16. D. J. Pepler and H. S. Ross, "The Effects of Play on Convergent and Divergent Problem Solving," *Child Development* 52 (1981): 1202–10.
17. Robert J. Sternberg, *The Triarchic Mind* (New York: Viking, 1988); Howard Gardner, *Frames of Mind* (New York: Basic Books, 1982).
18. A. K. Levy, "The Language of Play: The Role of Play in Language Development," *Early Childhood Development and Care* 17 (1984): 49–62; Colette Daivte, "Writing Play," *Spencer Foundation Newsletter* 3 (1988), p. 2; Dina Feitelson, Bracha Kita, and Zahava Goldstein, "Effects of Listening to Series Stories on First Graders' Comprehension and Use of Language," *Research in the Teaching of English* 20 (1986): 339–356; Dina Feitelson and Zahava Goldstein, "Patterns of Book Ownership and Reading in Young Children in Israeli School-Oriented and Nonschool-Oriented Families," *Reading Teacher* 39 (1986): 924–930; Dina Feitelson, *Facts and Fads in Beginning Reading* (Norwood, N.J.: Ablex, 1988).
19. P. H. Lewis, "The Relationship of Sociodramatic Play to Various Cognitive Abilities in Kindergarten" (Ph.D. diss., Ohio State University, 1973); Jerome L. Singer and Dorothy G. Singer, "Imaginative Play and Pretending in Early Childhood: Some Experimental Approaches," in *Child Personality and Psychopathology: Current Topics,* ed. Anthony Davids (New York: Wiley, 1976), pp. 69–112; Jerome L. Singer and Dorothy G. Singer, *Television, Imagination and Aggression: A Study of Preschoolers* (Hillsdale, N.J.: Erlbaum, 1981); Paula Olszewski, "Individual Differences in Preschool Children's Production of Verbal Fantasy Play," *Merrill-Palmer Quarterly* 33 (1987): 69–86.
20. Nelson and Seidman, "Playing with Scripts"; Lorraine McCune-Nicolich and Carol Bruskin, "Combinatorial Competency in Symbolic Play and Language," *Contributions to Human Development* 6 (1982): 30–45.
21. McCune-Nicolich and Bruskin, "Combinatorial Competency," pp. 41–42.
22. McCune-Nicolich and Bruskin, "Combinatorial Competency," p. 43.
23. Nelson and Seidman, "Playing with Scripts."
24. Singer and Singer, *Television, Imagination, and Aggression.*
25. Joan T. Freyberg, "Increasing the Imaginative Play of Urban Disadvantaged Kindergarten Children through Systematic Training," in *The Child's World of Make-Believe,* ed. Jerome L. Singer (New York: Academic Press, 1973), pp. 129–154; Eli Saltz and Jane Brodie, "Pretend-Play Training in Childhood: A Review and Critique," *Contributions to Human Development* 6 (1982): 97–113; Sara Smilansky, *The Effects of*

Sociodramatic Play on Disadvantaged Preschool Children (New York: Wiley, 1968).

26. Peter K. Smith, "Does Play Matter? Functional and Evolutionary Aspects of Animal and Human Play," *Behavioral and Brain Sciences* 5 (1982): 139–184.

27. Saltz and Brodie, "Pretend-Play Training"; Singer and Singer, *Television, Imagination and Aggression.*

28. C. J. Brainerd, "Effects of Group and Individualized Dramatic Play Training on Cognitive Development," *Contributions to Human Development* 6 (1982): 128.

29. Singer and Singer, *Television, Imagination, and Aggression.*

30. Robert Holt, "Imagery: The Return of the Ostracized," *American Psychologist* 19 (1964): 254–264; Jerome L. Singer, *Imagery and Daydream Methods in Psychotherapy and Behavior Modification* (New York: Academic Press, 1974).

31. W. D. Rohwer, "Images and Pictures in Children's Learning: Research Results and Implications," *Psychological Bulletin* 73 (1970): 393–403.

32. Mary Ann Pulaski, "Toys and Imaginative Play," in Singer, *The Child's World of Make-Believe.* pp. 74–103.

33. Alan Paivio, "Imagery and Language," in *The Adaptive Function of Imagery,* ed. S. Segal (New York: Academic Press, 1971); Singer and Singer, "Imaginative Play and Pretending"; Greta G. Fein, "Preschool Play: Creativity and Consciousness," in *Curiosity, Imagination and Play,* ed. Dietmar Gorlitz and Joachim Wohlwill (Hillsdale, N.J.: Erlbaum, 1987), pp. 281–304.

34. Schachtel, *Metamorphosis.*

35. Rohwer, "Images and Pictures in Children's Learning."

36. Jean Piaget and Barbel Inhelder, *Mental Imagery in the Child* (New York: Basic Books, 1971).

37. Alexander R. Luria, *The Nature of Human Conflicts* (New York: Liveright, 1932); Singer, *The Child's World of Make-Believe.*

38. Herbert Litt, "Imagery in Children's Thinking" (Ph.D. diss., Liverpool University, 1973).

39. James P. Guilford, *The Nature of Human Intelligence* (New York: McGraw-Hill, 1967).

40. Jerome L. Singer and S. Brown, "The Experience-Type: Some Behavioral Correlates and Theoretical Implications" in *Rorschach Psychology,* ed. M. C. Rickers-Ovsiankina (New York: Krieger, 1977).

41. Diane Franklin, "Block Play Modeling and Its Relationship to Imaginativeness, Impulsivity-Reflection, and Internal-External Control" (Unpublished prediss. research, Yale University, 1975).

42. Catherine Garvey and Rachel Berndt, "The Organization of Pretend Play" (Paper presented at the Symposium on Structure in Play and Fantasy, American Psychological Association, Chicago, September 1975); Catherine Garvey, *Play* (Cambridge, Mass.: Harvard University Press, 1977).

43. Dina Feitelson and G. S. Ross, "The Neglected Factor—Play," *Human*

Development 16 (1973): 202–223; Dina Feitelson, "Developing Imaginative Play in Pre-school Children as a Possible Approach to Fostering Creativity," *Early Childhood Development and Care* 1 (1972): 181–195; E. Paul Torrance, *Torrance Tests of Creative Thinking, Verbal, Forms A and B* (Princeton, N.J.: Personnel Press, 1966).

44. J. L. Dansky, and I. W. Silverman, "Effects of Play on Associative Fluency in Preschool-aged Children," *Developmental Psychology* 9 (1973): 38–43; J. L. Dansky and I. W. Silverman, "Play: A General Facilitator of Associative Fluency," *Developmental Psychology* 11 (1975): 104; J. L. Dansky, "Make-Believe: A Mediator of the Relationship between Play and Associative Fluency," *Child Development* 51 (1980): 576–579; S. W. Russ and A. Grossman-McKee, "Affective Expression in Children's Fantasy Play, Primary Process Thinking on the Rorschach and Divergent Thinking," *Journal of Personality Assessment* (1990): in press.

45. Eli Saltz, D. Dixon, and James Johnson, "Training Disadvantaged Preschoolers on Various Fantasy Activities: Effects on Cognitive Functioning and Impulse Control," *Child Development* 48 (1977): 367–380; Saltz and Brodie, "Pretend-Play Training in Childhood."

46. Pulaski, "Toys and Imaginative Play."

47. Jane Tucker, "The Role of Fantasy in Cognitive-Affective Functioning: Does Reality Make a Difference in Remembering?" (Ph.D. diss., Teachers College, Columbia University, 1975).

48. Anneliese A. Riess, "Study of Some Genetic Behavioral Correlates of Human Movement Responses in Children's Rorschach Protocols" (Ph.D. diss., New York University, 1957); George Spivack and Murray Levine, *Self-Regulation and Acting-out in Normal Adolescents,* Progress Report for the National Institute of Mental Health, Grant M-4531 (Devon, Pa.: Devereaux Foundation, 1964); H. H. Herskovitz, Murray Levine, and George Spivack, "Anti-Social Behavior of Adolescents from Higher Socio-Economic Groups," *Journal of Nervous and Mental Diseases* 125 (1959): 467–476.

49. Jerome L. Singer, "Imagination and Waiting Ability in Young Children," *Journal of Personality* 29 (1961): 396–413; Singer, *The Child's World of Make-Believe*; Franklin, *Block Play Modeling and Its Relation to Imaginativeness.*

50. Walter Mischel and N. Baker, "Cognitive Appraisals and Transformations in Delay Behavior," *Journal of Personality and Social Psychology* 31 (1975): 254–261.

51. Donald Meichenbaum and J. Goodman, "Training Impulsive Children to Talk to Themselves," *Journal of Abnormal Psychology* 77 (1971): 115–126.

52. Franklin, *Block Play Modeling and Its Relation to Imaginativeness.*

53. Shelley Taylor, *Positive Delusions: Creative Self-Deceptions and the Healthy Mind* (New York: Basic Books, 1989).

54. Saltz and Brodie, "Pretend-Play Training."

55. Sigmund Freud, "Civilization and Its Discontents" in *The Complete*

Psychological Works of Sigmund Freud, vol. 21 (London: Hogarth Press, 1930; 1962).

56. Rosalind Gould, *Child Studies through Fantasy* (New York: Quadrangle Books, 1972).

57. Gould, *Child Studies through Fantasy*, pp. 34, 22–24.

7. Creating an Environment for Imaginative Play

1. Carl R. Rogers, "Towards a Theory of Creativity," *ETC: A Review of General Semantics* 11 (1954): 249–260.

2. D. S. Feitelson, "Imaginative Play and the Educational Process," in *International Year of the Child: Child Advocacy 1979 Proceedings*, ed. S. Katz (New Haven: Yale University, 1979), pp. 185–197.

3. Nancy King, "Play and the Culture of Childhood," in *The Young Child at Play*, ed. Greta Fein and M. Rivkin (Washington, D.C.: National tional Association for the Education of Young Children, 1986), p. 30.

4. Helen B. Schwartzman, *Transformations* (New York: Plenum, 1978), p. 236.

5. Lev S. Vygotsky, *Mind in Society* (Cambridge, Mass.: Harvard University Press, 1978).

6. Barbara O'Connell and Inge Bretherton, "Toddler's Play, Alone and with Mother: The Role of Maternal Guidance," in *Symbolic Play*, ed. Inge Bretherton (Orlando: Academic Press, 1984), p. 366.

7. O'Connell and Bretherton, "Toddler's Play," p. 362.

8. Vygotsky, *Mind in Society*, p. 102.

9. Robert M. Hodapp, Eugene C. Goldfield, and Chris J. Boyatzis, "The Use and Effectiveness of Maternal Scaffolding in Mother-Infant Games," *Child Development* 55 (1984): 772–781.

10. Jay Belsky, Mary Kay Goode, and Robert K. Most, "Maternal Stimulation and Infant Exploratory Competence: Cross-Sectional, Correlational, and Experimental Analyses," *Child Development* 51 (1980): 1163–78.

11. Arietta Slade, "A Longitudinal Study of Maternal Involvement and Symbolic Play during the Toddler Period," *Child Development* 58 (1987): 367–375.

12. Joan Lucariello, "Spinning Fantasy: Themes, Structure, and the Knowledge Base," *Child Development* 58 (1987): 434–442.

13. Robert Kavanaugh, Sue Whittington, and Mark J. Cerbone, "Mothers' Use of Fantasy in Speech to Young Children," *Journal of Child Language* 10 (1983): 45–55.

14. Robert W. White, "Motivation Reconsidered: The Concept of Competence," *Psychological Review* 66 (1959): 297–333.

15. David M. Harrington, Jeanne H. Block, and Jack Block, "Testing Aspects of Carl Rogers' Theory of Creative Environments: Child-Rearing Antecedents of Creative Potential in Young Adolescents," *Journal of Personality and Social Psychology* 52 (1987): 851–856.

16. Harrington, Block, and Block, "Testing Aspects," p. 855.

17. Erik H. Erikson, *Identity: Youth and Crisis* (New York: Norton, 1968).

18. Diana Shmukler and Idva Naveh, "Structured vs. Unstructured Play Training with Economically Disadvantaged Preschoolers," *Imagination, Cognition and Personality* 4 (1984–1985): 293–304.

19. Shmukler and Naveh, "Structured vs. Unstructured Play Training," p. 302.

20. Diana Shmukler, "Mother-Child Interaction and Its Relationship to the Predisposition of Imaginative Play," *Genetic Psychology Monographs* 104 (1981): 215–235.

21. Jerome L. Singer, ed., *The Child's World of Make-Believe* (New York: Academic Press, 1973).

22. Jerome L. Singer and Dorothy G. Singer, *Television, Imagination, and Aggression: A Study of Preschoolers* (Hillsdale, N.J.: Erlbaum, 1981).

23. Wolf Mankowitz, *Dickens of London* (London: Weidenfield and Nicolson, 1976).

24. Jerome L. Singer, Dorothy G. Singer, and Wanda Rapaczynski, "Children's Imagination as Predicted by Family Patterns and Television Viewing: A Longitudinal Study," *Genetic Psychology Monographs* 110 (1984): 43–69.

25. Roni B. Tower, "The Influence of Parents' Values on Preschool Children's Behaviors" (Ph.D. diss., Yale University, 1980).

26. Eli Bower, A. Ilgaz-Carden and K. Noori, "Measurement of Play Structures: Cross-Cultural Considerations," *Journal of Cross-Cultural Psychology* 13 (1982): 315–329.

27. Tower, "The Influence of Parents' Values."

28. Merle B. Karnes, Allan M. Shwedel, and Deborah Steinberg, "Styles of Parenting among Parents of Young Gifted Children," *Roeper-Review* 6 (1984): 232–235.

29. Theodore Dix and Joan E. Grusec, "Parental Influence Techniques: An Attributional Analysis," *Child Development* 54 (1983): 645–652.

30. Kevin MacDonald, "Parent-Child Physical Play with Rejected, Neglected, and Popular Boys," *Developmental Psychology* 23 (1987): 705–711.

31. Kevin MacDonald and Ross D. Parke, "Bridging the Gap: Parent-Child Play Interaction and Peer Interactive Competence," *Child Development* 55 (1984): 1265–77.

32. MacDonald and Parke, "Bridging the Gap," p. 1272.

33. MacDonald and Parke, "Bridging the Gap," p. 1273.

34. L. A. Sroufe, E. Schork, F. Motti, N. Lawroski, and P. La Freniere, "The Role of Affect in Social Competence," in *Emotions, Cognition and Behavior,* ed. Carroll Izard, Jerome Kagan, and Robert Zajonc (New York: Plenum, 1983).

35. Neil Cohen and C. Tomlinson-Keasey, "The Effects of Peers and Mothers on Toddlers' Play," *Child Development* 51 (1980): 921–924.

36. Michael Deakin, *The Children on the Hill* (London: Andre Deutsch, 1972).

37. Deakin, *Children,* p. 37.

38. Deakin, *Children*, p. 61.
39. John Madden, John O'Hara and Phyllis Levenstein, "Home Again: Effects of the Mother-Child Home Program on Mother and Child," *Child Development* 55 (1984): 635–647; Sandra Scarr and Kathleeen McCartney, "Far from Home: An Experimental Evaluation of the Mother-Child Home Program in Bermuda," *Child Development* 59 (1988): 531–543.
40. Phyllis Levenstein, "Which Homes? A Response to Scarr and McCartney (1988)," *Child Development* 60 (1989): 514–516; Kathleen McCartney and Sandra Scarr, "Far from the Point: A Reply to Levenstein," *Child Development* 60 (1989): 517–518.
41. Bernard Spodek, *Teaching in the Early Years* (Englewood Cliffs, N.J.: Prentice-Hall, 1972), p. 212.
42. Spodek, *Teaching,* p. 215.
43. Marie Montessori, *Childhood Education* (New York: New American Library, 1955), p. 21.
44. Scarr and McCartney, "Far from Home," p. 542.
45. Montessori, *Childhood Education,* p. 44.
46. Sara Smilansky, *The Effects of Sociodramatic Play on Disadvantaged Preschool Children* (New York: Wiley, 1986), p. 3.
47. Smilansky, *The Effects of Sociodramatic Play,* p. 127.
48. Patricia Greenfield and Edward Tronick, *Infant Curriculum: The Bromley-Heath Guide to the Care of Infants in Groups,* rev. ed. (Santa Monica: Goodyear, 1980).
49. Greenfield and Tronick, *Infant Curriculum.*
50. Nellie McCaslin, *Creative Drama in the Classroom* (New York: Longman, 1984); Helane S. Rosenberg, *Creative Drama and Imagination* (New York: Holt, Rinehart and Winston, 1987); Patricia Monighan-Nourot, Barbara Scales, Judith Van Hoorn, and Millie Almy, *Looking at Children's Play* (New York: Teachers College Press, 1987); Dorothy G. Singer and Jerome L. Singer, *Make Believe: Games and Activities to Foster Imaginative Play in Young Children* (Glenview, Ill.: Scott, Foresman, 1985).
51. Helen Bonny and Louis Savary, *Music and Your Mind* (New York: Harper and Row, 1973); Elizabeth Kelley, *The Magic If* (New York: Drama Book Specialists, 1973); Marilyn Segal and Don Adcock, *Just Pretending* (Englewood Cliffs, N.J.: Prentice-Hall, 1981).
52. Carolyn L. Piazza and Susan Riggs, "Writing with a Computer: An Invitation to Play," *Early Child Development and Care* 17 (1984): 72.
53. Robert Reinhold, "Lending Libraries for Educational Toys," *New York Times,* May 4, 1975, p. 11.
54. Reinhold, "Lending Libraries."
55. Lisa Hammel, "What Is It? Anything Your Little Heart Desires," *New York Times,* August 14, 1976, p. 16.
56. Steven Silberman, "Cheese Tunnels, Ice Cream Slides," *Record,* January 13, 1989, sec. B, pp. 1–2.
57. Polly Hill, *An Overview of the Needs of Children and Youth in the*

Urban Community (Ottawa, Canada: Children's Environments Advisory Service, Central Mortgage and Housing Corporation, 1972).

58. Molly McGrath and Norman McGrath, *Children's Spaces* (New York: William Morrow, 1978); Alexandra Stoddard, *A Child's Place* (Garden City, N.Y.: Doubleday, 1977).

59. Stoddard, *A Child's Place,* p. xi.

60. Richard de Mille, *Put Your Mother on the Ceiling* (New York: Viking, 1973). De Mille, a psychologist, is related to the famous film director, Cecil B. deMille and to the choreographer Agnes de Mille.

8. Television-Viewing and the Imagination

1. Cecilia von Feilitzen, "Developing and Evaluating Prosocial Television Programming," in *International Year of the Child: Child Advocacy 1979 Proceedings* (New Haven: Yale University Press, 1979), p. 237.

2. Bradley S. Greenberg, "When Cable Television Comes Home," in *Children and the Media,* ed. Stanley Katz and Paul Vesin (Los Angeles: Children's Institute International, 1985), pp. 71–76.

3. Dorothy G. Singer, Jerome L. Singer, and Diana M. Zuckerman. *Teaching Television* (New York: Dial Press, 1981), p. 18.

4. Marshall McLuhan, *Understanding Media* (New York: New American Library, 1964).

5. Marlise Simons, "The Amazon's Savvy Indians," *New York Times Magazine,* February 26, 1989, p. 37.

6. A. C. Nielson Company, *1988 Nielson Report on Television* (Northbrook, Ill.: Nielson, 1988).

7. Aletha C. Huston, John C. Wright, Mabel L. Rice, Dennis Kerkman, and Michelle St. Peters. "The Development of Television Viewing Patterns in Early Childhood: A Longitudinal Investigation" (Paper presented at the Thirty-ninth Annual Conference of the International Communication Association, San Francisco, May 1989).

8. Huston et al., "Development of Television Viewing Patterns," p. 29.

9. David Pearl, Lorraine Bouthilet, and Joyce Lazar, eds., *Television and Behavior,* DHHS pub. no. ADM 82-1195, vol. 2 (Washington, D.C.: U.S. Government Printing Office, 1982).

10. Daniel R. Anderson and Patricia A. Collins, *The Impact on Children's Education: Television's Influence on Cognitive Development* (Washington, D.C.: U.S. Department of Education, 1988).

11. Lynette K. Friedrich and Aletha H. Stein, "Prosocial Television and Young Children: The Effects of Verbal Labeling and Role Playing on Learning and Behavior," *Child Development* 46 (1985): 27–38; Jerome L. Singer and Dorothy G. Singer, "Can TV Stimulate Imaginative Play?" *Journal of Communication* 26 (1976): 74–80.

12. Huston et al., "Development of Television Viewing Patterns."

13. Albert Hollenbeck and Ronald Slaby, "Infant Visual Response to Television," *Child Development* 50 (1979): 41–45; Daniel R. Anderson, "Home Television Viewing by Preschool Children and Their Families"

(Paper presented at the Biennial Convention of the Society for Research in Child Development, Detroit, 1983); Huston et al., "Development of Television Viewing Patterns."

14. Dafna Lemish and Mabel L. Rice, "Television as a Talking Picture Book: A Prop for Language Acquisition," *Journal of Child Language* 13 (1986): 251–274.

15. Lemish and Rice, "Television as a Talking Picture Book," p. 260.

16. Lemish and Rice, "Television as a Talking Picture Book," p. 267.

17. Albert Hollenbeck and Ronald Slaby, "Influence of a Televised Model's Vocalization Patterns on Infants," *Journal of Applied Developmental Psychology* 3 (1982): 57–65.

18. Jerome L. Singer and Dorothy G. Singer, *Television, Imagination, and Aggression: A Study of Preschoolers* (Hillsdale, N.J.: Erlbaum, 1981); L. Rowell Huesmann and Leonard D. Eron, eds., *Television and the Aggressive Child* (Hillsdale, N.J.: Erlbaum, 1986).

19. Jerome L. Singer, Dorothy G. Singer, Roger Desmond, Bennett Hirsch, and Anne Nichol, "Family Mediation and Children's Cognition, Aggression, and Comprehension of Television: A Longitudinal Study," *Journal of Applied Developmental Psychology* 9 (1988): 329–347.

20. Gavriel Salomon and Tamar Leigh, "Predispositions about Learning from Print and Television," *Journal of Communication* 34, no. 2 (1984): 119–135.

21. Paul Messaris and Dennis Kerr, "Mothers' Comments about TV: Relations to Family Communication Patterns," *Communication Research* 10 (1983): 175–194.

22. Roni B. Tower, Dorothy G. Singer, Jerome L. Singer, and Anne Biggs, "Differential Effects of Television Programming on Preschoolers' Cognition and Play," *Journal of Orthopsychiatry* 49 (1979): 265–281.

23. Anderson and Collins, *The Impact on Children's Education.*

24. Andrew N. Meltzoff, "Imitation of Televised Models by Infants," *Child Development* 59 (1988): 1221–29.

25. Julie M. Duck, Robert A. M. Gregson, Eileen B. J. Jones, Grant Noble, and Michael Noy, "Children's Visual Attention to 'Playschool': A Time Series Analysis," *Australian Journal of Psychology* 40 (1988): 413–421.

26. Duck et al., "Children's Visual Attention," p. 419.

27. Singer and Singer, "Can TV Stimulate Imaginative Play?"

28. Daniel R. Anderson, Huewon P. Choi, and Elizabeth P. Lorch, "Attentional Inertia Reduces Distractibility during Young Children's TV Viewing," *Child Development* 58 (1987): 798–806.

29. Morton J. Mendelson, "Attentional Inertia at Four and Seven Months?," *Child Development* 54 (1983): 677–685.

30. Deanne M. Argenta, Zolinda Stoneman, and Gene H. Brody, "The Effects of Three Different Television Programs on Young Children's Peer Interactions and Toy Play," *Journal of Applied Developmental Psychology* 7 (1986): 355–371; Singer and Singer, *Television, Imagination, and Aggression*; Zolinda Stoneman and Gene H. Brody, "Family Interaction

during Three Programs: Contextualist Observations," *Journal of Family Issues* 4 (1983): 349–366.

31. "The Talk of the Town: Notes and Comments," *New Yorker*. February 27, 1989, p. 24.

32. Mark A. Runco and Kathy Pezdek, "The Effects of Television and Radio on Children's Creativity," *Human Communication Research* 11 (1984): 109–120.

33. Jessica Beagles-Roos and Isabelle Gat, "Specific Impact of Radio and Television on Children's Story Comprehension," *Journal of Educational Psychology* 75 (1983): 128–137; Patricia Greenfield, Dorothea Farrar, and Jessica Beagles-Roos, "Is the Medium the Message?: An Experimental Comparison of the Effects of Radio and Television on Imagination," *Journal of Applied Developmental Psychology* 7 (1986): 201–218.

34. Patricia Greenfield and Jessica Beagles-Roos, "Radio vs. Television: Their Cognitive Impact on Children of Different Socioeconomic and Ethnic Groups," *Journal of Communication* 38 (1988): 86.

35. Beagles-Roos and Gat, "Specific Impact of Radio and Television."

36. D. Hayes, S. Kelly, and M. Mandel, "Media Differences in Children's Story Synopses: Radio and Television Contrasted," *Journal of Educational Psychology* 78 (1986): 341–347.

37. L. K. Meringoff, M. Vibbert, H. Kelly, and C. Char, " 'How Shall You Take Your Story, with or without Pictures?' Progress Report on a Program of Media Research with Children" (Paper presented at the Biennial Meeting of the Society for Research in Child Development, Boston, 1981).

38. Greenfield and Beagles-Roos, "Radio vs. Television."

39. Ray Bradbury, *Fahrenheit 451* (New York: Simon and Schuster, 1967), p. 14.

40. Singer and Singer, *Television, Imagination, and Aggression.*

41. John P. Murray and Kathy Krendl, "Television and Fantasy: Children's Viewing and Storytelling" (Unpublished manuscript, Department of Family and Child Development, Kansas State University, Manhattan, Kansas, 1989).

42. Singer and Singer, *Television, Imagination, and Aggression.*

43. Neil Postman, *Amusing Ourselves to Death* (New York: Viking, 1985).

44. Patrick Shannon and David E. Fernie, "Print and Television: Children's Use of the Medium Is the Message," *Elementary School Journal* 85 (1985): 663–672.

45. Linda Harrison and Tannis Williams, "Television and Cognitive Development," in *The Impact of Television: A Natural Experiment in Three Communities,* ed. T. M. Williams (New York: Academic Press, 1986), pp. 87–142.

46. Robert Hornik, "Television Access and Slowing of Cognitive Growth," *American Educational Research* 15 (1978): 1–15.

47. Takeo Furu, *The Functions of Television for Children and Adolescents* (Tokyo: Sophia University Press, 1971); Hilde T. Himmelweit, A. N.

Oppenheim, and Pamela Vince, *Television and the Child* (London: Oxford University Press, 1958); A. Werner, "The Effects of Television on Children and Adolescents: A Case of Sex and Class Socialization," *Journal of Communication* 25 (1975): 450.

48. P. Williams, E. Haertel, G. Haertel, and H. Walberg, "The Impact of Leisure-Time Television on School Learning: A Research Synthesis," *American Educational Research Journal* 19 (1982): 19–50.

49. Jerome L. Singer, Dorothy G. Singer, and Wanda Rapaczynski, "Children's Imagination as Predicted by Family Patterns and Television Viewing: A Longitudinal Study," *Genetic Psychology Monographs* 110 (1984): 43–69.

50. Thomas Cook, Hilary Appleton, Ross Conner, Ann Shaffer, Gary Tamkin, and Stephen Weber, *"Sesame Street" Revisited* (New York: Russell Sage Foundation, 1975); Harvey Lesser, *Television and the Preschool Child* (New York: Academic, 1977).

51. Singer et al., "Family Mediation"; L. Morrow, "Home and School Correlates of Early Interest in Literature," *Journal of Educational Research* 76 (1983): 221–230.

52. Singer et al., "Family Mediation."

53. S. Jay Samuels and Glenace Edwall, "The Role of Attention in Reading with Implications for the Learning Disabled Student," *Journal of Learning Disabilities* 14 (1981): 353–361, 368.

54. Singer, Singer, and Rapaczynski, "Children's Imagination."

55. Diana M. Zuckerman, Dorothy G. Singer, and Jerome L. Singer, "Television Viewing and Children's Reading and Related Classroom Behavior," *Journal of Communication* 30 (1980): 166–174.

56. Salomon and Leigh, "Predispositions about Learning."

57. K. Pezdek, A. Lehrer, and S. Simon, "The Relationship between Reading and Cognitive Processing of Television and Radio," *Child Development* 54 (1984): 1015–23.

58. Dolf Zillmann, "The Anatomy of Suspense," in *The Entertainment Function of Television,* ed. Percy Tannenbaum (Hillsdale, N.J.: Erlbaum, 1980), pp. 133–163; Elizabeth Hall, "Our Children Are Treated Like Idiots!" (Interview with Bruno Bettleheim), *Psychology Today* 15 (1981): 28–44.

59. George Gerbner and Lawrence Gross, "Living with Television: The Violence Profile," *Journal of Communication* 26 (1976): 173–199.

60. Robert D. McIlwraith and John R. Schallow, "Television Viewing and Styles of Children's Fantasy," *Imagination, Cognition and Personality* 2 (1982–1983): 323–331.

61. Dorothy G. Singer, "Television and the Developing Imagination of the Child," in *Television and Behavior: Ten Years of Scientific Progress and Implications for the Eighties,* ed. D. Pearl, L. Bouthilet, and S. J. Lazar, DHHS pub. no. ADM 82-1196, vol. 2 (Washington, D.C.: U.S. Government Printing Office, 1982), pp. 39–52.

62. Murray and Krendl, "Television and Fantasy."

63. Singer and Singer, *Teaching Television.*

64. Zuckerman, Singer, and Singer, "Television Viewing and Children's Reading."

65. R. A. Snow, "How Children Interpret TV Violence in Play Contexts," *Journalism Quarterly* 51 (1974): 13–21; Grant Noble, *Children in Front of the Small Screen* (London: Constable, 1975); Joyce Sprafkin, Kenneth D. Gadow, and Monique Dussault, "Reality Perceptions of Television: A Preliminary Comparison of Emotionally Disturbed and Nonhandicapped Children," *American Journal of Orthopsychiatry* 56 (1986): 147–152.

66. Dorothy G. Singer, Jerome L. Singer, and Diana M. Zuckerman, *Getting the Most Out of Television: Teacher's Manual and Children's Workbook* (Glenview, Ill.: Scott Foresman, 1981); *Getting the Most Out of Television* videotapes (Bend, Oreg.: New Dimension Films, 1981).

67. Singer et al., "Family Mediation."

68. Aryeh Wohl, "No Secrets to Reading: Developing a New Reading/Language Arts Learning Program Using Television in Israel," *The Reading Teacher*, January 1985, pp. 446–449; Robert Abelman, "Children and TV: The ABCs of TV Literacy," *Childhood Education* 60 (1984): 200–205; Robert Abelman, "Amplifying the Affective Level Effects of Television's Prosocial Fare through Curriculum Intervention," *Journal of Research and Development in Education* 20 (1987): 40–49.

69. Alan Wurtzel, Vice President, Standards and Practices, ABC-TV (Unpublished manuscript and personal communication, New York, 1979).

70. Rosemary Potter, *New Season: The Positive Use of Commercial Television with Children* (Cleveland, Ohio, Charles E. Merrill, 1976); *High School Curriculum* (San Francisco: Far West Laboratory for Educational Research, 1978). The address is 1855 Folsom Street, San Francisco, CA 94103; Heide L. Kane, ed., *Critical Television Viewing: A Language Skills Work-a-Text* (New York: Cambridge, The Basic Skills Company, 1980).

71. *Development of Critical Television Viewing Skills in Students* (Boston: Boston University School of Public Communication, 1978).

72. Thomas R. McDaniel, "Teaching Television Literacy to Teachers," *Educational Technology* 22 (1982): 13–16.

73. Gregory Sarlo, Leonard A. Jason, Cheryl Lonak, "Parents' Strategies for Limiting Children's Television Watching," *Psychological Reports* 63 (1988): 435–438.

74. Roger Desmond, Jerome L. Singer, Dorothy G. Singer, Rachel Calam, and Karen Colimore, "Family Mediation Patterns and Television Viewing: Young Children's Use and Grasp of the Medium," *Human Communication Research* 11 (1985): 461–480.

75. Pamela Tuchscherer, *TV Interactive Toys: The New High Tech Threat to Children* (Bend, Oreg.: Pinnaroo Publishing, 1988).

9. Play as Healing

1. Brian Vandenberg, "Play, Myth and Hope," in *Play, Play Therapy, Play Research,* ed. Rimmert van der Kooij and Joop Hellendoorn (Berwyn, The Netherlands: Swets North America, 1986), p. 86.

2. Sigmund Freud, "Sexuality in the Aetiology of the Neuroses" in *The Complete Psychological Works of Sigmund Freud,* vol. 3 (London: Hogarth, 1898; 1962), pp. 259–285; Sigmund Freud, "Three Essays on Sexuality" in *The Complete Psychological Works of Sigmund Freud,* vol. 7 (London: Hogarth, 1905; 1960), pp. 135–243; Seymour Fisher and Roger P. Greenberg, *The Scientific Credibility of Freud's Theories and Therapy* (New York: Basic, 1977).

3. Eleanor E. Maccoby, *Social Development* (New York: Harcourt Brace Jovanovich, 1980); Sandra Scarr, "Personality and Experience: Individual Encounters with the World," in *The Emergence of Personality,* ed. James Aronoff, Albert Rabin, and Robert Zucker (New York: Springer, 1987), pp. 49–78.

4. Scarr, "Personality and Experience"; Arnold Buss and Robert Plomin, *A Temperament Theory of Personality* (New York: Wiley, 1975); Arnold Buss, "Personality: Primate Heritage and Human Distinctiveness," in Aronoff, Rabin, and Zucker, *The Emergence of Personality,* pp. 13–48; Robert Hogan, "Personality Psychology: Back to Basics," in Aronoff, Rabin, and Zucker, *The Emergence of Personality,* pp. 79–104; Jerome Kagan, J. Steven Reznick, and Nancy Snidman, "Biological Bases of Childhood Shyness," *Science* 240 (1988): 167–171.

5. J. A. Singer and P. Salovey, "Mood and Memory: Evaluating the Network Theory of Affect," *Clinical Psychology Review* 8 (1988): 211–251.

6. Eleanor Pavenstedt, ed., *The Drifters* (Boston: Little, Brown, 1967).

7. E. A Mason, *Angels Don't Have Headlights: Children's Reactions to Death in the Family* (Videotape presented at the annual convention of the American Psychological Association, New Orleans, 1989).

8. Diana Shmukler, "Mother-Child Interaction and Its Relationship to the Predisposition of Imaginative Play," *Genetic Psychology Monographs* 104 (1981): 215–235; Roger J. Desmond, Jerome L. Singer, Dorothy G. Singer, Rachel Calam, and Karen Colimore, "Family Mediation Patterns and Television Viewing: Young Children's Use and Grasp of the Medium," *Human Communications Research* 11 (1985): 461–480; Jerome L. Singer, Dorothy G. Singer, Roger J. Desmond, Bennett Hirsch, and Anne Nichol, "Family Mediation and Children's Cognition, Aggression, and Comprehension of Television: A Longitudinal Study," *Journal of Applied Developmental Psychology* 9 (1988): 329–347.

9. Nadine J. Kaslow, Richard Tanenbaum, Lynn Abramson, Christopher Peterson, and Martin E. Seligman, "Problem Solving Deficits and Depressive Symptoms in Children," *Journal of Abnormal Child Psychology* 11 (1983): 497–502.

10. Joan Fineman, "Observations on the Development of Imaginative Play

in Early Childhood," *Journal of the American Academy of Child Psychiatry* 1 (1962): 167–181.

11. W. Corsaro and G. Tomlinson, "Spontaneous Play and Social Learning in the Nursery School," in *Play and Culture,* ed. H. B. Schwartzman (West Point, N.Y.: Leisure Press, 1980); Helen Giffin, "The Coordination of Meaning in the Creation of a Shared Make-Believe Reality," in *Symbolic Play,* ed. Inge Bretherton (New York: Academic Press, 1984); Nancy King, "Play and the Culture of Childhood," in *The Young Child at Play,* ed. Greta Fein and Mary Rivkin (Washington, D.C.: National Association for the Education of Young Children, 1986), pp. 29–41; Rosalind Gould, *Child Studies through Fantasy* (New York: Quadrangle Books, 1972).

12. Helen B. Schwartzman, *Transformations* (New York: Plenum, 1978).

13. Gould, *Child Studies through Fantasy,* pp. 60–61.

14. Heinz S. Herzka, "On the Anthropology of Play: Play as a Way of Dialogical Development," in van der Kooij and Hellendoorn, *Play, Play Therapy, Play Research,* pp. 29–30.

15. Bernard Segal, George Huba, and Jerome L. Singer, *Drugs, Daydreaming and Personality: A Study of College Youth* (Hillsdale, N.J: Erlbaum, 1980).

16. Herzka, "On the Anthropology of Play," p. 31.

17. M. R. Johnson, J. K. Witt, and B. Martin, "The Effect of Fantasy Facilitation of Anxiety in Chronically Ill and Healthy Children," *Journal of Pediatric Psychology* 12 (1987): 273–284.

18. Lonnie K. Zeltzer and Samuel LeBaron, "Fantasy in Children and Adolescents with Chronic Illness," *Journal of Developmental and Behavioral Pediatrics* 7 (1986): 195–198.

19. Jerome L. Singer and B. Streiner, "Imaginative Content in the Dream and Fantasy Play of Blind and Sighted Children," *Perceptual and Motor Skills* 22 (1966): 475–482; Dorothy G. Singer and M. L. Lenahan, "Imagination Content in the Dreams of Deaf Children," *American Annals of the Deaf* (February 1976): 44–48; S. Sloan, "Teaching the Handicapped Imagination," *Education of the Visually Handicapped* 15 (1983): 87–94; Joop Hellendoorn, E. Groothoff, P. Mostert, and F. Harinck, *Beeldcommunicatie: Een vorm van Kinderpsychotherapie* (Deventer, The Netherlands: Van Loghum Slaterus, 1981); van der Kooij and Hellendoorn, eds., *Play, Play Therapy, Play Research*; Charles E. Schaefer and Kevin J. O'Connor, eds., *Handbook of Play Therapy* (New York: Wiley, 1983).

20. Larke Nahme-Huang, Dorothy G. Singer, Jerome L. Singer, and A. B. Wheaton, "Imaginative Play Training and Perceptual-Motor Interventions with Emotionally-Disturbed Hospitalized Children," *American Journal of Orthopsychiatry* 47 (1977): 245.

21. J. D. Smith, R. T. Walsh, and M. A. Richardson, "The Clown Club: A Structured Fantasy Approach to Group Therapy with the Latency-Age Child," *International Journal of Group Psychotherapy* 35 (1985): 49–64.

22. Ollis Udwin, "Imaginative Play Training as an Intervention Method

with Institutionalized Preschool Children," *British Journal of Educational Psychology* 53 (1983): 32–39; Ephraim Biblow, "Imaginative Play and the Control of Aggressive Behavior," in *The Child's World of Make-Believe,* ed. Jerome L. Singer (New York: Academic Press, 1973) pp. 104–128.

23. Lynn Abramson, Martin E. Seligman, and J. Teasdale, "Learned Helplessness in Humans: Critique and Reformulation," *Journal of Abnormal Psychology* 87 (1978): 49–74; Loren Alloy and Lynn Abramson, "Judgment of Contingency in Depressed and Nondepressed Students: Sadder but Wiser?" *Journal of Experimental Psychology: General* 108 (1979): 441–485.

24. Kaslow et al., "Problem Solving Deficits and Depressive Symptoms in Children."

25. Tiffany Field, David Sandberg, Sheri Goldstein, Robert Garcia, Nitza Vega-Lahr, Kathleen Porter, and Monica Dowling, "Play Interactions and Interviews of Depressed and Conduct Disorder Children and Their Mothers," *Child Psychiatry and Human Development* 17 (1987): 213–234.

26. W. L. Stone, K. L. Lemanek, M. Fernandez, and P. T. Fishel, "Play and Imitative Skills in Autistic and Other Handicapped Preschoolers" (Paper presented at Ninety-fifth Annual Convention of the American Psychological Association, New York, August 1987).

27. Dorothy G. Singer and Jerome L. Singer, *Make Believe: Games and Activities to Foster Imagination and Creativity in Young Children* (Chicago: Scott, Foresman, 1985). Revised version of *Partners in Play* (New York: Harper and Row, 1977).

28. Dorothy G. Singer, "Encouraging Children's Imaginative Play: Suggestions for Parents and Teachers," in van der Kooij and Hellendoorn, *Play, Play Therapy, Play Research,* pp. 89–99.

29. Shlomo Ariel, "Family Play Therapy," in van der Kooij and Hellendoorn, *Play, Play Therapy, Play Research,* pp. 153–160.

30. Lois B. Murphy, and Associates, *Colin: A Normal Child, Personality in Young Children,* vol. 2 (New York: Basic, 1956), pp. 48, 54, 55, 72, 217.

31. H. Hug-Hellmuth, "On the Technique of Child-Analysis," *International Journal of Psycho-Analysis* 2 (1921): 287–305.

32. Melanie Klein, *The Psychoanalysis of Children* (London: Hogarth Press, 1932).

33. Anna Freud, *The Psychoanalytical Treatment of Children* (London: Imago Press, 1926; 1946).

34. Aaron H. Esman, "Psychoanalytic Play Therapy," in *Handbook of Play Therapy,* ed. Charles E. Schaefer and Kevin J. O'Connor (New York: Wiley, 1983), p. 11.

35. Hannah Segal, *Introduction to the Work of Melanie Klein* (New York: Basic, 1964), p. 55.

36. Donald J. Cohen, Steven Marans, Kristen Dahl, Wendy Marans, and Melvin Lewis, "Analytic Discussions with Oedipal Children," *Psychoanalytic Study of the Child* 42 (1987): 60.

37. Esman, "Psychoanalytic Play Therapy," p. 15.
38. Otto Rank, *Will Therapy* (New York: Knopf, 1936); Otto Rank, *Truth and Reality* (New York: Knopf, 1936).
39. Frederick H. Allen, *Psychotherapy with Children* (New York: Norton, 1944), p. 129.
40. Virginia M. Axline, *Play Therapy* (New York: Norton, 1947).
41. Clark Moustakas, *Psychotherapy with Children* (New York: Harper and Row, 1959); Bernard Guerney, *Relationship Enhancement* (San Francisco: Jossey-Bass, 1978); Louise F. Guerney, "Client-Centered (Nondirective) Therapy," in Schaefer and O'Connor, *Handbook of Play Therapy*, pp. 21–64.
42. Stefan Schmidtchen, "Practice and Research in Play Therapy," in van der Kooij and Hellendoorn, *Play, Play Therapy, Play Research*, pp. 169–195.
43. E. A. Vermeer, *Spel en Spelpaedagogische Problemen* (Utrecht: Bijleveld, 1962); Ina van Berckelaer-Onnes, "Different Play in Different Children: Implications for Treatment," in van der Kooij and Hellendoorn, *Play, Play Therapy, Play Research*, pp. 133–143; Hellendoorn et al., *Beeldcommunicatie*.
44. Guerney, "Client-Centered (Nondirective) Therapy," p. 51.
45. Guerney, "Client-Centered (Nondirective) Therapy."
46. T. W. Downey, "Notes on Play and Guilt in Child Analysis," *Psychoanalytic Study of the Child* 42 (1987): 109.
47. Virginia M. Axline, *Dibs: In Search of Self* (New York: Norton, 1964); Rudolf Ekstein, *Children of Time and Space, of Action and Impulse* (New York: Appleton, 1966).
48. R. J. Casey and J. S. Berman, "The Outcome of Psychotherapy with Children," *Psychological Bulletin* 98 (1985): 388–400.
49. John Weisz, Bahr Weiss, Mark D. Alicke, and M. L. Klotz, "Effectiveness of Psychotherapy with Children and Adolescents: Meta-Analytic Findings for Clinicians," *Journal of Consulting and Clinical Psychology* 55 (1987): 542–549; H. T. Prout and R. A. DeMartino, "A Meta-Analysis of School-Based Studies of Psychotherapy," *Journal of School Psychology* 24 (1986): 285–292.
50. I. Kolvin, R. Garside, A. Nicol, A. MacMillan, F. Wolstenholme, and I. Leitch, *Help Starts Here: The Maladjusted Child in the Ordinary School* (London: Tavistock, 1981); Alan E. Kazdin, "Developmental Psychopathology: Current Research, Issues and Directions," *American Psychologist* 44 (1989): 180–187; Alan E. Kazdin, *Child Psychotherapy: Developing and Identifying Effective Treatments* (New York: Pergamon, 1988).
51. E. J. Rave and G. L. Hannah, "The Use of Play Therapy to Increase Adaptive Behavior in the Classroom" (Paper presented at the Ninety-fifth Annual Convention of the American Psychological Association, New York, August 1987).
52. Shmukler, "Mother-Child Interaction"; Marc Gershowitz, *Fantasy Behavior of Clinic-Referred Children in Play Encounters with College Un-*

dergraduates (Ph.D. diss., Michigan State University, 1974); Tamaki Takahashi, "Verbal and Non-Verbal Communication in Mother-Child Relationship," *Hiyoshi Report,* no. 12 (1985): 11–24, published by the Department of General Arts and Literature, Japanese Women's University, Tokyo (in English); Tamaki Takahashi, *Imagination and Reality: The Child's World of Pretend Play* (Tokyo: Doshin, 1989) (in Japanese).

53. Heinz Kohut, *How Does Analysis Cure?* (Chicago: University of Chicago Press, 1984); Jerome L. Singer, "The Development of Imagination in Early Childhood: Foundations of Play Therapy," in van der Kooij and Hellendoorn, *Play, Play Therapy, Play Research.*

10. When Imaginative Play Goes Underground

1. Bill Boggs, "A Farewell to Toyland," *New York Times Magazine,* May 15, 1988, pp. 28, 30.
2. Calvin Trillin, "Profiles: Penn and Teller," *New Yorker,* May 15, 1989, pp. 58–86.
3. Jon Godden and Rumer Godden, *Two under the Indian Sun* (New York: Knopf, 1966), p. 55.
4. Alexander R. Luria, *The Nature of Human Conflicts* (New York: Liveright, 1932).
5. Stephen Mitchell, "Object Relations Theories and the Developmental Tilt," *Contemporary Psychoanalysis* 20 (1984): 473–499.
6. Jerome L. Singer, "Delayed Gratification and Ego-Development: Implications for Clinical and Experimental Research," *Journal of Consulting Psychology* 19 (1955): 259–266.
7. Jerome L. Singer and Serena Brown, "The Experience-Type: Some Behavioral Correlates and Theoretical Implications," in *Rorschach Psychology,* new ed., ed. Marie C. Rickers-Ovsiankina (New York: Krieger, 1977).
8. Jean Piaget, *Play, Dreams and Imitation in Childhood* (New York: Norton, 1962).
9. Piaget, *Play, Dreams and Imitation,* p. 145.
10. James Youniss, *Parents and Peers in Social Development* (Chicago: University of Chicago Press, 1980).
11. Reuven Kohen-Raz, *The Child from 9 to 13* (Chicago: Aldine-Atherton, 1971); J. M. Tanner, *Growth at Adolescence* (Springfield, Ill.: Charles C. Thomas, 1962).
12. D. Goldhaber, *Life-Span Human Development* (New York: Harcourt Brace Jovanovich, 1986); Kohen-Raz, *The Child from 9 to 13.*
13. Jean Piaget and Barbel Inhelder, *The Psychology of the Child* (New York: Basic Books, 1969).
14. S. G. Paris and B. K. Lindauer, "Constructive Aspects of Children's Comprehension and Memory," in *Perspectives on Development and Memory,* ed. R. V. Kail and J. W. Hagand (Hillsdale, N.J.: Erlbaum, 1977).

15. John H. Flavell, *Cognitive Development* (Englewood Cliffs, N.J.: Prentice-Hall, 1977).

16. Jean Piaget and Barbel Inhelder, *Mental Imagery in the Child* (New York: Basic Books, 1971).

17. L. S. Vygotsky, "Play and Its Role in the Mental Development of the Child," *Soviet Psychology* 12, no. 6 (1966): 62–76. Transcribed from lecture in 1933; Brian Sutton-Smith, *Play and Learning* (New York: Gardner, 1979).

18. M. G. Dias and P. L. Harris, "The Effect of Make-Believe Play on Deductive Reasoning," *British Journal of Developmental Psychology* 6 (1988): 207–221; E. Peisach and M. Hardeman, "Imaginative Play and Logical Thinking in Young Children," *Journal of Genetic Psychology* 146 (1985): 233–248; Alan M. Leslie, "Pretense and Representation: The Origins of 'Theory of Mind,'" Psychological Review 94 (1987): 412–426.

19. S. B. Silvern, P. A. Williamson, and T. A. Countermine, "Young Children's Story Recall as a Product of Play, Story Familiarity, and Adult Intervention," *Merrill-Palmer Quarterly* 32 (1986): 73–86.

20. C. Frankenstein, "School without Parents," *Megamoth* 12 (1962): 15.

21. Herschel D. Thornburg, *The Bubblegum Years* (Tucson: HELP Books, 1979); William McGuire, "Search for the Self: Going Beyond Self-esteem and the Reactive Self," in *Personality and the Prediction of Behavior,* ed. Robert Zucker, Joel Oronoff, and Albert Rabin (New York: Academic, 1984).

22. For studies examining popularity in relation to play communication and information exchange, see A. F. Newcomb and J. C. Meister, "The Initial Social Encounters of High and Low Social Effectiveness School-aged Children," *Journal of Abnormal Child Psychology* 13 (1985): 45–58; Elliott Medrich, Judith Roizen, Victor Rubin, and Stuart Buckley, *The Serious Business of Growing Up* (Berkeley: University of California Press, 1982).

23. Geoffrey R. Loftus and Elizabeth F. Loftus, *Mind at Play* (New York: Basic Books, 1983).

24. Daniel Kahneman and Amos Tversky, "The Psychology of Preferences," *Scientific American,* January 1982, pp. 160–173.

25. Thomas W. Malone, *What Makes Things Fun to Learn? A Study of Intrinsically Motivating Computer Games* (Palo Alto: Xerox, 1980).

26. Pamela Tuchscherer, *TV Interactive Toys: The New High Tech Threat to Children* (Bend, Oreg.: Pinnaroo Publishing, 1988).

27. Tuchscherer, *TV Interactive Toys.*

28. Patricia M. Greenfield, *Mind and Media* (Cambridge, Mass.: Harvard University Press, 1984).

29. James Levin and Yaacov Kareev, *Personal Computers and Education* (San Diego: University of California Center for Human Information Processing, 1980), pp. 40–41. For further references, see J. Brusca, "Effects of Video Game Playing on Children's Social Behavior," *Dissertation Abstracts International* 48 (1988): 3127–28; J. Cooper and

D. Mackie, "Video Games and Aggression in Children," *Journal of Applied Social Psychology* 16 (1986): 726–744; D. Graybill, M. Strawniak, T. Hunter, and M. O'Leary, "Effects of Playing versus Observing Violent Versus Non-Violent Video Games on Children's Aggression," *Psychology: A Quarterly Journal of Human Behavior* 24 (1987): 1–8; P. McClurg, and C. Chaille, "Computer Games: Environments for Developing Spatial Cognition?," *Journal of Educational Computing Research* 3 (1987): 95–111.

30. Philippe Ariès, *Centuries of Childhood* (New York: Vintage Books, 1962); Robert Louis Stevenson, *Virginibus Puerisque and other Papers* (London: Chatto and Windus, 1968); Jane Austen, *Mansfield Park* (Boston: Little, Brown, 1899).

31. Tuchscherer, *TV Interactive Toys.*

32. National Coalition on Television Violence, *NCTV News* 10 (1989): 1–16.

33. Nellie McCaslin, *Creative Drama in the Classroom,* 4th ed. (New York: Longman, 1984); Helane S. Rosenberg, *Creative Drama and Imagination* (New York: Holt, Rinehart and Winston, 1987).

34. Winifred Ward, *Drama with and for Children,* Bulletin 30 (Washington, D.C.: U. S. Department of Health, Education, and Welfare, 1960).

35. McCaslin, *Creative Drama in the Classroom.*

36. Rosenberg, *Creative Drama and Imagination,* p. 104.

37. Jacob L. Moreno, "Reflections on My Method of Group Psychotherapy and Psychodrama," in *Active Psychotherapy,* ed. Harold Greenwald (New York: Atherton, 1967), p. 131.

38. Thomas Maeder, " 'Does Your Father Analyze You?' " *Pennsylvania Gazette,* May 1989, pp. 34–39.

39. Charles E. Schaefer and Steven E. Reid, eds., *Game Play: Therapeutic Use of Childhood Games* (New York: Wiley, 1986).

40. Diane E. Frey, "Communication Boardgames with Children," in Schaefer and Reid, *Game Play,* pp. 21–39. Some of the games Frey cites include: R. Zakich and S. Monroe, *Reunion* (Placentia, Calif.: Ungame Company, 1979); Harold Burks, *Imagine* (Huntington Beach, Calif.: Arden, 1978); R. Burten, *Social Security* (Anaheim, Calif.: Ungame Company, 1976); Richard A. Gardner, *The Talking, Feeling, Doing Game* (Cresskill, N.J.: Creative Therapeutics, 1973); Nathan Kritzberg, *The Structured Therapeutic Game Method of Child Analytic Psychotherapy* (Hicksville, N.Y.: Exposition, 1975); Elaine A. Blechman, "The Family Contract Game," *The Family Coordinator* (July 1974): 269–281; T. Oden, *The Transactional Analysis Game* (New York: Harper and Row, 1976); S. Zitsman, *The Rational Emotive Game* (Unpublished manuscript, Wright State University, Dayton, Ohio, 1984).

41. Connie Behrens, "Therapeutic Games for Children," in Schaefer and Reid, *Game Play,* pp. 187–194.

42. Nathan I. Kritzberg, *The Structured Therapeutic Game Method of Child Analytic Psychotherapy* (Hicksville, N.Y.: Exposition, 1975); Gardner, *The Talking, Feeling, Doing Game.*

43. Elaine A. Blechman, Claire Rabin, and Michael J. McEnroe, "Family Communication and Problem Solving with Boardgames and Computer Games," in Schaefer and Reid, *Game Play,* pp. 129–145; E. F. Dubow, L. R. Huesmann, and L. D. Eron, "Mitigating Aggression and Promoting Prosocial Behavior in Aggressive Elementary Schoolboys," *Behavioral Research and Therapy* 25 (1987): 527–531.

44. Medrich et al., *The Serious Business of Growing Up,* p. 28.

45. Medrich et al., *The Serious Business of Growing Up.*

46. J. A. Seitz, "The Precursors of Creativity: Metaphor, Symbolic Play and Categorization in Early Childhood," *Dissertation Abstracts International* 48 (1987): 899; A. D. Pellegrini, "The Narrative Organisation of Children's Fantasy Play: The Effects of Age and Play Context," *Educational Psychology* 5 (1985): 17–25; A. K. Li, "Toward More Elaborate Pretend Play," *Mental Retardation* 23 (1985): 131–136.

47. David Forbes and Gary Yablick, "The Organization of Dramatic Content in Children's Fantasy Play," *New Directions for Child Development,* September 1984, no. 25, pp. 23–36.

48. D. A. Sleet, "Differences in the Social Complexity of Children's Play Choices," *Perceptual and Motor Skills* 60 (1985): 283–287.

49. Jerome L. Singer and Dorothy G. Singer, "Imaginative Play and Pretending in Early Childhood: Some Experimental Approaches," in *Child Personality and Psychopathology,* ed. Anthony Davids (New York: Wiley, 1976); J. F. Christie, "Training of Symbolic Play," *Early Childhood Development and Care* 19 (1985): 43–52; Dias and Harris, "The Effect of Make-Believe Play"; Peisach and Hardeman, "Imaginative Play and Logical Thinking"; R. J. Ottenstein, "Symbolic Play and Imaginative Predisposition: A Study of Their Relationship and the Impact of Cognitive Development and Gender," *Dissertation Abstracts International* 44 (1984): 3217; S. E. Portko, "A Study of Play Behavior in Elementary School Children," *Dissertation Abstracts International* 45 (1985): 3975; W. G. Pettigrew, "The Effects of Imaginative Play upon Intelligence Quotients, Symbolic Play, and Language Usage in Six-Year-Old Children," *Dissertation Abstracts International* 46 (1985): 69.

50. Newcomb and Meister, "The Initial Social Encounters of High and Low Social Effectiveness School-aged Children."

51. B. S. Engel, "Between Feeling and Fact: Listening to Children," *Harvard Educational Review* 54 (1984): 304–314.

52. G. H. Brody, A. D. Pellegrini, and I. E. Sigel, "Marital Quality and Mother-Child and Father-Child Interactions with School-aged Children," *Developmental Psychology* 22 (1986): 291–296.

53. B. L. Fineberg, "Bean Bag Chairs as Versatile Play Objects in Boys' Latency Groups," *International Journal of Group Psychotherapy* 34 (1984): 503–509; Dianna Kelly-Byrne, "Text and Context: Fabling in a Relationship," *New Directions for Child Development,* no. 25 (September 1984): 37–51; A. P. Copeland, "Self-control Ratings and Mother-Child Interaction," *Journal of Clinical Child Psychology* 14 (1985): 124–131.

54. Brody, Pellegrini, and Sigel, "Marital Quality and Mother-Child and Father-Child Interactions."

55. W. Crain, E. D'Alessio, B. McIntyre, and L. Smoke, "The Impact of Hearing a Fairy Tale on Children's Immediate Behavior," *Journal of Genetic Psychology* 143 (1983): 9–17.

56. Erica Rosenfeld, L. Rowell Huesmann, Leonard Eron, and J. V. Torney-Purta, "Measuring Patterns of Fantasy Behavior in Children," *Journal of Personality and Social Psychology* 42 (1982): 347–366.

57. Jerome L. Singer and John S. Antrobus, "Dimensions of Daydreaming: A Factor Analysis of Imaginal Processes and Personality Scales," in *The Function and Nature of Imagery,* ed. Peter Sheehan (New York: Academic Press, 1972).

58. Rosenfeld, et al., "Measuring Patterns of Fantasy Behavior," p. 363.

59. Rosenfeld, et al., "Measuring Patterns of Fantasy Behavior," p. 365.

60. Sigmund Freud, "Formulations on the Two Principles of Mental Functioning," in *The Complete Psychological Works of Sigmund Freud,* vol. 12 (London: Hogarth Press, 1911; 1962).

61. Albert Bandura, *Aggression: A Social Learning Analysis* (Englewood Cliffs, N.J.: Prentice-Hall, 1973); Robert A. Baron, *Human Aggression* (New York: Plenum, 1977); Jerome L. Singer, *The Human Personality* (New York: Harcourt Brace Jovanovich, 1984); Dolf Zillmann, *Hostility and Aggression* (Hillsdale, N.J.: Erlbaum, 1978).

62. L. Rowell Huesmann and Leonard D. Eron, "The Development of Aggression in American Children as a Consequence of Television Violence Viewing," in *Television and the Aggressive Child: A Cross-National Comparison,* ed. L. Rowell Huesmann and Leonard D. Eron (Hillsdale, N.J.: Erlbaum, 1986). pp. 44–80.

63. Dorothy G. Singer and Jerome L. Singer, "Television Viewing and Aggressive Behavior in Preschool Children: A Field Study," *Annals of the New York Academy of Science* 347 (1980): 292–303; Jerome L. Singer and Dorothy G. Singer, *Television, Imagination, and Aggression: A Study of Preschoolers* (Hillsdale, N.J.: Erlbaum, 1981); Jerome L. Singer, Dorothy G. Singer, and W. Rapaczynski, "Family Patterns and Television Viewing as Predictors of Children's Beliefs and Aggression," *Journal of Communication* 34 (1984): 73–89; Roger Desmond, Jerome L. Singer, Dorothy G. Singer, Rachel Calam, and Karen Colimore, "Family Mediation Patterns and Television-Viewing: Young Children's Use and Grasp of the Medium," *Human Communication Research* 2 (1985): 461–480.

64. L. Rowell Huesmann, "Cross-National Commonalities in the Learning of Aggression from Media Violence," in Huesmann and Eron, *Television and the Aggressive Child: A Cross-National Comparison,* p. 244.

65. Lawrence Kohlberg, "A Cognitive-Developmental Approach to Socialization-Morality and Psychosexuality" (Paper presented at the Midwestern meeting of the Society for Research in Child Development, Bowling Green, Ohio, 1966); Jerome L. Singer, *The Inner World of Daydreaming* (New York: Harper and Row, 1975).

66. Ephraim Biblow, "Imaginative Play and the Control of Aggressive Behavior," in *The Child's World of Make-Believe,* ed. Jerome L. Singer (New York: Academic Press, 1973), pp. 104–128.
67. Sybil Gottlieb, "Modeling Effects upon Fantasy," in Singer, *The Child's World of Make-Believe,* pp. 155–182.
68. Gottlieb, "Modeling Effects upon Fantasy," pp. 175–176.
69. E. Barbara Hariton and Jerome L. Singer, "Women's Fantasies during Sexual Intercourse: Normative and Theoretical Implications," *Journal of Consulting and Clinical Psychology* 42 (1974): 313–322.
70. Anthony F. Campagna, "Fantasy and Sexual Arousal in College Men: Normative and Functional Aspects," *Imagination, Cognition, and Personality* 5 (1985–1986): 3–20.
71. Philip Roth, *The Breast* (New York: Hold, Rinehart and Winston, 1972); Franz Kafka, *Metamorphosis* (New York: Vanguard, 1946); *Everything You Always Wanted to Know About Sex but Were Afraid to Ask,* directed by Woody Allen, 1972.
72. Singer and Antrobus, "Dimensions of Daydreaming"; S. J. Lynn and J. W. Rhue, "Fantasy Proneness: Hypnosis, Developmental Antecedents, and Psychopathology," *American Psychologist* 43 (1988): 35–44.
73. Thomas Berndt, "Age Changes and Changes over Time in Prosocial Intentions and Behavior between Friends," *Developmental Psychology* 17 (1981): 408–416; M. D. Storms, "Theories of Sexual Orientation," *Journal of Personality and Social Psychology* 38 (1980): 783–792.
74. Donald P. Spence, *The Freudian Metaphor* (New York: Norton, 1987).
75. George H. Lewes, *The Life of Goethe* (New York: Frederick Ungar, 1966).
76. Shelley Taylor, *Positive Illusions: Creative Self-Deception and the Healthy Mind* (New York: Basic Books, 1989); Singer, *The Inner World of Daydreaming.*

11. Toward the Creative Adult

1. Edith Cobb, *The Ecology of Imagination in Childhood* (New York: Columbia University Press, 1977), p. 54.
2. Cobb, *Ecology of Imagination,* p. 55.
3. Erik H. Erikson, *Identity: Youth and Crisis.* (New York: Norton, 1968), p. 129.
4. Danny Santiago, "The Somebody," in *Adolescence in Literature,* ed. Thomas West Gregory (New York: Longman, 1978), p. 372.
5. Teresa M. Amabile, "The Social Psychology of Creativity: A Componential Conceptualization," *Journal of Personality and Social Psychology* 45 (1983): 361.
6. Amabile, "Social Psychology of Creativity"; Graham Wallas, *The Art of Thought* (New York: Harcourt, 1926); Robin M. Hogarth, *Judgement and Choice* (Chichester, England: Wiley, 1980).
7. Ruth Richards, Dennis K. Kinney, Maria Benet, and Ann P. K. Merzel,

"Assessing Everyday Creativity: Characteristics of the Lifetime Creativity Scales and Validation with Three Large Samples," *Journal of Personality and Social Psychology* 54 (1988): 476–485.

8. Daniel Goleman, "A New Index Illuminates the Creative Life," *New York Times,* September 13, 1988, pp. C1, C9.

9. Richards et al., "Assessing Everyday Creativity."

10. David M. Harrington, Jack Block, and Jeanne H. Block, "Predicting Creativity in Preadolescence from Divergent Thinking in Early Childhood," *Journal of Personality and Social Psychology* 45 (1983): 609–623.

11. Harrington, Block, and Block, "Predicting Creativity," p. 619.

12. Charles E. Schaefer, "Imaginary Companions and Creative Adolescents," *Developmental Psychology* 1 (1969): 747–749.

13. Sidney J. Parnes, "Learning Creative Behavior," *The Futurist* 18 (1984): 30–32.

14. S. Elizabeth Bird, "Playing with Fear: Interpreting the Adolescent Legend Trip" (Paper presented at the Popular Communication Interest Group, International Communication Association, New Orleans, May 1988).

15. Bird, "Playing with Fear," p. 1.

16. Bird, "Playing with Fear," p. 2.

17. Bird, "Playing with Fear," p. 18.

18. Brian Sutton-Smith, "Creativity and the Vicissitudes of Play," *Adolescent Psychiatry* 15 (1988): 307–318.

19. Robert D. McIlwraith and Wendy L. Josephson, "Movies, Books, Music, and Adult Fantasy Life," *Journal of Communication* 35 (1985): 167–179.

20. Robert Frost "Directive," in *Complete Poems of Robert Frost* (New York: Henry Holt, 1949), p. 378.

21. Eugen Fink, "The Oasis of Happiness: Toward an Ontology of Play," in *Yale French Studies: Game, Play, Literature* 41 (1968): 22.

22. Suzanne Cassidy, "England's Merry Morris Men," *New York Times,* June 4, 1989, p. 19.

23. Lis Harris, "Annals of Intrigue: The Palio," *New Yorker,* June 5, 1989, pp. 83–104.

24. Harris, "Annals of Intrigue," p. 89.

25. Jules Older, "Show Turns Farm into Puppet State," *New York Times,* July 10, 1988, p. 32.

26. Older, "Show Turns Farm into Puppet State," p. 32.

27. National Public Radio, "Heaven-Hell Tour, Atlanta, Georgia" (interview with John Ludwig, creator of the eight-year-old Center for Puppetry Arts, June 23, 1989).

28. Vera Etzion, "Photograph," in an article by Joseph Hoffman, *Jerusalem Post,* March 16, 1989, p. 2.

29. Advertisement in the *New Yorker:* The North American School of the Artsy and Somewhat Musically Inclined, Dept. Y1, Box 10931, St. Paul, Minnesota 55110, October and November 1988 issues.

30. T. M. Luhrmann, *Persuasions of the Witch's Craft: Ritual Magic in*

Contemporary England (Cambridge, Mass.: Harvard University Press, 1989).

31. Roger Caillois, *Les Jeux et les Hommes* (Paris: Gallimard, 1958); Johan Huizinga, *Homo Ludens* (Boston: Beacon Press, 1950).

32. Clifford Geertz, "Deep Play: A Description of the Balinese Cockfight," in *Play,* ed. Jerome S. Bruner, A. Jolly, and K. Sylvia (New York: Basic Books, 1976), p. 674.

33. Mikhail Bakhtin, *Rabelais and His World* (Cambridge: MIT Press, 1968).

34. Jerome L. Singer, *The Inner World of Daydreaming* (New York: Harper and Row, 1975); Jerome L. Singer, *Daydreaming and Fantasy* (Oxford: Oxford University Press, 1981).

35. Sybil Gottlieb, "Modeling Effects upon Fantasy" in *The Child's World of Make-Believe,* ed. J. L. Singer (New York: Academic Press, 1973), pp. 155–182; Ulla Johnsson-Smaragdi and Keith Roe, "Teenagers in the New Media World," *Lund Research Papers in the Sociology of Communication,* no. 2 (1986): 1–79.

36. Singer, *Daydreaming and Fantasy*; Jerome L. Singer and John Kolligian, Jr., "Personality: Developments in the Study of Private Experience," *Annual Review of Psychology* 38 (1987); Jerome L. Singer and George A. Bonanno, "Personality and Private Experience: Individual Variations in Consciousness and in Attention to Subjective Phenomena," in *Handbook of Personality,* ed. Lawrence Pervin (New York: Guilford, 1990); L. M. Giambra, "Adult Male Daydreaming across the Life-span: A Replication, Further Analyses, and Tentative Norms Based upon Retrospective Reports," *International Journal of Aging and Human Development* 8 (1977): 197–228.

37. Jerome Bruner, *Actual Minds, Possible Worlds* (Cambridge, Mass.: Harvard University Press, 1986); Kenneth S. Pope and Jerome L. Singer, "Introduction: The Flow of Human Experience," in *The Stream of Consciousness,* ed. Kenneth S. Pope and Jerome L. Singer (New York: Plenum, 1978), pp. 1–6; Eric Klinger, "Modes of Normal Conscious Flow," in Pope and Singer, *The Stream of Consciousness,* pp. 225–258.

38. Mihalyi Csikszentmihalyi, *Beyond Boredom and Anxiety* (San Francisco: Jossey-Bass, 1975).

39. William James, *The Principles of Psychology,* 2 vols. (New York: Dover, 1890; 1952).

40. Julian Budden, *The Operas of Verdi,* vol. 1 (New York: Oxford University Press, 1978).

41. Jerome L. Singer, "Experimental Studies of Daydreaming and the Stream of Thought," in Pope and Singer, *The Stream of Consciousness,* pp. 187–223; Singer and Kollingian, "Personality"; Jerome L. Singer, "Sampling Ongoing Consciousness and Emotional Experience: Implications for Health," in *Psychodynamics and Cognition,* ed. Mardi J. Horowitz (Chicago: University of Chicago Press, 1988), pp. 297–346.

42. Singer, "Experimental Studies of Daydreaming"; Singer, "Sampling

Ongoing Consciousness"; Singer and Bonanno, "Personality and Private Experience."

43. Jerome L. Singer, *Imagery and Daydream Methods in Psychotherapy and Behavior Modification* (New York: Academic Press, 1974).

44. See the following for a somewhat different position: Marshall Edelson, *Psychoanalysis: A Theory in Crisis* (Chicago: University of Chicago Press, 1988); Marshall Edelson, "Introduction, The Nature of Psychoanalytic Theory: Implications for Psychoanalytic Research," *Psychoanalytic Inquiry* 9 (1989): 169–192.

45. Singer and Kolligian, "Personality"; Singer, "Sampling Ongoing Consciousness."

46. Singer, "Sampling Ongoing Consciousness" contains a description of Antrobus's unpublished study and other recent research; John S. Antrobus, Ronald Coleman, and Jerome L. Singer "Signal Detection Performance by Subjects Differing in Predisposition to Daydreaming," *Journal of Consulting Psychology* 31 (1967): 487–491.

47. Singer, "Sampling Ongoing Consciousness"; Russell T. Hurlburt, "Validation and Correlation of Thought Sampling with Retrospective Measures," *Cognitive Therapy and Research* 4 (1980): 235–238; Russell T. Hurlburt, *Sampling Normal and Schizophrenic Inner Experience* (New York: Plenum, 1990).

48. George H. Huba, Carol S. Aneshensel, and Jerome L. Singer, "Development of Scales for Three Second-Order Factors of Inner Experience," *Multivariate Behavioral Research* 16 (1981): 181–206; Steven Starker and R. Hasenfeld, "Daydream Styles and Sleep Disturbances," *Journal of Nervous and Mental Disease* 163 (1976): 391–400; Steven Starker and Annette Jolin, "Imagery and Fantasy in Vietnam Veteran Psychiatric Inpatients," *Imagination, Cognition and Personality* 2 (1982–1983): 15–22; Steven Starker, and Jerome L. Singer, "Daydreaming and Symptom Patterns of Psychiatric Patients: A Factor Analytic Study," *Journal of Abnormal Psychology* 84 (1975): 567–570.

49. Michael Barrios and Jerome L. Singer, "The Treatment of Creative Blocks: A Comparison of Waking Imagery, Hypnotic Dream, and Rational Discussion Techniques," *Imagination, Cognition and Personality* 1 (1981–1982): 89–109; Josephine R. Hilgard, "Imaginative and Sensory-Affective Involvements in Everyday Life and in Hypnosis," in *Hypnosis: Developments in Research and New Perspectives,* ed. Erika Fromm and Ronald E. Schor (New York: Aldine Press, 1979), pp. 483–518; Helen Crawford, "Hypnoting Ability, Daydreaming Styles, Imagery Vividness, and Absorption: A Multidimensional Study," *Journal of Personality and Social Psychology* 42 (1982): 915–926; Nicholas Spanos, "A Social Psychological Approach to Hypnotic Behavior," in *Integrations of Clinical and Social Psychology,* ed. G. Weary and H. Mirels (Oxford: Oxford University Press, 1982), pp. 231–271; Auke Tellegen and Gary Atkinson, "Openness to Absorbing and Self-Altering Experiences ("Absorption") and Hypnotic Susceptibility," *Journal of Abnormal Psychology* 83 (1974): 268–277.

50. Jean Piaget, *Possibility and Necessity,* 2 vols. (Minneapolis: University of Minnesota Press, 1980; 1987).
51. Singer, *The Inner World of Daydreaming.*
52. George Eliot, *Middlemarch,* in *The Works of George Eliot,* vol. 2 (New York: Peter Fenelon Collier, 1982), p. 42.
53. Kenneth S. Pope, "How Gender, Solitude, and Posture Influence the Stream of Consciousness," in Pope and Singer, *The Stream of Consciousness,* pp. 259–299; Hurlburt, *Sampling Normal and Schizophrenic Inner Experience.*
54. John S. Antrobus, "Dreaming for Cognition," in *The Mind in Sleep,* ed. Arthur Arkin, John S. Antrobus, and Steven Ellman (Hillsdale, N.J.: Erlbaum, 1978), pp. 569–581; John S. Antrobus, "Dreaming: Cortical Activation and Perceptual Threshholds," *Journal of Mind and Behavior* 7 (1986): 63–82.
55. Singer, *Imagery and Daydream Methods in Psychotherapy*; E. Caruth, "How You Play the Game: On Game as Play and Play as Game in the Psychoanalytic Process," *Psychoanalytic Psychology* 5 (1988): 179–192; T. DeAngelis, "Playfulness in Therapy Opens New Dimensions," *American Psychological Association Monitor* July 20, 1989, p. 27.
56. Donald P. Spence, *Narrative Truth and Historical Truth* (New York: Norton, 1982); Donald P. Spence, *The Freudian Metaphor* (New York: Norton, 1987).
57. Thomas Hobbes, *Leviathan* (Harmondsworth, England: Penguin, 1968); Thomas Hobbes, *Elementa Philosophica de Cive* (Garden City, N.J.: Anchor Books, 1972); G. W. von Leibniz, *Nouveaux essais* (New York: Cambridge University Press, 1981); Jerome L. Singer, "Towards the Scientific Study of Imagination," *Imagination, Cognition and Personality* 1 (1981–1982): 5–28.
58. Singer, "Experimental Studies in Daydreaming."
59. Richard de Mille, *Put Your Mother on the Ceiling* (New York: Viking Press, 1973).
60. Joseph E. Shorr, *Psychotherapy through Imagery* (New York: Intercontinental Medical, 1974); Joseph E. Shorr, *Go See the Movie in Your Head* (New York: Popular Library, 1977).
61. Singer, *Imagery and Daydream Methods in Psychotherapy*; Jerome L. Singer and Kenneth S. Pope, eds., *The Power of Human Imagination* (New York: Plenum, 1978); Jerome L. Singer and Ellen Switzer, *Mind Play: The Creative Uses of Fantasy* (Englewood Cliffs, N.J.: Prentice-Hall, 1980); Richard M. Suinn, "Body Thinking: Psychology for Olympic Champs," *Psychology Today* 10 (1976): 38–43.
62. Martha Graham, commentary for *Martha Graham: Three Contemporary Classics,* videotape produced by the Martha Graham Center for the Dance (New York: RCA-Ariola International, 1984).
63. Lawrence Weschler, "A Reporter at Large: The Great Exception. I. Liberty," *New Yorker,* April 3, 1989, p. 14.
64. Albert Rothenberg, *The Emerging Goddess: The Creative Process in Art, Science, and Other Fields* (Chicago: University of Chicago Press, 1979).

65. Victor Nell, *Lost in a Book* (New Haven: Yale University Press, 1988); E. Brown, "A Theory of Reading," *Journal of Communication Disorders* 14 (1981): 443–466.

66. Rainer Maria Rilke, poetic fragment cited in Eugen Fink, "The Oasis of Happiness: Toward an Ontology of Play," *Yale French Studies: Game Play, Literature* 41 (1968): 19–30.

Index